BORDER PEOPLE

BORDER PEOPLE

LIFE AND SOCIETY IN THE U.S.–MEXICO BORDERLANDS

OSCAR J. MARTÍNEZ

THE UNIVERSITY OF ARIZONA PRESS   TUCSON & LONDON

KGQ020I

24cm

352 p.

The University of Arizona Press
Copyright © 1994
The Arizona Board of Regents
All rights reserved
♾ This book is printed on acid-free, archival-quality paper.
Manufactured in the United States of America

99 98 97 96 95   6 5 4 3 2

Library of Congress Cataloging-in-Publication Data

Martínez, Oscar J. (Oscar Jáquez), 1943–
    Border people : life and society in the U.S.–Mexico borderlands /
Oscar J. Martínez.
        p.   cm.
    Includes bibliographical references and index.
    ISBN 0-8165-1396-1 (cloth). — ISBN 0-8165-1414-3 (pbk.)
    1. Mexican-American Border Region.   2. Mexican-American Border
Region—Population.   I. Title.
    F787.M36   1994
    972'.1—dc20
                                                        93-45298
                                                        CIP

British Cataloguing-in-Publication Data
A catalogue record for this book is available from the British
Library.

A portion of the material presented in Chapter 3 appeared in the
Journal of Borderlands Studies 5 (Spring 1990): 79–94. A portion
of the material presented in Chapter 4 appeared in the *Revista
Mexicana de Sociología* 53 (July–September 1991): 291–303. A
longer version of the statement by Soledad Fuente in Chapter 6
appeared in William A. Beezley and Judith Ewell, eds., *The Human
Tradition in Latin America: The Twentieth Century* (Wilmington,
Del.: Scholarly Resources, 1987), 195–206.

To border people
dedicated to the task of transcending
political and cultural boundaries

CONTENTS

FIGURES

TABLES

ACKNOWLEDGMENTS

I wish to thank the many people who assisted me with this project, giving generously of their time and expertise to facilitate the research, data processing, and preparation of the manuscript for publication. I owe the greatest gratitude to the interviewees who shared their personal stories with me. I am also indebted to many relatives, friends, colleagues, and acquaintances who for years have aided me in my quest to unravel the mysteries of the borderlands. Casual and formal conversations with people from many walks of life and observations of border phenomena in a variety of settings have given me insights that otherwise would have been very difficult to glean.

The project began in El Paso in the 1970s, where I received strong institutional support while teaching at the University of Texas at El Paso (UTEP). The professionalism and pleasant ambiance of the UTEP history department provided just the right atmosphere to carry on my work. Staff at the UTEP Institute of Oral History who contributed to the research in a variety of ways include Sarah E. John, Virgilio H. Sánchez, Mario Galdós, Arturo Hernández, Rhonda Hartman, and Manuela Barrón. A grant to the institute from the National Endowment for the Humanities facilitated my research with border workers during the late 1970s. At the University of Arizona, where I have taught since 1988, the history department also provided significant research and administrative support. Mary Sue Passe-Smith and Jim Lombardo typed the manuscript and used their considerable computer skills to improve the appearance of many of the graphics; Pat Foreman made final revisions. The following colleagues in the United States and Mexico provided encouragement, criticism, and suggestions that led to countless improvements throughout the book: A. I. Asiwaju, Jeffery T. Brannon, Jorge Bustamante, Paul Ganster, Virginia S. Kemendo, David E. Lorey, Michael C. Meyer, Kathleen Rubin-Fairbanks, Thomas E. Sheridan, John Sherman, Ellwyn R. Stoddard, David J. Weber, and James W. Wilkie. I am especially indebted to

Alan M. Schroder of the University of Arizona Press for his careful copyediting and excellent comments. My task in identifying candidates for interviews was made easier through the kind assistance of Denise Joseph, Cesar Caballero, Irasema Coronado, Ana María Osante, Rebeca Ramos, Isabel Robles, Juan Sandoval, and Don Shuffstall.

INTRODUCTION

When I began to research the U.S.–Mexico borderlands two decades ago, I determined that a study focused on border people would add significantly to our understanding of the region, and I proceeded to conduct preliminary fieldwork. Other commitments subsequently relegated the project to the back burner, although I steadily gathered data and sought to ascertain the most appropriate way of portraying the way of life of borderlanders. I decided early on that the study should be based largely on firsthand interviews with individuals from different walks of life and different borderland areas. This strategy necessarily increased the time required to do the research, but in retrospect the extended timetable allowed me to proceed with considerable selectivity and to crystallize my thinking on the scope of the study and its implications beyond the U.S.–Mexico borderlands.

As I conducted interviews, I found myself personally engrossed with what respondents revealed about their unique world, and as a borderlander myself I could easily relate to their experiences. Those stimulating conversations, many trips to numerous border communities, observations of border phenomena over many years, reflection on my own personal history, and previous work on the history of the region all contributed in significant ways to shaping this book.[1]

Since my own life is mirrored in my portrayal of border society and my interpretation of border phenomena, it seems appropriate to reveal some personal information. In the early twentieth century my paternal great-grandparents migrated from Jalisco, a state in central Mexico, to the U.S. borderlands, where my great-grandfather, and later my grandfather and father, labored in the fields and mines and on the railroads, frequently returning to Mexico for temporary stays. It was in about 1940 during one of those periods of residence in Mexico that my father met my mother in the Parral mining district in the state of Chihuahua. A few years later I was born in the mining town of San Francisco del Oro a few hundred miles from the border. Shortly thereafter my parents, Bernardo

Martínez Ramírez and Magdalena Jáquez de Martínez, moved to Ciudad Juárez, a prominent border city that my father subsequently used as a springboard for obtaining employment in the United States.

I spent most of my childhood on the Mexican side, but I lived in Colorado for a year and in Illinois for another while my father was employed as a railroad and factory worker. I also commuted from Juárez for several years to attend an American school in El Paso. When I was fourteen our family, which by then included five children, moved permanently to El Paso as legal U.S. residents. I then began to experience the borderlands from a U.S. perspective, building on what I already knew about the region from my years in Juárez. After I graduated from high school in El Paso, we moved to California, where I eventually attended various universities, finally receiving a Ph.D. from UCLA in 1975. That same year I accepted a full-time position at the University of Texas at El Paso (UTEP), eagerly returning to the border to teach, do research, and live as an adult borderlander. I remained at UTEP until 1988, when I moved to the University of Arizona in Tucson, about sixty miles from the border.

In all, I have spent more than three-fourths of my life amidst border people, experiencing and studying the forces that have shaped them. Even before I began my formal study of the region, I had a strong but vague feeling that borderlanders were somehow singular in their history, outlook, and behavior, and that their lifestyle deviated from the norms of central Mexico and the interior United States. That impression became stronger as I conducted research on various aspects of border history. In some respects, then, this book represents the culmination of a long personal and academic journey. The project has allowed me to develop a deeper understanding of, and appreciation for, the unique surroundings in which borderlanders live.

My early fieldwork with borderlanders led me to assume the directorship of the Institute of Oral History at UTEP in 1975. During the next seven years I conducted many oral history interviews myself and supervised the work of research assistants. Periodically we would travel to near and distant border locations to interview people from diverse backgrounds and ethnic groups. By the 1980s the institute had accumulated the largest oral history archive on borderlanders anywhere in the world.[2] As my work with oral history progressed, I decided to focus on the border experience since World War II; consequently I sought respondents who were directly involved in recent and present-day transnational and transcultural processes.

The fieldwork, as well as my own participation in transnational interaction, made the complexity of border society clear. Far from being a monolithic population, borderlanders on both sides of the dividing line manifested substantial diversity. While readily identifiable as distinct groups, border Mexicans, Mexican Americans, and Anglo Americans exhibited considerable internal heterogeneity as a result of the influence of the wide array of cross-border and cross-cultural ties, networks, and relationships. My challenge became to construct a paradigm to illustrate this multiformity, and I decided to devise typologies for each group. At that stage I felt compelled to abandon constraints imposed by my own discipline—history—in favor of methodological strategies and techniques that would best allow me to convey the meaning of the border in human terms. I embarked on this interdisciplinary adventure with some trepidation, but my strongly felt need to use whatever approach seemed most appropriate for the task at hand prompted me to experiment with conducting the research and formulating models to illustrate borderlands interaction. Where data are lacking, I have opted for presenting ideas and interpretations as hypotheses rather than conclusions. I hope I have not deviated too far from the scholarly practices of my colleagues in history, sociology, and anthropology.

This study is guided by the axiom that environmental factors play a determining role in shaping the lives of distinct populations. In traditional societies, for example, people who inhabit mountain areas develop a lifestyle that is necessarily different from those who live on the plains. The two groups function in contrasting terrains and ecological systems. In the mountains, constant movement is often necessitated by a scarce resource base, while on the plains a sedentary life is made possible by the presence of cultivable land. Similarly, mountain people are more isolated from the outside world than are plains people. In the modern world, with its highly effective communication and transportation systems, the natural environment has declined as a force in sustaining differences among unlike populations. Nevertheless, a host of environmental influences remain significant. Rural people continue to differ from urban people, inner-city residents from suburbanites, and working classes from upper classes because of their dissimilar economic, social, cultural, and political circumstances. In like fashion, borderlanders stand apart, especially in relation to people who live in heartland regions, because of the singular world in which they live.

In addition to seeking to explain the way of life of the population in the U.S.–Mexico borderlands, I also want to contribute a framework for describing border phenomena in general. Many patterns and structural relationships that are evident along the U.S.–Mexico border—including the evolution of transnational interaction, the emergence of societal subtypes in border society, and cross-boundary and cross-cultural links—are repeated in varying forms and to varying degrees in other border areas. Thus Chapter I addresses broad conceptual issues in order to establish the universality of this study's findings. In particular, the chapter presents models of borderlands interaction and the "borderlands milieu" that rely on data and examples from different border regions and different historical periods.

My thesis is that borderlanders live in a unique human environment shaped by physical distance from central areas and constant exposure to transnational processes. My laboratory is the U.S.–Mexico border region, but I believe many of the findings are applicable to other borderlands because of the universality of border phenomena. International boundaries have the same basic functions everywhere: to delimit one nation from another and to control the movement of people and goods from one side of the boundary to the other. Borderlands are generally situated at the periphery of nations, and to one degree or another all are subject to foreign influences. These characteristics are common to borderlanders from different parts of the globe. The determining influence of the border makes the lives of border peoples functionally similar irrespective of location, nationality, ethnicity, culture, and language. In other words, all borderlanders share the border experience.

This is not to deny the reality that different borderlands have their own particular identities owing to special environmental factors. For example, contiguous borderlands of nations in Asia, Africa, Europe, North America, and South America differ from one another because of the diverse local landscapes, political conditions, economic circumstances, and cultural milieus of groups living in frontier zones. Moreover, diversity is present in any borderlands population due to distinctions in race, class, and culture, not to mention the degree of cross-border and cross-ethnic contact. Hence, while all borderlands share functional similarities stemming from transboundary interaction, they also retain distinct identities arising from particular local settings.

In any human sphere, some people function in the center and others hover on the periphery, and this pattern is replicated in a border setting. Some borderlanders are situated at the center of the border experience, others are distant from it, and many people occupy positions in between. The distance separating an individual from the center of the borderlands milieu depends on his or her level of involvement in transnational processes and intercultural relationships. The more an individual functions in diverse settings, the greater is his or her propensity for living like a "genuine" borderlander and the greater is the contrast between him or her and an individual from the heartland. On the U.S.–Mexico border, as in any borderland, the human spectrum ranges from the quintessential border people (individuals highly immersed in transnational and transcultural interaction) to people who for one reason or another are influenced very little by the presence of the boundary and are therefore not much different from people living in interior areas.

This study focuses on the heart of the borderlands, that is, the border corridor where the U.S.–Mexican symbiotic urban complexes are situated. Since the mid twentieth century, twin cities like San Diego–Tijuana, El Paso–Ciudad Juárez, and Brownsville–Matamoros have experienced phenomenal population and economic growth, becoming premiere centers of international interdependence. Another part of the world that has undergone similar development is western Europe, where some cities located adjacent to international boundaries have expanded significantly in the decades following World War II. Two trinational urban regions, Basel (Switzerland)-Mulhouse (France)-Freiburg (Germany) and Maastricht (Holland)-Aachen (Germany)-Liège (Belgium) in many ways replicate the processes evident in the U.S.–Mexico border cities: pronounced transboundary movement, interdependence, and the creation of social systems that transcend national frontiers. The way of life of Mexican, Anglo American, and Mexican American borderlanders, then, may well provide important insights into trends that are also much in evidence in other parts of the world.

The dual concern in this work for the general and the specific places it within the broader literature on borderlands as well as the body of knowledge pertaining to U.S.–Mexico border studies. The study of international borders goes back many decades, and significant theoretical contributions have been made by scholars from a number of disciplines. Geographers, political scientists, sociologists, economists, historians, and others have expanded our understanding of such general issues as border conflict, border delimitation, border maintenance, border problem solving, migration, cross-border trade, regionalism in a border context, and border landscapes.[3] In addition, studies of specific border areas have been helpful for comprehending similarities and differences around the world.[4] Among the literature I have surveyed, the most insightful for comparative purposes has been the work of historian A. I. Asiwaju, a Nigerian borderlander and currently a member of his country's boundary commission.[5] But helpful as all these works are, their predominant concern has been with questions relating to official and institutional transnational relationships, not with the nature of border society.

Specialists in the U.S.–Mexico borderlands have also produced a rich literature, but little of it directly analyzes patterns in the lives of borderlanders. Almost every other subject, however, has been addressed by scores of capable American and Mexican scholars from many disciplines. Historians in particular have long been active in the field, producing outstanding works on the Spanish colonial period (from the early sixteenth century to 1821) and the nineteenth and twentieth centuries. Major topics examined by historians include Indian-Spanish relations, the Texas rebellion (1836–1845), the U.S.–Mexico War (1846–1848), post-1848 border controversies, filibustering, banditry, Indian raiding, the impact of the Mexican Revolution, cross-border migration, and the evolution of border cities. Scholars concerned with the contemporary scene have focused their attention primarily on such topics as decision making in a binational context, ethnic politics, Mexican American–Anglo American relations, drug trafficking, cross-border migration, binational urbanization, industrialization, environmental pollution, ecological crises, and poverty.[6]

I have grouped the chapters in this book into three parts. Chapters 1 and 2, which make up Part I, discuss general concepts pertaining to global border phenomena and transnational interaction in the U.S.–Mexico borderlands, respectively. Part II examines the nature of border society, with Chapters 3 through 5 presenting typologies and case histories of Mexicans, Mexican Americans, and Anglo Americans. Part III portrays the experience of border people through selections from oral history interviews, with Chapter 6 focusing on migrants and workers, Chapter 7 on functionaries and activists, and Chapter 8 on "mixers," or individuals with a high degree of involvement with people from the other side of the border and from other cultures. The conclusion addresses salient questions pertaining to contemporary borderlands society.

Each of the three sections of the book is distinct in its structure and approach, but they are unified by a common focus: the way of life in the borderlands. The interview summaries and oral histories in Parts II and III provide the human dimension implicit in the concepts, evolutionary trends, and contemporary circumstances delineated in Part I. The oral histories in particular, which constitute more than half the book, illuminate the drama found on the frontier. They offer a kaleidoscopic view of the world in which border people live and function.

PART I THE BORDER PHENOMENON

Isolation, underdevelopment, and neglect characterized the lives of many borderlanders around the world in the nineteenth century and the first half of the twentieth. Above all, an unstable international climate kept borderlands generally underpopulated and economically backward, as central governments hesitated to develop areas where the likelihood of fighting in time of war was the highest. After World War II, however, changes began to occur in the world that would profoundly affect many border regions, particularly in western Europe and North America. Territorial disputes declined appreciably, allowing formerly tense border zones to attain stability and to turn former locational disadvantages into assets for achieving growth and development. This turn of events reflected larger global transformations. Advances in air warfare diminished the importance of land-based combat, thus rendering borderlands much less significant as buffer zones to keep real and potential enemies at a secure distance from nations' heartlands. Concurrently, the global economic system became highly internationalized, and many countries drew closer together through interdependent networks that arose from greatly increased trade.

As frontline zones of contact, borderlands encountered opportunities previously unavailable to them. Their functions underwent substantial redefinition, from frequently ignored wastelands to dynamic centers of trade, commerce, and even industrialization. Many closed borders became open, allowing capital, people, and products to move from country to country in search of new opportunities. Borderlands that were enmeshed in this process developed economic activity sufficient to spur the growth of existing population centers and the emergence of new ones. Borderlanders affected by such trends, especially borderlanders from developed nations, found a new place in the world, playing roles long denied them by an international system previously driven by global tensions and the ideology of rigid national sovereignty.

Borderlands of nations on the periphery of world progress have also been affected by the post–World War II trend toward global integration but to a much lesser degree. In fact, in many conflict-ridden regions, such as the Middle East and parts of Africa, interaction across international boundaries has not increased appreciably. Thus, unfavorable conditions in countless areas continue to inhibit their borderlands from carrying on productive relationships with foreigners.

In today's world, many different types of borderlands may be found, some filled with tension, others peaceful; some impoverished, others prosperous; some sparsely populated, others overcrowded; some closed to commerce and immigration, others almost completely open to trade and the free movement of people. Variations in borderlands interaction is one of two topics taken up in Chapter 1; the other pertains to the unique political, social, and cultural forces that impact the lives of border people. Chapter 2 examines the historical evolution of the U.S.–Mexico borderlands in relation to changes in the level of binational interaction and identifies contemporary cross-border links for the purpose of establishing the context in which border Mexicans, Mexican Americans, and Anglo Americans function.

I

BORDERLANDS AND BORDERLANDERS

A border is a line that separates one nation from another or, in the case of internal entities, one province or locality from another. The essential functions of a border are to keep people in their own space and to prevent, control, or regulate interactions among them. A borderland is a region that lies adjacent to a border. The territorial limit of a borderland depends on the geographic reach of the interaction with the "other side." Some borderlands are physically small because foreign influences are confined to the immediate border area; others are large because such influences penetrate far beyond the border zone. I employ *border* and *borderland* interchangeably to refer to the place or region. A related term, *frontier,* denotes an area that is physically distant from the core of the nation; it is a zone of transition, a place where people and institutions are shaped by natural and human forces that are not felt in the heartland.

As frontier entities enveloped by international phenomena, borderlands share many functional commonalities with one another. European, African, Asian, and American borderlands manifest conditions unique to each continent and region, but the transnational interaction present in all borderlands provides universal links. For example, cross-boundary relationships and the movement of goods and people are driven by international trade, interdependence, and migrations, processes that are duplicated widely throughout the world. Regardless of location, then, borderlanders are subject to many similar experiences.[1]

To place the U.S.–Mexico borderlands in broader global context, this chapter considers some of the ways in which that shared experience is found in borderlands in general. I first examine four models of borderlands interaction and then discuss the concept of a borderlands milieu.

Models of Borderlands Interaction

In categorizing borderlands it is essential to assess cross-border movement and the forces that produce it. With that in mind, I would like to propose four models of borderlands interaction: alienated borderlands, coexistent borderlands, inter-dependent borderlands, and integrated borderlands (Figure 1.1).[2] Each model illustrates a different degree of cross-border interaction and prevailing tendencies in a borderland. There may be cases, of course, where borderlands simultane-ously manifest varying inclinations, but one of the four conditions tends to pre-dominate. For instance, today interdependence is overwhelmingly dominant in the U.S.–Mexico borderlands, and therefore the most appropriate designation for that binational zone is interdependent borderlands. But that does not mean that elements of alienation, coexistence, and even integration are not part of the scene; they are, but in the broadest sense of cross-border interaction, none of these other tendencies predominates.

Reflecting the recent evolutionary trend in various parts of the world from international conflict toward harmony, many borderlands have advanced in their cross-boundary relationships in stages that generally correspond to these models. The U.S.–Mexico borderlands again may be cited as an example of this temporal linear progression, and some borderlands in post–World War II western Europe have also evolved along that path. On the other hand, many borderlands have not experienced such evolutionary trends, and the notion of sequential change is not applicable to them. With such exceptions in mind, a discussion of the differ-ent forms of borderlands interaction follows.

Alienated Borderlands

This model refers to borderlands where routine cross-boundary interchange is practically nonexistent owing to extremely unfavorable conditions. Warfare, po-litical disputes, intense nationalism, ideological animosity, religious enmity, cul-tural dissimilarity, and ethnic rivalry constitute major causes of such alienation. International strife leads to militarization and the establishment of rigid controls over cross-border traffic.

To say the least, such a tension-filled climate seriously interferes with the efforts of local populations to lead normal lives. International trade and substan-tial people-to-people contacts are very difficult if not impossible to maintain. The ever-present possibility of large-scale violence keeps these unstable areas sparsely populated and underdeveloped. Borderlands that have gone through this stage in the past include the Scottish–English frontier in the fifteenth and six-teenth centuries and the U.S.–Mexico border for two generations after the Texas rebellion of the 1830s. Currently, alienated borderlands are found in the Middle East, Africa, Asia, and among the republics of the former Soviet Union.

Coexistent Borderlands

Coexistence arises between adjoining borderlands when their respective nations reduce international border-related conflicts to a manageable level or, in cases

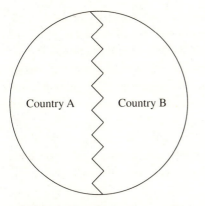

Alienated Borderlands
Tension Prevails. Border is functionally
closed, and cross-border interaction is
totally or almost totally absent. Residents
of each country interact as strangers.

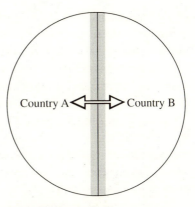

Coexistent Borderlands
Stability is an on-and-off proposition. The
border remains slightly open, allowing for
the development of limited binational
interaction. Residents of each country deal
with each other as casual acquaintances,
but borderlanders develop closer
relationships.

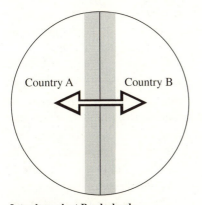

Interdependent Borderlands
Stability prevails most of the time.
Economic and social complementarity
prompts increased cross-border interaction,
leading to expansion of the borderlands.
Borderlanders carry on friendly and
cooperative relationships.

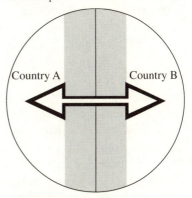

Integrated Borderlands
Stability is strong and permanent. The
economies of the two countries are functionally merged, and there is unrestricted
movement of people and goods across the
boundary. Borderlanders perceive themselves as members of one social system.

FIGURE I.I Models of borderlands interaction

where unfavorable internal conditions in one or both countries preclude binational cooperation, when such problems are resolved to the degree that minimal border stability can prevail. A scenario that reflects the evolution from a state of alienation to one of coexistence is one in which a serious dispute is resolved by two nations to the extent that international relations are possible but not to the point of allowing significant cross-border interaction. In effect, economic and social development that would normally take place in the region under more favorable circumstances is put on hold. For example, after prolonged strife two nations may reach a general agreement regarding the location of their common border but leave unresolved questions of the ownership of valuable natural resources in strategic border locales.

Another explanation for a condition of borderlands coexistence is simply the need for traditionally antagonistic neighbors to have enough time to get over the acrimony produced by conflicts endured during the period of alienation. Suspicion and distrust can only be overcome with the passage of time. Eventually the elimination of overt conflict allows for enough accommodation to stabilize the border, permitting borderlanders to interact with their counterparts across the boundary within the formal parameters established by the two nations.

An example of a domestic issue that limits the ability of borderlanders to interact with foreigners is regional fragmentation. National unity demands a certain degree of integration among disparate internal entities; in its absence, central governments will not risk "drift" at the periphery by allowing borderlanders to maintain substantial links with citizens of another country. In time, domestic sectionalism may be lessened through the spread of modern transportation, communication, and trade networks, diminishing the isolation of peripheries and giving the center strong control over independent-minded frontiersmen. Once sufficient internal unity has been achieved, central governments will be less concerned by contacts between their borderlanders and foreigners. Coexistence characterizes the Ecuador–Peru, Israel–Egypt, and Russia–China borderlands, to cite some examples.

Interdependent Borderlands

A condition of borderlands interdependence exists when a border region in one nation is symbiotically linked with the border region of an adjoining country. Such interdependence is made possible by relatively stable international relations and by the existence of a favorable economic climate that permits borderlanders on both sides of the line to pursue growth and development projects that are tied to foreign capital, markets, and labor. The greater the flow of economic and human resources across the border, the more the two economies are structurally bonded to each other. The result is a mutually beneficial economic system.

Interdependence implies that two more or less equal partners willingly agree to contribute to and extract from their relationship in approximately equal amounts. Reality may in fact approach this ideal state in some instances, but the prevalent pattern in binational regions throughout the world has been one of asymmetrical interdependence, in which one nation is stronger than its neighbor and consequently dominates it. In the case of two substantially unequal economies, the productive capacity of the wealthier country is often matched with raw materials and cheap labor in the poorer nation to create a complementarity that, while asymmetrical in nature, nonetheless yields proportional benefits to each side.

Economic interdependence creates many opportunities for borderlanders to establish social relationships across the boundary as well, allowing significant cultural transfer to take place. Thus the binational economic system produced by symbiosis spawns a binational social and cultural system. The degree of interdependence in the borderlands is contingent upon policies pertaining to the national interests of the two neighbors. Concerns over immigration, trade competition, smuggling, and ethnic nationalism compel the central governments to monitor the border carefully, keeping it open only to the extent that it serves national agendas.

The U.S.–Mexico borderlands are a good example of strong asymmetrical interdependence, while a more balanced interdependence may be found in parts of western Europe, where economic inequality among neighboring nations is less of a problem than in the Western Hemisphere or in other continents where Third World conditions predominate.

Integrated Borderlands

In integrated borderlands, neighboring nations eliminate all major political differences between them as well as existing barriers to trade and human movement across their mutual boundary. Borderlanders merge economically, with capital, products, and labor flowing from one side to the other without restrictions. Nationalism gives way to a new internationalist ideology that emphasizes peaceful relations and improvements in the quality of life of people in both nations through trade and the diffusion of technology. Each nation willingly relinquishes a significant part of its sovereignty for the sake of mutual progress.

Integration between two closely allied nations is most likely when both are politically stable, militarily secure, and economically strong. Ideally, the level of development is similar in both societies, and the resulting relationship is a relatively equal one. Population pressures are nonexistent in both nations, and neither side feels threatened by heavy immigration across the open border. Western Europe is far ahead of other regions in promoting multinational integration among the members of the European Community. For example, high levels of transborder integration are found between Belgium and its neighbors and in the

Regio Basiliensis transfrontier zone, where Switzerland, France, and Germany have pioneered new forms of international cooperation and planning.[3]

The Borderlands Milieu

Whether in a state of alienation, coexistence, interdependence, or integration, border zones stand out in their respective countries because of their location, which in many cases is far from the core, and because of the international climate produced by their being adjacent to another country. The unique forces, processes, and characteristics that set borderlands apart from interior zones include transnational interaction, international conflict and accommodation, ethnic conflict and accommodation, and separateness. In their totality, these elements constitute what might be called the borderlands milieu.

Infinite variations are to be expected in the borderlands milieu because of divergences in cross-border interaction as well as the heterogeneity of borderlands, which arises from differences in the size of nations, their political relationships, levels of development, and ethnic, cultural, and linguistic configurations. It would be difficult to identify one particular border region that has all the characteristics discussed below, but the U.S.–Mexico borderlands, with their longstanding, dynamic transborder interaction, provide many excellent illustrations of that milieu and are therefore frequently cited here as an example.

Transnational Interaction

Their location at the edge of a nation places borderlanders in international environments that have wide-ranging implications for those who function in or are affected by transborder interchange. This applies most directly where circumstances permit extensive cross-border movement, as in the case of interdependent and integrated borderlands. Relatively unimpaired interaction makes it possible for residents of contiguous borderlands to be active participants in transnational economic and social systems that foster substantial trade, consumerism, tourism, migration, information flow, cultural and educational exchange, and sundry personal relationships.

An open international environment exposes borderlanders to foreign values, ideas, customs, traditions, institutions, tastes, and behavior. Borderlanders find it easy to see how members of other societies make their living, how they cope with daily life, how they acquire an education, and how they exercise their responsibilities as citizens. Consumers are able to purchase foreign products, business people find it possible to expand their clientele beyond the boundary, and employers have access to foreign workers.

Transnational interaction thrives when border barriers dissolve, but even under less than favorable circumstances, cross-boundary exchange can still occur because total isolation from the outside world has become impossible. The level of transborder contact is fundamentally dependent on the relationship between adjoining nations, the concentration of population at the border, and the condition of the binational economy. In alienated borderlands, where the official policy is to maintain a closed border, movement from nation to nation may range from nonexistent in extreme cases to slight. Normally only borderlanders who have a compelling need to maintain ties with their neighbors are willing to risk the dangers of clandestine activity.

The existence of transborder interaction under extremely unfavorable conditions is illustrated in several alienated or coexistent borderlands. Along the Finnish–Soviet frontier in the late 1980s, legal trade as well as the smuggling of books, steroids, silver, gold, and paintings was much in evidence. Along the South Africa–Mozambique border, black workers commute in large numbers to mines in South Africa. In Cyprus the tense border that divides Greeks and Turks has not eliminated trade, commuting, and local cooperation.[4]

Transnational interaction increases as contiguous nations overcome mutual antagonisms and begin to allow substantial social and economic interchange at their common border. The levels of interaction vary from little or none in alienated borderlands to very high in integrated borderlands. Ethnic or cultural affinity among the peoples of adjacent borderlands enhances transnational interaction. Along the U.S.–Mexico border, for example, cross-boundary activity is intense partly because of the presence of large numbers of people of Mexican descent who live in the U.S. borderlands but who have maintained close ties with Mexicans south of the boundary for a long time.[5] Similarly, many African borderlands, whose levels of development and density of population are much lower, nonetheless experience substantial transnational interaction because of longstanding cross-border ethnic links.[6] Europe has numerous borderlands where culturally cohesive groups that are split by borders maintain extensive relationships, some with official approval and others despite government opposition.[7]

Unprecedented levels of transnational interaction have been achieved in Europe and North America in recent decades as a result of the rise in trade among Western industrialized nations. Niles Hansen has noted the remarkable changes that have prompted many border areas of western Europe to abandon traditional rivalries and ways of doing things in favor of closer ties with neighboring countries:

> In Western Europe old conflicts have steadily been submerged in favor of mutual economic development and cooperative efforts to promote the international mobility of people, goods, services, and information, with the result that international boundaries have become increasingly permeable. The importance of transboundary cooperation between border communities and regions has been officially recognized. All of the major governments have signed the European Outline Convention on Trans-

frontier Cooperation between Territorial Communities or Authorities, wherein they pledged "to promote such cooperation as far as possible and to contribute in this way to the economic and social progress of frontier regions and to the spirit of fellowship which unites the people of Europe."[8]

Dynamic transnational interaction is best exemplified along the U.S.–Mexico border, where about 5.1 million people on the U.S. side and about 3.8 million on the Mexican side live in a strong symbiotic relationship .[9] Here two different economies, cultures, and societies have fused to create a highly interdependent binational system. Transnational interaction manifests itself in myriad ways, including close cooperation among local authorities, cross-border living arrangements and employment patterns, the use of each other's educational and recreational facilities, and mutual celebration of holidays and festivals. The extraordinary transborder association is revealed in the massive numbers of people who cross the border at official entry points every year. In the late 1980s, such routine entries from Mexico into the United States reached almost 255 million annually; most were local people involved in daily personal or business routines, and a substantial number of crossers were non-border people passing through the area.

Twin-city complexes such as Brownsville–Matamoros, Laredo–Nuevo Laredo, Ciudad Juárez–El Paso, Douglas–Agua Prieta, Nogales–Nogales, Calexico–Mexicali, and San Diego–Tijuana are in the forefront of borderlands interaction. These urban centers function as unified entities despite the division imposed by the international boundary. A prominent borderlands scholar characterizes the urbanized border strip as "an overlap with a line drawn through the middle of it," while an experienced urban planner refers to the paired border communities as Siamese twins.[10]

Allowing for differences in city size, location, and level of economic development, binational border communities in other parts of the world function in essentially the same manner. Within the Western Hemisphere, analogous situations are manifested along the U.S.–Canadian boundary, the Venezuelan–Colombian frontier, and Argentina's borders with Brazil and Paraguay. In western Europe, interdependent urban centers may be found along the Italian–Yugoslavian border, the Swiss–German–French boundary, and the French–German frontier. A. I. Asiwaju notes similar patterns in Africa, although on that continent conditions vary in degree if not in kind because of the notorious arbitrariness of so many boundaries and the predominance of economic underdevelopment:

In the whole of Africa . . . there is perhaps no border location outside the singular case of Brazzaville (capital of . . . the Congo) and Kanshasa (formerly Leopoldville, capital . . . of Zaire) where, as in the U.S.–Mexico border, settlements of standard urban sizes are found in a twin-type location at several points along the binational frontierline. However, there are several equivalent mid-size towns not directly on the borders but within the borderlands, not to mention the innumerable village level communities of the same type of dual location along all Nigerian and African borders; and, as in the U.S.–Mexico case, there is the same degree of interdependence in social and economic matters and comparable extents of informal linkages across the borders.[11]

International Conflict and Accommodation

Borderlands strife is different from friction in other parts of nations because of the peculiar conditions in peripheries—they are vulnerable to international disputes and to crises produced by boundary instability.[12] Borderlanders face special challenges inherent in the boundary itself, while interior populations are shielded from such stresses.

Border people who are caught up in territorial or political struggles between their antagonistic nations will be subject to attack from foreigners or even from some of their countrymen, who may question their loyalty if they express a desire to remain neutral or simply to be left alone. Often fighting between rival countries continues for long periods, turning borderlands into battlefields. Perhaps the best historical example of this phenomenon is the Scottish–English border region, where international discord created an extremely unstable climate for several centuries. In his absorbing book *The Steel Bonnets: The Story of the Anglo-Scottish Border Reivers,* George MacDonald Fraser concludes that the protracted fighting between England and Scotland fashioned a very precarious environment at the border, with devastating consequences for the local people:

> Whoever gained in the end, the Border Country suffered fearfully in the process. It was the ring in which the champions met; armies marched and counter-marched and fought and fled across it; it was wasted and burned and despoiled, its people harried and robbed and slaughtered, on both sides, by both sides. Whatever the rights and wrongs, the Borderers were the people who bore the brunt; for almost 300 years, from the late thirteenth century to the middle of the sixteenth, they lived on a battlefield.[13]

The experience of *tejanos* (Texas Mexicans) resembles that of the Scottish and English Borderers, although the period of extreme instability was much shorter. During the Texas rebellion of the 1830s and the U.S.–Mexico War in the following decade, the Texas–Mexico border became a ravaged wasteland, forcing many borderlanders to choose between remaining in their war-torn land and abandoning it for safer ground. Scores of tejanos sought asylum in Mexican territory, returning to their homes years later after the issue of a permanent boundary had been settled.[14]

Boundaries established by warfare or power politics often elicit challenges by the losing side, which may entertain hopes of recovering lost territory. Or, to the chagrin of its already dismembered neighbor, the victorious nation may actually seek to acquire yet more territory. In either case, one important effect is the creation of great uncertainty in the borderlands, where violence remains a strong possibility as long as the border remains unsettled. On the U.S.–Mexico border, tensions remained high for decades after the ratification of the Guadalupe Hidalgo and Gadsden treaties (in 1848 and 1854 respectively) as a result of continued official U.S. interest in absorbing more Mexican lands and repeated filibustering excursions into northern Mexico led by American and French adventurers and soldiers of fortune.[15]

Border conflict is also rooted in disagreements about natural resources or shared space between communities on opposite sides of the dividing line. Centuries ago, French and Spanish border towns in Cerdanya feuded with each other over water rights, just as towns on the U.S.–Mexico border have contested water use along the Rio Grande and the Colorado rivers since 1900.[16]

A different source of friction along unstable borders pertains to the local feuding and raiding that in many cases mirror antagonisms between parent societies. For many generations, institutionalized border lawlessness prevailed on the Scottish–English border, cited above, where neither country could control the behavior of unruly Borderers, who raided their neighbors for both personal and nationalistic reasons. Literally thousands of cross-border forays, skirmishes, and fights kept that area in turmoil, especially in the fifteenth and sixteenth centuries. "One can be in no doubt," concludes James Reed, "that the [border was] a matter of some governmental concern. It was easy for family feuds to develop into political conflicts between the nations; it was equally easy for troops to be outwitted by hostile Borderers of either realm."[17] In a determined effort to bring peace to that troubled land, the Scotsman James VI, who became King James I of Great Britain in 1603, empowered a binational commission to suppress those involved in family feuds, robberies, and murders. Subsequently the authorities ruthlessly exercised their charge, hanging forty disorderly Borderers in April 1606 alone. According to Fraser, within a few years "the system of the frontier had been destroyed . . . the life of plunder and banditry . . . was over; the whole fabric of rustling and racketeering, of feud and organized mass foray, of beacon fire and blackmail, of warden court and hot trod, of local Border law and native custom, had vanished."[18] Sustained border peace, however, did not materialize until a century later, when economic progress diminished frontier isolation and offered new opportunities for personal improvement within conventional structures.[19]

As troubled borders achieve some stability through accommodation, the dangerous climate to which borderlanders are exposed diminishes, though conflict remains a constant feature. The bitterness and distrust produced by previous tumultuous eras may linger for decades or centuries in the memories of borderlanders, making it difficult to achieve significant cross-border cooperation and interchange. Any border incident, even if minor, has the potential to rekindle old hatreds and to produce confrontations.[20]

Beyond the residual effect of historical alienation, borderlanders must confront new challenges posed by changing border conditions. Economically dynamic borderlands that have progressed to the stage of interdependence may face frictions associated with international trade, smuggling, undocumented migration, heavy cross-border traffic, and international pollution. Thus, while the emergence of interdependent borderlands has diminished traditional strife related to location, it has not eliminated conflict. New disputes have been spawned by the intrinsic contradiction of maintaining border restrictions as the economies and societies of the two sides draw closer together.

For example, high tariffs and import-export restraints inevitably produce smuggling, and immigration controls spur illegal migration, upsetting central governments bent on maintaining tight controls over their borders. As international sparring takes place over these issues, borderlanders bear the brunt of any high-level diplomatic acrimony and whatever restrictive policies are imposed on the region by bureaucrats in distant capitals. Borderlanders who disagree with the decisions of the authorities find themselves in a middle ground between national and local interests. This is a familiar pattern along the U.S.–Mexico border, where borderlanders have constantly been at odds with federal officials over many policy matters. Over time, binational communities like El Paso–Ciudad Juárez have had to work closely together to minimize the local impact of international controversies, to adjust to bothersome federal regulations, and to solve local problems through "border-style" diplomacy.[21]

When binational borderlands reach the stage of integration, borderlanders are sometimes able to shed much of the burden of being the frontline targets of international conflict and controversy. Nevertheless, even in this ideal state, sources of friction are still present because fundamental questions about economic advantage, nationality, assimilation, and identity continue to cause distress. In short, conditions on the border may change, but the innateness of the boundary as a source of friction does not disappear unless the border itself completely disappears.

While the focus of the preceding discussion has been the discordant nature of borderlands, it is important to emphasize that the forces of cooperative interaction are equally powerful. Even under conditions of alienation, some borderlanders maintain cordial cross-border relations, and during particularly stressful periods, local peacemakers emerge to assist in putting out the fires. Most human beings prefer peace over conflict and accommodation over confrontation. Hence border populations always include individuals and groups that take the lead in dealing with the tension that is inherent in their environment, in building bridges across nations and across cultures, and in creating greater transnational understanding and cooperation.

Such a trend has been very much in evidence in western Europe, where in the last half century there has been a dramatic shift from transborder confrontation to cooperation. As Julian V. Minghi has pointed out, conflict has not disappeared, but its character is totally different from pre–World War II days:

> The [western European] borderland as a region of national confrontation, security dominance and potential war no longer exists. The issues are those of local and regional control in which national borderlands, hitherto denied that right in a straitjacket of national space separated by the boundary, team together in their own self-interest across the border to protect themselves from policies which, in a spirit of international cooperation, can work to the detriment of the borderland community.[22]

Ethnic Conflict and Accommodation

In contrast to populations in national heartlands, where cultural homogeneity is the norm, people of border regions are more likely to live in heterogeneous environments because of greater ethnic mixing and more extensive migration between contiguous countries. Cultural diversity inevitably produces interethnic friction, especially if the groups represented have a history of antagonism. The greater the differences in race, religion, customs, values, and level of economic development, the more pronounced the intergroup tension. Ethnic strife often originates with attempts of mainstream societies to assimilate all groups into the nation by force, precipitating strong resistance by peoples who are determined to preserve their different identities and lifestyles. Such opposition is found especially in cases where a group is more strongly tied to people of the same ethnic background who reside across the boundary than to the dominant society in its own country. For a country concerned with national integration, such a situation is particularly vexatious. For border minorities caught up in cultural tugs-of-war, the perplexities are equally difficult.

Nationalism and interethnic hatreds often run so deep that borderlands sizzle with agitation and violence. Jean Lang paints a depressing picture of ethnic turmoil along the Scottish-English border that endured for several centuries. For the Scots, who were eventually absorbed by their more powerful neighbors, "there was never a time when England ceased to be regarded as an enemy. . . . Scot and Englishman hated one another, and it was the Borderer's part never to allow Scotland's 'auld enemy' to forget that the Scots were an independent nation, their country a free land."[23] For many Scottish Borderers, raiding English settlements became the most satisfying means of striking back at their enemies. "There can be no doubt," writes Lang, "that the Scot who risked his life by riding over the Border to despoil the English had, originally, not only the gratification of securing for himself and his countrymen much-needed loot, but felt also an ennobling glow of real patriotism. He was spoiling the Egyptians, striking a blow at the hated enemy of the country that he loved. As . . . [the raiders returned home] they could feel that there were two or three fewer Englishmen left in the world, and, for the English, certainly less worldly wealth. With patriotism as a mainspring, reiving became a profession to which not only no shame attached, but which brought much credit in the event of a successful raid."[24]

In the case of relatively isolated villagers, discord with other groups may arise out of fear and resentment triggered by encroachment from outsiders. Settlement of unwelcome "aliens" in the homeland of the local group has an especially great potential to unleash confrontation. Such polarization has been recorded in the oral traditions and ballads of numerous conquered peoples. In the Spanish–French Cerdanya of the nineteenth century, for instance, the arrival of outsiders had the effect of hardening group loyalties and affirming identities.[25]

In his discussion of balladry among folk societies, Américo Paredes emphasizes the pervasiveness of ethnic and cultural clashes in border environments:

> In the histories of European balladries one finds the heroic ballad . . . arising in
> frontier areas where small, cohesive folk groups are in conflict with another people.
> The *romance* . . . developed in Castile, where the efforts to reconquer Spain from
> the Moors came to a focus, and where border conflicts were daily fare for centuries.
> Scottish balladry also was of border origin. In Russia the *bylini* arose from the bor-
> der struggles of the Russians against the nomads of the steppes. Entwistle speaks of
> the Akritic age in Greek balladry as "the oldest stratum of European balladry: an age
> when the Greek frontier was on the Euphrates and the Saracens were their enemies."
> It would appear then that the "oldest stratum of European balladry" was also a bal-
> ladry of border warfare.[26]

Along the U.S.–Mexico border, the Mexican folk of the Texas–Tamaulipas frontier waged their own sometimes violent struggle against Anglo American intruders during the late nineteenth and early twentieth centuries. Many events, as well as sentiments of the local population, were recorded in *corridos* (ballads). "The conflict on the Rio Grande," notes Paredes, "like that on the Scottish border, was most often on an individual rather than a national scale. The fighters operated in small bands, or they were individual fighting men."[27] Apart from glorifying individuals who fought injustice for the noblest of reasons, corridos also exalted those who flouted laws considered oppressive or those who challenged the power structure. Thus smugglers, cattle rustlers, and other normally shadowy figures became bandits with a cause who deserved to be admired for their bravado in opposing the enemies of the people.[28]

As with heroes of other borderlands immortalized in popular ballads, the heroes of corridos from the Lower Rio Grande attracted little attention outside their immediate surroundings, but their deeds and the support of the common folk for resistance movements were certainly matters of concern to national authorities. One local hero who stirred the passions of his people was Gregorio Cortez, who evaded pursuit by the Texas Rangers after shooting an Anglo American sheriff. Through his fascinating study of the ballad of Cortez, Paredes has illuminated the nature of Mexican folk culture in a border environment and has provided valuable insights into the strained relations that existed between Mexican Americans and Anglos at the beginning of the twentieth century.[29] Ethnic conflict, of course, extended far beyond the Lower Rio Grande. History is filled with both large- and small-scale encounters in the border areas of West Texas, New Mexico, Arizona, and California. To a significant degree, many important events in Chicano history—such as the Texas revolt, the U.S.–Mexico War, the Cortina raids (1859–60), the El Paso Salt War (1877), the Plan de San Diego raids (1915–16), and countless other less dramatic clashes—originated in ethnic and cultural antipathies that flourished in the border region.[30]

While ethnic conflict is commonplace in border settings, harmony and cooperation are also to be found in plenty. Scottish and English Borderers, for example, who had many reasons to hate each other, nonetheless coexisted successfully and sometimes even functioned as one community in the face of threats from the outside world. "Despite national rivalry," writes Fraser, "there was considerable fraternization and cooperation between Scots and English along the frontier, socially, commercially, and criminally. There was intermarriage on a large scale."[31] Peter Sahlins likewise reports strong ethnic and cross-boundary ties between Spanish and French borderlanders in Cerdanya. In several French border communities in 1866, for example, Spaniards made up more than a third of the population. In one town, almost half of all the marriages involved Spaniards.[32] In the U.S. borderlands, along with conflict between Anglos and Mexican Americans, there has also been substantial ethnic and cultural fusion. Here again, an indicator of that integration is the high incidence of intermarriage between the two groups, especially in recent decades.[33]

Separateness

Aware of the unique environment that shapes their lives, borderlanders think of themselves as different from people of interior zones, and outsiders perceive them that way as well. Feelings of "differentness" and "separateness" originate with such factors as unique physical surroundings, ethnicity, culture, isolation, internationality, social "deviance," or combinations thereof. Andrew F. Burghardt found such a sentiment strongly embedded in the minds of borderlanders in Burgenland, a frontier area of Austria. "We are a different people with a different history and a different way of life," he reports hearing repeatedly. That feeling of "differentness" sprang primarily from Burgenland's location in a transitional zone between East and West, which in turn engendered significant cultural, ethnic, linguistic, and religious distinctiveness in the local milieu. To the Viennese, whose perspective reflected heartland views, Burgenland seemed more Hungarian than Austrian. In fact, Hungarian cultural traits abounded, since Burgenland had once belonged to Hungary.[34] Similarly, Anglo Americans have been startled by the pronounced Mexican imprint in numerous U.S. communities along the border with Mexico. The explanation, of course, is that Spain and Mexico had sovereignty over the U.S. border area for centuries, and since the establishment of the modern border in 1848, ties with the Mexican side have steadily become stronger because of increased transnational interdependence.

Noting the ambivalent nature of borderlands societies that have heterogeneous populations, Raimondo Strassoldo identifies three simultaneous psychological currents:

> The first is the ambiguous identity of individuals who feel genuinely pulled in two directions for linguistic, cultural and economic reasons. The second is a lack of strong identification with the national State, the sense that we are sui generis and unlike the populations of the heartlands of States. The third is an extreme defensive nationalism based on real or imagined dangers from across the frontier. The peculiar and specific mixtures of ambivalence, rational calculation and anxiety have made the populations of frontier regions historically interesting and important.[35]

Defensive nationalism originates both from distrust and suspicion communicated by people from the heartland, who often doubt the loyalty of frontier people, and the need of borderlanders to retain their national identity in the face of foreign assimilative influences. In reality, however, strong nationalism will coexist with weak nationalism in a border environment. Remoteness from the heartland and sustained interaction with foreigners tend to dilute the national identity of many borderlanders. This is well illustrated in the French Cerdanya during the age of Napoleon I, when Spanish Catalonians chased French troops out of the bi-national region and, much to the dismay of the French authorities, French fron-tiersmen did little to help the motherland. At the time, draft avoidance was com-mon and desertion rates were very high, prompting one French officer to express great disenchantment with his tour of duty in the area, stating that he "would rather have gone to hell." [36]

Borderlanders with the weakest national loyalty are those with strong links to the population across the border, be it through intermarriage, social relation-ships, business ties, or property ownership. Such individuals develop an inter-nationalist vision that clashes with the official stance of core-oriented authorities.

Tolerance of ethnic and cultural differences is a major trademark of border-landers with a binational orientation. Because of their unique geographical cir-cumstances, border people are constantly exposed to foreign values and atti-tudes. This contact fosters open-mindedness and cosmopolitanism, impelling borderlanders to understand and appreciate the perspective of their neighbors much better than do people in interior zones. Members of interdependent or integrated binational communities in particular must weigh carefully what stands they take in international controversies. This is illustrated in the African novel *Destination Biafra,* by Nigerian borderlander Buchi Emecheta, when a resident of the frontier town of Agbor expresses alarm at the extension of the Biafran war to her area. "Our Obi has declared us neutral," she says. "We can't afford to take sides, since we are on the border. I don't know why they should be shooting here at all." [37] One of the most significant messages in *Destination Biafra* is that human progress will be enhanced if more people repudiate confining nationalism, rigid ideologies, and restrictive group loyalties.

Many borderlanders live and function in several different worlds: the world of their national culture, the world of the border environment, the world of their ethnic group if they are members of a minority population, and the world of the foreign culture on the other side of the boundary. Considerable versatility is required to be an active participant in all of these universes, including the ability to be multilingual and multicultural. By contrast, individuals from interior zones who live in homogeneous environments have no need to develop such multifaceted human proficiencies, or to be knowledgeable and sensitive to the perspectives of other peoples.

The sense of "otherness" in a borderlands context is most profoundly illustrated in the case of individuals who manipulate national identity to their advantage. The murky waters of a mixed ethnic/national population in a binational frontier make it possible for many people to acquire or to claim citizenship in different countries and to exercise rights and privileges accordingly. Obligations that accompany citizenship often take a back seat to personal interests. Sahlins documents many cases of borderlanders on the French–Spanish frontier who moved from one side of the border to the other or who changed their identities when it was convenient and profitable. Often the stakes were high: retention of property, exemption from taxation, or escape from conscription. Both French and Spanish authorities in the nineteenth century complained about the activities of "political amphibians," people who were "neither French nor Spanish" and whose only interest seemed to be to extract benefits from both nations while at the same time avoiding responsibilities. Commenting on the situation among the Spanish Cerdans in the 1980s, Sahlins concludes that they continue to be "unabashed manipulators of identity in the service of their interests, masters of the techniques of shaping identities." [38]

Geographic location, interaction with foreigners, and cultural diversity thus make the lives of borderlanders stand out from the national norm. In an article on the U.S.–Mexico border entitled "A World Apart," a U.S. news magazine captured this anomaly well:

> In truth [the border] is a world apart—a third very unsovereign nation, not wholly American and not quite Mexican either, with its own customs, mores, values, and even its own language, Spanglish. Family ties, religious roots, and economic interdependence knit the border region in both countries together to the point that [U.S.

border cities] have more in common with their sister towns in Mexico than they do
with most of the United States.[39]

Not surprisingly, the singular nature of life in border environments has elicited
engaging commentary from popular writers, novelists, and poets. Writers of Africa have portrayed borderlands in that part of the world as places where "the
hidden, the forbidden, and the inaccessible" serve as counterpoints "to the commonplace which often lacks appeal."[40] Nobel laureate Nadine Gordimer, a white
South African, describes the lurid fascination of her countrymen for the Mozambique frontier town of Maputo (formerly Lourenço Marques), where pleasures
of all sorts are readily available. A character in Gordimer's novel, *A Sport of
Nature,* is mesmerized by the Maputo nightlife: "She fell in love with the sleazy
dockside nightclubs, the sexuality and humidity, the freedom of prostitutes.
That's what she kept going back for. To wash off the Calvinism and koshering
of [South Africa]."[41]

In U.S. literature on the American Southwest and northern Mexico, descrip-
tions abound that depict the border region as a captivating and mysterious place.
In his autobiographical novel *Southwest,* John Houghton Allen finds the border
"strange, gorgeous, and exotic."[42] Graham Greene, the English novelist, writes
in *Another Mexico* that

> everything [at the Mexican border] is going to be different. . . . The man seeking
> scenery imagines strange woods and unheard of mountains; the romantic believes
> that the women over the border will be more beautiful and complaisant than those at
> home; the unhappy man imagines at least a different hell; the suicidal traveller ex-
> pects the death he never finds. The atmosphere of the border—it is like starting over
> again; there is something about it like a good confession: poised for a few happy
> moments between sin and sin. When people die on the border they call it "a happy
> death."[43]

Greene's characterization of the Mexican border as a haven for fantasy, pleasure,
and sin is standard fare with American writers. Among the world's borderlands,
the Mexican border has perhaps the most notorious reputation for vice, deca-
dence, and unlawful activity. In the nineteenth century, writers with a flair for
the sensational and the lurid began a tradition of spotlighting the "hellish" environment of the region. An essay in an American magazine published in 1880,
for example, described the area as "a land where there is compressed more
crime, licentiousness, and immorality per capita than in any other country claiming to rank with the civilized peoples of the world."[44]

By the 1920s, during the age of Prohibition in the United States, cities such
as Ciudad Juárez and Tijuana had achieved fame as playgrounds for pleasure-
seeking Americans. Throngs of visitors crossed into Mexico to drink, gamble,

and partake of other nighttime recreation not readily available back home. The stereotype of Mexican border towns as Sodoms and Gomorrahs was added to the already long list of negative images of Mexico. In the American mind the border came to represent a divide between progress and backwardness, between good and evil. That perception was dramatically captured in a Charlie Chaplin film in 1923. In the final scene of *The Pilgrim,* escaped convict Chaplin "runs along the . . . border, one foot on either side, unable to choose between the United States, representing law and order, . . . and Mexico, representing lawlessness and anarchism."[45]

Hollywood continued to portray the Mexican border in highly unflattering terms in many movies after the Chaplin era, even into the 1990s. Countless stories about the border told on the silver screen have used lawlessness, banditry, gangsterism, corruption, gambling, drug addiction, prostitution, and smuggling as central or subsidiary themes.[46] In so doing, U.S. moviemakers have given their audiences what they expect to see, that is, what the latter think they know, recognize, or understand about the border: deviancy, degradation, and disorder.[47]

On the other side of the boundary, Mexicans have similarly portrayed the border as undesirable, emphasizing that many of the people who live there are culturally and morally corrupt and that they live amidst a multitude of dangers. Accusations leveled at *fronterizos* (borderlanders) by their countrymen include an alleged tendency toward *agringamiento* (embracing the American culture at the expense of their own), an addiction to foreign products, and a shameful tolerance for all manner of illegal activity. Many Mexicans have also been very critical of conditions on the U.S. side, where they see Mexican immigrants and Mexican Americans victimized by American materialism, discrimination, poverty, social disintegration, and rampant crime. Numerous Mexican films have used such themes both to entertain and "educate" movie audiences concerning the evil environment of the border region.[48]

One particularly interesting phenomenon in the human drama found in border regions is the frequent concentration of displaced or misplaced peoples among local populations. Economic immigrants usually constitute the bulk of the uprooted, but refugees, exiles, expatriates, and miscellaneous nonconformists from other lands seek the shelter of friendly borderlands as well. The Scottish–English border, for instance, became a haven for witches, gypsies, and religious "deviants" during the centuries when frontier isolation prevailed and protection from persecutors and lawmen could easily be obtained in the hill country on either side of the boundary.[49] In the case of the Canadian border with the United States, several Hollywood films have portrayed the region as a place that has offered escape, a second chance, an opportunity to forget, and safety and comfort for those in need of it. In real life, American runaway slaves did indeed seek refuge in Canada in the nineteenth century, and draft dodgers did the same during several wars in the twentieth.[50]

The borderlanders' sense of being different often has far-reaching political consequences for both the borderlands and the nations to which they belong. By virtue of their distance and isolation from the heartlands, coupled with unique local ethnic and economic characteristics, borderlands frequently develop interests that clash with central governments or with mainstream cultures. Consequently, alienation from the core is not uncommon. In his perceptive analysis of the dynamics of frontier and border areas, K. D. Kristof writes that "frontiersmen tend to insist on a degree of detachment, autonomy, and differentness which sets them apart and is incompatible with the state interests and the rule of law as seen by the central government."[51]

Borderlanders clamor for recognition of their special needs by the authorities, often insisting that some national laws have detrimental regional effects and must therefore be changed or enforced differently in border zones. Statutes dictated by the national government that do not interfere with local customs or cross-border symbiotic relationships meet no resistance, but those that do are routinely circumvented or violated. For example, borderlanders find it morally and culturally acceptable to breach trade and immigration regulations that interfere with the "natural order" of cross-border interaction.

More than any other activity, smuggling exemplifies the tendency of borderlanders to function outside of established national rules. Surreptitious trade is found in border zones throughout the world, and it flourishes in those areas where economic disparity between one side of the border and the other creates special opportunities for entrepreneurs seeking to make a fortune, workers in search of more remunerative employment, and shoppers in quest of bargains.[52] High tariffs and rigid prohibitions against the importation of unwelcome products only encourage borderlanders to become more adroit in violating the law.[53] A popular justification for defying the state in this manner is that import regulations are often unrealistic because they fail to take into account the unique conditions in binational settings where interdependence is a way of life. Such laws, borderlanders insist, are made by distant, insensitive, and excessively nationalistic politicians. Moreover, the sentiments of borderlanders, whose usually sparse numbers and remoteness from the center of power limit their political clout, are said to be frequently ignored by decision makers.

In extreme cases, independent-minded groups living along the edge of a nation's territorial domain may function outside the established political and economic systems. Many merchants and traders in particular may come to think of themselves as members of a self-contained and self-directed border economic community rather than as "pure" citizens of a nation, whose behavior must conform strictly to national norms. This sense of economic independence emboldens them to ignore or circumvent laws they dislike and to carry on relationships with foreign neighbors that promote their own interests and those of their binational region. Frontiersmen with substantial cross-boundary links often function as a "joint community," according to Owen D. Lattimore, and "become a 'we' group to whom others of their own nationality, and especially the authorities, are 'they.' [Thus] it is not surprising that the ambivalent loyalties of frontier peoples are often conspicuous and historically important."[54]

Self-assertiveness vis-à-vis central authority may become widespread among different sectors of borderlands society, sometimes leading to subversive activity and even secessionism. For example, a strong sense of regionalism and rebelliousness existed in the Cerdanya in the seventeenth and eighteenth centuries, eliciting complaints from both Spanish and French officials regarding the recalcitrance of the frontiersmen.[55] To the present day, Spanish Cerdans continue to express strong nationalistic sentiments, as do the Basques on the opposite end of the Spanish–French border. In the case of China, regionalist Manchurians resisted the authority of the national government for many centuries. Even in recent times, Sinkiang province has been prone to separatism owing to its remoteness, different ethnic configuration, and proximity to the former Soviet Union. Ethnic and religious animosities coupled with resentment of Chinese rule triggered repeated regional uprisings along that periphery during the last century.[56] The most dramatic contemporary manifestation of frontier secessionism occurred in the Soviet Union following the collapse of communism in 1991. It is significant that the spirit of independence has been most pronounced in the republics located on the periphery of the former empire.

In the Mexican borderlands adjacent to the United States, strong regionalist sentiments fueled by ties to foreigners have at times escalated into full-scale rebellions against the control of Mexico City. To a significant degree, the Texas movement for independence in the 1830s grew out of dissatisfaction with central rule. In the late 1840s and early 1850s, an insurrection involving rebels from both sides of the border sought to create a Republic of Sierra Madre, whose territory would consist of a small portion of Texas along the Rio Grande and much of northeastern Mexico. More recently, strong regionalist sentiments have been expressed by Mexican borderlanders through repeated rejections at the polls of the Partido Revolucionario Institucional, the nation's ruling party.[57]

Conclusion

This chapter has presented a conceptual framework for understanding the functioning of borderlands, distinguishing among four types: alienated, coexistent, interdependent, and integrated borderlands. A binational region's location within this scheme depends on numerous factors, including topography and environment, distance from the heartland, demographic profile, ethnic and cultural patterns, level of economic development, and the international climate. The constellation and mix of these elements shape cross-border links.

By nature all borderlands, regardless of their location or level of interaction, function in an environment—here called the borderlands milieu—that springs from boundary-related phenomena. As the peripheries of nations, borderlands are subject to frontier forces and international influences that mold the unique way of life of borderlanders, prompting them to confront myriad challenges stemming from the paradoxical nature of the setting in which they live. Borders simultaneously divide and unite, repel and attract, separate and integrate. These opposing forces have the effect of pulling borderlanders in different directions, causing stress in both the private and public domains. Such inherent liabilities reveal only a one-side-of-the-border experience, however. To be a borderlander is to have opportunities unavailable to people from heartland areas. Through exposure to transnational interactions and transculturation, borderlanders are able to develop versatility in their human relationships, and access to a foreign economy increases employment possibilities and consumer choices.

At the level of the nation, the implications of intense ties between people of adjoining borderlands are profound. Transnational interaction implies diminished sovereignty on both sides of the border. The expansion of economic activity in a border zone means population growth at the margin of the nation and consequent migration, both documented and undocumented, back and forth across the boundary. Finally, questions of national identity emerge as borderlanders fuse their culture with that of their neighbors, creating new social patterns that people in heartland zones may find abhorrent.

2

THE U.S.–MEXICO BORDERLANDS

Functionally, the U.S.–Mexico borderlands resemble border regions in other parts of the world, but the high level of transboundary interchange makes this binational zone quite distinct. Nowhere else do so many millions of people from two so dissimilar nations live in such close proximity and interact with each other so intensely. Here the modern industrial world clashes and blends with the developing world, engendering myriad human relationships. Interestingly, this First World–Third World dichotomy has produced a vibrant binational economy and society that thrives on cultural adaptation and experimentation.

The dynamic interaction that characterizes the borderlands today derives from an evolutionary process that began centuries ago when European powers competed for control of North America. Both the United States and Mexico emerged as nations from this process, and their common border took shape when the struggle for territory reached a decisive stage in the mid nineteenth century. The first part of this chapter traces the major stages of historical interaction in the region, focusing on relations between the two countries and the ways in which cross-border interaction has been affected by international conditions. The second part examines contemporary transnational interaction within the framework of social, economic, and cultural links that bind U.S. and Mexican borderlanders.

The Evolution of the Borderlands

Using the model of borderlands interaction delineated in Chapter 1 and reaching back in time to the earliest days of European confrontation in northern New Spain, the history of the U.S.–Mexico borderlands may be divided into periods as follows:[1]

STAGE	PERIOD	MAJOR BORDER-RELATED DEVELOPMENTS
Alienation	1560s–1880	European competition for control of North American territory, beginning with skirmishes in the Caribbean area; the Louisiana controversy; the Texas revolt; the War of 1846–1848; the Gadsden Purchase; filibustering; Indian raids; banditry; pronounced ethnic conflict
Coexistence	1880–1920	1880–1910: Lessening of frontier lawlessness; flow of U.S. capital into northern Mexico; railroads crisscrossing the borderlands, connecting northern Mexico to the United States; growth of borderlands cities; Mexican migration to the United States 1910–1920: ebb and flow between coexistence and alienation caused by Mexican Revolution and anti-Americanism in Mexico
Interdependence	1920–Present	Border rectification agreements; water treaties; the Chamizal settlement; expansion of border trade, industrialization, tourism, and migration; extraordinary population and urban growth

Alienation, the 1560s to 1880

The International Political Climate

The historical political geography of the U.S.–Mexico borderlands is traced in Figures 2.1 to 2.6. The earliest stage unfolded in the sixteenth and seventeenth centuries, when Spain, Great Britain, and France established colonies in North America, initiating a spirited contest for ownership of the continent among themselves and with the diverse Native American groups. Spain advanced northward into what is now Florida and the U.S. Southwest from the Caribbean and central Mexico, France moved southward from the Great Lakes into the Mississippi Valley, and Britain planted colonies on the Atlantic coast from New England to South Carolina (Figure 2.1). The European powers sought to expand their possessions outward from these settlements, creating new borderlands with each advance. By the early 1700s Spanish, French, and British colonists were facing each other in three borderlands (Figure 2.2). In 1763, following the Seven Years' War, France transferred the Louisiana territory to Spain, and Spain ceded Florida to Britain, bringing about a new spatial configuration. Twenty years later Spain reacquired Florida from Britain as the United States struggled to survive as an independent nation (Figure 2.3).

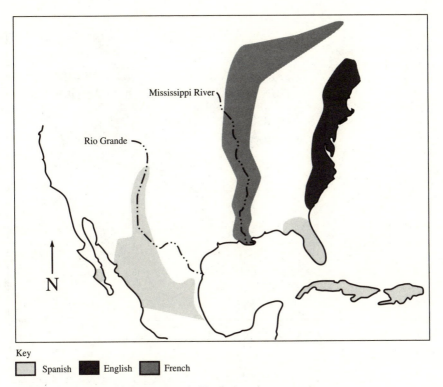

Key
Spanish   English   French

FIGURE 2.1 European frontier zones in North America, ca. 1700

Another major realignment took place in 1803 when the United States purchased Louisiana from France, which had reacquired it from Spain three years
earlier (Figure 2.4). Unfortunately, the precise location of Louisiana's western
border was unknown, leading Spain and the United States to engage in a prolonged and vigorous debate over the extent of each other's territorial claims. The
discussions resulted in the signing of the Adams-Onís Treaty of 1819, which
made East Florida an American possession and established the Sabine River as
the demarcation line between Louisiana and the northeastern frontier of New
Spain (Figure 2.5). Many Americans, however, denounced the treaty, accusing
Secretary of State John Quincy Adams of giving away Texas, a province that
they believed was an integral part of the Louisiana Territory. From the perspective of the treaty negotiators, however, the historical record did not support that
position, and the U.S. government had to renounce any claim to Texas.

Nevertheless, the desire to possess Texas persisted among American expan-
sionists. Once Mexico became an independent nation in 1821, the United States

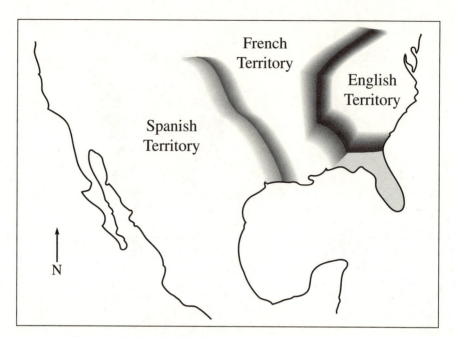

FIGURE 2.2 The Spanish–French–English borderlands, 1700–1763

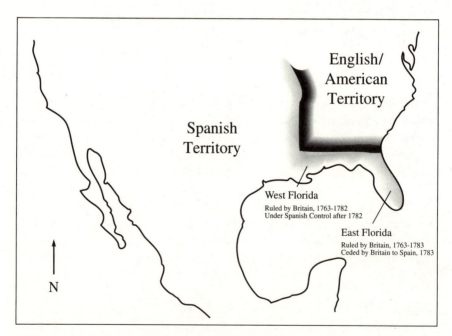

FIGURE 2.3 The Spanish–English–American borderlands, 1763–1800

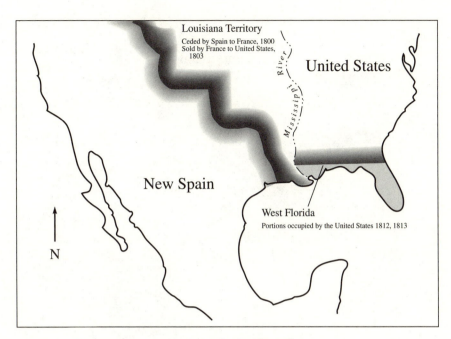

FIGURE 2.4 The Spanish–American borderlands, 1800–1819

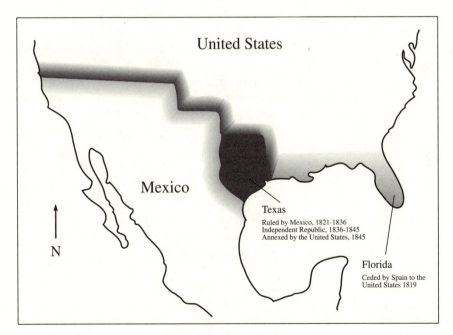

FIGURE 2.5 Mexican–U.S. borderlands, 1819–1848

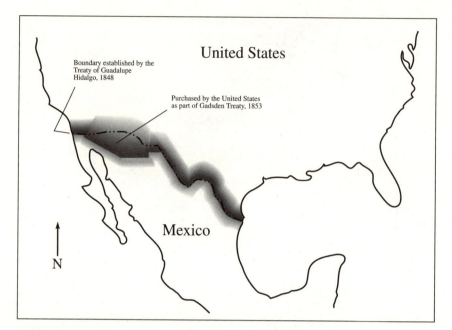

Boundary established by the
Treaty of Guadalupe
Hidalgo, 1848

United States

Purchased by the United States
as part of Gadsden Treaty, 1853

Mexico

N

FIGURE 2.6 Mexican–U.S. borderlands, 1848 to the present

repeatedly attempted to buy the province, along with New Mexico and California, but Mexico refused to sell any portion of its northern frontier. In the
1820s and 1830s large-scale American immigration into Texas precipitated a war
for independence and eventually annexation to the United States in 1845 (Figure 2.5). The loss of Texas worsened the already aggravated relations between
Mexico and the United States, and war erupted in 1846. When that conflict ended
almost two years later, Mexico was forced to agree to a new boundary that drastically altered the configuration of the borderlands. Uncertainties in the Treaty
of Guadalupe Hidalgo about the exact location of the new border were cleared
up with the Gadsden Treaty, which transferred additional Mexican lands in
southern New Mexico and southern Arizona to the United States (Figure 2.6).
Friction over the location of the boundary persisted for years after the signing
of the Gadsden Treaty because of a continuing desire among American expan-
sionists for more Mexican territory, but apart from minor refinements, no further
changes in the border took place.[2]

Chronic tension in the borderlands stemmed from the exploits of Indians,
bandits, filibusters, smugglers, cattle thieves, chasers of runaway slaves, trigger-
happy lawmen, and assorted adventurers and desperados who found a haven on

the isolated, sparsely populated frontier. Moreover, racial clashes continually plagued relations between Anglo Americans and people of Mexican ancestry.[3]

The foregoing events made life difficult for borderlanders during the long stage of alienation, but in reality there were also prolonged periods of peace and stability. Local residents tried hard to minimize conflict and to encourage trade and social interaction. By the late nineteenth century the people of the borderlands had drawn increasingly close, largely as a result of a steady rise in population and diminution of regional isolation. Two powerful countervailing forces— alienation and accommodation—actually worked simultaneously both to repel borderlanders and to unify them. In the struggle between the two, the tendency toward consolidation proved to be more enduring.

Regionalization and Cross-Border Economic Interaction

As early as the sixteenth century, Mexico's northern territories assumed distinctiveness as a distant frontier with its own identity. There was relatively little contact with the outside world—or even within the region itself—because of difficult geography, sweeping desert terrain, and vast distances between settlements. Communication and trade with the Mexican core took place along three land corridors that originated in central Mexico and ran northeast to Texas, north to New Mexico, and northwest to Arizona and California. The Mexican core also maintained sporadic contact with California via the sea. Despite the geographic obstacles, the people of the Spanish/Mexican borderlands managed to maintain regular internal contact via the main north–south corridors as well as some east–west trails, including those linking distant New Mexico to Arizona and California, which were developed at the end of the Spanish period.

The sense of frontier separateness and cultural distinctiveness remained constant up to the mid nineteenth century, when Mexico lost its northernmost provinces to the expansionist United States. Texas, New Mexico, Arizona, and California—the principal ceded lands—became the U.S. borderlands, and Tamaulipas, Nuevo León, Coahuila, Chihuahua, Sonora, and Baja California became the Mexican borderlands. Each border area now functioned in a different political environment, but in reality the new boundary did little to retard the process of economic convergence that had slowly been reshaping all these provinces from a collection of disparate parts into one relatively cohesive whole.

The regionalization of the borderlands had taken a significant step forward in the early 1800s when Anglo American spies, adventurers, trappers, traders, merchants, colonists, and assorted visitors began settling in the area. This infiltration grew to become a steady stream by the 1830s, with its greatest impact coming in Texas, New Mexico, and California as the newcomers established important trade routes between these provinces and the eastern United States.[4] By virtue of their location, Tamaulipas, Nuevo León, and Chihuahua also participated in the process of enhancing the region's external links. In short, the first half of the nineteenth century led to an increase in the area's population, improvements in its existing roads and the construction of new ones, a lessening of isolation, and the establishment of incipient transnational interaction.

From the 1850s through the 1870s the U.S. border region underwent gradual incorporation into the economy of the eastern United States and, to a lesser degree, so too did the Mexican borderlands. Texas, New Mexico, Arizona, California, Chihuahua, and Sonora supplied minerals, cattle, crops, and cheap labor for industries controlled by outside interests, establishing a pattern that would last well into the twentieth century.[5]

Coexistence, 1880–1920

The International Political Climate

By the early 1880s, international conflict had diminished considerably in the borderlands as a result of better relations between the United States and Mexico and a new climate that was conducive to regional growth and prosperity. The era of U.S. expansionism at the expense of Mexico had passed, troublesome Indians had been largely pacified, and general frontier lawlessness had been curbed. Porfirio Díaz, the Mexican dictator driven by the philosophy of "order and progress," is credited with bringing about enforced stability throughout Mexico, including the northern border. Díaz also actively cultivated good relations with the United States, and for the next several decades a formerly turbulent binational relationship evolved into a businesslike association.[6]

In 1910 the Mexican Revolution shattered the stability of the previous generation, plunging the two nations anew into numerous confrontations along the border and elsewhere. To a significant degree, U.S. intervention in the affairs of Mexico from 1913 to 1916 led to many of the diplomatic troubles, but chaotic conditions inside Mexico took their toll as well. For a decade, borderlanders on both sides witnessed continuous revolts, battles, raids, racial clashes, and displacement of the population. The Mexican border cities became major battlegrounds on several occasions, and fighting spilled over into the United States.[7] In 1916 a raid on Columbus, New Mexico, by the forces of Pancho Villa precipitated a "punitive" U.S. expedition onto Mexican soil, bringing the two nations dangerously close to war. The crisis passed, however, and the two neighbors gradually reestablished normal relations.[8]

The volatile climate of the revolutionary years seriously disrupted life in the borderlands, but as in previous eras, a spirit of coexistence prevailed much of the time, with the two sides doing their best to minimize the damage to the cooperative relationship they had built during the Porfiriato. In cities like El Paso and

Ciudad Juárez, the extant cross-border bonds endured despite repeated setbacks, assuring that the trend toward greater binational interchange would continue.[9]

Cross-Border Economic Interaction

The growth in U.S. investments in Mexico helped to assure the survival of the binational links even during difficult times. Throughout the Porfiriato, Mexico had opened its economy to foreigners as never before, and for the first time Anglo American investors ventured south of the border in significant numbers, pouring vast amounts of capital into transportation, mining, ranching, and agriculture. Díaz offered foreigners generous concessions, eliciting an enthusiastic response from capitalists interested in exploiting the economic potential of resource-rich states like Sonora and Chihuahua. Foreign railroad companies received cash subsidies, mineral rights, and tax exemptions, while land companies obtained a third of the land they surveyed and subdivided, with the option to purchase portions of the remaining land at bargain prices. Petroleum companies benefited substantially from changes in the Mexican mining codes in the 1880s and 1890s that transferred subsoil rights to mineral fuels from government to private ownership.[10]

These attractive incentives prompted U.S. conglomerates such as the Doheny interests to purchase thousands of acres for oil exploitation. In the mining sector, the Guggenheim interests bought mines, built smelters, and controlled other mining-related operations. Along the Sonora border, William C. Greene built the Cananea Consolidated Copper Company into a major copper-producing concern, and in Chihuahua the Hearst family acquired vast areas of prime farm and ranch land at bargain prices.[11] The railroads and mining companies hired large numbers of Mexican workers, creating a foreign economic orientation among key sectors of the population of northern Mexico. The tendency was reinforced by the steadily increasing migration of Mexicans to similar but better paying jobs in the U.S. borderlands.[12]

By 1910 the Mexican borderlands, linked in numerous ways with the economy of the U.S. Southwest, had been drawn into a well-established system that reached far beyond the boundary. Like their counterparts in the United States, the Mexican border states supplied raw materials and cheap labor to the industrial northeastern United States. Once the railroads were firmly in place on both sides of the border, the resources of the binational region became readily accessible, enticing distant Anglo American entrepreneurs to channel capital both to the U.S. Southwest and to northern Mexico. The production of primary goods rose substantially in the region, and both sides of the border figured prominently in the growth experienced by the United States as a whole at the turn of the century.

In the mining sector, the binational region participated in the exploitation of precious metals, namely gold and silver, and in the production of industrial metals such as copper. The latter product, mined heavily in New Mexico, Arizona, and Sonora, contributed significantly to the electrification of the United States. The railroads played a key role in mining by transporting ores to smelting centers in the borderlands and to industrial sites in the eastern United States. Railroads also facilitated the shipping of livestock and crops from the border region to distant urban markets. Agricultural production in the U.S. Southwest grew at a phenomenal pace in the early twentieth century as a result of the great infusion of investment capital and irrigation initiatives of the federal government. The Newlands Reclamation Act of 1902, for example, supported the construction of dams and canals that transformed many U.S. desert areas into productive fields.[13]

California benefitted more than any other state from government projects. It soon became the leading agricultural state in the United States, producing a wide variety of fruits, vegetables, and other crops. Between 1900 and 1920, orange growers quadrupled their production, and lemon growers increased theirs fivefold. During World War I, California growers were responsible for more than a third of all food production in the United States. Much of the labor needed to harvest the crops in California and other parts of the Southwest originated in the Mexican borderlands, underscoring the growing complementarity of the two sides of the boundary.[14]

Interdependence, 1920 to the Present

The International Political Climate

After the Mexican Revolution, the binational borderlands entered into a new relationship that mirrored the improved atmosphere between Washington and Mexico City. Unrest in Mexico, while still present, declined considerably as the nation turned its attention to rebuilding the political system and the economy. Intrigues and battles along the border became a thing of the past, and the intense nationalism of the previous decade subsided as the region shifted its focus to promoting growth and strengthening traditional cross-border links.

To be sure, in building the new relationship both nations had to overcome serious obstacles created by nineteenth-century conflicts and the legacy of the Revolution. One particularly thorny issue at the national level that had significant regional ramifications as well concerned the manner in which foreign capitalists conducted business in Mexico. The United States disapproved of the efforts of postrevolutionary governments to redefine the property rights of foreigners, especially in the extractive industries. As Mexico invoked its constitutionally mandated government ownership of subsoil resources, U.S. and British oil companies fought back with every means at their disposal. Compromises reached in the 1920s allowed the companies to continue extracting petroleum under new rules,

but in the 1930s a labor dispute escalated into a full-fledged confrontation between the companies and the Lázaro Cárdenas government when the former refused to abide by a ruling issued by the Mexican Supreme Court which favored
the workers. Reacting to the intransigence and arrogance of the companies, Cárdenas dealt them a fatal blow in 1938 by nationalizing the oil industry. Fears that
the United States would intervene on behalf of the companies vanished when the
Roosevelt administration acknowledged Mexico's right to expropriate property
belonging to foreigners, admonishing only that the companies be given fair and
prompt treatment.

Roosevelt's "Good Neighbor Policy" of the late 1930s and early 1940s improved relations between the two countries and enhanced cooperation and friendship in the borderlands. Frictions remained, but the focus of disagreement shifted
from fundamental questions to more routine quarrels. For example, in the area
of trade, the importation of certain Mexican agricultural products into the United
States elicited opposition from American protectionists, causing occasional confrontations along the border. Above all, the smuggling of drugs aroused the ire
of several administrations in Washington which focused attention on the border
communities where most of the trafficking took place. To this day, trade and
narcotics have remained constant irritants in the relationship between the two
countries.

The two nations have also skirmished for decades over the issue of Mexican
undocumented migration to the United States.[15] Tension has been steady and
constant, but the periods of greatest acrimony are as follows:

PERIOD	SOURCE OF CONTROVERSY
Early 1920s	U.S. debate on immigration quotas
Early 1930s	Repatriation of a half-million Mexicans from the United States
Late 1940s	Border incidents and disagreements over provisions of the Bracero Program
Early 1950s	Massive deportation of Mexicans under "Operation Wet-back"; border incidents
1960s-Present	Prolonged debate in the United States over legislation to curb undocumented immigration; a new restrictive law passed in 1986; border incidents; human rights abuses

Of the four problem areas that have troubled U.S.–Mexican border relations
since the 1920s—the property rights of foreigners in Mexico, protectionism,
drug trafficking, and undocumented immigration—only the first one has been
eliminated as an active source of tension. The others continue to create head-
aches for both nations, and this pattern will probably continue well beyond the

year 2000. Without minimizing the seriousness of these problems, however, it is important to emphasize that their very existence is a manifestation of the high degree of transnational interaction that has characterized life in the borderlands during the last seven decades.

Cross-Border Economic Interaction

The trend toward vigorous interdependence began in the 1920s, when Prohibition in the United States led to a tourist boom in the border cities. Twin-city complexes like San Diego–Tijuana and El Paso–Ciudad Juárez witnessed the emergence of a new level of economic symbiosis as throngs of Americans patronized Mexican tourist establishments and large numbers of Mexicans shopped in the expanding commercial centers of the U.S. border communities.[16] The Great Depression eroded some of the economic expansion recorded in the 1920s, but the trend toward increased interdependence continued. With the eruption of World War II, both sides received an unprecedented impulse for new regional development as a result of the growth of defense-related industries in the U.S. Southwest. The U.S. government expanded existing military installations, created new ones, and financed research facilities to develop modern weaponry. New industries that served the needs of the military stimulated other economic activity, which in turn attracted increasing numbers of people to formerly slow-growing centers of population in desert areas. Large government expenditures also went for improvements in the infrastructure, such as interstate highways and water projects, substantially raising the capacity of the region to sustain rapid urbanization.[17] Growth in the U.S. Southwest was further stimulated by the Korean and Vietnam wars and the shift of economic activity from the industrial Snowbelt to the southern and western Sunbelt.[18]

U.S. border cities benefitted substantially from these trends, expanding and diversifying their economies beyond the traditional agricultural, ranching, mining, trade, and service-oriented activities. For example, by the 1960s El Paso had boosted its agricultural and tourist sectors and had developed substantial labor-intensive industries that employed large numbers of low-wage workers, many of them from Mexico. The need for Mexican domestics went up dramatically as American women became wage earners in ever-increasing numbers and as a result needed help with housekeeping and child care. As El Paso became more integrated into the national economy, giant corporations established local operations. Soon modern commercial centers and shopping malls sprang up to serve the new middle-class suburbs.

The post–World War II boom affected the Mexican border cities just as forcefully, with the result that new waves of job-seeking migrants from the interior of Mexico began to make their way to the northern frontier. The economic growth along the border also reflected trends throughout Mexico, since the postwar years constituted a period of great national progress. *La frontera,* with its dynamic, U.S.–driven economy, surpassed most other regions of Mexico in the expansion of trade, industry, and tourism. As military installations in the U.S. borderlands enlarged their populations during the war years, soldiers, sailors, and marines by the millions visited such cities as Ciudad Juárez and Tijuana, stimulating local entertainment and other service-related activities. In addition, tourism continued to rise as more and more American families traveled in the U.S. Southwest and made short trips across the border, and as more visitors spent time at the border in preparation for trips to the interior of Mexico. Other sectors of the Mexican frontier economy such as commerce also grew rapidly as American shoppers from nearby U.S. cities, particularly Mexican Americans, crossed the border to buy a wide variety of Mexican products.

The strong symbiotic relationship between the U.S. and Mexican borderlands is best illustrated by the large-scale and steady flow of migrant workers northward across the boundary that has continued since the days of World War II. Starting in 1942, the Bracero Program, the bilateral labor-contract arrangement that supplied Mexican workers to U.S. agriculture well into the 1960s, created a stream of migration that swelled the population of the frontier communities. Initially *braceros* merely used the border cities as way stations in their journey to the U.S. interior, but eventually large numbers of these workers made *la frontera* their permanent home, especially after the termination of the program in 1964. The displaced braceros expanded an already sizable local labor force that was firmly oriented toward the U.S. economy. In the decades that followed, the migration of poor Mexican workers from the interior who were intent on obtaining better jobs in "El Norte" increased even more, solidifying the dependence of many U.S. borderland communities on foreign workers, many of them undocumented. The Mexican border cities played a key role in the system of labor exchange, acting as staging areas and springboards for the migrants.[19]

The high unemployment rate along the Mexican border caused by the termination of the Bracero Program constitutes a primary reason for one of the most significant borderland initiatives: the Border Industrialization Program (BIP).[20] Conceived by Mexican border entrepreneurs and quickly endorsed by Mexico City, since 1965 the BIP has permitted U.S. and other foreign companies to establish low-wage assembly plants, or *maquiladoras,* along the Mexican frontier. Although they grew at a modest rate in the first few years of the program, by the mid-1970s the maquiladoras had begun to take off, achieving phenomenal expansion when the continuous devaluation of the Mexican peso reduced labor costs to rock-bottom levels. By 1992 about 2,000 maquiladoras were employing close to 500,000 workers, with thousands of others employed in sectors of the border economy directly or indirectly related to the program. In less than a generation the maquiladoras had become the principal economic activity along the border, providing striking evidence of the area's overwhelming ties with the U.S. economy.

On the eve of the twenty-first century, transnational economic interaction has intensified as a result of Mexico's liberalization of foreign investment laws and drastic reduction in its tariffs. When the North American Free Trade Agreement is fully enacted, it will signal the beginning of a new phase in the bilateral relationship. The continuing process of increasing symbiosis will be greatly accelerated, and it could eventually culminate in the merger of the two economies. Free trade will speed the transformation of the borderlands from a condition of advanced interdependence to one of incipient integration. Free trade, however, while bringing benefits to both sides of the border, will not alter the fundamentally unequal relationship that has existed in the region since the creation of the boundary. The United States, with its powerful industrial economy, will continue to dominate Mexico's predominantly Third World economy. If anything, free trade will accentuate the asymmetry that now characterizes borderlands interdependence. In other words, the movement will be from asymmetrical interdependence to asymmetrical integration.

Contemporary Interaction in the Borderlands

As the historical record makes clear, transnational interaction in the borderlands has increased steadily since the mid nineteenth century and particularly in the last five decades. Territorial disputes, warfare, violations of sovereignty, banditry, raiding, ethnic conflicts, protectionism, smuggling, illegal migration, environmental pollution, and other border-related sources of friction certainly have taken their toll, but they have failed to stop the growth of cross-border interdependence. Today an extraordinary level of symbiosis is evident in the many economic and cultural bonds that fuse the destinies of the two sides of the boundary. This symbiosis is most obvious in the close relationships between the border urban complexes, which geographer Lawrence A. Herzog has described as

> a single functional spatial domain that transcends the international border . . . [a] transnational settlement functionally unified by common daily activity systems (work, shopping, school, social trips), shared natural resources and environmental features (air, water, flora, fauna), and product and labor markets that overlap the political boundary. . . . The transfrontier metropolis . . . embraces two forces—the traditional cities, as defined by national culture, and the integrated metropolis, defined by evolving social, cultural, and economic processes that connect the United States and Mexico across the border on a daily basis.[21]

This book is essentially a study of the border urban population involved in the processes outlined above. Thus, as used here the term *borderlands* usually refers

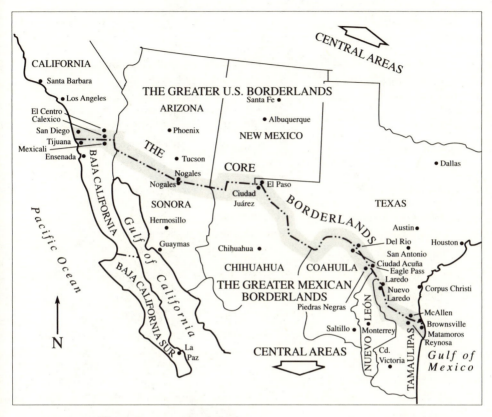

FIGURE 2.7 The contemporary borderlands

to the transborder metropolises, but at times it may apply to the entire border strip, consisting of forty-nine rural and urban U.S. border counties and thirty-six rural and urban Mexican *municipios* (municipalities); this corridor is the heart of the borderlands, or the core borderlands. The "greater" borderlands may be visualized as the U.S. and Mexican border states—Texas, New Mexico, Arizona, and California on the American side and Tamaulipas, Nuevo León, Coahuila, Chihuahua, Sonora, and Baja California on the Mexican side (Figure 2.7).

Population Groups

As of 1990, almost 9 million people lived along the U.S.–Mexico border, 3.8 million in the Mexican municipios and 5.1 million in the U.S. counties (see Tables 2.1 through 2.4).[22] Tijuana, Mexicali, and Ciudad Juárez, with populations of 742,686, 602,390, and 797,679 respectively, were the most populous Mexican border cities, while San Diego and El Paso, with populations of 1,110,140 and 503,325 respectively, led the U.S. border cities. Data for the U.S.

TABLE 2.1. Population of Mexican Border *Municipios*, 1980 and 1990

	1980	1990
BAJA CALIFORNIA		
Tijuana	461,257	742,686
Tecate	30,540	51,946
Mexicali	510,664	602,390
TOTAL	1,002,461	1,397,022
SONORA		
San Luis Río Colorado	92,790	111,508
Puerto Peñasco	26,775	26,200
Plutarco Elías Calles	—[a]	9,691
Caborca	50,452	58,516
Altar	6,029	6,431
Saric	2,250	2,075
Nogales	68,076	107,119
Santa Cruz	1,587	1,479
Cananea	25,327	27,026
Naco	4,441	4,636
Agua Prieta	34,380	39,045
TOTAL	312,107	384,035
CHIHUAHUA		
Janos	8,906	11,113
Ascención	11,985	16,565
Juárez	567,365	797,679
P. G. Guerrero	7,777	8,395
Guadalupe	8,876	9,109
Ojinaga	26,421	23,947
TOTAL	631,330	866,808
NUEVO LEÓN		
Anahuac	16,479	17,248
TOTAL	16,479	17,248

TABLE 2.1. *Continued*

	1980	1990
TAMAULIPAS		
Nuevo Laredo	203,286	217,912
Guerrero	4,191	4,315
Mier	6,382	6,032
Miguel Alemán	19,600	21,127
Camargo	16,014	15,029
Gustavo Díaz Ordaz	17,830	17,598
Reynosa	211,412	281,618
Río Bravo	83,522	93,931
Matamoros	238,840	303,392
TOTAL	801,177	960,954
COAHUILA		
Ocampo	9,000	7,952
Acuña	41,948	56,750
Jiménez	8,636	7,922
Piedras Negras	80,290	98,177
Guerrero	2,316	2,351
Hidalgo	751	1,192
TOTAL	142,941	174,344
TOTAL FOR ALL MUNICIPIOS	3,145,215	3,800,411

SOURCE: Mexico, *X censo general de población y vivienda, 1980*, Mexico,
   XI censo general de población y vivienda, 1990: Résultados preliminares.

[a] Part of Puerto Peñasco municipio in 1980.

TABLE 2.2. Population of Major Mexican Border Cities,
1980 and 1990

	1980	1990
Tijuana	461,257	742,686
Mexicali	510,664	602,390
Nogales	68,076	107,119
Ciudad Juárez	567,365	797,679
Piedras Negras	80,290	98,177
Nuevo Laredo	203,286	217,912
Reynosa	211,412	281,618
Matamoros	238,840	303,392

SOURCE: Mexico, *X censo general de población, 1980;* Mexico, *XI censo
general de población y vivienda, 1990: Resultados preliminares.*

border counties reveal that Anglo Americans comprised 50 percent of the population concentrated along the border, Mexican Americans 41 percent, and other
groups (African Americans, Native Americans, etc.) 9 percent. Anglos are numerically dominant in the California and Arizona borderlands, and Mexican
Americans predominate in the New Mexico and Texas borderlands. Eighteen of
the twenty-four border counties have Hispanic majorities, with Hispanics exceed-
ing 70 percent of the population in thirteen of them. In the eleven principal urban
centers, Anglos constitute the majority population in two border cities, and Hispanics in nine. Hispanics make up more than 90 percent of the population in the
cities of Calexico, Nogales, Laredo, and Brownsville, and over 60 percent in El
Centro, El Paso, Del Rio, and McAllen.

A comparison of the data from the 1980 and 1990 censuses reveals a highly
significant trend throughout the U.S. borderlands: the number of Hispanics has
risen much more rapidly than that of Anglos, with consequent major percentage
gains by Hispanics from California to Texas. In eleven border counties the
absolute number of Anglos has actually dropped. Eight of these counties are in
Texas, with El Paso County experiencing the largest decline in Anglo population, from 157,842 in 1980 to 151,313 in 1990. These population shifts reflect
high birth rates among Mexican Americans, heightened immigration from Mexico, and Anglo "flight" in a number of communities. The implications of changing demographics could be profound, and the matter is addressed in the conclusion to this book.

While the population of the borderlands includes people other than Mexicans,

Mexican Americans, and Anglos, I have chosen to focus on these three major groups because of their overwhelming numerical superiority and because they are the ones most directly involved in transnational interaction. African Americans, whose numbers are relatively low in the region, are affected by the border environment in a way similar to the Anglo Americans, and thus the patterns for Anglos identified here generally apply to blacks as well.[23] In the case of Native Americans, most live on reservations or in villages and are relatively isolated from the border urban centers. Few are engaged in the transnational processes emphasized in this study. Hence, whatever variations may exist in the lifestyles of groups of borderlanders not examined here should not alter my general findings. Nevertheless, it is appropriate to acknowledge the unique historical experience of indigenous peoples in the borderlands. Three groups in particular have been affected in fundamental ways by the existence of the border: the Kickapoo, Yaqui, and Tohono O'odham Indians.[24]

The Kickapoos, whose ancestors originated in the Great Lakes region in the United States, live on the Texas–Mexico border and maintain ties with their home village Nacimiento, located some 125 miles from the border in the state of Coahuila, Mexico. Approximately 600 strong, the Texas Kickapoos received official recognition from U.S. authorities in the 1980s as an American Indian band, allowing them to settle permanently in the United States after many generations of roaming between the two nations. For years they maintained a way station known as Kickapoo Village under the international bridge connecting Eagle Pass and Piedras Negras.

Because of their roots in the United States, their extended residence in Mexico (since the early nineteenth century), and their constant movement back and forth across the boundary, in a technical sense the Texas–Mexico Kickapoos have lived a binational lifestyle. Functionally, however, they have managed to retain their indigenous culture and group identity, and their involvement in the prevailing borderlands milieu has been very limited. Furthermore, their life pattern differs markedly from that of Mexicans, Mexican Americans, and Anglos, the groups that are heavily concentrated in the urban areas where the borderlands milieu thrives. In short, the Kickapoos have lived and worked in relative isolation from "mainstream" borderlanders, and the border experience for them does not include substantial participation in the modern, binational urban world.

The Yaquis of southern Arizona, whose population is estimated at 6,000, have participated much more directly than the Kickapoos in the borderlands milieu through cross-border migration and interaction. The Yaqui presence in southern Arizona dates from the late nineteenth century, when Yaqui refugees fled political persecution in Mexico directed against them by the Porfirio Díaz dictatorship. More migrants arrived in the Tucson and Phoenix areas during the Mexican Revolution of 1910 to 1920. Over several generations the Yaquis have

TABLE 2.3. Hispanic and Anglo Population in U.S. Border Counties, 1980 and 1990

| | Total | | Anglo | | | |
| | | | Number | | Percent | |
	1980	1990	1980	1990	1980	1990
CALIFORNIA						
San Diego	1,861,846	2,498,016	1,374,649	1,633,281	74	65
Imperial	92,110	109,303	35,411	31,742	38	29
TOTAL	1,953,956	2,607,319	1,410,060	1,665,023	72	64
ARIZONA						
Yuma	90,554	106,895	57,446	58,151	63	54
Pima	531,443	666,880	384,932	454,919	72	68
Santa Cruz	20,459	29,674	5,024	6,168	25	21
TOTAL	642,456	803,449	447,402	519,238	70	65
NEW MEXICO						
Hidalgo	6,049	5,958	3,144	2,917	52	49
Luna	15,585	18,110	9,084	9,113	58	50
Dona Ana	96,340	135,510	42,862	55,158	45	41
TOTAL	117,974	159,578	55,090	67,188	47	42
TEXAS						
El Paso	479,899	591,610	157,842	151,313	33	26
Hudspeth	2,728	2,915	1,114	956	41	33
Culberson	3,315	3,407	1,196	950	36	28
Jeff Davis	1,647	1,946	866	1,154	53	59
Presidio	5,188	6,637	1,188	1,197	23	18
Brewster	7,573	8,681	4,171	4,833	55	56
Terrell	1,595	1,410	899	651	56	46
Val Verde	35,910	38,721	12,237	10,418	34	27
Kinney	2,279	3,119	876	1,463	38	47
Maverick	31,398	36,378	2,275	1,571	7	4
Dimmit	11,367	10,433	2,416	1,655	21	16
Webb	99,258	133,239	8,124	7,427	8	6
Zapata	6,628	9,279	1,572	1,726	24	19
Starr	27,266	40,518	812	1,001	3	2
Hidalgo	283,229	383,545	51,719	54,259	18	14
Cameron	209,727	260,120	46,488	45,354	22	17
TOTAL	1,209,007	1,531,958	293,795	285,928	28	19
TOTAL FOR FOUR STATES	3,923,393	5,102,304	2,206,347	2,537,377	56	50

SOURCES: U.S., Bureau of the Census, *Census of Population, 1980*; U.S., Bureau of the Census, *Census of Population, 1990*.

[a] Less than 1 percent.

Hispanic				Other			
Number		Percent		Number		Percent	
1980	1990	1980	1990	1980	1990	1980	1990
275,177	510,781	15	20	212,020	353,954	11	14
51,384	71,935	56	66	5,315	5,626	6	5
326,351	582,716	17	35	217,335	359,580	11	14
26,638	43,388	29	41	6,470	5,356	7	5
111,418	163,262	21	25	35,093	48,699	7	7
15,229	23,221	74	78	206	285	1	—[a]
153,283	229,871	24	29	41,769	54,340	7	7
2,849	2,984	47	50 +	56	57	—[a]	—[a]
6,148	8,628	39	48	353	369	2	2
50,204	76,448	52	56	3,274	3,904	3	3
59,201	88,060	50	55	3,683	4,330	3	3
297,001	411,619	62	70	25,056	28,678	5	5
1,589	1,935	58	66	25	24	1	1
2,101	2,419	63	71	18	38	—[a]	1
866	770	47	40	4	22	—[a]	1
3,989	5,417	77	82	11	23	—[a]	—[a]
3,262	3,702	43	43	140	146	2	2
691	751	43	53	5	8	—[a]	1
22,601	27,299	63	71	1,027	1,004	3	3
1,310	1,570	58	50	93	86	4	3
28,366	34,024	90	94	757	783	2	2
8,845	8,688	78	83	106	90	1	1
90,842	125,069	91	94	292	743	1	1
5,042	7,519	76	81	14	34	—[a]	—[a]
26,428	39,390	97	97	26	127	—[a]	—[a]
230,212	326,972	81	85	1,298	2,314	—[a]	1
161,654	212,995	77	82	1,585	1,771	1	1
884,710	1,210,139	73	79	30,502	35,891	2	2
1,423,757	2,110,786	36	41	293,289	454,141	8	9

TABLE 2.4. Hispanic and Anglo Population in U.S. Border Cities, 1980 and 1990

| | Total | | Anglo | | | |
| | | | Number | | Percent | |
	1980	1990	1980	1990	1980	1990
San Diego	875,538	1,110,140	601,960	651,508	70	59
Chula Vista	83,927	135,163	57,132	67,302	68	50
National City	48,772	54,249	19,680	14,080	40	26
Calexico	14,412	18,633	513	416	4	2
El Centro	23,996	31,384	10,037	8,890	42	28
Nogales	15,683	19,489	2,201	1,410	14	7
El Paso	425,259	503,325	139,945	131,526	33	26
Del Rio	30,034	30,705	8,421	6,463	28	21
Laredo	91,449	117,149	6,120	6,323	7	5
McAllen	66,281	81,188	18,534	17,111	28	21
Brownsville	84,997	98,886	13,408	9,208	16	9

SOURCE: U.S., Bureau of the Census, *Census of Population, 1980*; U.S., Bureau of the Census, *Census of Population, 1990*.
[a]Less than 1 percent.

superimposed on their native culture traits from the Mexican, Mexican American, and Anglo cultures, while maintaining ties with the parent Yaqui "nation" in Sonora.

As a result of the Yaquis' close association with Mexicans and Mexican Americans, their pattern of cross-border interaction resembles that of those two groups in some ways—in terms of migratory trends, consumerism, and transculturation, for example. On the other hand, distinct experiences arising from their status as an indigenous people and residents of a reservation differentiate the border Yaquis from the rest of the people in the region.

Like the Yaquis, the Tohono O'odham (formerly called the Papago) manifest uniquely indigenous as well as "mainstream" patterns of borderlands interaction, but their degree of isolation from both Mexican and U.S. society is substantial. For centuries they have lived on desert land that overlaps the Arizona–Sonora border, with the 24,000 American O'odham occupying a 4,800-square-mile reservation, and the 4,000 Mexican O'odham scattered in farms and towns on the Mexican side. Over the years the O'odham have asserted their right to cross the boundary at will, so cross-border flow has been constant. Nevertheless, their

Hispanic				Other			
Number		Percent		Number		Percent	
1980	1990	1980	1990	1980	1990	1980	1990
130,455	229,341	15	21	143,123	229,291	16	21
19,624	50,376	23	37	7,171	17,485	9	13
18,708	26,914	38	50	10,384	13,255	21	24
13,566	17,806	94	96	333	411	2	2
11,983	20,482	50	65	1,976	2,012	8	6
13,337	17,924	85	92	145	155	1	1
265,819	348,687	63	69	19,495	23,112	5	5
21,036	23,698	70	77	577	544	2	2
85,076	110,151	93	94	253	675	—[a]	1
47,361	63,202	72	78	386	875	1	1
71,139	89,138	84	90	450	540	—[a]	1

crossing points are in remote, sparsely settled locations, and their exposure to urban borderlands interaction is extremely limited. The O'odham who live in Tucson or Nogales are the most exposed to the regional binational system. Involvement in cross-border interaction or transculturation is most pronounced among those individuals whose lifestyles resemble those of Mexican American or Anglo borderlanders.

Economic Interaction

The interdependence built up in the borderlands in recent generations is most visible in the close relationship between the U.S. and Mexican border communities. As Tables 2.5 and 2.6 illustrate, the cross-border traffic is now of monumental proportions, and major sectors of the economies of both sides are heavily dependent on foreign-oriented activities. On the U.S. side, commerce, banks, real estate and stock brokerage firms, and labor-intensive industries thrive on the importation of capital, products, and workers from Mexico, while the Mexican side derives substantial benefits from externally financed maquiladoras, U.S. tourists and shoppers, and U.S. jobs for many local workers.

TABLE 2.5. Cross-Border Traffic, 1989

TWO-WAY FLOW	
Routine border crossings (measured at U.S. ports of entry)	254,265,701
FROM THE UNITED STATES TO MEXICO	
Travelers (including tourists)	5,668,000
FROM MEXICO TO THE UNITED STATES	
Travelers (including tourists)	4,856,000
Legal immigrants to the United States	405,172
Undocumented Mexicans apprehended in the United States	865,292

SOURCES: U.S., Bureau of the Census, *Statistical Abstract of the United States, 1991*; U.S., Immigration and Naturalization Service, *Statistical Yearbook, 1989*.

Brownsville–Matamoros, El Paso–Ciudad Juárez, San Diego–Tijuana, and the other urban complexes along the border vibrate with the constant movement of people and goods from one side to the other. On any given day the long traffic lines congesting the international ports of entry include endless streams of maquiladora trucks, buses, automobiles, bicycles, and pedestrians. Malls and other shopping centers on the U.S. side depend heavily on Mexican customers, and during busy seasons such as Easter and Christmas, U.S. parking lots are full of cars with Mexican license plates. In downtown shopping districts in El Paso, Laredo, and Brownsville, the clientele is almost exclusively Mexican and Mexican American, and Spanish is probably spoken more than English. On the Mexican side, tourist strips such as the famous Avenida Revolución in Tijuana and Avenida Juárez in Ciudad Juárez lure millions of Americans every year, while sundry shops and supermarkets cater to ordinary shoppers, most of them Mexican Americans.

Interdependence provides both advantages and liabilities, prompting some segments of the border population to capitalize on opportunities where they exist and other segments to minimize the negative consequences that often arise from the asymmetrical relationship. For example, workers from Mexico have been attracted to the border area for the many possibilities it offers to make a living, with foreign-related economic activities generally topping the list of preferred employers. The workers have eagerly sought to work on the other side because of the prospect of earning higher wages paid in a stronger currency than that of their own country. Working conditions and benefits are also much better in the United States than at home. Further, as these workers integrate themselves into

TABLE 2.6. Foreign-Oriented Sectors of the Borderlands Economy

Sector	Salient Characteristics
U.S. SIDE	
Trade	Mexican imports include agricultural and mining products, light industrial goods, and handicrafts.
Commerce	Large numbers of merchants rely heavily on clientele from Mexico.
Banking	Mexicans have deposits in U.S. banks valued in the billions of dollars.
Real estate	Since the early 1980s, many affluent Mexicans have purchased residential and investment properties throughout the U.S. borderlands.
Business investments	Mexican entrepreneurs own shopping centers, hotels, restaurants, factories, car dealerships, farms, ranches, and other business establishments throughout the U.S. borderlands.
Labor-intensive industries	U.S. employers in both urban and rural areas employ low-wage Mexican workers in large numbers.
MEXICAN SIDE	
Maquiladoras	In 1992 some 2,000 assembly plants employed nearly 500,000 workers. This industry is now the dominant sector in several major border cities.
Tourism	Ubiquitous tourist attractions and tourism-related businesses constitute major sources of income and employment for local populations.
Services	U.S. consumers patronize a wide variety of Mexican service establishments.
Commuting workers	Tens of thousands of legal and undocumented workers cross daily to their jobs on the U.S. side.

the foreign economy, they improve their chance of obtaining permanent U.S. residence, and many do eventually move across the border.

Union workers from the United States have reacted differently to the border situation, perceiving labor from Mexico as a direct threat to their interests. They often accuse their Mexican competitors of undercutting wages, accepting substandard working conditions, and retarding unionization. They seek help from policymakers to keep "aliens" out of the U.S. domestic labor market, or at least to regulate their entry in such a way that the welfare of native workers is not harmed.

Acting on self-interest, employers on the U.S. side have welcomed the availability of abundant, cheap foreign labor, applauding (silently or otherwise) the tensions between the foreign and domestic workers, for such fragmentation has lessened the chance of their having to deal with a strong unionized labor force. By contrast, employers in Mexico, unable to compete with higher U.S. wages, have often experienced labor shortages as workers, particularly skilled workers, leave their local jobs in search of higher pay on the other side. To Mexican employers, then, the proximity of foreign jobs has represented a destabilizing element in the domestic labor force.

Investors on both sides, often acting on different motives and pursuing different objectives, have had opportunities to channel capital into profitable ventures in the neighboring nation. Historically, capital from the United States has flowed into basic sectors in Mexico, such as agriculture, ranching, mining, and urban industries that satisfy middle-class and elite consumers. Tourism has also attracted investment because of the strong attractions present in Mexico, including scenic beauty, a warm climate, alluring beaches, and archaeological remains from ancient civilizations. U.S. direct investment in Mexico has increased sharply with changes in Mexican regulations and the boom in maquiladoras in the 1980s. These trends will be reinforced with the signing of the North American Free Trade Agreement.

Although capital has traditionally been in short supply in Mexico, Mexican funds have moved across the border in the form of investments, as in real estate, that are calculated to yield attractive returns or to be safe. Afflicted by high inflation and constant monetary devaluations in their homeland, many Mexicans, seeking to protect their assets, have also converted their weak national currency into dollars and made large deposits in U.S. banks and brokerage firms along the border. Not surprisingly, this continuous flight of capital has had devastating consequences for the Mexican economy.

For consumers, the border zone has offered numerous opportunities to buy more for less, since the economic unevenness of the two sides has produced a dual system whereby certain goods and services are less expensive on one side than on the other. The seasoned border shopper plans purchases carefully, buying selectively in both countries. Sophisticated products such as personal computers or vcrs normally cost less in the more industrialized United States, and personal services such as haircuts or permanents are cheaper in Mexico, a labor-abundant country.

Smugglers have thrived in the U.S.–Mexico border environment because of strong consumer demand for prohibited foreign goods or products subject to high tariffs. Surreptitious trade has been especially dynamic in large population centers like El Paso–Ciudad Juárez, but smuggling networks have extended deep into the interiors of each nation. Interestingly, borderlanders accept smuggling as a normal activity because it is considered a natural part of the unique economic interaction in the binational region. While government intervention is expected for the purpose of enforcing national tariff laws or keeping out undesirable products, borderlanders also expect officials to be flexible and tolerant, allowing a certain amount of illegal traffic to go on in order to maintain the delicate interdependence between the two sides of the border.

Cultural Interaction

Out of economic necessity as well as a personal desire to venture into "other worlds," border Mexicans and Americans have intermingled at close range for many years, borrowing from as well as contributing to each other's way of life. This association, ranging from superficial contact to intimate relations, has produced unique patterns that make up key components of what is commonly referred to as "border culture." [25]

Border culture is rooted in the influence that the boundary exerts on the lives of borderlanders. In other words, the processes that make up the borderlands milieu—transnational interaction, international conflict and accommodation, ethnic conflict and accommodation, and separateness—are central elements in the values, thinking, and behavior of border people. But other factors play a significant role as well. Regionalism has been an important variable in the cultural configuration of the borderlands, with distinct subareas having their own characteristics, shaped by local environmental factors and the degree of contact with the outside world. Above all, the distinctiveness of border Mexicans and Anglos is embedded in the long-term incorporation of many traits from each other's culture, including cross-borrowing of such things as language, religion, values, customs, traditions, holidays, foods, clothing, and architecture.

Put another way, U.S.–Mexico borderlands culture is the product of forces and influences generated by the boundary itself, by regional phenomena from each nation, and by the transculturation shared by Mexicans and Americans. On the Mexican side, the national culture, implanted long ago by the Mexico City core zone, is intermixed with varieties of *norteño* culture as well as the cultures of migrants from major interior sending states such as Jalisco, Michoacán, Guanajuato, and Zacatecas. Similarly, the U.S. borderlands have combined the Anglo Saxon culture rooted in the northeastern United States with indigenous Southwestern cultures and those imported by migrants from all over the nation. The two resulting cultures are further recast by the elements of the borderlands milieu.

Borderlands culture is most vibrant in the core zone of the borderlands, the strip of territory where the population centers that abut the boundary are situated. Beyond the border area there is a secondary domain where borderlands culture is still strongly felt. Important cities in this region include Los Angeles, Tucson, Phoenix, Albuquerque, San Antonio, La Paz, Hermosillo, Chihuahua City, and Monterrey. The cultural impact of the borderlands diminishes in the interior sections of each nation, but certain areas of influence in both directions are readily apparent. For example, in the United States, places like San Jose, Denver, Dallas–Fort Worth, and Chicago have large Mexican American populations who maintain direct links with the borderlands. An important part of the link is maintained by migrants who constantly travel between Mexico and the interior United States. Within Mexico, significant spheres of borderlands cultural influence include Durango, Aguascalientes, Guadalajara, and Mexico City, to name a few large cities, and hundreds of towns and villages that serve as sending communities for emigrants to the borderlands or the interior of the United States.

Significantly, the vastness of the borderlands assures subregional variation in the manifestation of borderlands culture. Hence, while the lifestyles of borderlanders have fundamental characteristics in common regardless of their location, it is also true that local peculiarities shape the cultures of different places in distinct ways. Figure 2.8 depicts four major subregions within the greater borderlands. The first area, the southern California–Baja California borderlands, reflects the lifestyle of coastal metropolises such as Los Angeles, San Diego, and Tijuana as well as the exoticism of the Baja peninsula. Because of large-scale immigration of people from all over Mexico and the United States, this western zone is very cosmopolitan. Among Mexicans and Mexican Americans, the cultural imprint of Baja California predominates, but influences from Jalisco, Sinaloa, and Sonora, all places of origin of many migrants, are also strong. The second area, the Arizona–Sonora borderlands, with a relatively small population base, has been shaped by the harshness of the Sonoran Desert, by isolation, and by dominant industries such as copper mining and ranching. Sonoran culture is prevalent among Mexicans and Mexican Americans, while the Anglo population, which includes large numbers of retirees, generally reflects the U.S. cultural mainstream. The third area, the New Mexico–West Texas–Chihuahua borderlands, exhibits patterns characteristic of an isolated high-desert zone and a population heavily dependent on the major rivers in the region (the Rio Grande,

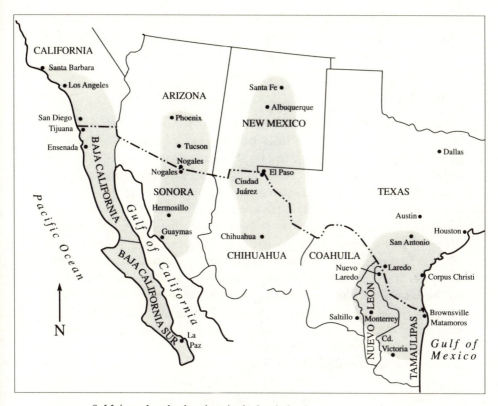

FIGURE 2.8 Major cultural subregions in the borderlands

the Pecos, and the Río Conchos). Cultural strains from Chihuahua and New Mexico are particularly strong here, but influences from Mexican states such as Durango, Coahuila, and Zacatecas and many U.S. states have made their presence felt in recent years with the arrival of many immigrants. Migration is of particular importance here because this zone has served as a major corridor between central Mexico and the U.S. Southwest for centuries. The fourth area, the southern Texas–northeastern Mexico borderlands, manifests influences arising from a subtropical climate, a large agricultural and ranching society, and a strong mix of Texas Anglo culture with Mexican *norteño* culture to form "Tex–Mex" culture. Important Mexican states that have contributed migrants include Tamaulipas, Nuevo León, and San Luis Potosí. In addition, deep and widespread poverty constitutes an important variable in the shaping of the culture of this zone.

Among the three major groups in the U.S.–Mexico borderlands, Mexican Americans most strongly manifest border culture, because their lifestyle embraces central elements of the borderlands milieu as well as vital strains from the

Mexican and U.S. mainstream and provincial cultures. Bicultural Mexicans and Anglos who have significant cross-border links also practice border culture, but their numbers are substantially smaller than for Mexican Americans.

Conclusion

Since the mid nineteenth century, when the border between the United States and Mexico became permanent, American and Mexican borderlanders have been engaged in forging a new society, building linkages that have thrived during the age of interdependence. Significantly, many cross-border bonds are rooted in the asymmetry that characterizes the binational relationship. Coveted jobs and consumer goods in the United States, the less dependent partner, serve as powerful magnets for Mexicans, and low-wage labor and tourism in Mexico, the more dependent partner, constitute strong lures for Americans. Today powerful transnational forces shape and define the daily lives of millions of borderlanders. Symbiosis is most clearly evident in the binational trade, tourism, migration, and industrialization that bind the U.S. and Mexican border communities. Transboundary fusion will probably accelerate even more rapidly in the future because both nations are on the verge of creating a free trade system that will further merge the two economies, paving the way for more intense and intimate social interaction. Subjected to an environment of vigorous transnational interaction for decades, El Pasoans, Juarenses, San Diegans, Tijuanenses, and residents of other frontier cities have fashioned a complex system of social organization that transcends the conventional dividing lines of nationality, race, ethnicity, and class. Internationalism and transculturalism have emerged as highly significant variables in the structuring of borderlands society.

PART II BORDER TYPES

INTRODUCTION

The chapters in this section present typologies of the three major population groups in the borderlands: Mexicans, Mexican Americans, and Anglo Americans. The term *Mexicans* refers to people whose nationality is Mexican and who reside on the Mexican side of the border, but it also embraces individuals born in the United States who maintain permanent residence in Mexico and whose identity and culture is unquestionably Mexican. *Mexican Americans* is used here to describe people of Mexican heritage who live permanently in the United States. I also employ *Chicano* as a synonymous term. At one end of the Mexican American or Chicano spectrum are individuals who are fully assimilated into U.S. society, while at the other extreme are newly arrived immigrants just beginning the journey toward integration. The terms *Anglo Americans* and *Anglos* refer to people of white European extraction (other than people of Spanish origin), who live permanently in the United States. Although it is far from ideal as a group identifier, *Anglo* nonetheless has been widely accepted throughout the borderlands as a self-referent by persons of English as well as non-English European descent.[1]

What differentiates border Mexicans, Mexican Americans, and Anglos from other people in the interior of Mexico and the United States is the environment of internationality inherent in the border zone. Powerful transnational forces pull large numbers of borderlanders into the orbit of the neighboring country, with a resulting array of cross-boundary relationships and lifestyles. Transnational interaction in the contemporary borderlands includes but is not limited to such phenomena as migration, employment, business transactions, tourism, trade, consumerism, cultural interchange, and social relationships.

Invariably, some sectors feel the impact of transnational interaction much more than others. Few who reside on the Mexican side are able to escape the overwhelming influence of the United States, and consequently most Mexican borderlanders have direct or indirect ties to the U.S. economy and to American culture. Such links have resulted in strong expressions of transnational interaction. On the U.S. side, vast numbers of Mexican Americans maintain substantial bonds with Mexico, and they live bicultural and transnational lifestyles to a far greater degree than any other sector of the borderlands population. Out of economic necessity and by the sheer force of the U.S. "melting pot" phenomenon, most Mexican American borderlanders, including many first-generation immigrants, have learned the English language and have absorbed large doses of American culture. At the same time, their proximity to Mexico has assured that Mexican Americans in the borderlands will strongly adhere to the Spanish language and Mexican culture. Generally speaking, then, Mexican American borderlanders are transnational in outlook and behavior.

By contrast, relatively few Anglo borderlanders manifest transnational characteristics, although some do have substantial relationships with Mexicans and Mexican Americans. The low incidence of transnational interaction and biculturalism among Anglos is principally explained by the lack of a compelling economic need to cross the border, learn Spanish, or become familiar with Mexican culture. Those few Anglos who do have such a need are generally the ones who speak Spanish and function comfortably in Mexican American and Mexican circles. Nevertheless, some Anglos have become bilingual and bicultural and participate in transnational activities for reasons other than economic interest.

The border population may be divided into two general types: national borderlanders and transnational borderlanders. National borderlanders are people who, while subject to foreign economic and cultural influences, have minimal or only superficial contacts with the opposite side of the border, owing either to their indifference to their next-door neighbors or their unwillingness or inability to function in any significant way in another society. Transnational borderlanders, on the other hand, are individuals who maintain significant ties with the neighboring nation. They seek to overcome obstacles that impede such contact and take advantage of every opportunity to visit, shop, work, study, or even live on the other side. Thus their lifestyles strongly reflect foreign influences. For some transnational borderlanders, such influences are modest, but for those who are deeply immersed in transborder interaction, foreign links govern central parts of their lives.

Among the variables that determine whether borderlanders are national or transnational and where they fit within each of those broad categories, are ties with interior areas, occupation, sources of income, level of education, family networks, and social relationships. Generally speaking, long-term border residents are more likely to reflect transnational characteristics than are newcomers. In the case of casual visitors and shoppers, the degree of difficulty in crossing the border often determines the extent of their contact with the other side. For example, many Anglo newcomers initially spend a considerable time on the

Mexican side, but the duration declines once the novelty of the experience wears off or if they encounter delays in returning to the United States. Inflated Mexican prices, inconveniences at the border, and perceptions of crime rates likewise impel long-term residents, both Anglos and Mexican Americans, to visit Mexico less frequently. Border-crossing patterns among Mexicans are affected in much the same manner. It must also be kept in mind that the border population includes both permanent and semipermanent residents plus large numbers of transients who spend little time in the border communities. Population fluidity and turnover are especially strong on the Mexican side.

In constructing the typologies that appear in Chapters 3 through 5, I used temporal, ideological, and economic criteria to differentiate among subgroups in the border population. The categories that follow, all of them common to the three major groups under discussion, introduce these criteria and describe the approach I used in creating the classification scheme. The temporal dimension is important in understanding the place in border society of borderlanders who are not native to the area. I define newcomers as people who have lived on the border less than five years and whose lifestyle and outlook reflect "mainstream" culture. I consider five years sufficiently long to establish a pattern of daily life that either continues to reflect overwhelming national tendencies or that moves in the direction of transnational and transcultural involvement. Ideological orientation is mirrored in such categories as uniculturalists (those people who are monocultural and monolingual), nationalists (uniculturalists who passionately assert the interests of their own nation and are opposed to influences from abroad), biculturalists (people whose lifestyles and mind-sets reflect two cultures), and binationalists (biculturalists whose lives are deeply enmeshed in the societies of the two nations and who consequently have a strongly international outlook). The importance of economics as a motive for engaging in transnational interaction is reflected in the lifestyles of commuters (people who cross the border on a daily basis to work in the neighboring nation) and binational consumers (people who do a substantial amount of shopping and/or consume numerous services in the neighboring nation). Figure II.1 provides a graphic representation of these standard border "types." Chapters 3 through 5 describe other types that are unique to each of the three major population groups being discussed.

Clearly, many borderlanders simultaneously fulfill multiple roles and could well be placed in various categories. This is particularly true with people in the transnational sector. For example, a binationalist is also a biculturalist and may also be a commuter and a binational consumer. The guiding principle for placing an individual in a specific category is the predominant force that currently drives his or her link with the neighboring country. In other words, a commuter may become a biculturalist through constant exposure to the way of life on the other side, but the essence of that person's current external link is his or her status as

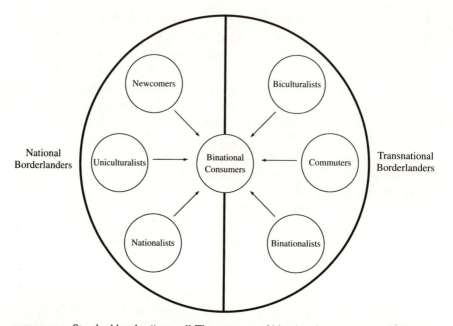

FIGURE II.I Standard border "types." The category of binational consumers includes individuals from all the subgroups.

a constant crosser of the international boundary for job-related purposes, and he or she is therefore identified as a commuter.

The heterogeneity of the borderlands population is revealed in the great variation found in the national–transnational dichotomy. At one extreme are individuals who live on the border but who are largely unaffected by it, and on the other are persons whose very lives personify the borderlands milieu. The latter may be referred to as core borderlanders and the former as peripheral borderlanders. People at the core are bilingual and bicultural, and they have a high degree of contact with the opposite side of the border. Those on the periphery are monolingual and monocultural, and their ties to foreigners or to countrymen who are racially, ethnically, or culturally different from themselves are slight or nonexistent. The mass of the borderlands population lies between these two poles, and their position varies in accordance with their orientation toward or away from transnational or transcultural interaction.

This conceptualization of who is at the core of borderlands society and who is on the periphery derives from my focus on a localized, transnational population. The central issue is not who holds political or economic power but rather who functions best in the binational, bicultural environment found in the borderlands. This criterion applies both to elite and non-elite borderlanders who, while functioning in different social milieus, still form part of a relatively self-contained transnational *system*. Hence my use of the terms *core* and *periphery* differs from the standard meaning found in world-systems and dependency literature in the sense that I am not concerned with historical or contemporary dominant–subordinate alignments, whether international, national, or regional.[2] I use the core-periphery concept to illustrate how people fit into the social and cultural environment of the transnational borderlands. Regardless of their political, economic, or social standing in society, individuals who have only a national orientation lack a full understanding of how the local system functions and are therefore situated on the fringes of that system. Conversely, borderlanders firmly anchored in the binational ambiance are at the center of the system and are much better positioned to benefit from it.[3]

The principal consideration for determining the various subtypes within the typologies developed in this section is the degree of interaction with the opposite side of the border and with people of a different ethnic group or culture, and how that interaction is presumed to affect one's lifestyle, self-perception, and outlook. Culture change is inferred through the person's exposure to foreign institutions, economic systems, consumerism, and cultural norms. Being employed, attending school, or carrying on significant social relationships on the other side are deemed to be especially powerful vehicles that engender or enhance contact with the neighboring nation's cultural system.

The major influences that shape the way of life of borderlanders include the borderlands milieu, education, social interaction, employment/income, consumerism, core culture, and popular culture. Exposure to the borderlands milieu means involvement in or observation of transborder and transcultural phenomena in the form of transnational interaction, international conflict and accommodation, ethnic conflict and accommodation, and a sense of separateness. Education refers to formal schooling at all levels, social interaction denotes familial and other human relationships, employment/income indicates sources of material sustenance, and consumerism means the consumption of products and services. The core culture embraces the culture's fundamental institutions, forms of human organization, values, and behavioral patterns, while popular culture is made up of surface cultural manifestations in society, including consumer products, food, entertainment, and images and messages communicated by print and visual media. The effect of these influences on the different types of borderlanders is assessed in the context of cross-border interaction.

To illustrate how the patterns identified for each border type function in the case of real persons, case histories are included throughout Chapters 3 through 5. With one exception (an account drawn from a published work), all are based on interviews conducted in various border communities during 1990 and 1991. In many instances I have used pseudonyms at the request of the interviewees,

and the places where the interviews took place are not identified. I am responsible for translations from Spanish to English.

One of the problems throughout this section is the limited quantitative data to
support some of the general conclusions I have made about the national and
transnational populations, core-periphery configurations, and the extent of cross-
border interaction for different borderland types. Hard evidence is simply unavailable, so I have had to rely on indirect, inferential, and intuitive means of
estimating what proportion of each group is national or transnational. More exact
measures would require highly specific data that could reveal patterns in transnational interaction and show how these patterns are distributed throughout the
borderlands population. Obviously it would take a monumental effort to generate
such hard data, necessitating fieldwork on a scale that would be both very costly
and difficult.

My estimates, however, do have some indirect quantitative basis, and the
extant literature allows for a certain amount of inference. The extraordinary size
of legal cross-border traffic (254 million crossings in 1989), in addition to the
great volume of crossings by undocumented people (865,000 apprehensions in
1989 alone), make it readily apparent that large numbers of borderlanders carry
on highly varied transnational interactions. On the Mexican side it is clear that
substantial numbers of people depend directly or indirectly on the United States
for their livelihood, which is my point of departure for inferring their external
ties. For example, an estimated 100,000 "Green Carders" (legal entrants who
reside on the Mexican side) commute to U.S. jobs on a daily basis. In 1991
nearly 2,000 externally controlled maquiladoras in the Mexican border cities
employed close to 500,000 people. Throngs of Mexicans cross the border every
day to shop in American stores. On the U.S. side, about a fifth of the Mexican
American population is foreign-born, which is a good indication of substantial,
continuous ties with Mexico. Anyone who has spent time in any of the U.S.
border cities will attest to the extremely high incidence of bilingualism and biculturalism among Mexican Americans, a fact that implies strongly that links
with Mexico or Mexican culture are a fundamental, continuing reality in the
Mexican American community. Few Mexican American borderlanders can escape the influences that flow from south of the boundary. As for Anglos, many
studies reveal a strong national orientation and a pattern of segregation (vis-à-vis
Mexican Americans and Mexicans) throughout the borderlands.[4] However, data
on Anglo intermarriage with Hispanics document that external links do exist,
although the level of intimate association between the two groups is much lower
on the border than in the nonborder areas of the U.S. border states.[5] Data on
Anglo bilingualism, biculturalism, and degree of involvement in transborder processes are lacking; consequently, I have relied on interviews and on what I have
observed over many years regarding the roles Anglos play in border society.

The absence of an empirical foundation should not, in my view, preclude efforts to delineate the structure of borderlands society. Speculation and the formation of hypotheses are especially appropriate in this study, where the central concern is with describing the nature of transnational and transcultural interaction rather than with quantifying precisely the size of the various sectors of the population. But having a general idea of which sectors are large and which are small helps in identifying the internal and external dynamics of the major groups, and consequently I have formed hypotheses on this matter freely throughout Chapters 3 through 6. My analysis, then, involves a certain degree of arbitrariness and simplification, which is the case with most classificatory schemas.

3

MEXICANS

Mexican borderlanders, or *fronterizos*, generally reflect Mexican mainstream society in their ethnic and social characteristics, but in many ways they differ significantly in their lifestyles as a result of close proximity to the United States. U.S. economic forces determine how large numbers of fronterizos make their living and how they assimilate foreign tastes and values. On the border, few Mexicans, even the very poor, are able to escape U.S. influence.[1]

This chapter examines the fronterizo population in the context of the international environment that surrounds it. Various subgroups are identified and analyzed according to their degree of involvement in transnational interaction. Figure 3.1 presents a typology of fronterizos, grouped into national and transnational sectors. National fronterizos likely constitute a majority of the population and include transient migrants, newcomers, nationalists, and uniculturalists. Transnational fronterizos consist of worker commuters (hereafter referred to as commuters), biculturalists, and binationalists. Binational consumers and settler migrants are found in both sectors, but especially on the transnational side. Figure 3.2 approximates the size of each subgroup and its location on a borderlands milieu core-periphery continuum, and Figure 3.3 compares the sources of cultural and lifestyle formation among the different types of borderlanders.

In the case of U.S.-born Mexicans who reside on the Mexican side, the question arises whether they are really an integral part of the Mexican fronterizo population. My view is that they are, because birthplace is culturally irrelevant for this subgroup. What counts is the environment in which they live and the customs, traditions, and values they adhere to. For U.S.-born fronterizos who live in Mexico, that way of life is naturally Mexican. Most important, they identify themselves strongly as *mexicanos*, not *americanos*, and that is reason enough to classify them as full-fledged Mexican fronterizos. To underline this point I have included several U.S.-born Mexicans in the case histories of fronterizos presented below. The first part of this chapter details the characteristics of different

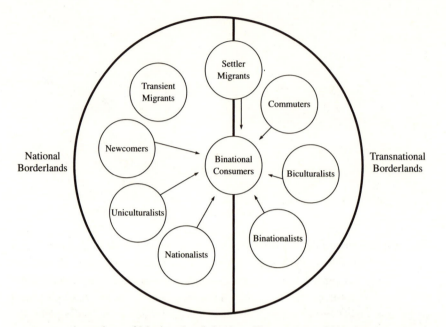

FIGURE 3.1 A typology of Mexican borderlanders. The category of binational consumers includes individuals from all the subgroups except transient migrants, who are mere passersby.

types of national fronterizos, and the second part examines the transnational subgroups. In each discussion, general definitions for fronterizo categories are followed by case histories.

National Fronterizos

Transient Migrants

Mexicans who pass through the border area on their way to the U.S. interior may be called transient migrants. Most of these individuals lack legal documentation, and their desire is to cross the international line as quickly as possible. They see the border primarily as a barrier to overcome; they give little or no thought to the frontier zone as a community unto itself. Their aim is to spend as little time at the border as possible, because lingering there consumes their resources and exposes them to danger. On the Mexican side, the migrants may be victimized by *coyotes* (smugglers of undocumented migrants), thieves, or even the police. On the U.S. side, the danger is primarily the possibility of being apprehended by *la migra* (the U.S. Border Patrol), but other threats include possible assault

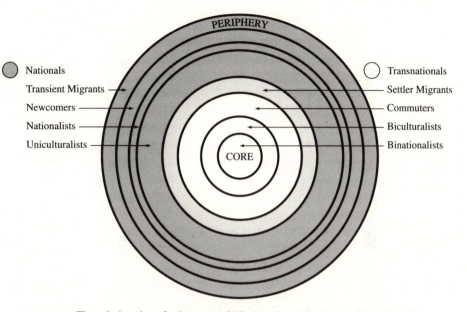

FIGURE 3.2 The relative size of subgroups of Mexican borderlanders and their location on the borderlands milieu core–periphery continuum. Binational consumers are not included here because they constitute a category comprised of members from all subgroups, particularly those in the transnational sector. Settler migrants are found in both national and transnational sectors.

or an accident. Once beyond the border zone, perhaps 100 miles into the United States, chances are good that undocumented migrants will reach their final destination. They will most likely remain there for a few months and then return to Mexico for a short visit, once again passing through the border area. The cycle will be repeated again and again, and each time the migrants will be better prepared to spend the least amount of time at the border and to avoid local dangers and traps. Thus, because of their need to be on the move, transient migrants are exposed to the borderlands milieu only to a very limited extent.

Jesús: Transient Migrant. / A central character in Ted Conover's *Coyotes,*[2] Jesús is a Mexican in his twenties who on several occasions has migrated from the interior of Mexico to the interior of the United States, entering U.S. soil without documentation. The worst part of his journey has been the crossing of the international line, where he has confronted a variety of dangers. Jesús is from Ahuacatlán, a remote village in Querétaro, a mountainous state in central Mex-

NATIONAL BORDERLANDERS

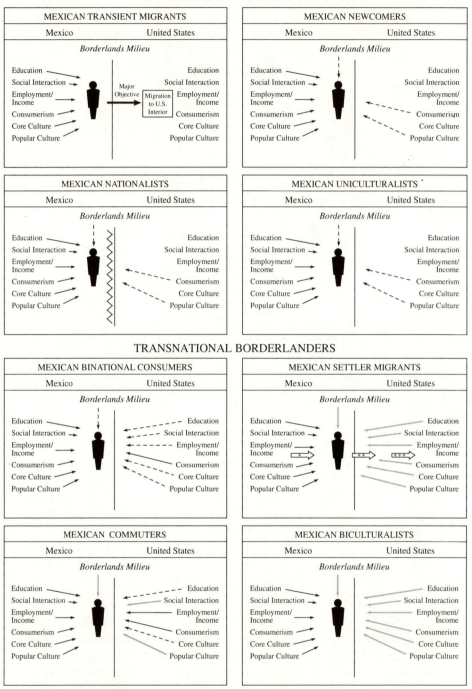

FIGURE 3.3 Major sources of cultural and lifestyle orientation among Mexican borderlanders.

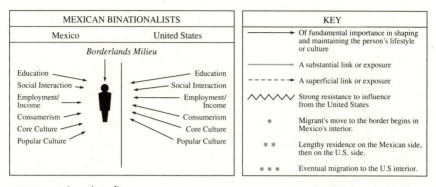

FIGURE 3.3 (*continued*)

ico. Like many other men in the town, his practice is to leave for the United States in the spring and return to his home in the fall. His current employer north of the border is a rancher in Idaho.

In the trip northward narrated by Conover, Jesús and other villagers travel by bus to Sonoita, Sonora, a Mexican border town in the midst of harsh desert terrain. As they approach the border, their bus is stopped by Mexican migration and customs inspectors, who extort money from two inexperienced migrants. Arriving very tired at the border, the group negotiates the cost of crossing the line with several *coyotes,* finally finding someone who is reasonable and can arrange transportation from the border to Phoenix. After they purchase food and supplies for their trip, a *coyote* accompanies Jesús and his friends to a designated spot outside Sonoita, where they meet other *coyotes* who are to take them across the border in a pickup truck. But the truck is intercepted by the *judiciales,* the Mexican federal police, and everyone is taken back to town for questioning. Some in the group are roughed up by the police, who accuse them of being drug smugglers. Finally, Jesús and the others pay off the judiciales, and the migrants are free to resume their journey.

After spending the night in a motel, they trek through the desert into the United States, where they are picked up by Indian *coyotes* and transported to a hiding place. Later, other *coyotes* provide transportation to their immediate destination, a ranch in the vicinity of Phoenix. From there Jesús and several others pile into an old car and proceed toward Idaho, intending to reach the ranch where they have worked in previous years. In Utah they are stopped by the police for "speeding" and are turned over to the Immigration and Naturalization Service, which deports them. It takes Jesús and the others four days to make their way back from Mexico to Phoenix. Once again they arrange for transportation to Idaho, and the second time they reach their final destination. After working several months for the Idaho rancher, Jesús and his friends return to Mexico to spend the winter.

Newcomers

Since the 1940s, large numbers of Mexicans from the interior have been attracted to the border for economic reasons, making newcomers a sizable portion of the population in the border cities. Studies conducted in the 1970s and 1980s yielded the following data pertaining to the size of the non-native population in the following communities: Reynosa, 47 percent; Ciudad Juárez, 53 percent; and Tijuana, 66 percent.[3] As with recent arrivals anywhere, it takes newcomers to the border time to integrate themselves into the local environment. Thus, during the period of adjustment—three to five years—newcomers may be said to be a part of the national population rather than the transnational population, although under special circumstances certain individuals may enter the world of transnational borderlanders in a relatively short time.

Generally speaking, the lifestyle and worldview of newcomers reflect the Mexican national perspective, or a regional variation of it. With the passage of time, that outlook is modified by exposure to the borderlands milieu. Many come to absorb in a substantial way influences that filter in from the United States. Those driven by cross-border economic, social, or cultural forces eventually make the transition from national to transnational borderlanders.

Alfredo Nuñez: Newcomer.   /   Alfredo Nuñez is a 40-year-old musician from a small village in Durango. He moved to Tijuana in 1989 and joined a *mariachi* band composed mostly of other men from his hometown who had arrived in Tijuana in the preceding two years. Mr. Nuñez figured he could earn a better living on the border, given that jobs in rural Durango paid very little. His wife and three children remained in Durango with his parents, but he hopes to bring them to the border as soon as it is economically feasible. At the moment he is not doing very well, since the demand for the services of mariachis is depressed. Moreover, there is substantial competition in the business. On one recent Saturday night, for example, eight bands congregated around one of the plazas in the tourist district waiting to be hired by private parties.

Mr. Nuñez is adjusting to life in Tijuana, which is very different from his hometown. He feels fortunate to be a part of the mariachi band because everybody knows one another very well, especially the men from Durango, who worked together before venturing northward. That has helped him with the difficult adjustment he has had to make to life in a very fast paced city. If Mr. Nuñez could find good employment back home, he would leave Tijuana, but that is not a likely prospect. Therefore he will persevere, hoping that his earnings will increase and that his family will be able to join him. Mr. Nuñez has no plans to migrate to the United States, although he has heard from several friends that jobs at good wages are available. He feels that with his skill he can eventually make a good living in Tijuana, and therefore he sees no need to risk humiliation by crossing illegally into the United States. At present he knows very little about life on the other side of the line.

Nationalists

Mexican nationalists are people who are strongly pro–Mexico and vehemently anti–United States. Their nationalism is revealed in their attitudes and opinions pertaining to such subjects as U.S. foreign policy, foreign investment in Mexico, American cultural influences, and the treatment of Mexicans north of the border. Nationalists deeply resent the historical domination by the United States and its intervention in Mexico and other parts of Latin America. They especially lament the loss to the gringos of half of Mexico's territory in the nineteenth century. Nationalists are generally distrustful of U.S. motives in the diplomatic relations between Washington and Mexico City. They see U.S. capital as undermining the sovereignty of their country, and they believe that Mexico's adoption of gringo cultural traits does great harm to the motherland. These sentiments make nationalists highly resistant to becoming seriously involved in any transnational process or activity. Nationalists consciously avoid dilution of their Mexican identity and are deeply bothered by the "demexicanization" they perceive among their countrymen. Nationalists are particularly visible in the intellectual community, which includes professors, students, journalists, writers, and artists. In all probability, nationalists constitute a very small portion of the Mexican border population, although they are more numerous in the interior of the country.[4]

Mónica García Montenegro: Nationalist. / Ms. García Montenegro is a fifty-year-old resident of a major Mexican border city, where she lives with her four children. Her strong nationalistic sentiments are exemplified by her refusal in the late 1950s to live in the United States and her continued dissatisfaction with American influences that filter across the border. Certain personal experiences in particular have shaped her views.

When she was growing up in a town in the Mexican border region, she heard negative stories about the United States from braceros, who related how they were discriminated against and exploited by American employers. She also heard accounts about the mistreatment of undocumented workers by *la migra.* At the age of thirteen, when she was having trouble getting along with her stepfather, her mother sent her to a Catholic school for troubled girls in a U.S. border city. Most of the students were *cholas,* or Mexican American girls from rough neighborhoods. She greatly resented having to leave her home to live in a country for which she had no affection. The next two years were difficult because she felt miserable in that school, facing numerous conflicts. She remembers fighting repeatedly with cholas who made negative comments about Mexicans.

Ms. García Montenegro particularly resented one Mexican American nun who showed disrespect toward Mexico. One September 16 (Mexican independence day) the nun announced that the students would be allowed to sing the Mexican national anthem. The nun had the students stand for the singing, but she herself remained seated. That made Ms. García Montenegro very angry, and when it came time to sing the U.S. anthem, she sat down while everyone else stood. The nun ordered her to stand, but she refused. For that she was prohibited from leaving the school grounds during the next two weekends. "That *monja pocha* [Americanized, or culturally corrupted, nun] really disliked me because of my patriotism for Mexico," recalls Ms. García Montenegro. She got along best with an Anglo nun who understood her feelings. Much of the time Ms. García Montenegro refused to speak English, so the Anglo nun allowed her to express herself in Spanish.

After her disagreeable experience at the school for girls, she went to live with her cousin Yolanda, who lived in Virginia with her husband, an Anglo sailor. Yolanda was pregnant at the time and needed assistance. Ms. García Montenegro spent a traumatic eight months in Virginia, and at one point half her face became paralyzed from the stress of living in such a strange environment. "Everyone was very cold," she recalls. "I didn't know my neighbors. I didn't like American food. Everything seemed so difficult." It was not a totally negative experience, however, since she was able to have some good times with an Anglo boyfriend. Although a "good guy," he thought very differently from her, and she objected to his advances and his failure to extend her basic courtesies. She felt he tried to take advantage of her, something she doubted he would do with Anglo women.

Upon her return to her hometown in Mexico, she met and agreed to marry a Mexican American who had lived in the United States for many years. He was an engineer who promised her many things. They decided to first have a civil wedding and be legally married, then to have her get her U.S. residency papers (her Green Card), and finally to formalize the marriage with a church ceremony. After that they would live permanently in the United States. She went through the first two steps but changed her mind about the marriage before the church wedding, which she considered to be the real and binding act of matrimony. During the three months that transpired after the civil ceremony, she decided marriage to that man would be a mistake because she could never be happy living with him outside of Mexico. Thus, legally married—but having never lived as man and wife—they got a divorce.

Besides the problem of having to live in the United States, Ms. García Montenegro had strong differences of opinion with her "ex" husband. He was staunchly pro–United States and anti–Mexico, and was especially critical of the Mexican government, which he characterized as "inefficient and corrupt." She in turn criticized the United States, pointing out to him that U.S. politicians were also corrupt. The only difference was that American officials "could hide such deficiencies better than Mexicans."

She remarried at age nineteen, but two years later got divorced again and this time moved to the border, where she believed a more liberal climate prevailed for divorced women. She lived with her sister, who had migrated there previously. With her knowledge of English, within a short time Ms. García Montenegro took a job as a cashier in a liquor store that catered to an American clientele. One day a Mexican-looking man came into the store and spoke to her in English, which she resented because she felt he should be speaking Spanish. She answered him in Spanish, but he didn't seem to understand, and that upset her even more because of her long-held belief that *pochos* (Anglicized Mexicans or Mexican Americans) should be able and willing to speak their native language. It turned out that the man was not a Mexican American but an American Indian, and she apologized for her curt behavior.

Within a short time of arriving at the border, Ms. García Montenegro went to the U.S. consulate and handed over her Green Card to an unbelieving consular official. He asked her if she was sure she wanted to give up her right to live or work in the United States. "Of course I'm sure," she said. "I don't need this Green Card. I'm not interested in living or working in the United States. I don't want to be in a country that exploits Mexicans. I don't want to be exploited or be part of an exploitative system. I'd rather stay in Mexico and exploit gringos." She then asked him for a *pasaporte local* (a local crossing card), which she believed would be good to have for occasional shopping trips to the U.S. side. The official just shook his head and began processing the necessary paperwork.

Though firmly committed to buying Mexican consumer products over U.S. goods, Ms. García Montenegro felt the need to purchase some "indispensables" across the border. In particular, she bought her underclothes in the United States because Mexican stores often did not have her size. On one of her shopping trips she had a confrontation with a U.S. immigration inspector at the border. He wanted to know why she was going to the United States. When she said "to shop," he demanded to see her money. She objected to his aggressive interrogative manner, but he became more abusive. He insulted and humiliated her in front of other people who were in line to cross. Infuriated, she placed her crossing card on the counter and said to the officer, "You can have your pasaporte! I don't need it!" As she started to walk away, the inspector apologized for his rudeness, gave her back her card, and let her cross.

Ms. García Montenegro feels highly incensed by such treatment of Mexicans at the border and by the discrimination suffered by Mexican workers in the United States. "It is not fair that the gringos treat us that way," she says. "We don't do that to them in Mexico. We let them in without any problems, and they do what they want here. Sometimes they break the law and go back to their country and nothing happens to them. On the other hand, our compatriots in the United States are treated differently." Ms. García Montenegro especially resents the presence and behavior of U.S. Drug Enforcement Agency agents in Mexico. She believes the Mexican government should not allow them to direct operations in her country. She is also offended by the pressure that the U.S. government often exerts in Mexico on foreign policy issues. She feels the United States needs to remember President Benito Juárez's admonition: "El respeto al derecho ajeno es la paz" (Respect for the rights of others is peace).

Regarding U.S. cultural influence on Mexico, Ms. García Montenegro is distressed that celebrations such as Halloween and Valentine's Day have been adopted by many border Mexicans. "We don't need a Valentine's day in Mexico," she says. "Here we practice love toward our fellowman on a daily basis. It is also ridiculous to celebrate Easter with egg hunts in the backyard or in the park. We Mexicans need to stick to our traditional ways and not imitate what the gringos do." It is highly ironic that despite her deep nationalism, Ms. García Montenegro has made her living by teaching English in various language schools at the border. Like so many other border Mexicans, she lives with personal contradictions that are more easily rationalized than eliminated.

Uniculturalists

Mexican borderlanders who by choice or circumstance remain largely unaffected by U.S. cultural influences may be called uniculturalists, or people whose lifestyles strictly reflect Mexican norms. Newcomers and nationalists, described above, by definition are uniculturalists, though for different reasons. "Classic" uniculturalists differ from newcomers in that the former have lived on the Mexican border for long periods yet have failed to absorb foreign traits or develop significant links with the U.S. side. Uniculturalists remain distanced from U.S. culture primarily because of personal indifference or because they have had few opportunities for exposure to what is on the other side of the border. Few Mexican uniculturalists, however, remain untouched by the United States. Samuel Ochoa, whose story is told below, counts among his experiences a short-lived adventure north of the border a long time ago.

Samuel Ochoa: Uniculturalist. / Mr. Ochoa is a seventy-eight-year-old man who, despite having lived in Matamoros almost fifty years, has had very limited interaction with the United States and has hardly been affected by American culture. Currently Mr. Ochoa works at odd jobs, saving money in hopes of retiring soon.

Mr. Ochoa is a native of Monterrey. As a young man, his friends persuaded him to seek employment in the United States. Thus he migrated to the border, obtained a local crossing card from the U.S. Immigration and Naturalization

Service, and entered the United States. He then made his way to the interior, where he got a job as a farm worker. The year was 1945. Unfortunately, within a few days he and his friends were apprehended by the Border Patrol and were sent back to Mexico. Mr. Ochoa believes that one of his fellow workers, who for some reason carried a grudge, turned them in to *la migra*. As a result, Mr. Ochoa lost his crossing card, and since then he has remained in Mexico.

He believed his expulsion from the United States meant that he would not be eligible to get a new crossing card, and he never pursued the matter after that. His unwillingness to risk apprehension again deterred him from crossing the border without documentation. That misfortune did not affect his opinion of the United States, however, which has remained positive. His attitude is based on his perception of opportunities available in the United States for ordinary workers. "The United States is a great country," he says. "Workers are treated well. When they get old, they are taken care of. Here in Mexico it is different. Workers are underpaid, and they have to struggle to get their pensions when they retire." Since 1945 Mr. Ochoa has held a variety of jobs in the construction industry. When he was younger he managed to work steadily and was able to make ends meet, but after the age of sixty he began to experience difficulties. He feels discriminated against because of his age.

With respect to his identity and culture, Mr. Ochoa sees himself as nothing but a Mexican. U.S. influences have not touched him in any significant way. He is a mexicano who happens to live on the northern border. He believes most of the people he knows are more or less like himself. He speculates that if he had been a regular border crosser or had spent more time in the United States he might be a different person today.

Transnational Fronterizos

Binational Consumers

Since the mid nineteenth century, Mexicans in the border zone have consumed a wide variety of American products because of quality and price advantages over goods produced in Mexico. Thus millions of Mexicans have crossed the border with great regularity simply to shop in the United States for anything from groceries to clothing to electronic gadgets. Many of them also purchase services, attend U.S. schools, partake of recreation and entertainment activities, and take vacations in the United States. This system has spawned the binational consumers, people who are very knowledgeable about the comparative advantages of making selected purchases at home and others abroad. The magnitude of transboundary consumerism is revealed in a 1991 study that indicated that direct purchases by Mexicans in Arizona amounted to almost 700 million dollars, with over 98 percent taking place in the border counties.[5] While on their shopping sprees to the United States, binational consumers often attend events or go to places (e.g., movie theaters) which further expose them to the U.S. way of life. Yet, despite that frequent contact with Americans, many binational consumers experience little acculturation to U.S. culture because the exposure seldom goes beyond the superficial level. In the case of people who "consume" U.S. education, however, the impact of American ways is much greater, and consequently many binational consumers are to some extent also biculturalists. For the Resendez family, consumerism has shaped its relationship to the United States even to the point of ensuring that all the children were born on the U.S. side.

The Resendez Family: Binational Consumers. / Now in their sixties, Margarita Ayala de Resendez and her husband, Antonio, have lived in a Mexican border city all their lives, making the most of opportunities offered by both sides of the international boundary. Despite being staunch Mexicans, their eight children were all born on the U.S. side because Mrs. Resendez preferred U.S. medical care and because U.S. citizenship gave her children access to education and other benefits in the United States. For the middle-class Resendez family, life at the border has been good because they have been able to take advantage of the low cost of living on the Mexican side and have enjoyed the consumer lifestyle characteristic of affluent Americans.

Apart from going to an Anglo pediatrician and using U.S. hospitals during her pregnancies, for many years Mrs. Resendez patronized American business establishments. She routinely purchased large quantities of groceries in U.S. supermarkets for her large family. She also bought most of the family's clothes and most of the household furniture and appliances in U.S. department stores. To avoid paying Mexican tariffs on highly taxed foreign products, Mrs. Resendez did what other borderlanders have always done—paid bribes to customs officials. The family frequented U.S. restaurants, movies, amusement parks, and attended special events such as Christmas pageants. Most important, several of her children went to U.S. schools, since she believed that was the best way for them to get a good education and learn the English language.

Although firmly committed to a Mexican lifestyle and to preserving native cultural traditions, Mrs. Resendez believed that her family's quality of life could be substantially improved by purchasing what the family could afford from the U.S. side. Many U.S. products clearly were superior in quality and price to Mexican products, and it was only natural for her to want to acquire them. Besides, many goods produced in Mexico's industrial centers simply did not reach the border, so the choice was to buy in the United States or do without. Mrs. Resendez, along with most people who could afford to buy on the other side, had no qualms about spending money in the United States. The family's tendency toward foreign consumerism was reinforced by the fact that Mr. Resendez's printing business depended on U.S. machinery, parts, supplies, and technological expertise.

The tradition of foreign consumerism is very much alive among Mrs. Resendez's children, who follow a pattern similar to that of their parents. For example, one of their married daughters, Margarita, now in her late thirties, has for many years crossed the border for the same reasons as her mother. Margarita even takes her own children to the same U.S. pediatrician who took care of her when she was a child. Margarita is a very interesting case because she is a U.S. citizen by birth, but in every respect she is thoroughly Mexican and wishes to be nothing else. Her family, her friends, and her social world are in Mexico. Her major connection with the United States basically amounts to frequent shopping trips and miscellaneous visits across the boundary. Her strong identification as a Mexican is underscored by her direct involvement in Mexican politics, including voting in elections and participating in demonstrations against the Partido Revolucionario Institucional, the country's ruling party.

Legally at her age she should not have dual citizenship, but like many other fronterizos she continues to hold on to both (without the knowledge of the authorities) because of the tremendous flexibility and advantages she derives from that status. Her stalwart Mexican identity will keep her from giving up her Mexican citizenship, and she will not voluntarily relinquish U.S. citizenship because she does not want to give up conveniences, opportunities, and benefits available north of the border that are hers by birth. For example, one of her U.S.-born children has Down's syndrome, and she is able to get free therapy for him in the United States. Such care is practically unavailable in Mexico. As a teenager Margarita was able to attend an American high school, and she intends to have her children do the same thing. But she strongly believes that they need to remain 100 percent Mexican, and she will be very careful to make sure their culture is not diluted by American influences.

Margarita says that friends from the interior of Mexico sometimes accuse her and other family members of being too Americanized, making it necessary to explain to them how things work at the border. "It's a special situation for us, and they have to understand that. Because we like what the United States has to offer doesn't mean we are anti-Mexico. It's unfair to call us *malinchistas* [traitors to Mexico]. Besides, many non-border Mexicans I know are just as familiar with popular American brands as we are, and they take U.S. vacations just like we do."

Settler Migrants

People classified as settler migrants arrive from the interior of Mexico with the primary intention of improving their economic circumstances, but unlike transient migrants, settler migrants stay at the border for prolonged periods. Family or other considerations govern their decision to live in the area for a few months or even a few years. The time spent at the border begins with residence on the Mexican side and later on the U.S. side as undocumented or documented persons. Many migrant settlers, eager to improve their economic circumstances, eventually find the U.S. interior the most appealing destination and move out of the border zone, but not before absorbing portions of its culture.

Having lived at the border proves extremely helpful because it allows these migrants to soften the cultural shock that transients experience when moving directly from the Mexican heartland to the U.S. interior. At the border settler migrants get a taste of the U.S. economy, meet Mexican Americans and Anglos, are exposed to the English language, and become partially acculturated to the American way of life. With those experiences behind them, settler migrants find it easier to cope with life in the United States than other Mexicans who lack preliminary exposure to U.S. culture.

The Domínguez Family: Settler Migrants. / The Domínguez family, consisting of the parents and five adult children, now live in Los Angeles after spending twelve years at the border. Their original home was a town in central Mexico that they left in the 1950s to seek a better life in a Mexican border city. Mr. Domínguez held a variety of low-paying jobs, including construction and agricultural work. After several years of struggling on the Mexican side, he decided to try his luck working on the U.S. side, commuting without documents on a weekly and monthly basis to better-paying but still unskilled jobs. The family continued to reside on the Mexican side. When work was scarce at the border, Mr. Domínguez traveled with other laborers like himself to pick crops in California. Sometimes he would be away from home for three to six months. Despite the problems of crossing the border and the constant absences from home, the family was better off economically than if Mr. Domínguez had continued to work on the Mexican side for Mexican wages. Two of the children even managed to attend school on the U.S. side, assuring that they would learn English and improve their chance of finding good employment later.

As time passed Mr. Domínguez became convinced that life would be better for his family if they could all move permanently to the United States. He managed to secure a letter of sponsorship from an employer (a farmer), which facilitated getting Green Cards for the entire family. They immediately moved to the U.S. side. Mr. Domínguez continued working for the employer who had helped him legalize his status, but after a few years of doing farm work he decided to seek a better job in the city, finding employment in a clothing factory. He now made more money and enjoyed health insurance and other benefits he had never had before. Meanwhile all of his children attended U.S. schools and were on their way to becoming Mexican Americans.

When the two older children graduated from high school, Mr. Domínguez decided that opportunities would be better for them in a large urban center away from the border, and the family moved to Los Angeles in 1970. Mr. Domínguez had friends in Los Angeles who had settled there some years before. They told him that good-paying jobs were available in California and that life was much better than in the depressed environment of the border. Mr. Domínguez considers the move to California the best decision he ever made. He got a good union job in construction and was able to buy a home in a nice neighborhood. Two of his children now work in construction and make good money, and the one who went to college is now a store manager. His two daughters are married and have families.

The Domínguez family illustrates a process of migration from the interior of Mexico to the United States which has been going on for many decades: the first step is the move from central Mexico to the Mexican side of the border; the second step is the move to the U.S. side; and the third and final step is the move to the U.S. interior. What drives most settler migrants to undertake this journey is the search for better economic opportunity.

Commuters

Whether originally from the Mexican interior or the border area, commuters are permanent residents of the Mexican frontier; their major distinguishing characteristic is dependence on employment on the U.S. side. The best-known commuters are the "Green Carders," legal U.S. immigrants who have chosen to live on Mexican soil to take advantage of the lower cost of living in Mexico. A second group of commuters are the people who misuse *pasaportes locales* to commute to unauthorized jobs on U.S. soil. Interestingly, holders of pasaportes locales cross the border legally but by virtue of working for pay in the United States become "undocumented" persons. Another group of commuters is composed of those individuals who cross the border at unauthorized points and without any documents whatsoever, risking apprehension from the moment they step over the dividing line.

As legal crossers, the Green Carders usually commute to their jobs on a daily basis, but "semi-documented" holders of pasaportes locales and totally undocumented workers may commute on a weekly or even monthly schedule to reduce the possibility of apprehension by *la migra*. Although employed outside their country, Mexican worker commuters generally live a predominantly Mexican lifestyle, with family and social networks and support systems mostly located on the Mexican side. Green Carders and U.S.-born Mexicans typically have more established links with the American way of life than the other commuter types because their legal status allows them to move about freely north of the border. Many Green Carders were formerly undocumented workers whose acquaintance with the United States began many years before they became legal U.S. immigrants. It is not easy to generalize about the extent of influence of U.S. culture on the semi-documented commuters and the undocumented workers. Crucial variables for both types include time spent in the United States; residence north of the boundary, or lack of it; and the degree of social ties with relatives or friends who may live in the United States.

Perhaps the least-known commuters are U.S.-born Mexicans who live on the Mexican side but cross the border to work on the U.S. side. Generally speaking, the only significant difference between U.S.-born commuters and Mexican-born commuters is place of birth. In other words, U.S.-born commuters are generally just as Mexican as other commuters, although there are exceptions to this rule. To underscore the point that place of birth does not disqualify a person from designation as a full-fledged Mexican fronterizo, I have included as my example of a commuter Diana Patricia Cruz Davidson. She was born in the United States, her mother was an Anglo, and she obtained her university education in the United States. Despite these foreign ties, Ms. Cruz Davidson is a Mexican, as is evident from her feelings about her identity. As a young professional, her situation differs greatly from most Mexican commuters, who tend to be unskilled, semi-skilled, or skilled workers. But the story is so compelling that I selected it for inclusion over a more typical case.

Diana Patricia Cruz Davidson: Commuter. / Ms. Cruz Davidson is a twenty-six-year-old, U.S.-born resident of a Mexican border city who commutes every day to her job as an administrator in a produce company on the U.S. side. Her father is Mexican and her mother Anglo. Despite her mixed ethnic background, her U.S. citizenship, her university education in the United States, and her U.S. employment, she considers herself totally Mexican.

Ms. Cruz Davidson's grandfather was an English dentist who practiced his profession in the U.S. border region. His daughter, going against the wishes of her Anglo mother, married a Mexican who was a principal in a school on the Mexican side. The couple settled in Mexico and eventually had seven children, all born in the United States because of the better medical facilities there. To make sure the children could legally function as citizens on both sides of the border, the parents "purchased" Mexican birth certificates for each of them. The youngest in the family, Ms. Cruz Davidson attended elementary and secondary schools in Mexico but got her bachelor's degree from a U.S. border area university. She was a student in the United States at a time when Mexican currency went through several steep devaluations, and her parents found it very difficult to pay her tuition and other bills because the family savings were deposited in Mexican banks in pesos, and the devaluations of the 1980s greatly eroded their value.

Since 1984 Ms. Cruz Davidson has worked for a produce company owned by a Mexican national but located on the U.S. side. She is in charge of the entire operation, supervising a staff of seven employees. The company sells Mexican tomatoes, bell peppers, cucumbers, squash, and chiles to buyers throughout the United States, Canada, and Japan. She enjoys her job but finds the daily commuting trip across the border increasingly frustrating because of the long lines at the crossing. Nevertheless, she will continue to live in Mexico simply because that is her home. She reports having had no problems at all because of her mixed ethnicity. Quite the contrary, the family has always been well accepted by their Mexican neighbors. Years ago her mother learned Spanish and became very active in social affairs in the community, serving in leadership positions in various organizations.

Ms. Cruz Davidson's loyalty and attachment to Mexico run deep despite her strong objections to the country's "bad government," which she blames for plunging the nation into economic crisis in the 1980s. She is particularly incensed at Mexican police, whom she characterizes as "terrible and very abusive." However, she believes that, in general, things have improved recently, and she sees greater national stability in the future. With regard to the United States, she resents the constant comparisons that Americans make between Mexico and their own country. "That is unfair," she says. "The United States is a huge, developed nation and Mexico is a relatively small Third World country. The unwarranted negative attitudes and criticisms of my country make me very angry." Ms. Cruz Davidson gets particularly upset at characterizations of Mexicans as "peasants." She feels Americans have formed warped opinions of the Mexican people from their constant contact with poor Mexican migrants in the United States, whom she describes as "uncultured and uneducated."

Ms. Cruz Davidson emphatically states that she is not a Mexican American, contrary to what people who do not know her often assume. But she understands why they would come to such a conclusion, given her family background, education, and the fact that she spends 80 percent of every working day on the U.S. side. Further, she admits that she watches U.S. television and movies almost exclusively, listens mostly to American music, and maintains extensive friendships with people on the U.S. side. She points out, however, that she speaks Spanish about 70 percent of the time, including in her workplace. Thus, even while she is physically on U.S. soil she continues to feel "muy mexicana" (very Mexican).

Biculturalists

Apart from being seasoned binational consumers, Mexican biculturalists are sufficiently familiar with the U.S. way of life that they can function with ease north of the border, where they spend a considerable amount of time. Strong Mexican roots plus economic and/or family links in the United States usually account for their biculturalism. Typically they are middle class, have attended both Mexican and American schools, maintain active ties with relatives and friends on both sides, and constantly move back and forth across the border, including taking trips to the U.S. interior. While their primary cultural orientation is Mexican, they are comfortable enough in American culture that if they felt it necessary to move permanently to the United States, they could do so with a minimum of trauma or adjustment.

Biculturalists should not be confused with bilingualists, or persons who learn English (either on the Mexican or U.S. side) primarily as a skill to be used on the job. While language facility gives bilingualists a means to learn about and participate more in American culture, sufficient opportunities to do so, are often not available, and they do not evolve into full-fledged biculturalists.

José Diego Lizárraga: Biculturalist. / José Diego Lizárraga has been director of the Museo de Historia y Arte in Ciudad Juárez since 1971. Now in his fifties, Mr. Lizárraga has for many years worked with his counterparts on the U.S. side to promote cultural activities along the border. His linguistic and cultural versatility is illustrated by his membership on several boards of U.S. cultural organizations, frequent attendance at and participation in U.S.-sponsored events, and numerous associations with Americans in various parts of the United States.

Mr. Lizárraga was born in Mexico City, but his parents moved to the border when he was just a few months old. He attended a private elementary school and began learning English in the fifth grade. Since he enjoyed languages, he continued to study English through secondary and preparatory schools, thus building a solid foundation that would facilitate his fluency later on. As a child he reinforced what he learned in the classroom with conversations with American tourists and other English speakers he met on the street. "I was full of curiosity and liked talking to lots of people," he says. "I found it entertaining to chatter with gringos and imitate the strange sounds they made." His knowledge of English served him well when he attended the Universidad Nacional Autónoma de México (UNAM) in Mexico City, for he was able to earn extra money by offering English classes. During an eleven-year absence from the border, he worked as an independent architect and held several positions with different firms, but eventually he decided to head back to Ciudad Juárez, becoming director of a new, government-sponsored museum catering to local Mexicans and foreign visitors.

His bilingualism and acquaintance with U.S. culture have been invaluable in carrying on the work of the museum and in assisting local authorities with promoting cross-border understanding, goodwill, and cooperation. With endorsement and help from American sympathizers and arts activists, he has been able to sponsor events such as art exhibits, musical presentations, and cultural conferences on the U.S. side. Conversely, he has organized presentations and performances by Americans on the Mexican side. For example, in the 1970s he and his collaborators on both sides of the boundary sponsored many activities around the theme of the blending of cultures.

After decades of interacting with Americans, Mr. Lizárraga has developed many positive attitudes toward the United States. He was particularly impressed with what he saw and experienced during a trip sponsored by the U.S. Information Agency to several major U.S. cities, which gave him a chance to visit many museums, cultural institutions, and centers of learning. He feels it is a great fallacy for so many Mexicans to feel that north of the border "there is no culture." He has found just the opposite and is critical of his countrymen who chauvinistically extol the superiority of Mexican culture. In order to correct such short-sightedness, he would like to see the creation of a center on the Mexican border that would focus on U.S. culture. He has made such a proposal to Mexican officials, but there has been little interest.

Because of the recent traffic delays and the frustrations of going through crowded border crossing points on a frequent basis, Mr. Lizárraga has reduced his daily interaction with the U.S. side. Nevertheless, he remains immersed in the cultures of both nations. He speaks English about 20 percent of the time, watches American television, and is constantly tuned in to a U.S. radio station. He visits American friends regularly and vacations in places like New York, Las Vegas, and Los Angeles.

Binationalists

One of the most interesting groups of fronterizos are those individuals who live a binational lifestyle, spending approximately equal time on each side of the border while interacting extensively with different subgroups, including Anglos. Most binationalists, whose ability to function in U.S. society surpasses that of biculturalists, come from the business and professional sectors of Mexican society. They may, for example, own retail establishments on both sides that require their close attention and their knowledge of business practices in both nations. To facilitate meeting social obligations and to enjoy the full benefits of two countries and two cultures, business binationalists may well maintain homes on both sides of the border. Professionals like physicians and college professors may not have the financial means to maintain multiple residences, but through their work in both countries they are able to live binational lifestyles both professionally and socially. This is especially true if they have relatives on the U.S. side who provide a strong social network and links with the Anglo community. At the low-income level, some workers lead a somewhat binational lifestyle when economic and family circumstances require working and living on both sides, but chances are that such individuals have little interaction with Anglos.

Mexican binationalists sometimes hold U.S. citizenship or Green Cards that allow them to work and move about legally in the United States. Thus such people are technically part of the immigrant community in the United States, but they retain their Mexican citizenship and continue to reside in their mother country because of their primary identification as Mexicans and for other personal or business reasons. Some Mexican binationalists who do not possess Green Cards act as if they do, spending long, unauthorized stretches of time on the U.S. side taking care of their businesses or properties, visiting relatives, shopping, or "seeing the sights." The illegal nature of their residence status is difficult to detect because of their affluent appearance and demeanor and their great ability to blend with the U.S. population.

The case of Roberto Carrasco again illustrates the irrelevance of place of birth. Like many of his friends and relatives, Carrasco was born in the United States as a result of his mother's preference for U.S. medical facilities. He has lived in Mexico most of his life but has worked mostly in the United States. He considers himself first and foremost a Mexican but consciously lives a binational lifestyle.

Roberto Carrasco: Binationalist / Mr. Carrasco is a forty-two-year-old, U.S.-born fronterizo who has extensive interaction with borderlanders in both countries. He is a highly educated professional who commutes on a daily basis from his home in Mexico to his teaching job in a U.S. university. Mr. Carrasco's Spanish is better than his English, but he is without question highly proficient in both languages. He spends more time in Mexico than in the United States, yet his friends and acquaintances are about equally divided among Mexicans, Mexican Americans, and Anglos.

Mr. Carrasco's father was born in Mexico, but he acquired his advanced education in the United States, attending a university located in an interior borderlands city. Mr. Carrasco's mother was born in a U.S. border city, and most of her relatives live in the interior of the United States. Carrasco family members, however, have lived on the Mexican border most of their lives.

Mr. Carrasco attended elementary school in Mexico and high school in the United States. He skipped the seventh and eighth grades because his parents concluded that the sixth-grade education he received in a private Mexican school prepared him well enough to proceed directly to high school on the U.S. side. Mr. Carrasco earned his bachelor's, master's, and Ph.D. degrees in U.S. border-area universities, with a specialty in Latin American literature. While a student in Mexico, Mr. Carrasco felt different from the other children because he was constantly reminded that he was not a Mexican citizen. The U.S. invasion of Mexico in the nineteenth century was always a topic of discussion. A question that the U.S.-born children in the school asked themselves constantly was what they would do if Mexico and the United States went to war. On whose side would they fight? Mr. Carrasco decided that he would never fight against Mexico, and that feeling remains very strong to the present day. In the Jesuit high school he attended in the United States, his main problem was insufficient knowledge of English, as well as total ignorance of American and English history and literature. Fellow students made him feel stupid for knowing very little about the United States. Students caught speaking Spanish were given demerits, and the only way to remove them was to walk laps after school, which created great inconvenience for his car pool because everyone would have to wait for those children walking off their demerits.

Mr. Carrasco has lived on the Mexican border most of his life, but he has also resided in Mexico City; Albuquerque; Seattle; and Newport, Rhode Island. While in the U.S. Navy in the late 1960s, he was also able to travel abroad. After his discharge from the navy he returned to college and held a variety of jobs on both sides of the border, including selling tickets at a racetrack and selling stereos at an electronics store. In graduate school he worked as a janitor and a research assistant. Upon receiving his Ph.D. he obtained employment at the U.S. border university where he teaches now. Over the years he has also taught in two Mexican border universities on a part-time basis.

Mr. Carrasco has participated in many community activities on both sides of the border, focusing his energies on civil rights and cultural issues. Once during a Chicano demonstration in the United States he was gassed by the police when a tear-gas canister landed in front of him. Mr. Carrasco takes advantage of recreation from both sides of the border. He enjoys watching classic Mexican movies and listening to Latin American music. Most movies he sees in public theaters are from the United States, partly because so few good Mexican and Latin American films are available on the border. Mr. Carrasco also likes to listen to U.S. pop music from the thirties to the sixties. Vacation destinations for Mr. Carrasco and his family include U.S. coastal and mountain resorts, and Mexican resorts and interior centers such as Mexico City and Veracruz.

Mr. Carrasco is simultaneously euphoric and ambivalent about his binationalism. He is foremost a Mexican and has a deep love for the country in which he lives, and he also has strong affection for the United States. Nevertheless, there are elements of both societies that disturb him. He comments:

> You ask me about my feelings toward Mexico. Let me put it this way. How does one think about one's mother? You have a love for her that is immeasurable. That's how I feel. Mexico is rich in culture. It has a long history, a long tradition. In Mexico there is real culture. We have the archaeological ruins and a rich *mestizaje* [racial mix-

ture]. Mexico is always creating. There is, of course, American influence, but Mexico's culture is so strong and deep that it is not being altered by foreigners. What I don't like about Mexico is its political system, corruption, the constant compromising of principles, how the poor are treated, inefficiency, underdevelopment, inertia. . . .

I like the United States for its people, its modernity, its inventiveness, its technology, its recognition of the contributions of people like me. U.S. strength and power is a real deterrent to world disorder. Gringos as a whole are easier to deal with than other nationalities. But I don't think there is an American culture. The United States has not developed its own culture. American culture is personified by Donald Duck, by superficiality, and a philosophy of screwing anyone who lets himself be screwed. The United States has its own interests, and everyone else be damned. Why does it not behave like the Christian nation it purports to be? These feelings about both countries create inner conflict for me. But I make a conscious effort to not let negative influences enter my life.

Conclusion

The salient heterogeneity of Mexican fronterizos is a product of the recent growth of population and its myriad links with the United States, whose effects are felt by large sectors of society. Many people are directly or indirectly dependent economically on the United States, and consequently they are drawn into the orbit of the neighboring country. Tens of thousands of fronterizos have jobs on the U.S. side, and hundreds of thousands work in foreign-oriented sectors on the Mexican side such as maquiladoras and tourism. Moreover, family ties and other social relationships link many fronterizos to the Mexican American population north of the boundary. Finally, there is heavy consumption of U.S. products and continuous American cultural penetration via television, movies, and music. Hence it is not surprising that large numbers of fronterizos manifest transnational characteristics.

Binational consumers, who include representatives from all sectors of fronterizo society (except transient migrants), most vividly illustrate the intense interaction with the U.S. side. But the most substantial cross-border links are carried on by binationalists, biculturalists, commuters, and settler migrants. The least affected by foreign influences are uniculturalists and nationalists. It is significant that nationalists are not numerically strong in the Mexican border region. The explanation lies in the deep economic ties that exist with the U.S. side and in the largely favorable attitudes toward Americans that have developed among fronterizos in the last several decades.

In general, fronterizos have accepted the reality of their unique relationship with the United States, and they have sought to capitalize on the benefits it brings. Interior Mexicans, by contrast, remain highly dubious that the border situation is in the best interests of their nation. They fear economic, cultural, and political drift by fronterizos. The difference in the perception of the status of the border population is an old theme in the relations between the periphery and the center, and the debate is bound to continue into the twenty-first century.

The major distinction between Mexican borderlanders and their counterparts across the border—that is, Mexican Americans and Anglos—is economic necessity, which drives fronterizos to take part so extensively in transnational interaction. Rather than being economically motivated, the strong transnational links among Mexican Americans derive mainly from familial, social, cultural, and consumer ties. Anglos, who also largely lack an economic incentive and who have no personal stake in Mexican society, have a relatively low level of participation in transnational interaction. These differences among the three groups constitute central concerns in the following two chapters.

4

MEXICAN AMERICANS

Although some Mexican Americans on the border are descended from colonial Spanish-Mexican families, most trace their presence in the region to the waves of immigrants from Mexico that began at the outbreak of the Mexican Revolution in 1910.[1] Those who arrived after 1940 are particularly numerous because of the much heavier migration flow during the half-century of extraordinary economic expansion in the U.S. Southwest that was initiated by World War II. Physical proximity to Mexico has assured strong adherence to Mexican cultural norms and the maintenance of the Spanish language. The overwhelming predominance of Spanish speakers on the border is indicated in data gathered by the U.S. census (see Table 4.1). In 1980 the proportion of Hispanics who spoke a language other than English at home ranged from 73.3 percent in San Diego to 96.3 percent in the Brownsville–Harlingen–San Benito area. At the same time, the need to function effectively in American society has supported fluency in English and familiarity with the ways of the mainstream Anglo culture. In the border areas described in Table 4.1, about three-fourths of the Hispanic population spoke English well. These circumstances, then, predispose border Mexican Americans as a group to be bilingual and bicultural, and to maintain substantial links with their ancestral homeland.

The degree of Mexican American integration into the U.S. mainstream depends on many variables associated with personal and societal circumstances. Generally speaking, people who have lived longer in the United States are more highly assimilated than recent immigrants. Those Mexican Americans who were descended from border pioneer families long ago learned how to function with proficiency outside their own group. Additionally, Mexican Americans descended from immigrants who arrived several generations ago have had the advantage of time and experience to ease the adjustment to U.S. society. By contrast, newly arrived immigrants are just beginning to acquaint themselves with U.S. society, and it will take them many years to become assimilated.

TABLE 4.1 Socioeconomic Characteristics of Hispanics in Three Border
        SMSAS,* 1980

	Brownsville–Harlingen–San Benito	El Paso	San Diego
Percent foreign-born	23.5	29.3	37.5
Percent who speak a language other than English (i.e., Spanish) at home	96.5	93.8	73.3
Percent who do not speak English well or at all	29.3	26.3	25.8
Percent who resided in a different SMSA in 1975	6.0	5.5	13.6
Income distribution, by household			
Less than $14,999	67.9	63.3	53.1
$15,000–$24,999	22.4	22.9	27.2
$25,000–$34,999	6.8	8.5	12.1
$35,000 or more	3.3	4.2	7.6
Percent of families below poverty level	33.7	26.5	18.1

SOURCE: U.S., Bureau of the Census. *Census of Population, 1980. Census Tracts.*
*Standard Metropolitan Statistical Areas

Class status also plays an important role in the process of integration. As a general rule, the higher the socioeconomic level of Mexican Americans, the greater the likelihood that they will merge with the dominant Anglo culture. For example, nineteenth-century Mexican American businesspeople and Mexican exiles of elite backgrounds who arrived during the Mexican Revolution found greater acceptance in the United States than the poor, uneducated immigrant masses. Yet in recent decades greater numbers of Mexican Americans from disadvantaged backgrounds have been able to rise to middle-class status quicker than previous generations as a result of better economic opportunities and a more favorable ethnic climate. Social advancement in the United States has caused many of these immigrants and their descendants to distance themselves from their cultural roots to a greater degree than earlier immigrants, who experienced very slow and limited mobility. Yet whether rich or poor, old-timers or newcomers, most Mexican American borderlanders retain their mixed culture because of the ever-present opportunities to function in the various social environments of the border.

Using as the main criterion the degree of interaction with the Mexican side and with Anglo society, Figure 4.1 presents a typology of Mexican American borderlanders, and Figure 4.2 gives an indication of the approximate relative size of each group and its location on the borderlands milieu core–periphery continuum. A small proportion of the Mexican American population is classified as national borderlanders, with one subgroup referred to as assimilationists and the other as newcomers. Those classified as transnational borderlanders, who constitute the vast majority within the whole cohort, include disadvantaged immigrants, advantaged immigrants, commuters, biculturalists, and binationalists. Binational consumers are part of both the national and transnational sectors but tilt toward the latter. As Figure 4.2 shows, newcomers and assimilationists, located on the periphery of the borderlands milieu, make up relatively small categories, and immigrants and biculturalists, in the core region, comprise the largest subgroups. Figure 4.3 provides a comparative overview of the cross-border links and influences in the lives of the nine Mexican American borderlands types. Relevant socioeconomic data from the 1980 census in three major Standard Metropolitan Statistical Areas on the border appear in Table 4.1.

National Mexican Americans

Assimilationists

As a nation of immigrants, the United States has historically played host to millions of individuals from many nationalities who have given up much of their own culture as they assimilated to another. Such individuals have been present in the Mexican American border community as well, although to a lesser degree than other ethnic groups because of the constant strong reinforcement of the native culture from nearby Mexico. Nevertheless, recent socioeconomic advances in the U.S. borderlands have made it possible for increasing numbers of Mexican Americans to be absorbed into the Anglo mainstream, resulting in a significant loss of Hispanic cultural traits. These people may be referred to as Mexican American assimilationists. One measure of assimilationist tendencies in the group is provided in Table 4.1, which indicates that 3.5 percent of the Hispanic population on the Texas side of the Lower Rio Grande Valley, 6.2 percent in El Paso, and 26.7 percent in San Diego speak English (as opposed to Spanish) at home. These percentages may be taken as rough estimates of the size of the assimilationist sector in each locality.

Perhaps the most common Mexican American assimilationists are people who wish to master the English language and obtain a thorough understanding of Anglo society in order to succeed economically and achieve social "respect-

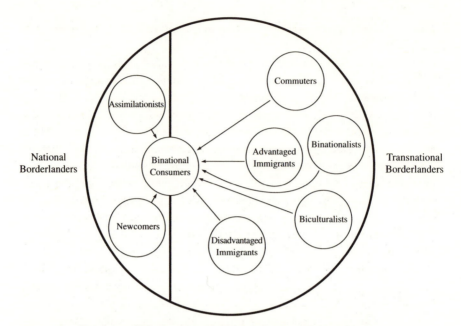

FIGURE 4.1 Typology of Mexican American borderlanders. The binational consumers category is composed of individuals from all subgroups.

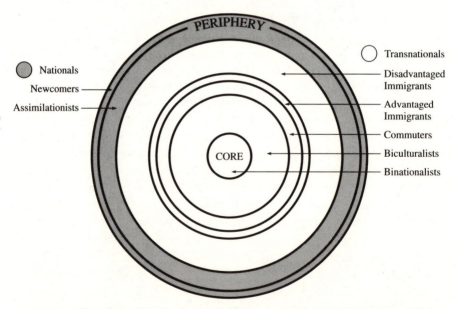

FIGURE 4.2 The relative size of subgroups of Mexican American borderlanders and their location on the borderlands milieu core–periphery continuum. Binational consumers are not included here because they constitute a category composed of members from all subgroups, particularly those in the transnational sector.

ability" for themselves and their children. In pursuing higher social status, they gradually distance themselves from their own culture, and with time their way of life becomes highly Anglicized. Opportunities to speak Spanish or be involved in Mexican-related activities diminish, and ties with Mexico become very weak. These people are essentially pragmatic assimilationists.

At the other end of the assimilationist spectrum are people who, in striving to achieve the American Dream of material comfort, status, and acceptability in U.S. society, consciously and overtly reject their Mexicanness because they see it as an impediment to personal progress. They are embarrassed by the poverty and other social problems that prevail in the Hispanic community and by the negative publicity that Mexicans constantly receive in the U.S. media. They are often very critical of their cultural background and the land of their forebears, and they work hard at shedding their "negative" baggage. Thus, the mind-set of these eager assimilationists is not conducive to carrying on substantial cross-border relationships.

The case histories that follow typify the assimilationist syndrome among young Mexican Americans highly exposed to the Anglo way of life. The first individual, Juan Hinojosa, reports that his parents have consciously steered him in the direction of the dominant society and away from Mexican culture. The second, Daniel Fisher, represents a growing segment of the population along the border, people of Mexican-Anglo extraction. Fisher has faced strong pressures to "be" Anglo because of the influence of his Anglo father and his close association with members of the mainstream society.

Juan Hinojosa: Assimilationist / John Hinojosa is a twenty-year-old U.S.-born university student who attended predominantly Anglo public schools in a major U.S. border city. He has little in common with the mass of Mexican American young people in the borderlands, who are strongly bilingual and bicultural. While physically he looks very Hispanic, his mind-set, mannerisms, and speech strongly reflect Anglo culture. His command of the English language is impressive, and he speaks without an accent. Conversely, his Spanish is extremely weak and his understanding of Mexican American and Mexican cultures is very shallow.

Hinojosa traces the loss of his native culture to the day he started kindergarten. At that time he knew only Spanish and had a hard time understanding what was happening in class. Sensing his predicament, his parents, both U.S.-born Mexican Americans, decided to speak only English to him. Since that time he himself has spoken very little Spanish, although he has heard it spoken around him. The strategy followed by his parents worked well, and he was able to become highly proficient in English and a very successful student.

His mother was especially instrumental in directing him toward Anglo cul-

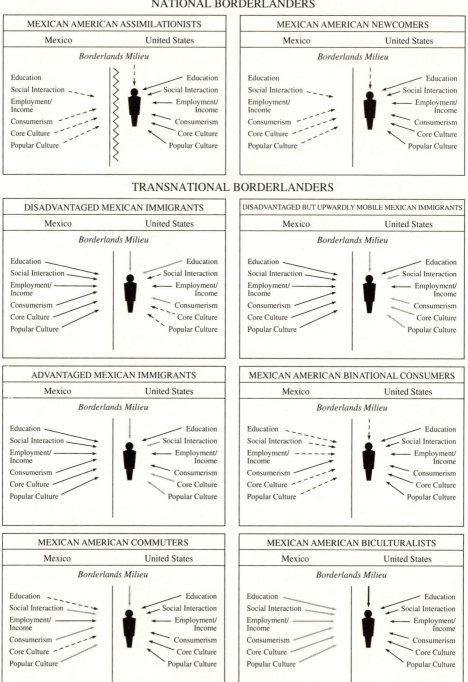

FIGURE 4.3 Major sources of cultural and lifestyle orientation among Mexican American borderlanders

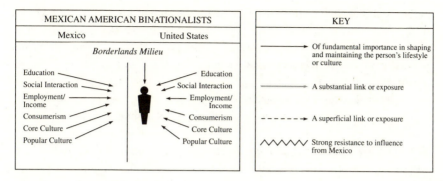

FIGURE 4.3 (*continued*)

ture. She wanted him to learn the English that is spoken in the eastern United States. A college graduate with training in English and journalism, she worked diligently with him on building vocabulary skills and insisted that he read classic works of U.S. and English literature, which she loved. Titles he readily remembers include Emily Bronte's *Wuthering Heights,* Pearl Buck's *The Good Earth,* Thomas Hardy's *The Return of the Native,* Aldous Huxley's *Brave New World,* and John Steinbeck's *The Grapes of Wrath.* He also recalls discussing these books with his mother.

Hinojosa explains that as a second-generation American his mother lost effective contact with Mexico. Despite growing up in a disadvantaged Mexican American neighborhood, she early developed a strong orientation toward Anglo society and away from her Mexican roots. Further, she was determined that her children would become well-educated, obtain white-collar jobs, and lead middle-class lives. To do that they would have to master the English language. Other relatives on her side of the family reflect that orientation as well. He does not recall much being said about Mexico or about Hispanic culture by members of his mother's family.

His father's family, on the other hand, identify strongly with their Mexican heritage, and this has created problems for his mother and for him. They accuse her of being aloof and too Anglo-oriented. They are always making snide remarks about the middle-class neighborhood in which they live and the predominantly Anglo schools her children have attended. They assume that John has mostly Anglo friends and that his Hispanic friends are as Anglicized as he is.

Hinojosa has traveled throughout Texas, New Mexico, Arizona, and California, and he would like to visit the northeastern United States, especially Boston and New York City. His firsthand knowledge of Mexico is confined to brief visits to the city on the other side of the boundary. He relates that his mother has discouraged him from crossing the border, fearing that he will be assaulted or get in trouble with the Mexican police. Thus the land of his ancestors remains a mystery to him. He has a vague impression that the Mexican government is corrupt, undemocratic, and cares little for the poor. He is embarrassed by the pervasive poverty he has seen in the neighboring Mexican city. Hinojosa seems unperturbed by the fact that he knows little about his Mexican heritage. He understands that his circumstances have put him in the position where he is today. In this sense he appears to be a well-adjusted assimilationist.

Daniel Fisher: Mexican American–Anglo Assimilationist / Daniel Fisher is a twenty-seven-year-old university student who is culturally Anglo, although his mother is a native of Mexico. His father is a retired Anglo army sergeant who feels positively toward Mexican culture but who has paid little attention to the task of cultivating a dual heritage in his children. His mother, on the other hand, has adhered strongly to Mexican values, but Fisher has always resisted her attempts to Mexicanize him. Thus, throughout his life Fisher has sought to be like other mainstream Americans, shunning his Mexican identity.

When he was a child, his mother spoke Spanish to him and he understood her, but he never developed the ability to speak it. What's more, he had a fear of speaking Spanish because he was inclined to identify with people who spoke English. His father spoke English to him, as did all his friends. "I wanted to Americanize," he says. "There was a lot of pressure everywhere around me to speak English." He relates that the kids at school considered English superior to Spanish and Americans superior to Mexicans. The teachers discouraged students from speaking Spanish, criticizing and even punishing them when they did not speak English. Mexico was also the object of much criticism. It was said that Mexicans were poor by choice, that they were lazy, and that they wanted to remain backward. He recalls jokes and insults hurled at Mexicans, and he grew up believing much of what he heard. The presence of *cholos* (poor Chicano kids who ran around in gangs) at school made it worse for Fisher because they seemed to personify what Mexicans were. "I did not want to be associated with them," he says.

Thus he felt very ambivalent about his Mexican background. His Anglo last name gave him an advantage, because others assumed he was not a Mexican. He deliberately associated with Anglo children or with Anglicized Mexican Americans. One of his lifelong apprehensions has been that other Mexicans will find out he is half Mexican and consequently assume he will tend to think like them. At that point they will discover how different he is, creating an uncomfortable situation for him and for them. So he avoids settings in which that might happen and continues to associate predominantly with Anglos and assimilated Mexican Americans.

Looking back, he regrets viewing Mexico so negatively and rejecting the Spanish language. He now sees speaking Spanish as an asset and plans to study it. However, he remains steadfast about his commitment to being a mainstream American, and that is how he plans to raise his children. He is strongly opposed to certain Mexican cultural values, and he has had disagreements with his mother over them. His main problem is Catholicism. As a child he went to church with his mother, taking the teachings of the Catholic church at face value, but he gradually became confused and alienated. By the time he was in high school he had stopped going to church, and his mother reluctantly accepted his decision.

Fisher also believes that certain values in Mexican culture hold people back. For example, he believes that the closeness of families makes family members "too dependent on each other." This keeps the children from developing a "sense of independence," and from venturing "out on their own." Fisher is particularly critical of *machismo* (male dominance). He sees Mexican women being placed at a great disadvantage because of it. He attributes the academic and job success of his three sisters to the absence of a *macho* environment when they were growing up.

Newcomers

Like other sectors of borderlands society, the Mexican American community includes individuals from the U.S. interior who are new to the border region and who, despite their ethnic affinity with Chicano/Mexicano borderlanders, lack the experience and ability to engage in a substantial way in transcultural and transnational processes. Such newcomers typically come from U.S. heartland communities where their families settled permanently when they immigrated from Mexico. Having grown up and lived far from the border, their level of assimilation into U.S. society is relatively high. Many of them, for example, are not very proficient in the Spanish language. Mexican Americans from places like Chicago, Kansas City, and Denver may be found in the large border cities. Most tend to be professionals or businesspeople who have relocated to the borderlands because of job changes or advancement opportunities. Data in Table 4.1 confirm the small size of the Mexican American newcomer sector on the border: approximately 6 percent in the Lower Rio Grande Valley, 5.5 percent in El Paso, and 13.6 percent in San Diego.

These newcomers are able to function effectively in the Anglo and middle-class Mexican American communities, but they have little in common with poor border Chicanos or with Mexican nationals. Thus their interaction with the latter two sectors is limited. Mexican American newcomers generally have little understanding of how things work on the Mexican side. Those who are interested in increasing their bilingual and bicultural proficiency take advantage of opportunities to do so, and if they stay at the border long enough, they become more like standard Chicano borderlanders. Many even make an effort to visit the Mexican side regularly, and in time they may even become true transnational borderlanders. Greg Rocha, whose newcomer status is described below, appears headed in that direction. A fair number of Mexican American newcomers, however, will likely never transcend their status as national borderlanders.

Greg Rocha: Newcomer / A native of Iowa, forty-year-old Greg Rocha has lived in a major U.S. border city for almost four years. He is a highly educated professional who finds the border environment substantially different from the interior United States, especially from the perspective of a Chicano who grew up in an Anglo world. Rocha's family migrated from Guanajuato, Mexico, to Iowa during the Mexican Revolution. His grandfather wanted to get as far away as possible from the violence that was engulfing his country. His father was a sheet-metal worker who raised four sons in a working-class community outside of Des Moines. To lessen the possibility of discrimination against them for their lack of language skills, his father and mother spoke only English to the children. Rocha relates that his mother in particular experienced discrimination at different times in her life. Inevitably Rocha became Anglicized, but constant visits from relatives kept alive his feeling of Mexicanness. Even though he had nothing in common with his relatives and could not communicate with them in Spanish, he saw them as his link to the land of his ancestors. He maintained a curiosity about Mexico, wanting to visit there sometime.

When he arrived at the border, two things overwhelmed him. One was the great number of Chicanos. Having grown up in a small circle of Mexican American relatives and friends and surrounded by Anglos, he had never seen anything like it. All of a sudden he felt a part of a majority group rather than a minority person. For the first time in his life he could just "melt" into the population, no longer subjected to "those looks" from people (Anglos in Iowa) who made him feel different. His world seemed completely turned around. He was overcome with different emotions, for the most part centered on a feeling of great satisfaction. He was also startled by the many Mexican American businesses all over town. Back home, the only Chicano businessmen he had seen were barber shop and restaurant owners. Having grown up with ubiquitous stereotypes about "lazy" Mexicans, this was a most pleasant surprise. There were prosperous-looking Mexican Americans everywhere.

On the negative side, the poverty on the border bothered him greatly. He was especially struck by the undocumented migrants who crossed the Rio Grande in such great numbers. As he drove by the river every day, he saw many people desperately making their way into the United States. The sight of families making a "dash for it" across the highway stunned him. In time he came to know some of these people, and he was impressed with their simplicity and friendliness.

The first time he crossed into Mexico he had the feeling that he was returning home, but he quickly realized that he was very much a stranger in a foreign country. He was a U.S. citizen and culturally an American, not a Mexican, or even a "Mexicanized" Chicano. He knew relatively little Spanish, and his behavior and clothes were different. Because he looked Mexican, some people would initially treat him as one of them, but then they would quickly find out that he was an American. His inability to communicate easily in Spanish would create awkward and uncomfortable situations. He resolved this problem in his own mind and heart by accepting the reality of his predicament. When the need arose, he would let others know right away that he was a Mexican by ancestry but that his roots and cultural formation were in the interior of the United States. He reports that this approach has worked well in his dealings with Mexicans, whom he describes as very accepting.

While at first Rocha had to make some big adjustments to his new surroundings, he now feels very comfortable on the border. He has taken a "180-degree turn" in his life. Whereas once he believed that getting away from his Mexican heritage was the thing to do, living on the border has changed his thinking. He now identifies strongly with his ethnicity and is making an effort to learn more Spanish.

Transnational Mexican Americans

Disadvantaged Immigrants

Most Mexican immigrants who have recently arrived in the United States may be classified as underprivileged because they reach their adopted country with little education, limited employment skills, and a lack of knowledge of how things function in the United States.[2] Furthermore, numerous hurdles built into U.S. society block their path toward rapid upward mobility, and they usually remain in the lowest economic sector for many years. Clues about the size of the disadvantaged immigrant population on the border can be found in Table 4.1. The Brownsville–Harlingen–San Benito, El Paso, and San Diego SMSAS have large proportions of foreign-born Hispanics, most of whom are poor. Additionally, the percentage of people who speak little or no English ranges from 25.8 to 29.3 percent in the three areas.

Historically, the U.S. border region has served as a major destination for masses of immigrants. There they find employment in the agricultural fields or in low-paying occupations in the cities. For example, the Lower Rio Grande Valley of Texas, the West Texas–southern New Mexico region, the Yuma–San Luis portion of Arizona, and the Imperial Valley of California have large numbers of poor immigrants whose main occupation is picking crops. Major border urban areas such as Brownsville, El Paso, and San Diego have sizable concentrations of immigrant laborers who work as maids, gardeners, busboys, and janitors.

Uneducated and unable to speak English well, these immigrants function on the margin of U.S. border society. They live in poor neighborhoods that often lack basic services such as water, and their life is a constant struggle. The schools attended by their children are often substandard, diminishing the chance for improvement among members of the second generation. Under these conditions, absorbing U.S. cultural norms is very difficult. Conversely, interaction with the Mexican side remains strong.

Despite the pervasive deprivation, however, some underprivileged immigrants somehow beat the odds and escape to better environments, enhancing their opportunities for achieving success in the world of the dominant society. Although not large in number, such upwardly mobile immigrants illustrate the possibility of making the transition in a short time from the bottom of the social order to the middle class. In general, underprivileged immigrant children are in the best position to experience such rapid social change.

The success of disadvantaged but upwardly mobile immigrants springs above all from unusually favorable economic or educational circumstances, but other important factors include hard work, a drive to succeed, and luck. In contrast to other underprivileged immigrants, upwardly mobile persons are able to overcome obstacles in their adoptive society quickly, improve their living standard, and diminish the marginality inherent in their immigrant status. In many cases they are fortunate enough to receive assistance from relatives or friends at crucial points in their lives. Such success stories are usually found in urban centers where opportunities exist to obtain a good education, well-paying jobs, and beneficial interaction with people from the mainstream. Immigrants who are trapped in poor, segregated *barrios* (neighborhoods) lack access to these things, and rural areas present even fewer possibilities for socioeconomic improvement. Residents of such disadvantaged communities face the prospect of long-term isolation and deprivation.

Upwardly mobile immigrants with access to opportunity and a determination to make the best of it make the transition from Mexicans to Mexican Americans relatively soon after their arrival in the United States. They strive to learn English and to become participants in their new surroundings. They see the United States as their new home; Mexico quickly becomes the "old country." To illustrate the phenomenon of relatively rapid rise to middle-class status among some immigrants, the case of an upwardly mobile person follows the case of a more typical disadvantaged individual who has lived at the lower end of the economic order all her life.

Juanita Vargas: Disadvantaged Immigrant / Born in Sinaloa in 1920, Mrs. Juanita Vargas migrated northward with her mother and brothers and sisters following the death of her father. The family first settled in Mexicali and then Tijuana, where Mrs. Vargas attended school through the fourth grade. She dropped out because she was needed to help out at home and because she had no transportation to attend the nearest school, located some five miles from where she lived. When she was sixteen, she attempted to finish elementary school but considered herself too old and felt out of place. In 1940 Mrs. Vargas married Leonardo Vargas, a U.S.-born Mexican who had settled in Tijuana with his family following their repatriation from San Diego during the Depression. Mr. Vargas recalls very difficult times in Tijuana when he was a young man. He worked at odd jobs, including serving as a helper in his brother's small grocery store. In time Mr. Vargas got a permanent job with a small egg company on the U.S. side and worked for thirty years as a foreman making modest wages.

The Vargases have four children, which Mrs. Vargas helped to support by working in a fish cannery in San Diego. Like her husband, she crossed the border every day until the family moved permanently to San Diego in 1955. Life became a little easier after that, but circumstances required that she continue to work. She eventually retired in 1982 at the age of sixty-two. Mrs. Vargas remembers that the work at the cannery was very demanding, but there were opportunities to make extra money by doing piecework rather than working by the hour. Since the plant was unionized, employees also enjoyed some protection. When workers went on strike, however, there was no income. She recalls one strike that lasted for four months. During that time she worked at a chile cannery to maintain some income.

Today Mr. and Mrs. Vargas live in a modest home in Chula Vista in a predominantly working-class Hispanic area. They are satisfied with the way their lives have turned out, and they are especially pleased that their children are gainfully employed. One is an accountant, another is a personnel administrator, another works in a gun shop, and the fourth is a maintenance worker. Mrs. Vargas is proud that their children are bilingual, something she strived to develop in them at an early age. She recalls she spoke Spanish to them at home, although they answered in English. Mrs. Vargas herself speaks English but is not completely fluent; she is much more comfortable speaking Spanish. Her life has revolved around her family, her work, and her church. Both she and her husband are active in their parish, assisting with a variety of chores and participating in many church activities. Living close to Tijuana and having friends and relatives there have helped them maintain continuous contact with Mexico.

Elena Matthews: Upwardly Mobile Immigrant / Elena Matthews is a thirty-six-year-old woman who immigrated to the United States in the mid-1970s following the marriage of her mother to an American who adopted her children. Today Ms. Matthews is making the transition from Mexican immigrant to Mexican American. She reports that she does not feel like a genuine Mexican anymore because of her residence in the United States for over a decade, but she does not see herself as a Mexican American yet. She still does not speak English fluently enough, nor has she mastered U.S. culture sufficiently. She finds herself at an "in-between" stage, but there is no question she is experiencing profound cultural and social change.

Life in Mexico was very difficult for Ms. Matthews and her seven siblings since their mother, who was raped and abused at an early age, was abandoned by a number of men with whom she had her children. Ms. Matthews suffered many privations when she and several of her brothers were left in the care of her grandmother in a small town in their native Coahuila while their mother worked on the border, where she eventually met her American husband in a brothel during her first day on the job.

The tragic and poverty-stricken life she led in Mexico has made Ms. Matthews deeply grateful for the family's good fortune in being able to immigrate to the United States. She has taken advantage of educational and other opportunities in her adoptive land to become a journalist and community activist. Her case is unusual in that in a relatively short time she has risen from destitution in a Third World country to middle-class status in the United States. Once the family immigrated to the United States, she attended college while holding a full-time job and helping to raise her younger siblings. Now married to a retired Anglo educator who is very supportive of her quest to improve herself, she has been able to participate in many career-enhancement activities, including attending international conferences and studying abroad.

She is ecstatic about her life in the United States. She says she has adapted well to U.S. culture. In her view, this is largely due to her natural interest in other cultures and her ability to accommodate to whatever conditions she encounters, whether in the United States or in other countries. "I adore the United States," she says. "I love Anglo Americans and their culture. I have learned many things from them. I could never return to Mexico. I would not be able to fulfill myself there like I can here." Her fondness for U.S. culture has not eroded her deep affection for Mexican culture, which she practices continuously: "I thrive on Mexican art, music, dance. . . . The parties I enjoy the most are Mexican parties. They leave me with a great deal of satisfaction." Like many other Mexican immigrants, what she dislikes about her homeland is the harshness of the life of the poor and the oppression of the government and those who have economic power. "I feel sad about Mexico," she says. "It is a very difficult world. The more power a person has there, the more he squashes those beneath him. To survive, you need to know the system very well. Being a woman presents special problems. Mexican men are tough to deal with because of their feelings of domination toward women."

Ms. Matthews and her husband currently reside in a major U.S. border city. Her parents are deceased. She has an older brother whom she has not seen since his disappearance in Mexico at age sixteen. Her remaining three brothers and three sisters are all married and have children. One of the brothers lives in Monterrey, Mexico, where he has "three wives and lots of kids." The others live in the United States with their families.

Advantaged Immigrants

Mexicans from the "advantaged" sectors of society who have relocated to the United States have received relatively little attention from scholars. Perhaps the reason is that these immigrants constitute a relatively small proportion of the overall Mexican immigrant community, which historically has been dominated by people from the working class. Nevertheless, the flow across the border has always included middle, upper middle, and upper class people who left Mexico for economic, political, or personal reasons. During the period of the Mexican Revolution, for example, thousands of affluent Mexicans fled the chaos in their homeland and settled in U.S. border cities. Although some returned to Mexico after the Revolution, others stayed permanently in the United States and eventually became part of the Mexican American community.

In the 1980s another crisis, this time an economic one, again drove affluent immigrants into the United States in significant numbers. Mexico faced bankruptcy as a result of a massive foreign debt and a drastic drop in the price of oil, the nation's most important export. Suddenly the Mexican people confronted a drastically devalued national currency, scarce investment capital, business failures, massive unemployment, and galloping inflation. In their desperation to protect their shrinking assets, many wealthy Mexicans deposited huge sums in U.S. banks, while others purchased real estate or invested in business enterprises in the U.S. border region. Many also bought homes in exclusive neighborhoods in select cities. For example, between 1982 and 1985 an estimated 600 wealthy Mexican families settled in San Diego, many of them in the plush La Jolla area.

Less privileged but still affluent persons such as professionals also immigrated in higher than normal numbers during the 1970s and 1980s. For instance, many Mexican physicians left their country for better opportunities north of the border. Such was the case with Dr. Salvador Montes, who decided it would be best for himself and his family to stay permanently in the United States following a long temporary residence there in connection with his work. Cristina Montes, his wife, relates how the family has adjusted to life in the United States. Contrary to the prevailing pattern, in which adult immigrants, especially affluent ones, seek integration into U.S. society in a passive manner at most, she has actively pursued it. This is not to say, however, that she has abandoned her traditional lifestyle. She and other members of the family maintain strong ties with relatives and friends in Mexico, frequently crossing the border. What is more, Mrs. Montes closely follows political developments south of the border.

Cristina Montes: Advantaged Immigrant / Mrs. Montes is a housewife in her early forties and is married to a physician with a very successful practice in a major U.S. border city. They first came to the United States in the 1970s when Dr. Montes, who had received his medical training in Mexico, got an "exchange visitor" permit from the U.S. Immigration and Naturalization Service to do his residency in a hospital in Minnesota. Two years later, the family moved to Chicago, where Dr. Montes continued his residency, and that was followed by a year at Baylor University Medical School, where he received specialized training. They then spent some time in Houston, followed by a move to the Texas border, where they made the decision to apply for permanent U.S. residency. By then the family included three U.S.-born children.

In the early 1980s it became very difficult for foreign physicians to obtain U.S. immigrant visas, but an immigration judge who knew the family advised them to persevere until the law was modified. Following a long struggle to become legal U.S. residents, including periods when they had no legal status, Dr. and Mrs. Montes finally managed to get Green Cards in 1984. Mrs. Montes explains that initially she and her husband intended to return to Mexico at the end of his medical residency. At home they had always had a very secure lifestyle, as both came from wealthy Mexican families. As their stay north of the border lengthened, however, their desire to go back weakened as they became accustomed to American life. Dr. Montes realized that if he returned home he would have to start all over again because all his professional experience was in the United States. He would also not be able to utilize fully all the advanced training he had received outside Mexico. Furthermore, conditions greatly deteriorated in his homeland with the onset of the devastating economic crisis of 1982, and the prospects for establishing a good practice and living a comfortable lifestyle looked very unpromising. "It was a great relief when we finally legalized our status," recalls Mrs. Montes. "You cannot believe the feeling. We had been in limbo for so long." She explains that years before they became permanent immigrants she had already begun to feel that she belonged in the United States. She had developed a love for the country. "Once at a baseball game in Chicago I felt very emotional when they played the national anthem," she says. "I also would cry when I would see Vietnam veterans go unappreciated. I would get angry because nobody seemed to care about them."

Mrs. Montes feels very happy about the way things have turned out. Her husband has a fulfilling and lucrative career, and the family lives well. "It is just like a miracle," she says. "We are very fortunate and feel very grateful. The United States has given us great opportunities. Here, if you want to make it, you can do it. Unlike Mexico, here your success is not dependent upon who you know or who you bribe. It is up to you." Mrs. Montes became a U.S. citizen in 1989 as soon as she became eligible to apply. She was anxious to be a participant in U.S. society, especially to be able to vote. She feels her voice will be better heard in her adopted country, in contrast to her experience in Mexico, where she felt the system made little allowance for participation by ordinary citizens. "We are now Americans," she says. "My kids are not Mexicans. Sometimes we even feel that we are not liked in Mexico. So this is our home now. We will make our stand and fight our battles in the United States."

Binational Consumers

Attracted by bargains, Mexican Americans along the border do a considerable amount of shopping on the Mexican side, purchasing items such as food, shoes, and clothing, and patronizing service establishments like barber shops, beauty parlors, tailor shops, and upholstery shops. Special occasions such as weddings or *quinceañeras* (debutante parties) often include activities south of the border, like taking group photographs in a Mexican studio or holding a dance in a Mexican hotel or hall. When the price of gasoline is cheaper in Mexico than in the United States, filling up at the PEMEX service stations is also popular. Finally, recreation provided by Mexican movie theaters, dance halls, discotheques, taverns, and other establishments attracts many Mexican Americans to the Mexican side on weekends.

Consumer patterns vary according to class status, with poor Mexican Americans being attracted in particular by the low prices of certain Mexican foodstuffs, and middle-class Mexican Americans lured especially by inexpensive gasoline, services, and recreation. Among many Chicanos, eating in Mexican restaurants and partying in Mexican night spots are favorite activities. Such trips across the border provide language and cultural reinforcement for Mexican Americans. However, because the establishments visited by consumers tend to be concentrated at or near the tourist districts, little substantial acculturation to Mexican mainstream values and institutions actually takes place. Nevertheless, consumer-motivated border crossings remain culturally significant for many Mexican Americans because they are the only real links they have with the land of their forebears. The case that follows illustrates how superficial such a link can be when the consumers are young Chicanos interested only in the "good times" Mexico can offer them.

Joe Maldonado: Mexican American Binational Consumer / Joe Maldonado is a twenty-year-old college student who resides in Chula Vista, California, and who regularly frequents the *discotecas* of Tijuana. He believes the nightlife on the Mexican side is much better than on the U.S. side because "the atmosphere is much more relaxed, there are more women, and I can drink" (California's legal drinking age is 21). Apart from crossing the border to party, Mr. Maldonado sometimes does some shopping and eats in restaurants in the tourist district. On occasion he also has his car serviced and washed. Over the past three years he has visited Tijuana an average of twice a month, usually on Saturday nights.

Mr. Maldonado feels his Mexican background and knowledge of Spanish give him an edge on the Mexican side over gringo tourists and partygoers. "The waiters are nicer to me because I can speak some Spanish to them," he says. "I can also communicate with Mexican women." Mr. Maldonado recognizes that his knowledge of Mexico and Mexican culture is very superficial, since his only exposure to the land of his parents is the border area. He also realizes that Tijuana is different from the rest of Mexico, but at least his weekend forays give him a chance to speak some Spanish and mingle with Mexicans even if it is in an environment heavily influenced by the United States.

Commuters

In comparison to Mexicans who commute to jobs in the United States—whose numbers are sizable—there are relatively few Mexican Americans who hold jobs in Mexico. The explanation is relatively simple: on the Mexican side there is an abundance of labor and wages are relatively low. Thus there is no demand for unskilled Mexican American workers. However, in some sectors of the Mexican border economy, such as business, education, health, and the maquiladoras, the services that can be provided by educated, bilingual/bicultural Mexican Americans are needed and sought after. Perhaps the most prevalent types of Mexican American commuters are managers, supervisors, and engineers who work for maquiladoras. In the case study below, however, I have chosen a more unusual type of commuter, a teacher who held on to her job in Mexico for many years. Because of the considerable time they spend in Mexico, Mexican American commuters are strong transnational borderlanders. They must function in the Mexican environment, speak Spanish much of the time, and interact socially with Mexicans. Thus the commuting experience considerably strengthens their biculturalism and their understanding of Mexican society.

Gloria Sandoval Caples: Commuter   /   Ms. Sandoval Caples is a forty-two-year-old former elementary school teacher in Mexico who lives on the U.S. side with her Anglo husband and four children. Since she moved to the United States in the late 1960s, she has been in a state of cultural transition, but her ties with Mexico have remained very strong. She continues to think of herself as both

Mexican and Mexican American but sees her children as definitely Mexican Americans.

Ms. Sandoval Caples's parents migrated to the Mexican border city where she grew up when she was six years old. Two years later her father passed away, leaving her mother and the four children in some financial difficulty. She eventually became a teacher and taught school for more than twenty years. She met her Anglo husband under casual circumstances on a shopping trip to the U.S. side. Following several friendly conversations, one day he walked back to Mexico with her and her mother to help with some home repairs. At the time he worked in construction. After that Ms. Sandoval Caples and her new friend saw each other frequently, enjoying each other's company even though she spoke almost no English and he spoke almost no Spanish. They married in 1967 and established their home in the United States. She immediately became a legal, permanent U.S. resident.

Despite the problems crossing the border on a daily basis and earning a salary paid in constantly devalued pesos, she kept her teaching job on the Mexican side, commuting from one country to the other during the ensuing two decades. As she began to have children, the trips across the border became more problematic, but being able to drop them off at her mother's house (on the Mexican side) for day care helped considerably. When the children were of school age, Ms. Sandoval Caples simply enrolled them in the school where she taught, figuring that she could be physically close to them. Further, attending a Mexican school would allow the children to learn Spanish well and to establish a strong Mexican identity. Her husband supported her in that decision. In order to avoid legal or bureaucratic problems with Mexican officials, who would surely object to a teacher living in the United States and working in Mexico and having her U.S.-born children in the same school, she never notified the authorities of her change in address. As far as they were concerned, she continued to reside on the Mexican side and her children were Mexican-born. Only the principal at the school and a few teachers who were close friends knew that she resided in the United States and that her children were U.S. citizens.

Like many other Mexicans who had moved across the border, Ms. Sandoval Caples considered life much easier in the United States. She was glad to have the conveniences that are often difficult to find in Mexico. She had been especially bothered by shortages of basic commodities in the stores and frequent interruptions in utility services. Erratic water service had been especially troublesome. In the United States, utility services were very dependable and shopping was easy and convenient, and that made a big difference to her as a working mother. Ms. Sandoval Caples left her teaching job in 1987 when the value of the Mexican currency plunged so low that her earnings became minuscule, given that she had to convert the pesos into dollars for spending on the U.S. side. She felt great sympathy for her fellow teachers who could not quit as easily as she could, especially those with families who were forced to take second and third jobs to survive. Many teachers wound up working evening and night shifts in *maquiladoras*.

Ms. Sandoval Caples is generally happy with her life in the United States. She loves Mexico for its beauty and great culture, but she is saddened by the many problems the Mexican people have to confront. She sees no genuine democracy in the political system. For Mexicans, she says, "democracy is only a dream." At the same time, she is concerned about certain deficiencies in U.S. society. She does not like some U.S. values and customs, especially as they pertain to family life. "Families are badly neglected," she says. "Parents are too liberal. There is too much divorce. There is little unity among parents and children. Children need more attention." With respect to Mexican Americans, Ms. Sandoval Caples believes they need to develop more pride in their cultural heritage and their native language. They also need to overcome feelings of inferiority and social problems within the group. They need to "incorporate" themselves better into the national system, avoiding behavior that keeps them on the fringes of U.S. society.

Biculturalists

The typical Mexican American who lives in the border environment is by definition a bicultural person, given that she or he has a firm grounding in Mexican culture and, through long-term residence in the United States, has become substantially Americanized. The Mexican American biculturalist maintains that biculturalism through constant interaction with others of similar background and through frequent trips to Mexico as a shopper, tourist, or family visitor. At one end of the biculturalist spectrum is the economically disadvantaged person who knows both Spanish and English but because of limited education lacks mastery over either one and because of his or her marginal status does not have the ability to interact effectively with either affluent Mexicans or Anglos. In many instances the disadvantaged biculturalist lives in a world of isolation, material deprivation, and cultural alienation. The opposite is true for the versatile biculturalist at the other end of the spectrum, typically a middle-class person with sufficient formal education and knowledge of U.S. and Mexican culture to function comfortably in both, enriching his or her own Mexican American lifestyle by picking and choosing from what the Mexican and Anglo worlds have to offer. Some parents, for example, enroll their children in private schools on the Mexican side to assure they will learn Spanish well and become familiarized with Mexican culture at an early age.

Most Mexican American biculturalists take their biculturalism for granted, accepting it as a normal feature of life in the region. There is a feeling that border society has always functioned this way and there is no reason to believe that things will change. There are some, however, who feel that the group cannot afford to take the extant climate for granted. They see real danger in the activities of U.S. groups that seek to safeguard the "purity" of American culture and the English language. The response of many Mexican American biculturalists to English Only movements and attacks on bilingual education is to promote multicultural awareness and understanding while strengthening the biculturalism of the Mexican American community by disseminating knowledge about Mexican history and culture.

I include in the biculturalist category militant Chicanos who may speak out against assimilation into the U.S. mainstream and who may also promote the idea of the creation of a Chicano "nation." This type of rhetoric was common among the youth in the borderlands during the Chicano Movement of the 1960s, especially in California. Since then such talk has almost disappeared, and few Chicanos actively pursue separatist agendas. In reality, the great majority of those who have advocated separatism have used the issue primarily to attract media and government attention to community problems. Ironically, some Chicano leaders (especially in the interior borderlands) have been highly assimilated individuals who have often had limited command of the Spanish language and have not practiced Mexican culture in a substantial way. Their rage originates in large measure from their feeling cut off from their own heritage because of pervasive anti-Mexicanism in Anglo society, especially within educational institutions. In short, the only difference between typical Mexican American biculturalists and Chicano militants is that the former follow a rather low-key approach to group issues, while the latter aggressively advocate on behalf of their community and include preservation of the native culture as one of their main objectives. The case below fits somewhere in the middle of the ideological activist spectrum.

Ana María Osante Zubia: Biculturalist / Ana María Osante Zubia is a U.S.-born Mexican American secretary in her fifties who has lived in the U.S. border area most of her life. Her parents were immigrants who instilled pride in her Mexican heritage and made sure she learned Spanish well. Ms. Osante Zubia exemplifies the Mexican American biculturalist who is able to function very effectively in her own group as well as among Mexicans and Anglos. She reports that she speaks English half the time and Spanish the other half, and that about three-fourths of her friends and acquaintances are Mexican Americans and the rest about equally divided between Mexicans and Anglos. She enjoys both Mexican and U.S. pop culture from television to music and dancing.

As a young woman, Ms. Osante Zubia married a wealthy Spanish engineer who lived in the United States. Shortly thereafter he took her to Mexico City, where they lived for five years. After they returned to the United States, they got a divorce. The marriage produced two daughters. Following her divorce, Ms. Osante Zubia began working as a secretary in a university but later worked in the private sector and in a civil-service position. Eventually she returned to the university, where she remains employed.

A politically and community minded citizen, Ms. Osante Zubia was active in one of the councils of the League of United Latin American Citizens (LULAC) for ten years. She served in several positions, including Secretary and Council President. She has also been active in a Spanish-speaking chapter of Toastmaster's International, rising to be president of the group. Her other community activities include membership in a state commission for women and in Hispanic women's organizations.

Ms. Osante Zubia is very fond of Mexico because of the positive attitudes passed on by her parents and because of her direct experience of living in that country. Her father used to tell her, "Don't forget who you are." As a child she used to spend summers with relatives in a Mexican city a few hundred miles from the border. Her years in Mexico City during her marriage also left positive impressions about the people and the culture. She believes Mexicans are generally happier than Americans, that they express more love within the family, and that they are more generous. But Ms. Osante Zubia is highly critical of Mexico's political system and social structure. She believes that the government does terrible things and that many in the upper classes live hypocritical lives. When she lived among the affluent in Mexico City, she noticed a hypocritical attitude among many women. They criticized the *pocho* (culturally corrupted) lifestyle of Mexican Americans but in many ways lived like that themselves. For example, they preferred U.S. products and took vacations abroad. Many of them also drank excessively and had lovers.

Ms. Osante Zubia likes her life in the United States and believes that Anglos are not terribly different from Mexican Americans. Most are good people. She sees U.S. culture as a mixture of many cultures, a melting pot that nevertheless allows her to enjoy her own culture. She also believes that, with all its faults, the United States has the best political system in the world, and she feels very patriotic toward her country. Her political allegiance to the United States is revealed in two incidents in which she was involved. Once when she was at a party in Mexico City, a young Mexican activist arrived from an anti-U.S. demonstration with a torn-up U.S. flag. The guests seemed to relish the young man's anti-U.S. rhetoric and demonstrated disdain for the U.S. flag. She was offended by their behavior and asked how *they* would feel if they found themselves in the United

States and someone walked into a party with a torn Mexican flag. She then left the party. On another occasion in the United States she saw some Chicano demonstrators carrying the Mexican flag. She told them they were wrong to do that, that they should carry the U.S. flag instead because they were Americans.

Despite her strong identification with and support of the United States, Ms. Osante Zubia does not feel fully integrated into U.S. society. She sees herself as a person of Mexican descent who resides in the United States. She has experienced an inner struggle because of her different ethnic background and cultural dualism. At times she has wondered who she really is. Her ambivalence is illustrated by her lack of enthusiasm for some American holidays, such as Thanksgiving. "I cannot relate to a big table with a turkey and all the trimmings, but I can relate to *mole, tamales,* and *champurrado* because that is what we would have on Thanksgiving Day when I was a child. My father did not like turkey, so my mother fixed Mexican dishes. We went to mass on that day. It was just like a Sunday. My parents were not anti-Anglo. That is just the way *they* celebrated Thanksgiving."

She considers her daughters fortunate for having grown up totally in the U.S. milieu without any direct personal connection with Mexico. This has spared them the insecurities and confusion she has often felt, knowing that she is neither a Mexican nor a "mainstream" American. She sees her daughters living a life just like other young people in the United States. They speak English fluently and practice the dominant culture, including listening to Anglo music almost all the time. One daughter is engaged to a young Anglo man, and Ms. Osante Zubia has gotten to know her future in-laws and likes their lifestyle. She has even celebrated a traditional Anglo Thanksgiving with them.

Binationalists

Mexican American binationalists have deep cross-border roots and strong, intense, and constant interaction with people from both countries. These individuals are usually of a middle class or higher background and have business interests, investments, or property in both countries, and their families straddle the border. In many cases, the extended family includes Anglos who have intermarried with family members. Mexican American binationalists live on the U.S. side, but they spend so much time on the Mexican side—including frequent overnight stays in connection with business or personal matters—that Mexico provides a secondary residence and/or place of business or employment.

By definition, Mexican American binationalists are also biculturalists, and in many cases business or professional commuters as well. As consumers of goods and services from both nations, they are also binational consumers. In short, Mexican American binationalists, more than members of other categories, personify in the widest range possible the process of transnational interaction and transculturation. They are truly major bridges of cultural bonding and of understanding and cooperation across the border.

Lillian González: Binationalist   /   Ms. González is a thirty-six-year-old professional who has held a variety of jobs on both sides of the border related to language training, social work, and health care. Currently she works for an international health organization as a coordinator and trainer in preventive care pertaining to venereal diseases, including AIDS. She spends most of her working time on the Mexican side while maintaining a residence on the U.S. side. At the personal level, she splits her time between one side of the border and the other, since some family members and friends live and work in the United States and others in Mexico.

Ms. González's process of becoming a binationalist began when her grandmother, who was then living in a Mexican border area city, chose to give birth to Lillian's mother in a U.S. border city where medical services were better than those available on the Mexican side, though the family continued to live in Mexico. Years later, Lillian's mother followed her mother's example and had her children in the United States as well, so Lillian became an instant U.S. citizen at her birth. The family remained on Mexican soil, however, and Lillian attended elementary and secondary schools in Mexico. She attended high school in the United States during her senior year, which she remembers as a traumatic experience because the social adjustment proved very difficult for her. Though her knowledge of English was limited, she did well academically because of the good foundation provided by the Mexican private schools she had attended. What proved challenging was getting used to the "barbarian" American students, the football players who almost knocked her down once, the drug users, and the biased individuals who had terribly distorted perceptions of Mexico. Upon graduation, Lillian attended a U.S. border area university but then transferred to the University of the Americas in Puebla, Mexico, and later to William Smith College in New York, where she received her B.A. She also did graduate work in other Mexican and U.S. universities, finally receiving an M.A. in public health from the University of North Carolina.

Her parents moved to the U.S. side in 1981 at a time of great inflation in Mexico when the cost of housing seemed lower north of the border. They lived in a big house in Mexico and wanted a smaller one but could find nothing suitable on the Mexican side. Since her mother was a U.S. citizen, the move did not present any problems for her. Her father, however, had to become a legal U.S. resident, though for some time he lived on the U.S. side without the documentation required by U.S. authorities. In effect, for her parents the move from one country to another meant little more than moving from one neighborhood to another. They still own the big house in Mexico and constantly go back and forth across the boundary.

Unlike her parents, who remain culturally Mexican despite their U.S. residence, Ms. González is thoroughly bicultural and bilingual and functions with equal effectiveness on both sides of the border. She has been able to obtain grants from the U.S. federal government to conduct health-related projects on the U.S. side and to work for Mexican organizations, carrying on her duties on the Mexican side. Her versatility in being able to function professionally in both environments is remarkable.

In response to questions about her feelings toward the two societies of which she is a part, Ms. González expresses gratification as well as ambivalence. "Mexico," she says, "evokes emotions in me similar to what I feel about my mother. All the nurturing that I have received as a human being has come from Mexico. Thus I feel many things and have many memories, but not all are pleasant. It pains me that Mexico lacks democracy, that a group of people controls the country." Ms. González expresses admiration for the United States because of its democratic system and the freedoms enjoyed by its people. "I feel very comfortable with Anglo culture. I know Mexicans who are antagonistic that way, but they tend to be oversensitive. However, I dislike American values like consumerism, materialism, and preoccupation with social status." She also deplores American interventionism abroad, especially in Latin America, and the discriminatory treatment of ethnic minorities such as African Americans, Mexican Americans, and Indians.

She considers herself a Mexican American, but some of the implications of being identified that way bother her. Her strong cultural identification with Mexico makes it imperative that she not be put in a situation where her personal identity becomes diluted in the great U.S. melting pot. "Sometimes I feel at the margin of Mexican American society," she says. "I find it especially hard to identify with assimilated Mexican Americans. I can't stand someone who rejects Mexican culture. That upsets me because I feel personally rejected, because I am at heart Mexican."

Her binational orientation is most clearly seen in her conscious decision not to become a voter in either Mexico or the United States. Despite her U.S. birth, should she wish to vote in Mexico she could do so because she retains "functional" dual citizenship, arranged long ago by her parents for the purpose of bestowing upon her the widest possible latitude during her life. "I have Mexican papers," she says. "When I was eighteen I thought of turning in my U.S. papers and declaring myself solely as a Mexican citizen, but my parents didn't let me. They thought I was too young to decide." Now she does not feel like a citizen of either country, and she has placed her own limit on her political rights. She feels entitled to engage in political activity in both countries, such as attending demonstrations in Mexico and participating in political campaigns in the United States, both of which she has done. But she considers actually casting a ballot too decisive a step to take. "Voting in one country," she says, "will invalidate belonging to the other, and I want to be a part of both. I am a part of both." As time passes, however, she feels more and more attracted to U.S. politics, especially as they affect the interests of Mexican Americans and other minority groups. If she does become a voter in the future, she thinks it will be in the United States, both because of her concern with the conditions among U.S. minorities and because "a vote in the United States counts more than a vote in Mexico."

Conclusion

Mexican American borderlanders are an important segment of the larger Hispanic population that has spread throughout the United States and whose assimilation into the mainstream society is following patterns reminiscent of other ethnic groups. Such trends are clearly evident along the border, but the proximity to Mexico inevitably has slowed the rate of integration for many people, in particular those in the ranks of the disadvantaged.

The most salient characteristic of Mexican American borderlanders is the intensity of their transnationalism, which is not surprising, because powerful historical forces have shaped a profound and enduring relationship with the Mexican side. Of the three major groups discussed in this work, Mexican Americans most closely resemble a transborder population, people whose living space transcends an international boundary. In many ways they are an in-between population, caught between competing ways of life and contrasting worldviews. But long ago they came to terms with their minority status in the United States and their ambivalent relationship with Mexico. Their adjustment to a dual way of life has been eased by direct and substantial participation in the shaping of the transboundary system in which they function, and on the whole they have managed to cope well enough with the challenges posed by cultural marginality.

In seeking a way to summarize in human terms what it means to be a Mexican American from the border, I decided to venture into the realm of poetry, notwithstanding my lack of experience with this medium.

CHICANO BORDERLANDER

A Chicano borderlander,
I am.
Part Mexican, part American.

Two currents feed my soul:
one southern, mestizo, Third World,
one northern, Anglo-Saxon, First World.

Straddling two nations, two cultures,
belonging to both, belonging to neither.
One moment totally sure of who I am,
the next baffled by my duality.

Bilingual, bicultural, binational,
embracing two social systems,
assuming multiple identities,
criss-crossing ethnic boundaries,
negotiating and taming opposing worlds.

Spare me the hellish choice
of taking sides
between the United States and Mexico.
One is my home, the other my nurturer.

On the border,
conflict of the heart or of the nation
has but one cure:
recognition of jointness
and jointness in resolution.

5

ANGLO AMERICANS

As with Mexican American borderlanders, the bulk of the contemporary Anglo population in the region derives from post-1940 migratory movements. Deeply rooted in the binational economy and culture of the borderlands, the "old-time" Anglos seem to have a greater disposition to view links across cultures and across the border in a positive way than is the case with the more recent arrivals. With shallow knowledge of border history and limited experience with culturally distinct groups, Anglo newcomers appear to be more uncomfortable than are old-timers with the proximity to a Third World country and with having Mexicans and Mexican Americans living in their midst.[1]

As with Mexicans and Mexican Americans, Anglo borderlanders manifest considerable internal diversity, ranging from those individuals who are affected very little by border conditions to those who are heavily immersed in biculturalism and binationalism. Yet compared to the other two groups, only a relatively small proportion of the Anglo community can be characterized as transnational. For the most part, the orientation among Anglo borderlanders is inward rather than outward, and only small numbers identify the Mexican side as part of their life space or see Mexicans or U.S. Hispanics as groups with whom to carry on substantial relationships. In short, Anglos are overwhelmingly national border-landers, as Figure 5.1 illustrates. Specific national types include nationalists, uniculturalists, newcomers, and winter residents. Transnational types include commuters, biculturalists, binationalists, and binational consumers, who spill over into the national sector as well. An additional transnational subgroup consists of Anglo residents in the Mexican border area, who are functionally an extension of the Anglo population from the U.S. side rather than an integral part of the Mexican border population.

Figure 5.2 provides an approximation of the relative size of each subgroup in the overall Anglo borderlander population and places the subgroups in the appro-

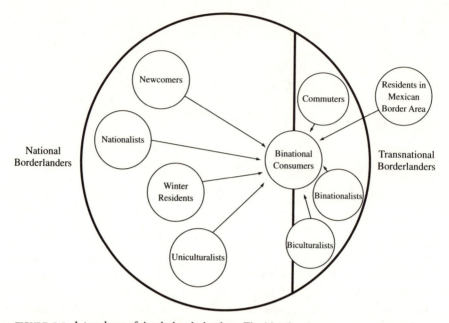

FIGURE 5.1 A typology of Anglo borderlanders. The binational consumers category is composed of individuals from all subgroups.

priate position on the borderlands milieu core–periphery continuum. The largest categories are newcomers and uniculturalists, both of which are located in the periphery section, and the smallest are the three types that make up the core: commuters, biculturalists, and binationalists. Figures 5.3 reveals the variation among the different Anglo types in the context of U.S. and Mexican influences affecting cultural and lifestyle orientations.

The degree of transnational interaction among Anglos correlates closely with the degree of ethnic interaction in the United States. That is, the greater the contact with the Mexican side, the greater the prospect that Anglo transnationals will carry on substantial ties with Mexican Americans. Hence, the links across the border described in the illustrations in this chapter to a significant extent also reveal patterns of Anglo–Mexican American interaction.

National Borderlanders

Newcomers

Recently arrived Anglos (those who have lived in the borderlands less than five years) who lack knowledge about the region and experience in dealing with Mexico may be thought of as newcomers.[2] Their lifestyles reflect the ways of main-

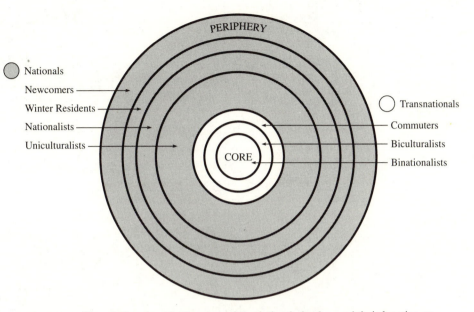

FIGURE 5.2 The relative size of subgroups of Anglo borderlanders and their location on the borderlands milieu core–periphery continuum. Binational consumers are not included here because they constitute a category composed of members from all subgroups, particularly those in the transnational sector.

stream U.S. society. Reactions to the borderlands milieu vary among Anglo newcomers, but apparently most are simply indifferent to it, wishing to continue living a "conventional" American lifestyle. In areas where Anglos are solid majorities or where Anglo enclaves are well insulated, such a goal can easily be accomplished, but where Mexican Americans predominate or are highly visible, it becomes more difficult. Contact with non-Anglos is unavoidable, and the impact of the Mexican side is felt immediately. Such situations often engender culture shock among Anglo newcomers. Being surrounded by foreign-looking people and hearing Spanish spoken everywhere can provoke great discomfort for many. Frequently they feel like strangers in their own country.

Some react negatively to their disconcerting situation, openly expressing disapproval of the prevailing social context. Their perspective is very much in line with that of Anglo nationalists and uniculturalists, who are discussed below. Others with a more pragmatic outlook, however, make a conscious decision to accommodate to the local way of doing things in order to avoid problems. Negative attitudes and opinions remain in the private domain, expressed only within their own group. Consciously or unconsciously, many newcomers minimize interaction with non-Anglos or keep much of the contact with Hispanics at

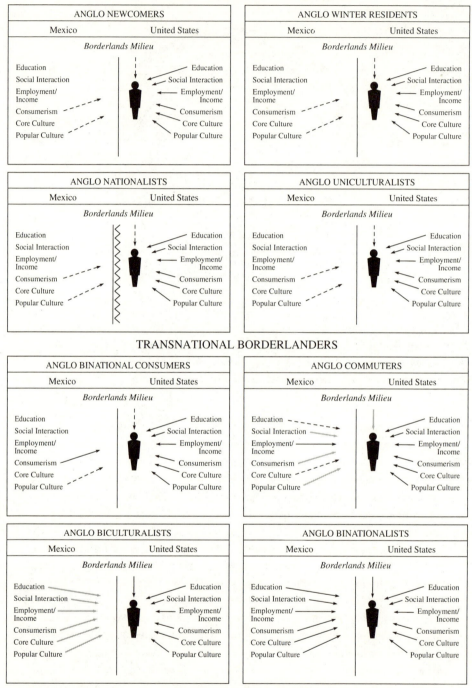

FIGURE 5.3 Major sources of cultural and lifestyle orientation among Anglo borderlanders

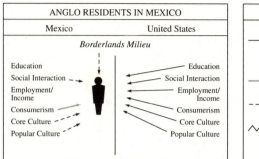
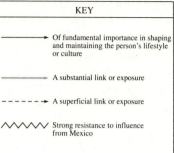

FIGURE 5.3 (*continued*)

superficial levels, thus phasing themselves into a way of life characteristic of uniculturalists.

The ranks of newcomers also include, of course, adventurous and culturally curious people who welcome opportunities to interact with a foreign nation and with people different from themselves. Such newcomers engage in transnational activities, and in time some of them become biculturalists. The case history below illustrates the latter type of individual.

Ann Richeson: Newcomer / A highly educated professional in her forties, Ann Richeson has lived in a major border city for almost two years. She is cognizant of the vast differences between the border and the interior United States and is consciously trying to understand better the cultural systems of both sides, yet she admits that her residence in the area has been brief and that she has a long way to go before she becomes well informed about how things function locally. Ms. Richeson differs from the typical Anglo newcomer in that she finds Mexico intriguing and is willing to invest time to learn more about her neighbors. She has visited the Mexican side as a tourist on numerous occasions and has had direct contact with both Mexicans and Mexican Americans. Her interest in social dynamics has prompted her to draw comparisons between these two groups and to form impressions of border Chicanos as compared to Chicanos from the interior of the United States, with whom she had some contact before moving to the border.

Ms. Richeson's spirit of adventure is illustrated by her boldness in going to places on both sides of the border that most Anglos consider unsafe. She believes that Anglos in general are very fearful of venturing onto the Mexican side, where they believe crime is rampant. "I think they're chicken," she says. "I'm not afraid. I use caution." What has bothered her a great deal is the poverty that she has seen on both sides but especially in Mexico. She finds it difficult to believe that so many people lack essentials like drinking water. When she first inter-

viewed for the job she now holds, those who hired her talked about such problems, and they became a concern for her. She admits to some culture shock
arising from the dismal social conditions and also from the ubiquitous presence
of Mexicans and Mexican Americans. The first time she went downtown (on the
U.S. side) she felt like she was in another country because there were almost no
Anglos walking around or shopping. She felt self-conscious because she was a
güera (blondie). Nonetheless, she adjusted quickly to the situation and found
much to appreciate in the central square and other key landmarks in her new city.

If Ms. Richeson's stay at the border turns out to be lengthy and if she maintains her current high level of curiosity and interest in the borderlands milieu,
she may eventually learn Spanish and even become a biculturalist. For now, she
remains essentially a newcomer uniculturalist, but her conviction that "You only
have one life to live, and if you live it in the closet, it's not much fun" sets her
apart from the vast majority of Anglo newcomers, who do in fact tend to live in
a closet.

Winter Residents

Anglos from the interior of the United States who spend the winter in the relatively mild climate of the borderlands are referred to as winter residents, winter
visitors, or just snowbirds. Most are permanent residents of Midwestern states.
In addition, many Canadians also make the seasonal trek to the borderlands. Two
favorite destinations for the winter visitors are the Lower Rio Grande Valley and
the Arizona border, in particular the Yuma area. They are predominantly retirees
who like the border area because of the abundant sunshine and the relatively low
cost of living.

Winter residents are largely uniculturalists who have very little interest in
Mexico, Mexican culture, or U.S. Hispanics. They tend to live in self-contained
enclaves that provide a "home away from home." They associate and socialize
primarily with people like themselves. Their major objective at the border is to
pass the winter as warm and problem-free as possible and to relax and enjoy
themselves. It is largely in the context of their search for recreational activities
that they sometimes venture onto the Mexican side as tourists and shoppers. In
the process they are exposed, even if superficially, to the way of life in the neighboring country.

Archie and Arlene Sanders: Winter Residents / Archie and Arlene Sanders
are a retired couple from Michigan who have spent twenty-one winters in a Texas
border city in the Lower Rio Grande Valley. When Mr. Sanders quit his job in
the late 1960s, a friend told him about the good weather and nice people in the
valley, so he and his wife decided to visit the area. They both liked what they

saw, and thus in 1969 they began to reside part of the year in Michigan and part in Texas, with periodic trips abroad to Europe and Asia. Mr. and Mrs. Sanders had considered wintering in Florida but decided against it because they did not feel comfortable there. They had visited Florida with friends, but there seemed to be too much "boozing and partying" there. The Sanders preferred a quieter and more peaceful environment. South Texas offered what they were looking for.

Their first visit lasted three months, and subsequently they stayed longer and longer, eventually spending six months of the year in Texas. With disposable income and experience in the real estate business (Mrs. Sanders had been a real estate agent in Michigan), they bought homes at the border, lived in them for a time, and then sold them for a profit. Over the twenty-one years of visiting the valley they have bought and sold twelve homes and apartment buildings. They no longer "wheel and deal" in real estate but do own a trailer home, a spacious and comfortable structure in a very nice trailer park. They also own property in Michigan.

During the early years in the valley, the Sanders crossed the border frequently to shop and to attend parties given by Mexican merchants seeking to attract the snowbird trade. Often they would eat in Mexican restaurants. Recently they have stopped doing that because their stomachs have become "weaker." The Sanders say they have never felt uncomfortable in the border environment, but they know many Anglos who do not like Hispanics, referring to them as "those damn Mexicans." Mr. Sanders reports that these unfriendly Anglos treat Mexicans as inferiors and especially resent the fact that Hispanics are in positions of authority. "We have to remind the Anglos," says Mr. Sanders, "that this is not their country, that the Hispanics are the natives and the winter Texans are the outsiders." Mr. Sanders believes that the key to getting along well with Mexicans is to treat them as equals.

Mr. Sanders emphasizes that the Anglos he knows who harbor anti-Mexican sentiments seldom go beyond the point of making disparaging comments. They hurl insults and register complaints, but things stop there: "It is mostly talk." Mr. Sanders acknowledges some friction with local people because of the added traffic and increase in demand for local services that the winter visitors bring. Competition for space and resources thus combines with ethnic differences to create tensions in the valley from time to time. Despite the long period that the Sanders have spent at the border and their benevolent attitudes toward Mexicans and Mexican Americans, they reflect little acculturation to the local way of life. As with most other winter visitors, the Sanders have spent their time largely in retirement communities, physically in close proximity to Hispanics but separated from them by high social and cultural walls.

Nationalists

Anglos who forcefully assert the interests of the United States and who see Mexicans as posing a threat to those interests may be called nationalists. Such persons have xenophobic tendencies and constantly criticize Mexico for its backwardness and for exporting its problems to the United States. They are alarmed at the growing "Mexicanization" along the U.S. border, resent immigration, oppose bilingual education, and, depending on the level of personal antipathy toward racially or ethnically different people, may even avoid interaction with Mexicans and Mexican Americans other than on a casual basis.

Nationalists see the presence of large numbers of Hispanics in the U.S. borderlands as an economic, cultural, and political liability for the country. Driven by a strong desire to halt the further "dilution" of the dominant Anglo culture, nationalists strongly support such causes as the English Only movement, which seeks to legislate English as the official language of the United States. Dislike for "foreign" influences causes nationalists to live in a rather confined Anglo environment, surrounded by but in relative isolation from U.S. Hispanics and Mexican nationals. Nevertheless, nationalists may still experience some superficial transculturation from occasional trips across the border or from chance or unavoidable encounters with Mexican Americans. Some nationalists actually have an elementary familiarity with select aspects of the popular cultures of Mexicans and Chicanos. The degree of nationalism varies among individuals, depending on personal circumstances and political philosophy.[3] In the case history presented below, the subject expresses very strong nationalistic tendencies through her public activities, although she is quick to deny anti-Mexican sentiments.

Muriel Watson: Nationalist   /   A twenty-year veteran of the anti-Mexican-immigration movement in the United States, Muriel Watson is the widow of a Border Patrol pilot and the leader of the recent Light Up the Border campaign in San Diego. "Light Up," as Mrs. Watson refers to her cause, allows people alarmed by the migration of undocumented people from Mexico to make their sentiments known in dramatic demonstrations at the border. Several nighttime rallies in 1989 and 1990 attracted hundreds of demonstrators who shined their cars' headlights in the direction of Mexico toward areas where undocumented migrants tended to congregate. This gesture was intended to call attention to the illegal migration problem and symbolically to support the efforts of the Border Patrol.

Mrs. Watson explains that she began Light Up in 1989 because she saw the illegal alien problem getting worse. She was especially bothered by the constant violence at the border, and she was frustrated by the "failure" of the Immigration Reform and Control Act of 1986. In her view, the greatest shortcoming of that law is the lack of adequate funding for the Border Patrol. With her knowledge of the problem and experience as a longtime activist, she felt she could not sit idly by, so she proposed the idea of high-profile border demonstrations to other concerned citizens. Light Up evolved from there.

Mrs. Watson has been strongly criticized by Mexicans and Chicanos for stirring the emotions of nativist-oriented Americans and for creating a potentially explosive climate at the border. She has been accused of being a reactionary and a racist. She denies she is either, explaining that her only desire is to bring an end to the "mess" at the border. She says she is not anti-Mexican or anti-immigrant, only anti-illegal-immigration. Mrs. Watson is proud of the attention and results her movement have generated. She claims credit for the installation by the Border Patrol of fourteen permanent sets of stadium lights that illuminate the San Diego side of the border. She feels her movement also pressured the U.S. Army Corps of Engineers to remove brush from large fields adjacent to the border and to level hills that once offered hiding places for illegal aliens.

Uniculturalists

Anglo uniculturalists reflect the lifestyle of mainstream U.S. society, embracing little or nothing from the Mexican or Chicano cultures. Such persons make up the bulk of the Anglo population along the border. They are generally uninterested in what transpires in Mexico or in the U.S. Hispanic community and have little or no desire to learn about or participate in a culture other than their own. Exerting no effort to take part in binational or bicultural activities, uniculturalists avoid becoming acculturated to the Mexican way of life, although they may acquire some knowledge of Mexicans through sporadic casual contacts in shopping centers, restaurants, workplaces, or by interacting with domestics.

With amenities and conveniences that typify U.S. lifestyles readily available in most parts of the border area, uniculturalists are generally able to live much the same as Anglos in the interior of the country. Of course, the conditions that foster cultural insularity (numerical superiority, economic and political dominance, and social segregation) are present to varying degrees in the border communities. In major urban centers such as El Paso and San Diego, large proportions of the Anglo population are able to carry on their lives relatively unaffected by border-related phenomena. Such an existence becomes more difficult, however, in places like Brownsville and Laredo, where Mexican Americans constitute more than 80 percent of the total population and where cross-border interaction permeates local society.

The behavior of uniculturalists is conditioned primarily by indifference toward the "foreign" qualities of the borderlands, and in that respect it generally reflects the apathy of most Americans to other nations and cultures. But lack of interest in learning about another culture does not necessarily mean total uncon-cern regarding foreign influences. When uniculturalists come to share the per-ception of nationalists that the integrity of U.S. culture is threatened by having too many Mexicans in their midst or too much Hispanic influence on their insti-tutions, or by the belief that foreigners are becoming too costly to U.S. taxpay-ers, many among them may be counted on to support preservationist measures advocated by xenophobic groups.

As with all other subgroups, there are many degrees of insularity among An-glo uniculturalists. Extremists in the group come close to being nationalists, but at the other end of the spectrum are found uniculturalists who claim affection for Mexicans and their culture but who, for one reason or another, are not personally touched by them. The case history below falls somewhere in between these two extremes.

Gladys Anderson: Uniculturalist / A native of a small town in the U.S. in-terior, eighty-one-year-old Mrs. Anderson has resided since 1935 in a major border city with a predominantly Mexican American population. Despite more than half a century of living next to Mexico and being exposed to Mexican culture, Mrs. Anderson remains largely unaware of the way of life of her neigh-bors. She says she has managed to learn only four words in Spanish, "because that language is too hard, and those people speak too fast."

Mrs. Anderson and her husband moved to the border during the Depression when he was transferred by his company to manage a local department store. Shortly thereafter, Mr. Anderson was killed in an automobile accident, leaving Mrs. Anderson with the responsibility of raising two young children. Struggling to support them, she returned to school and received an Associate of Arts degree at a community college. She then got a job as a public relations specialist with the local chamber of commerce, where she has worked ever since. Today she has a part-time job giving information to tourists and visitors.

When she was younger, Mrs. Anderson visited the interior of Mexico and describes it as beautiful. Mexico City, however, was "too big, too crowded, and too noisy." In years past she also visited the neighboring Mexican border city, mainly to shop. But she cut down on such trips because the downtown market "was not too clean" and "there were too many bars." Her infrequent visits to Mexico and her casual contacts with Mexicans and Mexican Americans consti-tute the extent of Mrs. Anderson's involvement with people ethnically different from herself. One type of contact that has upset her is illegal aliens "who are on welfare and use food stamps." She says she has seen "those people" buying steaks and other expensive foods at the supermarket, while she can only afford hamburger. "I resent it," she says. Nevertheless, she is not hostile toward illegal aliens as a group, because she understands that they cross the border out of necessity. "I don't blame them," she says.

Transnational Borderlanders

Binational Consumers

Anglo binational consumers typically go on shopping expeditions, "nights on the town," weekend trips, and vacations in Mexico. They are the counterparts of Mexican and Mexican American binational consumers. Anglos who like to shop in Mexico are attracted by such products as foodstuffs, crafts, artwork, furniture, and clothes, especially "traditional" embroidered dresses and *guaya-beras* (loose-fitting, dressy, summer shirts). Those who have adopted a Mexican motif for their homes are especially fond of wall hangings, pottery, and miscellaneous objects that reflect "typical" Mexican culture. Many Anglos regularly have lunch or dinner in favorite Mexican restaurants. Some enjoy meeting in Mexican bars for "happy hour," while others spend Friday or Saturday nights in popular nightclubs and discotheques, not to mention brothels.

For those with an inclination to venture beyond the border zone, weekends or extended vacations in Mexico are popular. For example, large numbers of Anglos from southern California like to frequent such spots as Rosarito Beach and Ensenada. Arizona borderlanders find Rocky Point (Puerto Peñasco, Sonora) an accessible beach resort. Anglos from the Texas border enjoy short visits to places like Chihuahua City and Monterrey. Many of these Anglo visitors actually own homes or condominiums in Mexico, especially in beach communities in Baja California and Sonora. As with most Americans who vacation in the interior of Mexico, many Anglo borderlanders often head to major beach resorts such as Cancún, Acapulco, Puerto Vallarta, and Mazatlán, or popular interior points such as Guanajuato, Mexico City, or Oaxaca. Owning a condominium in one of these places is also popular among affluent Anglos.

Jack Tolbert: Binational Consumer   /   Originally from San Antonio, Jack Tolbert moved to the border in 1972 following his professional training at a major university. The border environment was not new to him; he had visited border towns on several occasions from the time he was a child, so he "knew what to expect." Mr. Tolbert's major links with Mexico over the years have been shopping and recreational expeditions, mostly to the city across the border from where he resides. In the "old days" he would frequently go with friends to lunch and dinner on the Mexican side, but in recent years that practice has diminished because of the chronic delays in crossing the international boundary. Additionally, Mexican restaurant prices are no longer as attractive as they used to be.

Bargains have disappeared as well in many of the shops he frequented regularly.

During the heyday of his shopping sprees in Mexico, Mr. Tolbert bought a wide variety of products, including beef, seafood, bread, vegetables, canned goods, cigarettes, sugar, and liquor. He calculates he derived savings of 40 to 50 percent by purchasing these items on the Mexican side. In addition to food-stuffs, he also bought glassware and pottery, which he used mainly for decorating. He also has had two cars upholstered and painted in Mexico and has had several suits made by Mexican tailors. He reports a high degree of satisfaction with these products and services but stresses that in recent years the comparative advantage of shopping in Mexico has eroded. He continues to patronize Mexican establishments, albeit not as fervently as before.

These short visits to the Mexican frontier as well as a few trips into the Mexican interior have afforded opportunities for Mr. Tolbert to get a sense of Mexico and its people. Thus, in his case some acculturation has taken place, but by his own admission it has been limited. When asked about his ability to speak Spanish, he gave a one-word response—"nonexistent." Actually, he possesses a basic vocabulary in Spanish, acquired not only during his visits to Mexico but also via his Mexican American wife.

Commuters

Anglo commuters are typically managerial or professional people who cross into Mexico on a daily basis to work in maquiladoras. Because their jobs demand it, Anglo commuters must make a rapid adjustment to the special circumstances of the border, becoming functionally educated in the business and industrial climate of Mexico, at least minimally fluent in Spanish, and sufficiently informed about local customs to get along reasonably well with Mexican employees, associates, and functionaries.

Although frequently superficial and often short-lived, their knowledge about the border, accumulated on and off the job, leads to the formation of opinions about Mexico and Mexican border culture, thus making commuters important sources of information and attitude formation for other Americans. Commuters are frequently called upon to explain how things "really" function south of the border. As employees they are subject to corporate transfer policies, so their stints at the border often are of short duration. Just as they are getting used to the unique arrangement of living in one country and working in the other, many must depart for their next assignment. Thus the process of becoming acculturated to the Mexican way of life is interrupted, perhaps forever, as most will not return to the border to live and work under similar circumstances. In effect, corporate commuters resemble officers in the diplomatic corps, who transfer often and have only fleeting experiences with foreign cultures.

Anglo commuters who work for locally owned companies are not subject to transfers, and over prolonged periods such persons may become highly binationalized, serving as significant economic and cultural bridges between the two sides of the border. The case history of Ray Simmons typifies this pattern. Simmons has become thoroughly integrated into the transnational system, but at the same time he remains a "100 percent" American. His case is noteworthy because he is an African American, and although not technically an Anglo, he functions on the Mexican side much the same as an Anglo would.

Ray Simmons: Commuter / Ray Simmons is a retired U.S. Army colonel who since 1971 has been in charge of the promotion and development of maquiladoras for one of the largest industrial concerns in Mexico. Simmons resides on the U.S. side of the border and commutes daily to his job on the Mexican side. In accumulating a vast knowledge of low-wage industrialization, he has also developed considerable expertise in the working of Mexican society, culture, politics, and the world of business.

Simmons was drafted in 1943 into the U.S. Army, and after serving in World War II he returned to his native Ohio to attend Ohio State University. He graduated in 1948, decided on a military career, and spent the next twenty-eight years in uniform, serving as an officer in the artillery, intelligence, nuclear weaponry, inspector general, and instructional sectors of the army. In 1969 he chose the U.S. border area as the place to retire because, he says, "the cost of living was low and the environment was better for blacks." For the next two years he worked for various U.S. firms, but in 1971 he was hired by his current Mexican employer and charged with the task of developing a system for promoting maquiladoras among industrial concerns in the United States that wished to establish "off-shore" operations. He recommended the creation of a foreign-oriented marketing department and quickly became the marketing manager for the company. In the years that followed, he pioneered successful strategies to lure non-Mexican companies to establish factories in his company's industrial parks on the Mexican side of the border. By 1990 the presence of many U.S., European, and Japanese maquiladoras in these industrial parks testified to Simmons's success as a promoter of assembly operations.

As part of his job, Simmons has had to deal with Mexicans from both the public and private sectors. He was shocked at first when many Mexicans, including government officials, resisted the idea of having maquiladoras in their country. Once he even heard a cabinet minister give an antimaquiladora speech. Simmons soon learned that there was much resentment against the United States, that Mexicans were very nationalistic and proud. When he was asked to give a talk before a Mexican civic group on the subject of U.S.–Mexico relations, he considered a number of historical themes but had trouble coming up with a non-controversial topic. Finally he played it safe and talked about the friendship between Abraham Lincoln and Benito Juárez.

He describes his experience with Mexicans as "very pleasant," as something that has enriched his life. He feels he has gotten to know the Mexican psyche, which he finds "absolutely different." It took him some time to adjust to the culture, and he admits making mistakes along the way. "At times it has been frustrating as hell," he says. "But I have really gotten to know my fellowman." Commuting daily from one side of the border to the other has presented some interesting challenges. One moment he is functioning in American culture and the next in Mexican culture. He often feels like Dr. Jekyll and Mr. Hyde, constantly having to change his identity. One major difference in the cultures that has made a strong impression on him is the great respect and formality with which Mexicans deal with each other. He has also been struck by the domination of males over females and the deferential behavior of the poor toward the affluent and of employees toward their superiors. He is so used to that system now that when he is in the United States he has to remind himself that he needs to act differently. His wife has told him to "leave that Mexican stuff in Mexico" before he steps into their home.

Simmons feels that living and working in a binational environment has forced him to become more aware of things around him and to be more sensitive to and appreciative of differences among people. He sees multicultural tolerance and understanding as absolutely essential for carrying on personal relationships and doing business in another country. He agrees strongly that there is a "border perspective," that border people do think of themselves as different from their compatriots in the heartland. He has heard many complaints about neglect of the border on the part of federal officials in both countries. He relates that on one occasion someone in a business meeting suggested that the border area should declare itself an independent republic, that there would be "no problem at all with either government because it would take Washington, D.C., and Mexico City ten years to find out what was going on."

Biculturalists

In contrast to uniculturalists and nationalists, Anglo biculturalists have a broad vision of the world and a keen appreciation of cultural differences. Consequently they see the internationalism of the borderlands in a positive way. They tend to believe that the United States derives significant benefits from its close proximity to Mexico, and they approve of bilingualism and biculturalism on the U.S. side. If they are motivated to experience Mexican culture firsthand, Anglo biculturalists strive to learn Spanish well and take advantage of opportunities to mix with Mexicans and visit Mexico. Some parents may even send their children to private schools in Mexico for their elementary education, allowing them to become bilingual and bicultural at an early age. Numerically, Anglo biculturalists lag far behind uniculturalists, but the former play very important roles as agents of good neighborliness between the two countries and among the area's subgroups.

Mexicans and Mexican Americans are appreciative of Anglos who sincerely like Mexican culture and who seek to learn and practice it. Thus Anglo biculturalists are often the subject of affection and admiration. Many occupy a special place in the hearts of Hispanics accustomed to the attitudes and behavior of most Anglos, which largely mirror the uniculturalist and nationalist perspectives. The case history below is representative of Anglo biculturalists whose intense interaction with Mexico springs primarily from occupational and business activities. Yet among many Anglo biculturalists—and it is true of Frank McKnight—the interest in Mexico goes beyond economic motivation. As they learn the culture and interact with Mexicans on a personal level, they develop a genuine fondness for Mexico and a desire to maintain connections with it. Their interest is expressed through such activities as keeping up with Mexican events, becoming actively involved with binational affairs, attending Mexican cultural functions, maintaining friendships across the border, and frequently visiting Mexico.

Frank McKnight: Biculturalist / Frank McKnight is a sixty-five-year-old retired U.S. Army colonel and former bank official who has worked extensively in Mexico and the border area. In the mid and late 1970s he served as defense attaché in the U.S. embassy in Mexico City, becoming very familiar with the country and its people. Before that assignment, McKnight received language training and was given the opportunity to travel extensively throughout Mexico on his own. That preparation greatly facilitated his work with Mexican military officials and people in other sectors of society. When he left the military in 1979, McKnight capitalized on his intimate knowledge of and experience with Mexico by taking a job with a U.S. border area bank in the international department, rising to vice president after eight years. Following his bank experience, McKnight took a position as marketing director for a U.S. firm that had maquiladoras in Mexico. Subsequently he became chief editor of a newsletter on economic conditions and business opportunities along the border and has also acted as a consultant for multinational companies that are considering setting up operations in the border zone.

Years of interacting directly with Mexicans have provided McKnight with a deep understanding of Mexico and the border. He relates that his level of acceptance among Mexican soldiers and officers was higher than that accorded to two other U.S. military attachés who had also served in Mexico City, both of whom happened to be Mexican Americans. According to McKnight, the Mexicans seemed resentful and suspicious of his Mexican American colleagues, but he never encountered any problems. "I was there as a legitimate spy, but it never bothered anybody," says McKnight. Cooperation and goodwill among Mexican business associates have prevailed in his other jobs as well, he adds.

McKnight says he has developed an attachment to Mexico to the extent that he feels he is a part of that country. He has many friends and acquaintances on the Mexican side and crosses the border frequently for personal and business purposes. As a banker, businessman, consultant, and civic leader (he has served on several international committees and commissions), he has spent a considerable amount of time in Mexico. Thus his Spanish language skills remain strong, as does his grasp of conditions south of the border.

Binationalists

Like biculturalists, Anglo binationalists thrive on the internationalism of the borderlands, but the latter are much more directly and intensely immersed in that environment. Anglo binationalists typically come from old border families with business interests in Mexico. Their economic links necessitate constant movement across the border and close interaction with Mexicans. Often Anglo binationalists own a home in Mexico and spend extended periods there. It is not uncommon for binationalists to be directly tied to the elite sector of Mexican society through business partnerships and in some cases even by marriage. Such intimate ties with Mexicans allow binationalists to learn Spanish well and to master Mexican culture. Being bilingual and bicultural permits them to move easily between one country and the other and between both ways of life.

A special type of Anglo binationalist is the individual who does missionary or social work south of the border and who thus becomes thoroughly acculturated to the Mexican way of life and develops strong sympathies toward Mexico. Binationalists may also be found among the ranks of Anglo retirees and others who have established residences in the Mexican borderlands, although many of the retirees tend to live in enclaves that have few substantial ties with Mexican society.

Michael Peter Diamos: Binationalist   /   Michael Peter Diamos is a prominent U.S. border businessman with extensive experience in Mexico, where he has had substantial business interests, property, and social relationships. Recently he and his Mexican-born wife, a former beauty queen, celebrated their fiftieth wedding anniversary. Mr. Diamos, whose father immigrated to the United States from Greece, grew up in a bilingual, bicultural environment in a U.S. border city. His childhood friends were Mexicans and Mexican Americans, and Mr. Diamos remembers being punished at school for speaking Spanish. As a teenager he belonged to a barrio gang, and his friends called him El Alemán (The German) because of his fair skin and blond hair.

His father ran a restaurant and his grandmother had a sheet-metal shop, and as a young man Mr. Diamos worked with them both, picking up valuable business experience. When his grandmother expanded the sheet-metal shop to twenty employees, she asked him to join the business full-time. He learned fast, and by 1942 Mr. Diamos had taken over the business and expanded its operations into New Mexico, Arizona, California, and across the border into Mexico. The sheet-metal shop continued to grow. By the late 1950s Mr. Diamos was doing substantial business in Mexico, building packinghouses and cold-storage plants and installing air conditioning units for commercial firms as well as private residences in several cities in the north. Later Mr. Diamos made parts for Mexican electronics companies, including a firm owned by one of the wealthiest families in Mexico.

As Mr. Diamos and his family spent more time south of the border, he decided to buy a large ranch that happened to be right next to a ranch owned by one of Mexico's former presidents. Mr. Diamos grew wheat, beans, and cotton in addition to using the property for recreation and relaxation. In the mid-1960s, however, he decided to sell it because he could not get permission to dig additional wells (there was a fear that he might drain the ex-president's wells in the adjoining ranch). Subsequently Mr. Diamos gave up other interests in Mexico because of problems with labor unions. Nevertheless, he held on to some concerns and continued many of the relationships he had made over many years of cross-border business dealings.

Mr. Diamos expresses great satisfaction with his experiences in Mexico. He says he has never lost money there and has not had any problems with Mexican officials. He believes the key to his success in business is that he has always been forthright with Mexican businessmen and politicians, treating them with respect and without condescension. His mastery of the Spanish language, deep familiarity with Mexican culture, and Mexican family have also been of enormous help. In short, he has been well accepted by the Mexicans, who appreciate his biculturalism and "up front" business style. He relates stories of other American businessmen he has known who have failed in Mexico because of their ignorance of the country and their greedy tendencies. One problem in particular is their lack of understanding of how the system works in Mexico. "A lot of Americans go down there expecting to make a killing," he says. "They are not on top of what is going on. They expect Mexicans to bow down to them because they are Americans. That attitude dooms them." Over the years Mr. Diamos and his family have interacted socially with many prominent Mexican officials, including mayors, governors, and presidents. In addition, they have formed strong friendships with countless business associates. Attending weddings, receptions, and parties in Mexico has been a routine practice for the Diamos family for a long time.

Currently the family runs three separate companies. Mr. Diamos operates a sheet-metal company, his wife oversees a machine company, and his children run a firm that is heavily involved in international trade and cross-border industrialization. One of the services provided by the latter company is to make available warehouse space for maquiladoras. At the time of the interview, the family was very excited about the prospect of a free-trade agreement between the United States and Mexico. When that comes to pass, their companies will be ideally situated to expand their international operations in a big way.

Residents in the Mexican Border Area

In recent years an increasing number of aging Anglos have chosen to retire in selected areas of the Mexican borderlands, while many younger people have opted to live on the Mexican side and commute to their jobs on the U.S. side. The phenomenon of Anglo communities of expatriates is most pronounced in Baja California, where thousands live along the coast in popular resorts like Rosarito and Ensenada. Young Anglo professionals and other skilled workers who work on the U.S. side are largely concentrated in Tijuana. The lower cost of living in Mexico is the major reason Anglos give for their decision to relocate. They cite astronomical inflation in California real estate prices during the 1970s and 1980s as the most powerful push factor. Older people, especially those on fixed incomes, saw their purchasing power diminish dramatically, and for many of them the solution was to live on the Mexican side.

Casual observation of the lifestyles of these Anglo expatriates suggests that there is relatively little integration into the local society or acculturation to Mexican culture. Retirees tend to live in enclaves, where they strive to replicate as much of the North American way of life as they can. Material security, physical comfort, access to recreation, and a nonhectic daily routine are central concerns for the retirees. Social needs are largely met within the retirement communities themselves, thus obviating the need for mingling in a substantial way with the locals. Retirees maintain regular contact with the U.S. side, going there periodically to renew their legal documents, to shop, to visit relatives and friends, and to reacquaint themselves with the States. Nonretired expatriates cross the border for the same reasons and in many cases also to work. Among younger Anglos who live in Tijuana and other Mexican border cities, the contact with Mexican society is much deeper. Thus biculturalists are not uncommon in this smaller subgroup.

Hank Brewer: Resident in Mexico   /   For the past twenty-one years, Hank and Katie Brewer have lived in an American beach community near Ensenada, Baja California. It is both a housing development and a trailer park. Mr. Brewer is a retired U.S. Marine sergeant who had been stationed all over the world during his active duty. Prior to his retirement he was based at Camp Pendleton, California, and lived in nearby Oceanside. He and his family, including three children, started visiting Baja California on weekends. The more they went into Mexico, the more convinced he became that retirement there would be much better than in the United States. Life would be cheaper and much less hectic. "When I was still in the service," he says, "I couldn't wait for weekends to arrive so we could escape the problems on the U.S. side and head for the tranquility of Baja." Once the Brewers completed their life in the military, they bought a trailer home and rented a space in the Baja community where they now live. Later they sold it and bought a small house. To make their new home more livable and big enough to allow visits from their children, the Brewers added several rooms and made various improvements. Today their two-story home is one of the largest structures in the complex.

Mr. Brewer reports great satisfaction with his decision to live in Baja California. His retirement pay is plenty to support their lifestyle, which is modest by American standards but comfortable by Mexican standards. He supplements their income by assisting the owners of the complex with administrative tasks, especially collecting rent from his fellow Americans. The Brewers try to minimize trips to the United States because of the congestion at the border and the fast-paced life in the San Diego area. Recently they have averaged one trip each month to San Diego, primarily to shop in the commissary at Camp Pendleton, but there have been periods when they have been able to avoid crossing the border for three months at a time when their cupboards and freezers have been well stocked with American provisions.

The Brewers spend much of their time relaxing, enjoying the beach, and socializing with their neighbors. Television watching is a favorite activity; a satellite dish gives them access to more than a hundred channels, and they are easily able to keep up with events in the United States. Their small community does not have a social club, but they belong to the Amigos Club in Ensenada and participate in some of its activities. One of their neighbors is the secretary of the club and keeps them well informed of events. For example, during Easter 1991, the club sponsored a parade, and the Brewers attended it.

Interaction with Mexicans is limited and superficial since the Brewers are surrounded by American neighbors and spend most of their time within the complex. Mr. Brewer says he is somewhat able to read the local newspaper (in Spanish) and understands spoken Spanish, but he is unable to carry on a conversation. His biggest regret is that the Ensenada area has grown so much in recent years that "things are getting much as they are in the United States." There are too many tourists, too much traffic, and goods and services are getting too expensive. Nevertheless, for his wife and him, life is still much better in Mexico than it could be north of the border.

Conclusion

The complexity of the Anglo population in the U.S. borderlands is illustrated by the different kinds of national and transnational borderlanders within this group. Anglos replicate some of the important subgroups found among Mexicans and Mexican Americans, but significant differences are readily apparent. Anglos are strongly national in their orientation, with uniculturalists making up the bulk of the population. Winter residents on the U.S. side and expatriates on the Mexican side are categories unique to Anglos. In contrast to most Mexican Americans, whose cross-border ties spring from their status as a minority group in an area physically adjacent to their traditional homeland, transnational interaction is not inherently a part of the experience of most Anglo borderlanders. Consequently, Anglo binationalists and biculturalists are few in number.

Those Anglos who lack economic or social ties to Mexicans or Mexican Americans must exert considerable effort to function effectively with their neighbors, given that the United States does relatively little to facilitate international experiences or to promote multiculturalism. Despite such obstacles, as well as the anti-Mexican prejudices that exist in U.S. society, a small number of Anglos in communities from Brownsville to San Diego have ventured beyond their group boundaries into other worlds. Transnational interaction among border Anglos will likely increase as the economies of both countries draw closer together. When a free-trade system is formalized, the process will be accelerated because interdependence will deepen, drawing more and more Anglo borderlanders into cross-border webs and networks.

PART III THE BORDER EXPERIENCE

INTRODUCTION

This section focuses on border people who are directly and indirectly involved in transnational interaction and transculturation, two processes at the center of the border experience. The major themes addressed in the three chapters that follow are cross-border migration, interdependence, labor, border management, ethnic confrontation, cultural fusion, and social activism. In contrast to Part II, where case histories of individuals illustrate specific categories within different typologies, here borderlanders from many sectors of society recount—entirely in their own words—events in their lives related to their life on the frontier. The interviewees come from the ranks of immigrants (both legal and undocumented), workers, bureaucrats, Border Patrol agents, customs agents, clergymen, labor leaders, labor organizers, grass-roots activists, businesspeople, professionals, and housewives. My intention is to convey what border living has meant to people who have found themselves in the midst of the borderlands milieu, how their lives have been shaped, what special situations and problems they have confronted, and how they have responded to personal challenges. By hearing directly from borderlanders, readers will be able to understand them better as real people and to appreciate their feelings, viewpoints, frustrations, triumphs, and failures.

Some of the themes pertaining to the borderlands milieu discussed previously in abstract terms come into sharper focus in these interviews. For example, key aspects of transnational interaction are made clearer by information provided by respondents who have lived and worked on both sides of the border over extended periods. The means by which people cross the border without documents and find and maintain jobs in the United States bring to light important aspects of the system of labor exchange. Similarly, dilemmas and predicaments associated with cultural adaptation are revealed in the stories of individuals who have undergone assimilation or have intermarried into a group outside their own.

The value of using oral history interviews to elucidate the past has been demonstrated by historians for generations, but this method gained new popularity in the 1960s, when inexpensive tape recorders made it possible for anyone to gather large amounts of data via the interview process.[1] In the case of the borderlands, some studies have appeared that have used the oral history approach, but their topical and chronological emphases are different from what is presented here.[2] This book is the first attempt to present the collective experience of borderlanders in the recent past.

With a few exceptions, the interviews were tape recorded and transcribed.[3] I extracted relevant information from each manuscript, sometimes taking paragraphs, sentences, or phrases located in different parts of the document and stringing them together to obtain coherence and an orderly sequence. Many of the interviews were in Spanish, and I translated them into English. Generally the respondents' speech is presented verbatim, but wherever necessary I have eliminated hesitations and repetitions, reordered material, and injected transitional words. In editing, I have exercised great care to maintain the meaning and to preserve the style of conversation of the interviewees.

With all its faults, the interview method remains one of the most important means of uncovering information about human behavior. Undeniably, there will be biases in how individuals relate information about their lives, and memory loss among some older people will raise doubts about the accuracy of incidents and events that occurred long ago. But any evidence gathered retrospectively from people and subsequently used as the basis for a written document, report, or story is subject to the same difficulties. With regard to memory loss, the problem is not as serious as is often thought. As Paul Thompson has pointed out, "Memory loss is . . . concentrated during and immediately after the perception of an event. There are numerous old people who retain a remarkably full and accurate memory of their earlier years."[4] In the case of this book, these problems are greatly minimized because what is important here is patterns of life rather than factual details. The individuals whose recollections follow have spoken with candor. They have been eager to share their lives and to make a contribution to knowledge, and I have no reason to doubt the veracity of their accounts. Those who have had limited contact with poor, uneducated Mexicans and Mexican Americans may wonder about the lucidity of the stories. For me, one of the greatest discoveries in doing the fieldwork was learning how articulate people are, whether affluent or underprivileged, highly educated or illiterate, Mexican or Anglo. Indeed, most of the respondents turned out to be masterful storytellers, and I thoroughly enjoyed spending time with them.

I conducted most of the interviews, but some were done by research assistants under my direction. Interviewees were generally identified through referrals provided by key individuals in the community. This included educators, businesspeople, history buffs, and leaders. But often the best leads came from ordinary people in restaurants, bars, and town squares. Between the early 1970s and the early 1990s I made numerous research trips to Brownsville–Matamoros, Laredo–Nuevo Laredo, El Paso–Ciudad Juárez, Nogales–Nogales, and San Diego–Tijuana, identifying appropriate subjects for the study. Because of its strategic location, superb social "laboratory" conditions, and easy accessibility, the El Paso–Ciudad Juárez area proved to be the richest source of interviewees.

All of the selections are edited extracts of interviews. Most transcriptions are quite lengthy, and space considerations have made it impossible to include longer versions of the memoirs. A brief introduction is provided at the beginning of each chapter, and notes preceding each interview give biographical details on interviewees and comment on the significance of their experiences. Each respondent is classified in accordance with the typologies previously presented. These interviews, however, are broad in scope and go beyond illustrating cultural and lifestyle orientation. Some do not address that issue at all. Categorization, then, is not of primary concern in this section.

6

MIGRANTS AND WORKERS

Workers from the interior of Mexico have been migrating to the borderlands in significant numbers for more than a century, but the most pronounced movements date from 1940 to the present.[1] During World War II the United States and Mexico launched the Bracero Program, a labor contract arrangement that supplied Mexican workers to U.S. employers, predominantly in the agricultural sector. Millions worked as braceros until the program ended in 1964 following a protracted campaign by U.S. labor unions to eliminate it. The Bracero Program greatly stimulated cross-border migration and precipitated rapid growth in the border cities. When the program ended, many braceros joined the ranks of the unemployed, increasing job competition in the area.

Throughout these years a parallel movement of undocumented migrants took place as well. Many braceros tired of bureaucratic requirements and opted instead for illegal entry into the United States. Some were encouraged to follow this route by unscrupulous and greedy employers anxious to be free of government regulations. Millions of Mexicans skipped the bracero experience altogether, crossing the border year after year without official authorization. Like the braceros, many among the undocumented eventually settled at the border. Between the 1960s and the early 1990s, undocumented migration continued unabated, and hundreds of thousands of Mexicans also became legal U.S. immigrants, producing further movement across the border. The legal immigrants had access to better employment opportunities than the undocumented, and their status as permanent U.S. residents gave them additional rights and benefits.

A major consequence of the post–World War II population movements has been the creation of a vast army of laborers on the Mexican side who are readily accessible to U.S. employers. Newcomers have been constantly incorporated into the established system of cheap labor exchange at the border. Legions of poor people have become transborder commuters, living in Mexico and working in the United States. For Mexican workers, the economic environment on the border presents opportunities unavailable elsewhere. Jobs and wages are far more attractive at *la frontera* than in most parts of Mexico. Steady employment in a U.S.-owned maquiladora, for example, represents the fulfillment of a dream for many young people from depressed rural areas. Once on the border, workers become aware that conditions are even better, actually far better, on the U.S. side than on the Mexican side, and those with ambition and drive find ways of penetrating the foreign labor market.

The pressures that compel Mexicans to seek employment on foreign soil work to the advantage of American employers, who are eager to hire them at wages that are exploitative by U.S. standards but very desirable by Mexican standards. Not surprisingly, the employment of large numbers of undocumented workers is commonplace throughout the U.S. borderlands. Though the Immigration Reform and Control Act of 1986 imposed stiff penalties for hiring such workers, border-landers have found loopholes in the law, and the practice continues as before. Indeed, the illegal labor system is so entrenched and institutionalized along the border that legislation, regulations, apprehensions, deportations, and other measures aimed at discouraging the surreptitious flow of migrants have failed time and again.

From the perspective of the workers, crossing the boundary without documentation entails many risks, as is amply illustrated in the stories presented below. *Indocumentados* are easy prey for unscrupulous *coyotes,* dishonest policemen, sadistic U.S. Border Patrol officers, shameless thieves, shady lawyers, crooked bureaucrats, and oppressive employers. In the face of such vulnerability, the indocumentados must find strength within themselves and must constantly seek the help of kindhearted strangers. For those who are alone in a foreign and often hostile world, the daily struggles and loneliness are especially poignant. In short, these workers live in unpredictable and sometimes dangerous environments that require considerable survival skills, persistence, and character. That so many are able to survive and to accomplish their objectives is a powerful testament to the human spirit and the will to progress. One remarkable characteristic of the recollections of many indocumentados is their use of humor in relating stories of struggle and suffering. By focusing on the light side of difficult situations, the indocumentados can successfully cast off potentially self-destructive feelings about their unfortunate fate in life or the people who have abused them along the way. It was striking to hear them laugh at themselves and even at harrowing incidents that have touched their lives. Seldom did I encounter bitterness or pessimism as I conducted interviews with this segment of the border population.

A subject that comes up repeatedly in the interviews is abuse by agents of the Border Patrol. This has become a highly emotional issue because numerous shooting incidents during the 1980s and 1990s have led to deaths among the immigrants. In 1992 the American Friends Service Committee issued a report that cited 1,274 abuses along the border between May 5, 1989, and May 4, 1991, most involving the Border Patrol. The report grouped the abuses into the following categories: psychological or verbal abuse (28.3%), physical abuse (22.4%), illegal or inappropriate searches (15.7%), denial of due process (14.4%), illegal or inappropriate seizure of a person (11.2%), seizure or destruction of property (4.3%), violations of the right of Native Americans to cross the border freely (1.0%), and other abuses (2.7%). Incidents involving physical abuse—including shootings, beatings, sexual assaults, injury by vehicles, and high-speed chases— resulted in seven deaths during the two-year period.[2]

This chapter begins with several accounts that focus on the experiences of undocumented migrants, including their lives in Mexico, the circumstances that caused them to migrate, the border crossing, and the struggle to make a living in a foreign environment. In some cases the events related by the protagonists take place in the interior of the United States rather than at the border, but the border figures prominently in their lives. The first two memoirs provide some historical depth, drawing on events and personal experiences dating to the 1940s and 1950s. The recollections of a domestic worker are of special interest because she is part of a large segment of the border labor force who work in an environment that exposes them to considerable risk.

Another important sector of the border labor force is composed of people who work in the tourist districts of cities like Ciudad Juárez and Tijuana, and three of the interviews spotlight some of their experiences. For most of the twentieth century, tourism has been a cornerstone of the border economy, and thousands have made their living as guides, salespeople, waiters, bartenders, entertainers, taxi drivers, and prostitutes. Commercial establishments are intermixed with bars, discotheques, and nightclubs in the tourist strips, attracting a wide array of clients. Workers who come in contact with foreigners often have opportunities to make extra money by "hustling" their customers, especially inexperienced Americans visiting the border for the first time. On the strip the view prevails that visitors are fair game for fleecing, and naïveté invites swindling. But dishonesty can come from different directions; sometimes foreigners victimize local workers. The interviews with a taxi driver and a prostitute offer glimpses of the downside of life in the tourist strips. The rest of the selections include two men who recall interesting experiences during their childhoods when they spent considerable time on the street selling newspapers, shining shoes, and doing other odd jobs; a woman who worked in a maquiladora for several years; and a male supervisor of a maquiladora who reveals personal liaisons between management and workers. Most of the interviews in this chapter were conducted in El Paso– Ciudad Juárez, a major gateway from Mexico to the United States and long the "heart" of the borderlands.

"I wasn't about to stay at the border."

—MANUEL PADILLA

During the 1940s and 1950s, large numbers of Mexicans worked in the United States under the Bracero Program and as undocumented workers. Manuel Padilla, a settler migrant and native of Jalisco, did both, but he preferred the undocumented option because of his impatience with bureaucracy. His story illustrates important aspects of the migratory experience of that period, including step migration within Mexico, use of the border as a home base, problems faced by workers in getting bracero contracts, and the consequences of apprehension by the U.S. Border Patrol. In addition, Padilla reveals the renegade spirit characteristic of independent-minded and restless migrants.

As a child, I dreamed of riding on the train, of coming to the United States after dollars. And that's what I did. I left my hometown in 1936 and went to Aguascalientes. From there I climbed aboard a train that was headed north. It was in December, about one in the morning, and it was cold, but I was wearing a good jacket. We traveled for a few hours and made it to Opal, where the train had to change engines. One of the conductors saw me and told me to get down, that I couldn't travel up on the boxcar. I asked him why not, that I had been on that train since Aguascalientes. He started throwing rocks at me and I had to get off.

I hid behind a water tank, waiting for the next train. I was angry that I had to wait. The other train arrived and I climbed aboard. After a while I felt the train slowing down, and I saw some soldiers coming after me. The conductor probably saw me and told the soldiers to get me. I decided to jump, but when I landed I hurt my arm badly. I would have broken my neck if I had landed on my head! The train didn't wait for me; it just kept on going. I thought, "What now?" I decided not to turn back but to continue to Camacho, the next town, which was about twenty kilometers away. Some truckers who were headed south told me that at the pace I was walking I'd make it to Camacho late that afternoon. My arm was really hurting; I was sure I had broken a bone.

When I got to Camacho I went into a cantina and ordered a tequila. I started talking to the man who was beside me, and he asked me where I was headed. When I told him I was going to Torreón he told me there were thousands of people waiting for work there and that I would have problems. Instead, he suggested I go with him to Zacatecas, where I might be able to get a job loading sacks of corn, which was what he did. I told him my arm was in bad shape, but he said rubbing a certain kind of oil on it would heal it. (Later I would find out that his remedy would not work.) He convinced me and we left for Zacatecas. He bought a train ticket and rode in the passenger section, and I climbed aboard one of the engines. The engineers let me ride there. It was warm, but there was a lot of smoke everywhere.

When we got to Zacatecas, I didn't see my friend at the station, but I had his address and took a bus to a restaurant where he said he would meet me. The bus driver told me where to get off, and I found him there drinking coffee. He said, "Paisano [friend], you made it! I thought that you had decided to go to Torreón." He told me where I could stay and where I could get the oil for my arm. After two or three days my arm had not improved. Then my friend went on strike at his job, and I felt embarrassed living there, not doing anything. I told him, "Things are bad here. I don't feel good staying here. I have a buddy in Torreón with whom I can work." He said, "Do as you wish."

I left to catch the train about four in the morning. Again I was a tramp and managed to sneak my way to Torreón. We arrived at four in the afternoon, and I started looking for my buddy, whom I had known since childhood. I finally found him, but he told me there was no work. He said the only thing I could do was to go to the union hall and see if they could help me out, if they could send me somewhere. I stayed with him and several others who slept in a small room. They slept on the floor, like pigs, with their clothes hanging everywhere. It was a real dump. There was a little old lady who brought us food. I stayed there for three weeks. I would get up at three in the morning and milk some cows, and then I would go to the union hall to see what there was. I thought to myself, "This is no good!"

One day I met another old friend from Aguascalientes who told me there was a vacancy for a hotel clerk. It paid ten pesos a month plus food. He said, "The pay isn't much, but there is a way to make a little extra money. After rooms have been vacated, you can go in, clean them up, rent them on your own, and keep the money." I took the job. One afternoon I was sitting by the door when one of the girls ran by and swung the door hard, hitting my toe. It really hurt. I didn't say anything, I just swung the door hard back at her. She got angry and went to get her brother. He was angry and demanded to know why I had insulted his sister. I told him what had happened, mentioning that I had not said a word to her. He told me I no longer had a job. I said, "Well, stick the job up your nose! Pay me, I'm leaving."

I went back to my friend from the labor union. He asked me, "What happened?" I said, "I got fired. I got in a fight with one of the girls. It's just one of those things." I continued checking with the union hall for another three days, but there was nothing. I got tired of that. I then decided to sell wood on Saturdays and Sundays. I would buy a bundle wholesale for 5 or 6 pesos in Torreón and resell it on the streets in Gómez Palacios. I would make about 10 pesos profit. It was pretty good money. But then some people came over and told me I had to belong to the union to be able to sell that wood. I argued with them, but it did no good. I gave that up. Later I sold tomatoes, but things didn't go well. It was just like the man from Zacatecas had told me. There was no work in Torreón. I decided to look for work in agriculture nearby in La Laguna, an area that had beautifully cultivated fields. I knew some people who were working there. I finally found a job in an *ejido* [community farm] with some former revolutionaries who had been given land that used to belong to the rich. They let me sleep in a granary where they kept hay for the animals. I stayed there about four months.

One day someone killed a man from Atotonilco. It happened on a Saturday or Sunday night. He was laying there in a spot where the cotton seeds were kept, and there were people looking at him. We noticed that one of the workers was missing, and we suspected he had killed the man because they had had a fight the previous day. The police arrived and started asking questions.

"Did you know this man?"

I said, "Yes, we worked together. He and the other worker got into a fight."

The police then told us to wait while they went to a nearby hacienda. They said they wanted us to take care of the dead man. While they were gone I took off. I didn't want to be picking up a corpse! Those fat . . . policemen! I needed to collect some money that was owed to me at a ranch about four miles away.

Well, since I left the scene, the police thought I had killed the man or that I knew something about the crime. On my way back from the ranch, I saw their car approaching. I suspected they were coming after me and thought of running, but I didn't, figuring that they would then think I had something to hide. I met the police car, and when they asked me where I had been I explained, but they said, "Get in the car, you bastard!" I said, "Look, I haven't done anything!" But they said, "Let's go and see if that is true!" Sons of bitches, they took me to San Pedro and locked me up for the night. The next day they had me give them all the details I knew about the dead person and the murder suspect. The police then ordered the victim brought over, and the workers had to bury him. We put him in a wooden casket, threw dirt over him, and left. Then I was told, "Now you are free. You don't owe anything." Bastards. . . .

I returned to the ejido and found out that the police had been through my things and had taken a dagger that I had. I went back and asked them to return it, but I was told that it had been sent to San Pedro. *They* had stolen it, and I didn't like it. That afternoon I went to Torreón to catch the train to Chihuahua. I had a brother and sister there. I stayed with them a few days and got work with an American mining company in Los Azules. Then I got a place to live in company housing.

At that time I had two brothers who were in the Mexican military in Jalisco. I wrote to them, "Leave that bullshit. You've been soldiers I don't know how many years, and you have nothing to show for it. Come to Chihuahua. Things are good here; the work is with a company, and they pay well. The mine is not very deep. Come join me!" The Mexican military was a big waste of time. The common soldiers were paid a pittance. In the United States, if a soldier is killed in action, at least his children receive money, but in Mexico what do they get? You get killed and your children suffer from hunger. It is bullshit. Panchito left the service first and then Angel. Angel was actually kicked out because he almost killed another soldier in a fight. They told him he was unstable, that he could not control himself. They both joined me in Chihuahua and got jobs in Santa Barbara.

The silver mine where I worked was about 900 meters deep. It had fourteen or fifteen levels. It was very hot down there, and we would work half naked, carrying sacks all day long. At times there was no air. The water would run through the ditches, and it was so hot that it would vaporize. It was dangerous work. My father ruined his life working in the copper mines of Arizona. At the time he was working, the machines that crushed the ores did not have water to settle the dust. He breathed that dust, and after some time his respiratory system was plugged up. He would wake up in the middle of the night choking and yelling. It was terrible. He suffered for seven or eight years and finally committed suicide in 1933.

In 1940 I met a schoolteacher in Los Azules. I invited her to have some ice cream, and she accepted. At first we were friends, but later we went to a 5 de mayo [national holiday] dance. Within three months we got married and went to Torreón for our honeymoon.

I worked in Los Azules and then in San Francisco del Oro until 1944, when I decided to leave the mine and become a bracero. I went to Juárez, waited for nineteen days, but I could not get a contract. The politicians had decided that the workers should go to Mexico City to get the documentation, so I went to Mexico City with a leave of absence from the mine. In one day I was able to get my contract; there weren't too many people. That year I worked in San Bernardino, California. The following year I had to go to Mexico City once again to get my documents, but this time there were many thousands of people who wanted to go to the United States. Lines would form during the night, because the workers wanted to be ready for the following morning. They would sleep sitting down, covering themselves with their blankets. The people had great need; they were hungry. Many had been waiting around for two months without being able to get into the office. When the doors opened in the morning, there were some who would disrupt the line to create confusion so they themselves could go to the front. I saw someone throw some burning oakum, and that sure made the bunch scatter. Then the mob would form the line again.

Once there was so much confusion that one of the guards started shooting his gun into the crowd. He hit some workers who were blameless. Others soon went after the man with the gun. Then the officials sent for firemen, who came with hoses and shot water at the people to disperse them. It was a real mess, something terrible. There were some who got killed in the disorder, who were trampled as those in front ran back. Later they brought in some troops, who kept order with their rifles and bayonets.

For three weeks those of us from Chihuahua tried to get in, but we couldn't. We were afraid to be in line because of the tremendous crowding. About thirty or forty of us decided to go to Chihuahua City to see if the governor there could help us with a letter that we could then use to get in. We managed to get the letter, and the group took it to Mexico City, but I stayed behind in Chihuahua for a few days. When I returned to Mexico City, everyone on the list in the governor's letter had left. They had all been called over the loudspeaker and had gotten in. My brother Panchito was among them. I found a friend who gave me a note Panchito had left for me. He wrote that I and others on that list who had not been there when the names were called should contact a certain person to get our cards. The only problem was to get into the office. It was difficult because there were still so many people waiting in line. At noon I decided to go to the back entrance, and I told the guard that my name was on that list, and he let me in. I saw the official, and he signed my card right away, and that year I went to Idaho. In 1946 I got my contract in Aguascalientes, and later on I signed up about three times in Mexicali.

When I worked in the fields as a bracero, at times there were some foremen who were abusive, who would punish or fire you if you defended your rights. Once when I was loading lemons on trucks, the foreman left me to do the job of two people when he took away the other man who was helping me. I got angry and thought to myself, "Does he think I am going to do this alone all day long? He can go to hell! As soon as I have a chance I'm going to the rest room." That's what I did, but he came over and asked, "Why did you leave?" I told him I couldn't work all day long without going to the toilet, but he reported me to the "big foreman." The "big foreman" forgave me, but later I had the same trouble again and I got fired. I said, "The hell with it!"

They sent me someplace else to pick oranges, but there I got into a fight with another bracero who was one of the foreman's favorites. I was with him when he was driving a truck, and I opened the door because it was very hot. We were still in the fields; we had not entered the highway. He told me to shut the door because it would get damaged. I said, "The truck isn't yours. If the door is damaged, let the company buy another one. They have lots of money." He said, "Yes, but I am in command in this truck." I replied, "Well, you may be in command of the truck, but not of the door. I won't close it until we get to the highway." He stopped the truck, and we got into a fistfight. The "field boss" caught us fighting, and since I was new there, the following day they told me to get my things together, and I was sent to another camp nearby where it was very hot and where

I didn't like the food. Also, I didn't like the scissors they gave me to do the picking.

I said, "Give me another pair. These are no good. I don't want them."

"Well, we don't have any more. You'll have to wait until the 'field boss' comes."

When he got there, he didn't have anything, so I threw the scissors at him, saying, "This thing is no good. I'm just going to pick with my bare hands." He got angry and told me to get in the truck, that he was taking me back to the camp.

At the camp I decided to desert my contract. I left without telling anyone. I went to Palo Alto, where I had an aunt. I worked there for about a month and a half, and then I went to Fresno, where I worked until the end of the year. The *migra* caught me and I was sent to Juárez, where my family was now living. I had written to my wife and had told her to move to the border, that possibly things were better there. I told her it would be better for her and the kids to be at the border so I wouldn't have to go all the way to San Francisco del Oro to see them. I spent about three months in Juárez, and then I returned to the United States, hiding from the migra. I went to the state of Washington to pick apples. I knew I could earn good money there. After that, that is the way I did it for about ten years. I would return to Juárez at Christmastime, stay until April or May, and then go back to the United States.

I didn't like Juárez because of the climate; it got too hot there. Secondly, you couldn't work [on the American side] without papers because the migra patrolled the border all the time. Many from Juárez would work in El Paso with their local crossing cards, but when they were caught, they would lose them. I would head into the interior of the United States, where I had more opportunity to evade the migra. There the migra was not on top of you all the time. You could work for some time before they would come around. And if you could "escape" when they arrived, then you could stay longer. Also, the jobs around El Paso didn't pay much. If you wanted a factory job, you would have to wait for your turn to come up. If you worked in the fields, you could make about $2.50 a day maximum at that time. In California you could get a job right away, without having to apply or anything. If you picked fruit, you could work by piece-rate and earn as much as twenty-five or thirty dollars a day. I wasn't about to stay at the border.

Once I did try working in Las Cruces, New Mexico, which is near El Paso. I didn't like it. I worked weeding cotton for three dollars a day. I said to myself, "I can earn more than that in one hour picking cherries in California." I lasted two weeks on the job and then went to California. In two months I would earn more than a thousand dollars picking cherries, but I had to work from sunrise until dusk. In some orchards they would let you work as much as you wanted. I would take food and spend the whole day there. There were many good pickers who would earn more than forty-five dollars a day. Since the season was only two months long, we would try hard to earn as much as we could. After cherry picking was over, I would go pick apricots, then peaches, and then pears. I preferred to work in the fields because there it was easier to avoid the migra. I felt bad leaving the family at the border all the time. But what could I do? I had to earn money so we could all eat.

In 1946 when I was in the state of Washington, I didn't like it and went on to Idaho, where I thought the migra would not bother me. I worked loading potatoes on trucks for two or three weeks, and I earned pretty good money. When I least expected it, two plainclothes officials arrived. I never thought they were immigration inspectors.

"Padilla," one of them said, "come over here!"

I thought, "Who can that be?"

He said, "Do you have papers?"

I answered, "No, I don't have papers. What papers are you talking about?"

He said, "Your papers that allow you to be here. I am an immigration inspector. You'll have to come with us."

I said, "Well, all right."

Soon the farmer came over and paid me with a check. They locked me up for about a week in a nearby town and then took me to Spokane to a big jail, where they kept me for forty-six days. We ate twice a day. It was regular food; it filled us up. I would spend a lot of time playing cards, waiting for my turn to leave. Finally one day they took my group at two in the morning, and we left by plane to El Paso. I was lucky. Imagine, if they had taken us to another part of the border as punishment! When they let me go, I went to my home in Juárez.

Another time I was caught working in *el traque* [on the railroad] in Kansas. I was locked up in Kansas City also about forty-seven days, and from there they took us to San Antonio by train. We were on our way to Laredo, but I was taken off the train with a few others who had lied about their names. I had made a mistake when I told them my last name. It was back to jail again, this time in San Antonio for two or three weeks. Then they took us to Laredo. When I crossed the border, the Mexican immigration official gave me a bus ticket saying, "Here, take this. We don't want you here. Leave right away." Thief! From there I made my way back to Juárez through Monterrey and Torreón.

I spent two or three weeks in Juárez and re-crossed the border. I worked in Kansas for about a month, and then I was caught again. Back in Juárez I decided Kansas was too cold, so the next time I went to California. This was in 1948 or 1949. I spent about a year in Stockton and then returned to Juárez. I continued doing that for years, working for part of the year and then returning to Mexico in time for Christmas.

In 1956 I finally fixed my papers and became a permanent resident of the United States, but it was a hell of a chore. They required many documents— letters from the police and other such crap. It took me about two months to get the papers. The thing that gave me the most trouble was the letter from my job sponsor. I got that from a scoundrel woman in Juárez who used to sell those letters. I paid about $150 for that letter; later they were being sold for $500. The day I paid her I told her I wanted the letter that same week, and she said she would have it for me. Two months went by. During that time she was looking for someone to get it from. She had said she already had the letter, but she was lying. She was a rascal. She got those letters from American employers. Mine came from a construction contractor in El Paso, but when I went to get work with him, he said he didn't want anything to do with people who had gotten "bad" letters. He would not require such people to work for him; he said he just gave those letters to help them out. Of course, he was getting paid for those letters. I guess paying these people was better than getting robbed by those shameless officials at the international bridge.

"Why do I need to go around on my knees in Mexico when there is lots of work in the United States?"

— ANTONIO ORENDAIN

In the following selection, Antonio Orendain, a bicultural settler-migrant and one of the major leaders in farm labor organizing in the United States, relates his early experiences as an undocumented worker. Born in 1930 in Etzatlán, Jalisco, he was raised by his grandparents following the death of his father from a bullet wound. His family worked in agriculture, and as a boy Orendain dreamed of being a pilot. At age sixteen he joined the Mexican Air Force, where he worked as a radio technician but never fulfilled his dream of flying. After three and a half years of service, he left the military, disillusioned with the lack of opportunity for poor boys like himself and disgusted with the corruption that he observed among the officers. Orendain decided to try his luck in the United States, crossing the border at Tijuana in 1950 without documents. As an unregistered worker in California, Oregon, Montana, and Idaho, Orendain lived with the constant fear of apprehension by *la migra* until he became a legal U.S. resident in 1956.

When I arrived in Tijuana, I was completely disillusioned with Mexico. I thought to myself, "Why do I need to go around on my knees in Mexico when there is lots of work in the United States? Why do I need to sacrifice myself studying and having to be outstanding in Mexico when in the United States there is abundance? There I probably don't have to study. I can just go and work." I got that impression reading the newspapers and listening to the radio. I also saw how much money braceros would bring back from the United States. Some even wore good army clothes, and even air force jackets. That was a false idea that affected the youth in Mexico.

At the time I arrived at the border, the migra had a policy of shaving the head of anyone who had been caught as an illegal three times. I saw many people with their heads completely shaved. That worried me because I intended to cross illegally, and I wondered what would happen to me if I were caught three times. Actually, I was caught many times, even five times one day. To avoid the head shaving, I gave a different name every time I was caught. I gave the names of friends I knew in the Mexican military. I remembered details about them, such as their parents' names and their hometowns. The day I was caught five times I was beaten by an immigration agent because he wanted me to admit I was the same one who had been caught before. It made me angry that they would hit me.

Six of us who were upset at the policy of shaving heads and abusing people got together and caught two American blondes who had long, pretty hair and shaved their heads. It was late in the afternoon and it was dark as the women were crossing a bridge near the border. Things got really hot in Tijuana, and we decided to cross into the United States and hide. The Mexican police arrested many people, hoping that they would catch those responsible for shaving the women. We spent about eight days in hiding in San Ysidro, California [directly across from Tijuana], eating tomatoes. After that they stopped shaving the Mexicans who were caught.

I spent about two years as an illegal in California until I was caught in a dance in Fresno and was sent back to Tijuana. A friend and I then decided to reenter the United States, hoping to catch a train to San Diego late one night. The tracks ran through an area that had canyons and bridges where one could hide. We bought a bottle of tequila and went to an arroyo to wait for the train. It was cold and we made a fire. After a while, two other people joined us and we passed the tequila around. Then more people arrived, and pretty soon there were about ten of us. By then we had a big bonfire, and people were shouting, "We are Mexican! We are in Mexican territory!" And this and that.

We finished the tequila and flipped a coin to see who would go back to Tijuana to get some more. I lost, so they gave me money to go get it. Once on the Mexican side I could hear the yelling, "Long live the Revolution! Long live Pancho Villa! Long live *la cucaracha*!" I could also see the flames from the fire at the spot where we were supposedly hiding. I bought the tequila and ran back, saying, "Hey! Don't make so much noise! Your yelling can be heard all the way to Mexico! And the flames can be seen as well! They're going to find us!" But I was told, "You're a coward! Don't you know this is our land? This is Mexican territory that Santa Anna sold [to the United States]!"

A few minutes later we heard a voice, "Hey, boys! Put out that fire, and line up in twos! Go back to Mexico!" It was the migra. They didn't even ask us our names. They just made us put out the fire, lined us up, pointed to Mexico, and sent us back. As we walked toward the Mexican side, I said, "Didn't you say we were in Mexican territory? What happened?"

As soon as we got to Tijuana I said to my friend, "Let's cross again. But this time let's not go wait for the train. Let's go directly to the bus depot in San Ysidro." That's what we did. The depot was empty, and we bought our tickets. We got on the bus and no one bothered us. All the immigration officers and the police were in the area where the train would go by. That whole area was full of people who expected to jump on the train. We made it to San Diego without any problems.

Once I joined with three other illegals from Jalisco, and we crossed the border at Mexicali. We jumped on a train and rode it for two days. When we got off we saw some people working in a cornfield. Since we hadn't eaten for almost a day, we asked them if they could give us water and something to eat. They said yes. Then we asked if there was work, and one of them said he would find out. "Go ahead and prepare your food, whatever you want, and I'll ask the boss." Several of them went to talk to the boss. Others started making tortillas and cooking meat. They were very nice to us, but it turned out there was no work for us. Then one of them said, "Go ahead and eat. Make a lunch and be on your way. We are very brotherly here because we're all from Michoacán and people from Michoacán like to treat strangers well. We're not like those sons of bitches from Jalisco. Once I was in a camp where those from Jalisco claimed they were American citizens, and they wanted to turn me over to the migra. Those bastards. Here we help each other out. By the way, where are you from?" One of the *compañeros* said, "I'm from Zacatecas." "And you?" "I'm from Durango." And when it came my turn I said, "I'm from Yucatán." After we left, I commented, "That's terrible that all of you denied your home state." They answered, "Yeah, what about you? You not only denied it, you claimed to be all the way from the end of Mexico."

One year on the day of the Revolution, November 20, another compañero and I decided to cross at San Ysidro and walk to Encanto, California. To get there one would walk north all night in a straight line until coming to a red light, which was the light of a radio station in the town. That was the only guide along the way. One would have to jump over fences and risk dog attacks and even gunfire. On several occasions I had been shot at from houses along the way. Upon arriving at Encanto there was a spot where one would find water, bread, and other food. It was customary for those who passed that spot to leave something behind for those who were to come later. I knew the route well; I had experience.

My friend and I bought what we needed and started walking as soon as the sun went down. Since we were close to the ocean, we could feel the cool breeze hitting us from our left, or from the west. But my friend was from Los Altos de Jalisco, where cold wind comes from the north, and he kept saying that we should be walking into the breeze because that was the way north. I explained that the cool breeze was coming from the ocean and told him to listen to the sounds of the port at San Diego. As long as the cold wind was coming from our left, we were walking north for sure. But he kept insisting that cold winds came from the north.

At one point we came upon a small hill by an arroyo, and I stumbled onto a stake which I thought would make a good walking stick. But it turned out to be a water pipe which I could not uproot. We kept on walking, and my friend kept talking about the northern winds. It turned out that we got lost, but I explained to him that I knew how to find the way by figuring out in what direction the moon was moving. I could not convince him. By then we were desperate because we had encountered several dogs and we had been shot at. So I said to him, "Okay, just so you stop complaining, let's walk straight into the 'northern' breeze. But I'm sure we will hit the sea. Then we'll see what you will do. We'll see if you can walk on the water."

We walked the rest of the night looking for the sea, but we didn't find it. We wanted to find San Diego but couldn't do that either. Then, as it was getting light, we got to a small hill and crossed an arroyo. I told my compañero, "Stop. Look at the tracks around here and see if they fit our shoes." Sure enough, we had been through there before. I said, "You see. Because of your stupid idea of following the northern winds we have walked around in a circle. If we had planned it that way, we never would have done it, but we did it, and we walked all night." He didn't believe me, so after a while we saw someone around there hunting rabbits. He said, "Go ask that man." So I asked him where we were, and it turned out we were in Otay River, which was about two miles from the border. I was really angry.

We were out of food, and we just hid and waited for nightfall. When darkness came I told him, "This time you shut up about your northern winds. I don't want to hear anything about Los Altos de Jalisco." So we walked all night again. We drank water in the arroyos along the way, and when we got to the edge of San Diego, we stopped and bought milk and food and kept on walking. We made it to El Cajon, and by that time we were very dirty. As we headed down a hill, a dog started barking at us, and this lady yelled at us to go to her house. She said, "You are headed straight for the immigration station. Come in." She was an American lady whose husband was a doctor in the merchant marine.

She gave us towels so we could take a bath, and then she told us to hide behind her house because the migra would come looking for us. Sure enough, in a while the migra was asking if two illegals had been seen around her house. She said no. Then she gave us a good meal. Since I hadn't eaten for so long, I stuffed myself and got sick. At that time I really liked Fig Newton cookies, and I ate too many of those. I also drank too much milk. The night before in my dreams I had longed to drink a carton of milk, and she gave me one exactly as I had dreamed it. So I drank all of it. I got sick, but she cured me. She gave me something to settle my stomach. Then she said, "I'll go see if they need lemon pickers in Escondido." She left the door to her house open and told us we could go in and eat whatever there was in the refrigerator.

But my compañero got restless while we were waiting. He said, "They're going to turn us in to the migra. Let's go. We're wasting time here." We started walking again at night and headed for Ramona, where he wanted to go. We got there about 7 A.M., but there was no work for us there. I started to scold him again. Later as we rested I fell asleep, and when I woke up he was gone. I thought to myself, "What do I do now?" I had no money; I had nothing. I had no choice but to walk through one of the major streets in Ramona, hoping the police would pick me up. Two highway patrol cars went by, but they said nothing. A policeman went by, and he said nothing. Then as I came to a turkey farm some Mexican workers called me over. They fed me, made me a lunch, and gave me eighty cents for the trip. I continued walking toward Escondido. I said to myself, "I hope the police or the migra picks me up. At least I'll get a ride to Mexico." But nobody picked me up.

I got to Escondido that night. It was getting cold, and I covered myself with dried avocado leaves as I tried to sleep. I felt like a rattlesnake; I was shaking from the cold, and the dried leaves were making a rattlesnake-like noise. I spent the whole night like that, and the next day I determined to find the migra. I walked through the main street in Escondido, but the migra did not pick me up. I went through the whole town, and nothing. Then I turned around and walked through again, but again nothing happened. Finally this Italian man picked me up. He had two men with him, and I was told one of them was an illegal. They took me to a farm, and I was able to work there for some time.

Orendain's adventures as an undocumented person ended when he became a legal U.S. resident in 1956. His sensitivity and concern for the dismal conditions among the poor led him to establish contact in the late 1950s with activists from California who were involved in registering Mexican American voters and unionizing farm workers. By the mid-1960s he had become one of the key organizers for Cesar Chavez's fledgling union, which became known as the United Farm Workers. Orendain's experiences in Texas as a labor organizer are included in Chapter 7.

*"One of the men from migración had a mustache, and we called him
Pancho Villa. I said to him, 'Don't be cruel, Pancho Villa. Let us go.'"*
—TERESA VILLANUEVA

Crossing the international boundary, evading the U.S. Border Patrol, and finding work
are three imposing challenges confronted constantly by undocumented people. For
women, however, the problems are greatly compounded by the dangers that exist
at the border, on city streets, and even on the job. Often, women who cross the Rio
Grande from Ciudad Juárez to El Paso must first get through mobs of extortion-
minded and abusive men who hang around the riverbank. Having cleared that hurdle,
the women must then make their way across a sometimes water-filled river without
being detected and finally walk or ride public buses to their place of employment.
The trip includes multiple humiliations and indignities, especially if the women are
caught by *la migra*. On the job, they are frequently the victims of exploitation and
sexual harassment, as the case of Teresa Villanueva well illustrates. Villanueva, a
settler migrant, grew up on a farm in the vicinity of Torreón, where she lived with
her father after her parents separated. Her relationship with an irresponsible man produced several children who had to be supported, and Villanueva migrated to the border in the early 1970s looking for work. During the six years covered by this interview, Villanueva went through many difficult experiences but managed to keep a
positive outlook while seeking to better her situation. In telling her story, Villanueva
exhibited a sense of humor, which no doubt helped her cope with recurring family
and job-related crises.

I lived in Torreón with my boyfriend. He was one of those men who run around
with other women. We didn't get married, and I had a child. He treated me very
badly, and I put up with everything. I left him, but he would visit me at home.
Then I got pregnant again. He continued running around. Just before I delivered
my baby, I saw him with another woman and it upset me very much. She was a
woman of the streets, but he preferred her to me. I left the children with my
mother and took off for Juárez. Two months later I received a letter informing
me that my baby had died, so I returned to Torreón. I think the baby died from
the anger that I had felt when I saw my boyfriend with the other woman. I then
found out he had married a teacher, and she was supporting him. He didn't want
to work. She bought him a car, and they lived in a house she was renting.

When he learned I was back, he began looking for me. He told me that he
was living with the teacher only for convenience and that he loved only me. I
didn't know if it was really love, but I did look a lot better than when I had left.
I wasn't as skinny as before, and I was better dressed. I didn't pay any attention
to him, but he kept after me. He would force his way into my mother's house.
Well, I sneaked out of Torreón again and returned to Juárez, but he followed me

and took me back by force. I hid from him, which was easy because he lived with his wife and couldn't keep track of me. I returned to Juárez again.

When I got to Juárez, they stole my money at the bus station. I went to the bathroom to change clothes, and I set my purse where they put the toilet paper. I forgot it there when I left the station, and when I went back I couldn't find it. I even opened the door of one of the stalls, and a lady was in there. I went looking for some girlfriends I had but couldn't find them. I didn't want to go to my brother's house (I had a brother in Juárez) because we had had a fight three years before. I had gone to see him and he scolded me, so I didn't go back. I thought to myself, "Now how am I going to get downtown?" Then I met a man who was fixing some toilets, and I asked him if he would give me a peso, and he did. With that money I got downtown, and finally I found one of my girlfriends who lived out in the hills. That was in 1973.

I told her I wanted to go to El Paso to work, and she agreed to call a woman for whom she had worked before. After we called, I asked her to lend me some money for bus fare, and she did. The next day I got up around four in the morning and waited for the bus, but it didn't come. So I had to walk in the dark by myself from the hills to downtown Juárez. I was really scared, but I kept going because I wanted to cross the border early. When I got downtown I felt better because there were people there. This other woman named Manuela and I then tried to cross the border, but we turned back when we saw the immigration officers. I had crossed the border illegally several times before. Finally we crossed, but they caught us. It was one Mexican American and two Anglos. They joked around with us in the car, saying nasty things. Manuela made a comment that they should let us go because she was very hungry, and they said, "Well, wouldn't you like some American *huevos* [eggs, i.e., testicles] with American *chorizo* [sausage, i.e., penis]?" They would say things like that and laugh out loud. Manuela became very quiet. She was very embarrassed at what they had said to her. They detained us for about an hour and then let us go.

We decided to try again, this time going farther upriver. We crossed the river with some help from an old man, but they caught us again. The next time we went farther still, and we came to a spot where about seven other women were crossing. I said to Manuela, "Let's wait until after those women cross, and when the immigration officers catch them, they'll have to take them in, and then there will be no one to catch us." As we ran across the river [it was mostly dry] Manuela stepped into a big puddle of water and got mud all over herself. We made it across and took the bus into town. The driver was very kind. He waited for us and even gave Manuela a Kleenex to clean herself. We got to the plaza, and there I saw a girl I knew, and she gave us a quarter each so we could go get a cup of coffee. Then we were approached by this Anglo lady in a white station wagon, and she asked us if we were looking for work. We said yes. She said she lived in Las Cruces [in New Mexico, about 40 miles from El Paso], and she would pay one of us twenty-five dollars a week with weekends off or thirty dollars without weekends off. We told her both of us needed work, and she said, "I'll take both of you and try to find work for the other one. If I don't find her something, I'll bring her back to El Paso." So we left for Las Cruces.

She took us to her home [a farmhouse in Las Cruces] and gave us something to eat. When her husband got home, he looked us over, and I became embarrassed. He seemed to be a flirt. His wife—I assumed it was his wife, I didn't know—was very ugly. Her legs were like gelatin. I said to my friend, "Why don't you stay?" Then the lady asked her husband, "Which one do you want?" He said, "The one with the nicest legs." And he pointed to me. I thought to myself, "I know what this guy is up to." I said to Manuela, "Look at that. What a who-knows-what old man. Who does he think he is? Let's get out of here." Manuela answered, "Without any money? No, look, you stay here and I'll work someplace else, and then we'll return to El Paso." The lady got Manuela work with one of her friends, but it was only for three days. Manuela was then taken back to El Paso, and I never saw her again.

So I stayed there. The first week was fine, but then . . . one night I went to the kitchen and there was the man without any clothes on. I saw him and ran to the room where I slept with their three children. He took off after me, and I was afraid. I hid behind a clothes basket in the closet, and I didn't open the door until it got light. After a while I think he took a shower and got dressed, and that was it. But that night the same thing happened again. I was in bed with their little girl, and since the room had no lock, I had pushed the bed against the door just in case. Around midnight I felt the bed being pushed by the door, and I ran to one of the big closets and hid there. But he came toward me, so I ran to the living room and hid in a corner behind the sofa. As time passed, I would look into the bedroom to see if he had left, because he was in my bed. I suppose he was waiting for me. Just before daybreak I left my hiding place and went to the kitchen, but I saw him coming again. I ran outside to where the trash cans were, and I hid there until it got completely light. After a while he left for work.

For the next week he treated me very badly. He was angry with me and wouldn't talk to me. He threw things at me. One night he and his wife returned from a party around two or three in the morning. He was drunk, and I thought to myself, "He'll be coming to my room shortly!" The lady went to bed and fell asleep right away. Once she was asleep, no one could wake her up. Then the man pushed the door to our room as hard as he could, and the bed went to one side. He grabbed my hair and jerked me. I started crying and calling for his wife, but she was sound asleep. He closed the door and pulled my wrist, hurting it. In the dark I screamed and ran to the closet, and when he turned I pushed him aside and went to the bed where the two little boys slept and got between them. I thought to myself, "He won't take me from here!" I don't know how, but his wife heard the noise and got up. She said to him, "What are you doing?" He answered, "None of your business! You get out of here! You've got nothing to do with this!" Then he went to bed and left me alone.

I put up with that [and with no pay] for a month and a half. When the first two weeks went by and she had not paid me a cent, I wrote fake letters from my mother in which she "asked" me for money for my children. I showed them to the lady, but she didn't believe me. After all that time I was anxious to leave. I had to return home because I was going to be godmother to a pair of twins. I told the lady I needed my money, and she said she would give me sixty dollars and the rest when I returned. I told her I didn't know if I would return, and she said she would pay me more if I did. I told her okay, and I took the sixty dollars and left. I did not return. No way! I wasn't crazy!

I spent a week in Torreón and then returned to the border. I got work with this señora in Coronado [an affluent neighborhood in El Paso] who was very jealous. She would get upset if I fixed my hair, and she would make me lower the hemline on my dresses because she thought they were too short. She would say, "Muy corto, muy corto! Yo quiero muy largo! [Too short, too short! I want it very long!]" I didn't like to wear long dresses, and I must admit sometimes I wore them too short. One day she scolded me because I raised the hemline on my uniform and borrowed hair curlers from a friend next door. The señora said, "You know what? In this house the only one who needs to get all dressed up is me." She was a strange person, one of those Anglo women who look like old horses. She paid me sixteen dollars a week. One day I told her I was sick and needed to see the doctor. It wasn't true; I only wanted to leave. So I went back to Torreón and stayed for about eight months. My old boyfriend came around again, and he started to promise me the stars and the moon. Well, we lived together for a few months, and I got pregnant again. I stayed in Torreón until the baby was born. I saw that my boyfriend was still friendly with that other woman, and I decided to leave Torreón and never return. I left the baby with my mother and went back to Juárez.

I worked for this lady for three years, and I was happy, although she would pass me around to her cousin and another woman, and they worked me very hard. They would have me clean floors and iron big baskets of clothes. Since they paid me three dollars a day, they figured they could do with me as they pleased, passing me around like a toy. I didn't mind, though, because I had money to send to my children.

Once I saw the husband of another señora I worked for on the street. He asked me, "Where are you going?" I said, "Home."

"Do you want a ride?"

I thought he must be up to something, but he was my *patrón* [boss], so I couldn't say anything. I got in the car.

Then he asked me, "Do you only work for us?"

"No, I also have a job in an office, but in my free time I go work in homes or take care of children." Of course, it wasn't true that I worked in an office, but I didn't want to tell him the truth.

"Well, how about working for me in my office?"

"No, thanks. They pay me well in the office where I work."

"But wouldn't you like to earn an extra twenty dollars?"

"Not really. Why would I want twenty dollars? What kind of work is it anyway?"

"Well, first tell me if you're interested."

"No, I'm not."

After a while he said, "What a nice body you have."

"Is that so? Don't make fun of me."

"No, really. I like your body a lot."

"You like it? Well, thank you. Now, I insist you tell me, what kind of work do you have for me?"

"Do you like to dance?"

"Sure I like to dance."

So then he said he wanted me to dance naked on top of a table.

I said, "No, no, I'm not looking for that kind of work. There are places where you can go see women dance like that. Why don't you go there?"

"Yeah, but I'm attracted to you."

"No, I'll see you later. Let me off." I got out of the car and went home. I never returned to work for them again.

On another occasion I was on my way home when a *gabacho* [Anglo man] held up some dollar bills through his car window. I thought, "Who does he think he is? He must think I'm for sale or for rent, or I'm on special." He kept staring at me and went wild showing me his money. I said, "He's crazy."

Little by little I began to open my eyes wider, and I started making five, six, seven, eight dollars per day cleaning homes. I didn't like to work by the week any longer; I preferred working by the day. By that time [1976–1977] my sister and I were living with this family we had met years before. They were all very nice people. They treated us very well.

One day the *migración* [Border Patrol] caught my sister Alicia and me at the bus stop, and they shipped us to Mexico through Tijuana! There was no time to tell the señora I was working for what had happened. We made our way to Torreón and then came back to El Paso, and I explained everything to the señora.

Alicia and this other girl and I used to run around together, going everywhere and having a good time. Once after a dance we stopped to buy a soda, and two young gabachos invited us to go with them to play tennis. We said yes, but as we talked they took out some marijuana, and they parked their car all wrong. I said, "You'd better move your car before the police see you." They said the police would do nothing to them. I said to the girls, "Let's go!" We walked away from there, and soon the police went over to where the men were and gave them a ticket. The gabachos then told the police that we were asking them for a ride, but that was not true. We had only been sitting on a bench at the bus stop. So the police came over, and they started asking us questions. It was a man and a woman, and she was pretty mean. She talked to my sister a lot, but Alicia just listened like a donkey, not understanding anything. She had arrived from Torreón only a short time before. The police asked us what we were doing, and we answered we were just drinking a soda. They asked where we lived, and I gave them the señora's address. They said, "It can't be that girls who don't speak English live in El Paso. Get in the car." I explained to the police that Alicia was my sister and the other girl was visiting from Chihuahua, but they still told us to get in the car. I thought, "They're going to accuse us of stealing or something, and we haven't done anything."

When we got to the house the señora was out front, and when she saw us arrive in a police car, her legs started shaking. We said to ourselves, "Híjole! We're going to get scolded."

The police asked the señora about us, and she said we were her nieces. We added that we had come to El Paso because our grandmother was very sick and also told them we had *pasaportes* [local crossing cards]. I asked the police if they wanted me to bring my pasaporte to them, and they said no. But they told us we should always carry our pasaportes with us. They said, "Okay, thank you," and then left. The other girl started crying, but my sister and I just laughed about what had happened. The señora said, "You see what can happen? Don't go wandering around. If my husband finds out, he'll let all of us have it."

The following Saturday, my sister and I went dancing again. We came across some *chavalas* [girls] who thought they were hot stuff, wearing fancy boots and skirts. They treated us like we were their inferiors. I said, "Look at how great they think they are!" Later we went out to get some fresh air, and the presumptuous chavalas came out also. All of a sudden the *migración* swooped down on them and us too. I said to my sister, "Well, look at where the elegant ones are now!" My sister and I sat in the front of the [Border Patrol] car, and the other girls in the back. We were pretty crowded in there; I almost sat on top of one of the officers. They were pretty nice people. I said to them, "Why don't you let us go? Don't be cruel. Let us go!" One of them answered, "We can't do that, because they will fire us, and then we won't get paid. Would you support us?" And we answered, "Sure, of course we will!" And he said, "No, it's better if you go to Juárez." I then invited them to go out to eat, but they said no.

So they sent us back to Juárez, and once there we went dancing until daybreak. We then went to our brother's house, and he asked what we were doing there. I said, "Ahh, we felt like dancing, so we came over to Juárez." I didn't tell him the rest of the story. We would never tell him the truth because if we did, then he wouldn't feel like helping us cross the border again. He would accompany us to the spot where we crossed because there was some danger at the river's edge with so many men hanging around there accosting the women or throwing them in the water. So he went with us to the river, and my sister and I returned to El Paso. The next Saturday the same thing happened again. We went dancing in El Paso, they caught us and sent us back to Juárez, and we finished up our dancing [in Mexico] and then crossed into El Paso. It was easy for us to cross the border.

On another occasion, this other girl and I went dancing at this place where the migración had apprehended all the waiters the night before. There were a few people in there, but things were kind of dead. So this man that we knew offered to take us someplace else, but we thought we would find the same thing elsewhere because the migración was going around to all the dance halls. As we talked about leaving, five immigration officers and six policemen with several big dogs entered the dance hall and stopped the music. When they questioned me, I answered in English, insisting that I had my pasaporte at home. When they asked where that was, I said, "It's not true." The thing is that I was embarrassed with all those people there, especially these girls who disliked us because we would beat them to a good table every week. They were able to show their pasaportes, and we had nothing [to show]. So the migración crowded us into this van and took us away.

At the detention center we saw the migración humiliate some men by making them undress and then hang their underpants from a pole. They would treat the men pretty badly. They would beat them. What brutes! We were able to see those naked men through this small window in the room where we were, which was next to the room where the men were. And the women, if they had wigs, the migración would take them off and play with them. One of the men from migración had a mustache, and we called him Pancho Villa. I said to him, "Don't be cruel, Pancho Villa. Let us go." He said, "Sure, in a little while." Soon they sent us back to Mexico, and we went dancing again!

After that I began asking around where I could find a school to learn English. The señora I worked for told me that she would find out for me and that she would give me a chance to go to school. But she never did, so I left that job. I found a language school and attended classes for about a year and a half. I graduated and got a diploma. After I learned enough English, I would go to Juárez more often. I crossed the border several times, declaring that I was an American. I saved money and got together the papers I needed to apply for a pasaporte. The American consulate gave me a form to take to the international bridge, and I was given an appointment six months from when I had applied. They said, "Go there on January 12." I was happy about that. I said to myself, "I think God is going to help me, and I am going to get that pasaporte."

[At the time] I was staying with my sister in Juárez, but after three months she was able to emigrate to the United States because her husband helped her fix her papers. I had to stay behind. The six-month waiting period seemed so long. I just kept counting the months. Four days after my sister left, I decided to go to El Paso. I said to myself, "I'm going to cross the bridge, and if they send me back, so be it." When I got to the bridge it was just my luck that I got in a line that had a bald-headed Mexican American migración officer. I thought to myself, "Why did I choose this line? The Mexican American officers ask more questions than the Anglo officers, but I'll have to chance it." I said, "American [citizen]." He said, "Where were you born?"

"In El Paso."

"When?"

"In 1950."

"What school did you attend?"

"Bel Air [High School]."

"When did you graduate?"

"1970."

"And what was the school mascot?"

I chuckled and thought for awhile. I wasn't nervous, really. I said, "Oh, sorry. I forgot, because I finished my school a long time ago."

"When did you say you graduated?"

"1970."

"Well, it's the Highlanders."

"Okay."

"Well, go ahead."

So he let me cross. But I was shaking with fear and twisted one of my feet, and the migración officers burst out laughing. I didn't pay attention to them. I just kept walking.

On January 12 I went at 8 A.M. to get my pasaporte. It turned out that the bald-headed man who had asked me all those questions was at one of the windows where I had to go. I thought, "Híjole! What am I going to do? Which window will I get? What if they call me and I have to go see him? Will he recognize me? How can I move away from here? Maybe I should go buy myself some glasses." I tried to stay out of his line of vision as well as I could. I couldn't figure out what to do. I went through several hours of anxiety, walking in and out of there, hiding. When the people in front of me moved, I switched to another spot. I would say to myself, "If he calls me, should I respond?" I kept debating, first thinking yes, then no. Around noon he left for lunch, and I thought, "I've got it made." Then I was called and I ran over to the window. The officer asked me, "Do you have your Form 13?" I responded, "Yes."

"What other documents do you have?"

"That's all. This is the only thing I was asked to bring."

"Well, you need a letter from your place of employment in Mexico."

"But I wasn't told anything about that. I'm working in Chihuahua City."

"Well, I'm sorry. Let me see your Form 13." Then he put me down for another appointment in six months.

I said to myself, "Go to hell with your six months. I'm not coming back."

I called my sister and said, "Those devils denied me the pasaporte. But I'm going to get back to El Paso." I then prayed to San Lorenzo. I have a lot of faith in him. Whenever I find myself in trouble, I go to him. I said, "San Lorencito, if you put blinders on those *viejos* [the immigration officers] I will take you some candles." That afternoon at five I crossed at the same spot where all the viejos were. They didn't notice me. I said, "American." And San Lorenzo helped me. I crossed without any problem.

Villanueva continued crossing the border as an "American." She tried to bring her children to El Paso, but they preferred to remain with her mother in Torreón. In 1979 Villanueva was making plans to marry her boyfriend from El Paso, who had joined the U.S. Army and was in basic training. She was tired of working as a maid and was anxious to move away from the border, where she could get a better job. She had no intention of returning to Mexico, feeling much more at home in the United States.

"I'm not really afraid because I got used to it; I know all the ways to escape the Border Patrol."
                                                        —SANTIAGO MALDONADO

The thousands of illegal crossings that take place every day on the border create myriad situations that often lead to conflict between *indocumentados* and the Border Patrol. Additionally, the interplay between Mexican nationals and Chicanos at times brings to the surface the antipathy that exists between these two groups, a hostility rooted in economic differences and questions of identity. As a resident of Chihuahuita, a poor Chicano neighborhood in El Paso adjacent to the border, biculturalist Santiago Maldonado has had direct involvement with such issues. Maldonado's experiences as an underage farm worker, as a challenger to Border Patrol abuses, and as a pseudo-*coyote* speak eloquently of the tough environment in places like Chihuahuita. (Maldonado's community activism is the subject of a selection in Chapter 7.)

When I was about eight years old, I worked in the cotton fields in the El Paso area. I used to chop weeds and pick chiles and onions. I averaged ten or twelve dollars a day. It all depended on how much I would pick. Even though the child labor laws prohibit kids from working all day long like I was doing, it was common for the parents to take *all* the family to the field. My neighbors used to do it. In any case, sometimes I would go by myself, sometimes with friends, sometimes with relatives. People used to be transported to the fields every day. There was this place *right* across the international bridge coming from Juárez on El Paso Street. Every morning from 4:00 to 5:30 A.M. the buses would leave and go to the farm fields. I would make it a habit to be there on time around 4:00 every morning and get aboard the buses.

The majority who got on the buses were people from Juárez or people from South El Paso. The people from Juárez were Green Carders. I recall one evening when certain Mexican aliens were on the buses and the Immigration and Naturalization Service officials came aboard the buses to inspect to see if anybody was an illegal alien. Somebody behind me got nervous when they saw him. He got all panicky and decided to get out of the bus through the back door. He started running. An officer started running after him. He caught up with him, and what I saw was really something. He beat him up completely. I could hear the Mexican yelling and yelling for the agent to stop beating him up. He was beating him with a club stick, a *macana*. Finally he stopped. The man was put in a van and detained. I guess he was transported back to Mexico. The illegal alien didn't provoke or resist the officer when he was caught. The officer just wanted to make it look like the illegal was really doing all the resisting, and he wasn't. He seemed like a very good man when he was in the bus.

I recall many instances in Dell City and in El Paso when the Immigration raided the fields. The majority of my friends in the fields were illegal aliens. All the time they would talk about being afraid of getting caught by the Border Patrol, which had a habit of checking the fields. Every time we could see they were coming, the Mexicans would run and hide. It was a daily routine, always going on. Some were lucky and some weren't. The Border Patrol also had air surveys at that time, and sometimes it was real hard for these illegal aliens to hide.

At times the Immigration has stopped me simply because I have the same features that a lot of my Mexican friends do. But I always have some identification to provide, and they let me go, with the exception of the time that I was stopped in the Chihuahuita area. This happened when I was fourteen or fifteen. My friends and I decided to travel to Juárez to get some bottles of tequila. We decided that if we went over the bridge the normal, legal way, it was going to take a long time to get there, and we felt that the shortest route was over the railroad bridge. Besides, we didn't have enough money to pay the import tax and we were underage. We went across to the U.S. side, were spotted and detained. One of my friends, who was crippled, was really getting harassed by the officer. That got to me because he couldn't defend himself, so I stepped in. I said, "How come you're harassing him? He already showed you identification. And I'll show you mine." And the agent said, "Well, you know you're not supposed to cross through there, and you're supposed to pay the tax." And I said, "I know. I know we are guilty of doing that." And he said, "Can I see some identification?" I was talking to him in English, but still he had this feeling that I was a Mexican alien. I showed my identification, and he still didn't believe me, so he tried to grab me. He was about my size and I said, "Well, I know I can defend myself," so I started wrestling with him—throwing punches and kicks and everything. I had him on the ground when all of a sudden he starts yelling for another Border Patrol officer to come help him.

Out of nowhere comes this big guy, and he starts hitting me from behind. It all started in the alley near my house, and we went wrestling for about half a block, stopping in front of my house. By then the incident had gotten the attention of the whole neighborhood. My grandfather came out really upset, yelling at the officers to let me go, to stop hitting me. But when nobody was looking, they would really pound at me. I had had a couple of drinks, but I wasn't drunk, and I knew what I was doing. As a matter of fact, I wasn't booked for being drunk; I was booked for assaulting a federal officer. Nobody even knew that I had had a couple of drinks. The Border Patrol turned me over to the police, who took me to the Juvenile Detention Center. I slept there. I was released the next day. My grandparents really scolded me; they didn't like the idea of me passing liquor to this side, but they didn't like the way I was treated, either.

There are other experiences that I recall we had with people from Juárez. I always liked to go to the river and bathe because I didn't have to pay as in the swimming pools in El Paso. People from the U.S. side and people from the Mexican side would bathe together and fights would always erupt. Once some kids from Juárez came at me with a knife, demanding my belt and my shoes. They primarily were kids who liked to sniff glue, and they went around molesting people, wanting what they had. I gave them what I had.

Those incidents caused a lot of ill feelings between both sides. You would see about a hundred people from *that* side and about fifty people from *this* side throwing rocks at each other, right across the river. The problem would spread to the U.S. side and reach to the *presidios* [tenements]. After that, a lot of people didn't go back to the river to bathe. These people from Juárez have also been responsible for a lot of burglaries, a lot of fires, a lot of assaults, and a lot of rapes. I guess to counteract that, when Chicanos saw them coming, they would assault them also. It really got bad. When the police officers and Border Patrol were called in to stop all these acts of violence, they would get pelted with rocks also. It has calmed down quite a bit since about two years ago, when this problem reached its peak and lasted a couple of months. Occasionally you still find sporadic acts of violence.

In terms of Mexicans crossing illegally, I would say that the main crossing point along the entire boundary would be the area half a block from Chihuahuita, adjacent to the river, two blocks to the west of the El Paso–Juárez bridge. More people cross at that point than any other point that I can think of. I've talked to people who have come all the way from South America and from the interior of Mexico, but the majority are usually from Juárez. The reason I'd talk to them is because I live close to the presidios where the aliens used to hide from the Border Patrol, especially in the rest rooms, on the roofs, under cars—you name it, you'll find them everyplace. Sometimes I do my best to help them. I'll tell them, "The Border Patrol is hiding here and there. I would recommend that you cross at this point so you won't be caught." If I have a car, I'll give them a ride. If I can't get transportation, I'll call a taxi to help them. I've done this a lot.

I'm not really afraid because I got used to it. I know all the ways to escape the Border Patrol. I know where to look. I just don't even think about it. My grandfather was caught twice for transporting illegal aliens in the Sierra Blanca area, and he served two jail sentences. The last time he was put on probation. I got a lot of encouragement from him because I really looked up to him, and that's why I started doing it. Plus it was the fun of obtaining money. I don't charge high prices. As a matter of fact, in the majority of the cases I don't even charge. Sometimes if I don't have gasoline in my car, I ask them for a dollar or two. I just do it to help them. When my grandfather was doing this, a lot of illegal aliens were being arrested, rounded up, and transported back to Mexico. The growers were in desperate need of more cheap labor. My grandfather didn't have a job at that time. That was the only avenue he had, and he took it.

People cross at every hour of the day and night. Occasionally Border Patrolmen station themselves in my neighborhood, but because of a lack of manpower and so many people crossing, they have to turn their attention to other locations, so that leaves the opportunity for more people to cross close to my home.

"I used to make twenty to thirty dollars a week selling newspapers, so I really liked it."
—JOSÉ GABALDÓN

The border labor force includes many children who work in the informal sector, engaging in such activities as shining shoes, selling newspapers, peddling candy, cleaning windshields, and serving as "guides" for tourists. Tragically, many of these children drop out of school at an early age, and as adults they wind up in unskilled, low-paying, dead-end jobs. José Gabaldón, a disadvantaged forty-six-year-old immigrant working as a janitor in a U.S. border city, illustrates this life pattern. When he was a child, his family was abandoned by his father, which created many hardships for his mother and his four siblings. José managed to complete five years of schooling in Mexico, but after that he started working in typical odd jobs on the Mexican side. In time he learned about the higher wages paid in the United States, and he began to cross the border illegally. Below he recalls some of his experiences shining shoes and selling newspapers. Of special interest are his recollections of abuses perpetrated by the U.S. Border Patrol.

I started shining shoes when I was about twelve years old and living in Mexico. After school I would go home, eat, grab my shoeshine box, and take off. I made enough to buy whatever I needed, including food, clothes, notebooks, and pencils. Later I sold newspapers. I would get up at four in the morning. At times I would stand by the international bridge, selling newspapers to people who crossed the border. I did good business there because many people would buy them. After that I sold gum and lemons on the street and in the poor *colonias* [neighborhoods].

I remember some bad experiences from those days. Once my drunken uncle threw me out of the house, and I survived in the streets by shining shoes. For two weeks I slept in the cantinas. I would fight with my uncle because he treated us very badly. Then one day he was killed in an explosion in the United States. Another time I was thrown out of a cantina. The owner grabbed me and took my shoeshine box and threw it out in the street. I cried when I saw how the polish and other things I had in the box were scattered all over the place. I was also robbed on one occasion. Three guys took all the money I had.

When I was fourteen some friends who sold newspapers on the U.S. side invited me to join them. I crossed the border by saying I was "American." Many times we stayed overnight in the office where we picked up the newspapers. The guy in charge would let us stay there. He would lock up the place so *la migra* would not catch us. I slept in other places as well, including stairwells in hotels, at the post office, and in rest rooms. Once several of us stayed on the roof of a bank building. It was summertime. Someone saw us and called the police. Suddenly we were awakened by these bright lights that were shined on us. The police must have thought we were there for some other reason, but they checked the roof and found out we were just sleeping, so they let us go.

I used to make twenty to thirty dollars a week selling newspapers. So I really liked it. That was a lot more money than what I could make in Mexico. I helped out my family by giving them money and buying groceries. I also took care of myself. I used to like to dress well so that I wouldn't attract the attention of *la migra*. I crossed the border only on weekends, to avoid problems. *La migra* gave me plenty of trouble. I was caught often. My mother would bring me clean clothes every Wednesday, and at times I would cross into Mexico just to take my dirty clothes home.

Once *la migra* took away all the money I had, which was close to twenty dollars. At that time I would fill up little boxes with dimes. Each box would open automatically when I had put in five dollars. What I would do was to fill each one up to $4.90, and then I would leave them with the boss at the newspaper office for safekeeping. On Saturday nights he would return them to me, because he did not work on Sundays. One Saturday he returned four of those little boxes to me, and I carried them around as I sold the Sunday paper. But *la migra* caught me and threw me across the border. What upset me the most was that they took my boxes. In the car I said to them, "Why are you taking my money?" They just said, "Shut up!" I heard them say something like, "Now we have enough money for breakfast." They talked to each other in English and I couldn't understand everything, but I could make out more or less what they were talking about. So I lost the twenty dollars plus what I had expected to earn that day. Sunday was when one made the most money because the newspapers cost more, and there was more profit. Another time I was apprehended and beaten with a tree branch and then thrown in the river. I didn't want to go into the water; it was kind of cold. The immigration officers just laughed at me.

On another occasion after I was deported I lost a new pair of shoes, but this time that happened on the Mexican side. I had put those shoes on layaway two weeks before, and I had just gotten them from the store when *la migra* apprehended me and sent me back to Mexico. As I was trying to cross back into the United States, two guys who were hanging around at the border assaulted me. One pulled out a dagger, and the other took the shoes off my feet. I was very angry because of the great sacrifice I had made to buy the shoes. I had worn them for only three days. I crossed barefoot and went to a friend's house. He let me wear a pair of his tennis shoes. About three weeks later I was selling newspapers on the street and saw one of the guys walking by. He was wearing my shoes! I didn't say anything to him; I just followed him. Fortunately, he walked in the direction where I knew a friend of mine would be, and I thought, "Between the two of us we'll get this guy." So I explained to my friend what had happened, and we took off after him. We gave him a good beating, but I decided not to get my shoes back. There was no reason to. They were very dirty and didn't look good anymore.

"I had to make my move when there was enough money on the sidewalk."
—SEBASTIAN GONZÁLEZ

For children who work in the streets of border cities, the potential for getting into mischief is ever-present. They frequently succumb to the temptation to cheat and steal in order to make money. Sebastian González, a bicultural professional educator in his forties, was part of the army of young people on the border who earned an honest income from street jobs, but there were times when he ventured into the world of deviant "hustling." He has not forgotten the time he figured out a way to get his hands on some extra cash in broad daylight and right in front of people.

When I was about twelve years old, I was selling newspapers in front of the post office in El Paso. It was Christmastime. There was a lady from the Salvation Army right in front of me, ringing her bell, inviting passersby to make a contribution. She had a "pot" where one could put in a donation, or if away from her one could drop money along a rectangle that had been drawn with chalk along the sidewalk extending for some twenty feet from where she stood. At that time I was easily influenced by what other newspaper boys did, and stealing was a common activity. Kids would routinely go into dime stores, sporting goods stores, or other such places and shoplift. We would also figure out ways to extract money from telephone booths, Coke machines, and candy machines. In other words, we were constantly hustling for money, so seeing all that change on the sidewalk right in front of me presented a big temptation. I started thinking about how to get some of it.

I couldn't very well just grab at it. The Salvation Army lady was too close, and she wouldn't turn her head very often. Once in a while she would gather up all the coins on the sidewalk and put them in her pot. I had to make my move when there was enough money on the sidewalk and just before she decided to collect it. After thinking about it for a while, I devised a plan. I went across the street to a drug store and bought about five big balls of bubble gum. I put as much as I could in my mouth and chewed on it for a while. After the sweetness was gone, I took it out of my mouth and went behind one of the columns of the building, and once out of sight I lit a match to the gum. This made it very sticky. I split the ball in two and applied it to the bottoms of my shoes. I then went back to my usual spot walking on my toes, making sure my unusual movements were not noticed, especially by the Salvation Army lady.

I waited for the right moment when she turned her head, and then I pretended that someone across the street had signaled me to bring a newspaper to him. This was common, and I was running across the street all the time. Before I took off on my fake run I charted my course right over a spot which had quite a few quarters and half dollars. I tore off and pressed my shoes hard over that spot and made it across the street, trying to avoid running too hard so the coins I had picked up would not drop off. I made it to an alley and found a spot out of view from the street. There I took off my shoes and counted my booty. I had picked up a half dollar, three quarters, four dimes, and three nickels—a total of $1.80. This was really good, since in order to earn that much selling newspapers I would have to sell 120 [based on a profit of one and a half cents per newspaper sold]. It would take me a whole day to do that, and here I had done it in less than thirty seconds. I was proud of myself and the ingenious plan I had devised.

I cleaned off the gum from the coins and from my shoes, but it wasn't easy because the gum had become very sticky. It took some time to clean off the shoes. I returned to my spot, somewhat fearful that the Salvation Army lady might have noticed what I had done. She hadn't, and even gave me a friendly smile when I passed by.

In later years I remembered the incident with a mixture of pride and shame. I vowed I would go back and put the money I had stolen in a Salvation Army pot and ease my conscience. Finally during the Christmas season in 1980 I found one of the Salvation Army ladies ringing her little bell, and I dropped a ten-dollar bill into the pot. She smiled and thanked me. I thought to myself, "If she only knew what this is about."

"Just speak softly and carry a big stick."
—FRANCISCO HIDALGO

Taxi drivers around the world are known for their street wisdom and hustling tendencies. In the Mexican border cities, many drivers fit that profile, and their antics are legendary. Francisco Hidalgo, a biculturalist and youthful driver brimming with bravado, reveals *la movida*, the tricks of the trade, in Ciudad Juárez, a city visited by millions of tourists each year. While Hidalgo confirms stereotypes about drivers who are constantly "on the make," he also informs readers of the vulnerabilities and dangers faced by drivers stemming from not knowing the real state of mind or trustworthiness of their customers. (Francisco's struggles to fit into U.S. society are detailed in Chapter 8.)

When my dad decided to be a taxi driver, I started helping him on weekends. I was told that since I knew how to speak English I would be able to "hustle fish" by taking them to Irma's, Caesar's Palace, the Doll House, and all those places [well-known brothels in Juárez]. The other taxi drivers told me all about the system. I liked driving a taxi because I could see that I could make ten dollars in just a short time. *A toda madre* [Fantastic]. I worked Friday night, Saturday night, and Sunday afternoon. I was fifteen at the time, and my grandmother got me the driver's license in Camargo [a town about 230 miles south of Juárez]. I wasn't old enough, but with *feria* [money], one can get it at any age. I didn't have to pay *mordida* [a bribe], though, because my grandmother knew the local traffic chief. I just went one weekend, took the "exam," got the license, and returned to Juárez. The legal age for getting any license is eighteen, and for a chauffeur's license it is twenty-one. For the chauffeur's license, one also needs to take a more difficult oral exam. But I was asked only one question during the exam. If the examiner wants you to pass, he will say your answer is all right; if not, he will say it's not all right. To make sure it will be all right, one tells him, "Help me out and I will give you some feria." That way you pass quickly, no? But I didn't have to pay anything because of my grandmother.

At first I didn't do too well driving the taxi because I was so green and I got embarrassed easily. I didn't know the movida. I would make just a few trips here and there, taking people home at night for a dollar or two dollars. Then the other drivers turned against me because of the way I would answer questions gabachos asked me. They would want to know where the bullring was, and I would say, "Take that street and walk two blocks and you will be there." The drivers jumped on me. "Don't be stupid. Look, here is the way you do it. When they ask you where the bullring is, you tell them, 'Man, it's way out at *la chingada* [fucking far]. I'll take you for two dollars and save you some trouble.'" The idea was to take them all around the side streets, take a one-way street going down, and a one-way street coming up, and make it look like a real trip. Of course, all along we were in the downtown area, but they didn't know the difference. I wasn't stupid, I learned about that right away, and I started doing it. For a gabacho, two dollars was nothing, but for me it was a lot of money, no?

Later I learned more about la movida. Gabachos would come up to you and ask, "Where can I find good-looking chicks?," and all that stuff. Well, there were places all around the downtown area and elsewhere where I could get commissions. I would take them to Irma's, Caesar's Palace, the Doll House, the Horizon Club, El Horizonte, or the Bunny Club. There were a lot of places to take your "fish." We would go in, and the bartender would ask, "What would you like to drink?" The gabacho would order, and the bartender would say, "And for the driver?" The gabacho would then be forced to buy me a drink. "Well, whatever he wants." So I would ask for a *pisto* if I wanted liquor, but if not, I would say, "Give me a *cayetana*." The bartender knew. Cayetana was a drink that looked like beer but it was nothing more than apple cider in a beer bottle. The gabacho was charged for a beer, at a dollar apiece. Later the bartender would give me the money the gabacho paid for what I drank, whether those drinks were "straight" or not. The driver's drinks were on the house, all the time. If the customer just drank, if he didn't go with one of the girls, I would charge him one or two dollars for the trip. I would keep track of the time and try to get more for trips that took longer, but some would not want to pay more. I tried anyway.

When the customer went with a girl, I made more money. If he didn't like the girls in one place, we would go to another. I had to be really alert to collect my 40 percent cut from the girl because she and the customer made their own deal in the room. Of course, the girl collected in advance. She might charge twenty dollars, but she would come out and say, "He paid only ten," and keep the other ten. The girl got 30 percent, the house 30 percent, and I got the rest. Then there was the room charge. They would charge the customer three or five dollars, depending on how much money he had. If he had no more money left, that was the end of it, but if they knew he had money and he didn't want to pay for the room, they would pressure him by telling him that there was no way he could get back the money he had paid the girl. So the guy was forced to pay it, and the driver got 50 percent of that. All that added up for the driver. But I had to be very alert while that went on. Afterward I would say to the customer, "Man, that girl was really fine. How much did she charge you?" If he said twenty dollars, I would go back inside and report her. "This *cabróna* [bitch] charged twenty dollars but reported only ten." Then she would really be in trouble with the house. But I wasn't robbed too often, because the girls liked me since I was so young, and they thought I was cute.

Sometimes I made quite a bit because I would take several gabachos at one time. They would buy me four or five pistos, and then they would go with the girls. I would make twenty, thirty, or forty dollars at one shot. This happened especially during paydays at Fort Bliss, Texas [near El Paso]. I would take two or three soldiers at a time on those trips and then back to Fort Bliss. Of course, many times I would only make five or six dollars a day when I just had a few one-dollar trips, such as taking Mexicans around town. But even then there were opportunities to increase the take. For example, I had this customer, this waiter who always had a lot of quarters. He was always drunk when he took the taxi. Before he got on, he paid me seventy-five cents; that's what I always charged him. We would go one block and he would ask, "I already paid you, right?" I would answer no, and he would give me another seventy-five cents. He would pay me several times. I wasn't robbing him, at least not intentionally. I didn't want to, but . . . everybody worked that way.

Another movida was to sell things to guys who would come around thinking that buying *mota* [marijuana] is as easy as buying cigarettes. They would say,

"Come on, give me a joint." I would tell them I didn't have any mota, but they would insist. I didn't like to be sought after for mota, so I would get angry. I would tell them, "Look, I'll meet you at the rest room at that bar. Just wait for me there." I would then go and buy a box of Faros [the cheapest Mexican cigarettes], trim the ends of each cigarette, loosen them, and reroll them. The Faros would then look like joints, no? At that time I could buy twenty Faros for thirty cents. Pure junk, no? I would go to the bathroom and sell each of them to that guy for a dollar. They would also ask for pills, and I sold them Mejoralitos, the Mexican baby aspirins. I passed them off as speed and bennies. If they doubted these were the real thing, I would say, "The heart-shaped ones are no longer being sold, and we're out of mini whites and mini crosses, but these are better." I sold each one for a quarter or fifty cents, or five dollars a bottle, which had ten or twenty Mejoralitos. How much I charged depended on the customer. Most of them were drunk and wouldn't recognize me if they came around later. Also, whenever I burned someone, I would never drop him off at my cab stand. I would take him to the other side of the strip. When he returned there, he wouldn't find me. There were an infinite number of tricks.

The movida I liked the most was to find a steady customer with money who wanted an arrangement with a woman on a regular basis. I knew so-and-so, who was a prostitute but who had a little class. She was undeclared, no? It was good for her to get a job like that because she could live the whole week just on what she made that day. Then she could get other jobs. I would go where she lived and tell her I had a customer who paid twenty or thirty dollars. Some old men paid twenty dollars, and the chicks laid them right away. The girl and I went fifty-fifty. I was one of the more honest ones. Some *cabrones* [jerks, referring to other taxi drivers] would collect twenty, thirty dollars from the guy and pay the girl only three or five dollars. We met the girls in the bars, at Curley's, at Noa Noa. We saw them hustling there. One day they would be with a black guy and the next with a gabacho, and so on. I got to know them. I would kid around with them. At night they would take a taxi home, so I got to talking to them, and soon I would tell them that I would bring them a customer. Since I was more or less educated and not very corrupted, they trusted me. I would take them a customer, and they wouldn't burn him too badly. They did good work. Later the guy would return and ask me to take him to the same girl. "Orale, simón [Sure, man]."

. . . .

One day a gabacho, a truck driver who worked for the Bekins Moving Company, was at the bar next door to the cab stand, and the owner of the bar, who knew me well, came over and asked me to go see what the gabacho wanted. He was talking and talking, and she couldn't understand him. I found out he wanted to get married to a Mexican woman and live a Mexican lifestyle in El Paso. So I told him, "Sure, that will be easy." The cabrón was quite drunk; he didn't know what he was doing. So I took him to Caesar's Palace, but he didn't like it there because he didn't want a girl who worked in a bar. He wanted something good but cheap. So I said, "Well, let's see. I know some chicks who might want to marry you. If you want, I will introduce you, and if you like them, you can get married." So then I took him to this girl's house, a call girl, but she wasn't home. Next we went to the taxi stand, and I asked one of the drivers if he knew some-one who could do this job. "Simón [Sure]." We quickly went and picked up a girl he knew and took the gabacho and her to a motel so he could get laid and everything would end there. We never thought this guy was taking the whole thing seriously, but he really was. Since we knew he had money with him, be-cause every few minutes he would ask how much he owed us, we drove him everywhere. By the time we got to the motel, he had paid me twenty-five dollars. We expected to get fifty dollars from him for the judge, no? That's what the judges charged for marrying someone. But where were we going to find a judge in Juárez at two in the morning?

We needed to have a base of operations, so we picked the motel. We got the fifty dollars from the gabacho and left him and the girl there and went to get a drink nearby, thinking that the guy would knock out soon. Our plan was to go get the girl when that happened and take off. But when we returned she said, "This guy is crazy. He doesn't want to do anything until we are married." We asked her if she wanted to get married, and she answered, "Well, yes, he seems like a good *chavo* [guy]," and this and that. The gabacho told the girl he was serious about getting married, that he would work in El Paso. So we thought about what we might do. The girl was about twenty-three or twenty-four, and she had two kids. She must have told him about the kids, although I don't know, but since they talked and talked for an hour they must have talked about something. The broad spoke a little English. We said to the guy, "The judge was not avail-able, but we left the fifty dollars with the secretary so tomorrow he is obligated to take care of us. First thing in the morning, man. Where do you want to go? Do you want to stay here with her?" He said he wanted to return to his truck and get his things, for us to drop off the girl at her house and then he would return to Juárez.

By then he didn't seem so crazy; he seemed under control. *Híjole,* things got interesting, no? We split the fifty dollars. The girl got ten, the other driver got twenty, and I got twenty. I dropped off the girl, then the other driver and I took the gabacho to El Paso. I figured he owed me another fifteen dollars because we had made several trips since the last time he paid me when we went to the motel. He said he had more money in the truck. When we got to the truck, the other driver, who was his nephew, was there waiting. He found out what his uncle had been up to and said, "You're crazy. They gypped you, man. Forget about it." The kid had experience. Then he turned to me.

"And you, what are you doing here?"

"I'm the cab driver."

"What do you want?"

"I want to get paid, and he wants me to take him back to Juárez."

"Well, he's not going back and you're not getting paid."

"How come?"

"Because I don't think you deserve fifteen dollars."

"Ask him. I drove him all over town all night. I drove him anywhere he wanted to go, and I'm only charging him fifteen dollars."

"Well, I'm not going to pay you."

The other gabacho said, "Yeah, pay him, man! Pay him!" But no, he didn't want to. He said, "See you later." And he closed the door and started the engine. I was enraged. He wouldn't pay any attention to me, so I got in front of the truck and started throwing fingers and told him to come down and have it out. I threw rocks and whatnot at the truck. We were at the El Paso Terminal, next to the train depot, and there were a lot of trucks parked real close together. I think the guy got really angry at my obscenities because he took off fast toward me. "Hijo de su chingada madre! [Son of a bitch!]" I saw that big truck approaching, it was so wide, and there I was in the middle. The only thing I could do was to grab on to a handle by one of the windows, and there I went, hanging on the truck. I was ready to cry! But the truck slowed down when we came to the overpass. He gave me a chance to get off, so I did.

I walked back and found out he had wrecked trucks on the right and the left when he took off from the parking lot. His own truck was scraped on both sides. By then cops had arrived, because the station attendant had tried to stop him. He had seen me hanging on and had seen the guy hit the other trucks. The cops had radioed the state police, and I found out they stopped him at the New Mexico state line. In the meantime, the migra arrived and questioned me, but I spoke English and had my U.S. citizenship card, so they left. They didn't even find out that I was a cab driver from Juárez and that my car was parked there. I thought about the whole thing and decided to leave. I figured the bastard would come with the cops and tell them he tried to kill me because I tried to rob him, or that I robbed him, and this and that. I said, "It's not worth it." I also had to consider that I was living in Juárez and attending school in El Paso, and that was crooked, no? So I thought, "Let it die here." Who knows what happened eventually. He must have been arrested for hit and run and all that stuff. As far as what he did to me was concerned, they probably didn't do anything because there was no habeas corpus, because I wasn't there. I returned to Juárez, still frightened. I had diarrhea for about three days, and my stomach hurt all over. That was the worst thing that happened to me as a cab driver. It took me about a week to recover from that big one. Afterward, I was tougher and had more anger. I wanted to get revenge from other gabachos.

At other times, customers didn't want to pay me, but a few punches took care of it—and some running. I knew about the danger taxi drivers faced because my dad had warned me from the beginning, especially about the soldiers from Fort Bliss. He had told me, "Look, every new driver will get lost at least once at Fort Bliss, someone will not pay you, and you will suffer a *chinga* [beating]." Once a *camarada* [fellow taxi driver] from the stand next to ours took a load to Fort Bliss, returned, and later they found him dead in a bathroom bar. Almost all drivers have their bar where they go to the bathroom and all that. He had been stabbed at Fort Bliss, and he had gone to that bathroom to find out how bad it was. They had stabbed him with an ice pick and who knows what else. When he got there, he died. His car was full of blood. They said the stabbing had happened in El Paso, but how could the assailants ever be found?

On one occasion, one guy didn't pay me at Fort Bliss. He was a sergeant. The cabrón even left his cap with me and said, "I'll be right back," and so on. We had bullshitted on the way; he became very friendly. He said he was going to pay me double because he didn't have any money. He was very honest before he got on, saying, "I don't have any money. I'm not trying to bull jive you. Nobody wants to take me, but you understand. I'm going to pay you double for your trouble." And so on. We got there, and he never came out, so I went into the barracks, and the MPs quickly took me out. I told them who I was looking for, but the guy had given me a fictitious name. Another time I got lost at Fort Bliss and wound up about seven miles out of town. But I was never attacked, thank God. That's why Juárez drivers carry a *tarifa* [meter] next to them. It is a club they call a tarifa because taxis have meters that tell customers the rates, but nobody pays attention to those; they will pay attention to the club, though. I had one that I made from a pool cue. I taped it up and whatnot. They paid attention to that. That was the tarifa. I kept it under the seat, and I could take it out quickly and swing it. I used it two or three times, but only with drunks, and just to poke them here and there. That's one thing about drunks. They are all right in the car, but once they get to their *colonia,* where they can find rocks and where their *camaradas* are, then they think they're tough. So you poke them, and that's all it takes. Just speak softly and carry a big stick.

"Prostitution is not easy. . . . You have to do it because you need the money."

—SOLEDAD FUENTE

Prostitution is a well-known feature of life along Mexico's northern border. Tijuana
    and Ciudad Juárez in particular were famous as "centers of sin" not only during Pro-
    hibition in the United States but also during World War II, when large numbers of
    American soldiers sought diversion south of the border. In recent years, the U.S.
    "sexual revolution" diminished prostitution in the border cities, though it remains
    important economically. Its social implications are, of course, equally significant.
    When interviewed in Ciudad Juárez in 1976, twenty-eight-year-old Soledad Fuente, a
    uniculturalist, was working in the tourist district. The product of a broken home,
    Soledad rebelled against her domineering mother and her abusive uncle. By the time
    she was fourteen, she was drinking heavily and staying out late at night. Eventually
    she had an affair with a married man and gave birth to a child. Her difficult family
    and economic circumstances led her into prostitution at age sixteen. The portion of
    her story presented below begins with her initial involvement with Anglo men who
    patronized the Juárez red-light district.[3]

One day one of my girlfriends and I went dancing at Curley's Bar. I got all
dressed up and was feeling good. By then I didn't want to drink sodas; I only
wanted hard liquor. I drank quite a bit, and she wanted to take me home, but I
said, "I'm staying here. I have no one, no home, nothing. Leave me alone." She
left. After that I drank heavily every day. Then a friend said to me, "Look,
Chole, don't be dumb. If you're going to be doing that around here, take advantage of it. Don't just drink to drink; use it to make some money from the gabachos." I caught on to that and started making lots of money with the gabachos.
Then I got a job as a go-go dancer at the Crystal Palace, even though I was a
minor. There were six of us dancing there. One day the police raided the place,
and they took us to the juvenile hall, but they let us go and we continued to
dance. I was arrested again and decided to go someplace else, but I had trouble
getting work because I was a minor. Three months before I turned eighteen I was
put in the juvenile hall. Since I was the oldest, they put me in charge of making
sure the girls took showers, but after having to hit someone who didn't want to
shower, I told them I didn't want to do that. They said I would have to, and when
I refused they shaved off my head. I cried loudly.

   That night one of the big shots came to the juvenile hall, asking which girls
had had their heads shaved off. I said to him, "Can't you see, you stupid man,
you son of a bitch." That's what I told him. He said, "You know what, miss?
Neither your mother nor I are at fault that you are here." I answered, "Then,
who is? The mother of your *chingada madre* [fucking mother]?" I was so mad
because they had cut off my hair. He didn't say anything else, he just left. I didn't

care if they put me in jail. Nobody else talked to him that way. The other girls got a big kick out of it.

When I turned eighteen, they let me go. I remember I wore a red scarf over my bare head. My mother was told I was being released, but she didn't bother to pick me up. I said to myself, "So be it. Now where am I going to go without money or anything? And without a wig? Oh, my God!" I walked down the street, crying. I went to my grandmother's house, but it turned out she and her family were in Los Angeles. I decided to go to a friend's house, the girl with whom I had stayed the first time I ran away from home. When she saw me she said, "Jesus, what happened to you?" I explained everything to her, and then I asked her mother if I could stay with them. She said yes, and I lived there for a while. They gave me a wig. But I would keep asking myself, "Why live off these people, always confusing this lady?" I thanked her for her help and told her I was old enough to find my own way in life. I returned to the bar called Noa Noa. Three or four other *pelonas* [hairless women] were there, but of course they had wigs on. Once one of them got drunk and became hysterical. She yelled and cried and took off her wig. She told me to take off mine, but I said no, that if she tried to take it off of me I would kill her. That would have been an embarrassment for me as a woman; hair is what adorns the face. The girls got scared. They told me not to pay any attention to her, that she was drunk and was only kidding. Nothing happened and she left.

At that time my ovaries began to hurt from all the relations I had with men. My stomach would become inflamed, and I would shout like a crazy woman from the pain. When I danced it would hurt especially bad. One of the girls took me to a pharmacy, and I got an injection. Then I raised my feet and the pain eased. But I couldn't work very well. I would have to stay in my room at the hotel where I lived. I would run out of money and wouldn't have enough to pay the rent, so I would tell the manager to give me credit, that I would pay him later. I lived at that hotel for seven years.

Once the father of my daughter looked for me and found me in the hotel. I started to cry. I asked him why he had arranged to have my child taken from me. "You were married and had your own kids. You had no need to take my daughter." He said, "No, it was my mother who did all that. Why would I want the child if I knew she was with you?" But I hated him and his mother. They would bring me my daughter so I could see her, but I would tell his mother not to come near me. He asked me for forgiveness, but I said, "You think that will bring back what I loved so much, my first dream and all of that?" A child is a child; her blood is my blood. One loves them from the time one is carrying them. I cry a lot when I see my child.

In my life, the thing that bothers me the most is that I have always had bad luck with men—always. The first *bato* [guy] I lived with loved me very much.

He gave me everything I wanted. He supported me and gave me a home. Then, wham! He went to California. When he returned, he was crazy. So it was not meant to be with that man. And that's the way things continued to be. I have lived with *batos* who love me and everything, but then one thing or another happens and that's it.

. . . .

I would cross into El Paso with *americanos,* and one night I crossed with three of them. I hid on the floor of the car, and they put their legs over me so the immigration inspector couldn't see me. I heard them say we were going to the airport, but when we stopped we were in the desert. They said, "Take off your clothes." I refused, so one of them threatened me with a knife. "So you won't take them off?" He scared me. I undressed and laid all three. Then they told me to give them a blow job, but I said, "I won't do it. If I don't do that to a Mexican, why would I do it to you?" They put the knife to my stomach, but I said, "I will not do that." They tried to scare me. Then they kicked me out of the car and threw my clothes at me. One of them hit me on the head and blood came out. They got scared and took off without turning their lights on. They must have thought I was going to look at the license plates. I walked, and rocks kept getting into my sandals, and stickers clung to my pants. I cried and cried, and the blood just kept dripping out. Then a Jeep full of soldiers came by, and they tried to put me aboard, but since I was still traumatized, I shouted and tried to scratch them. Only when they slapped me did I regain control. "What happened to you?" They forced me into the Jeep and took me to an office where I was asked if I was a prostitute. I said no, but then one of them said, "Hi, Chole." I thought, "I've had it."

A Puerto Rican soldier took me aside and cleaned my face. He thought he was translating for me, but I was answering all the questions in English. I was asked what punishment I wanted to see the soldiers get. I said three years in jail for the leader and six months for each of the other two. From there they took me to the base hospital, where I was looked after. When the doctor was taking care of me, I thought to myself, "I feel like laying this guy right here." I still didn't realize what had happened to me. I was then taken to the Border Patrol, and one of them kept asking me if I was a whore. I told him that it was none of his business, to leave me in peace. He wouldn't let up, so finally I complained that he was bothering me. He got chewed out and was told to leave. Then they took me home. Later they assigned a lawyer to my case, and I would cross into El Paso and look at soldiers through a two-way mirror. They found the guilty ones because the police found my red brassiere in their car. That was the only thing they had not thrown to me. They must have hidden it in their car and thought that everything was over.

Even after that I continued to accept rides from strangers, from Mexicans or whoever. Sometimes when someone refused to pay me, I would leave the motel or wherever I was and start walking on the highway. Getting a ride was easy. Once I was taken away from the center of town and beaten by one guy while the other one just looked on. I asked him to help me, but the idiot didn't do anything. I yelled and the man bit me; I still have two scars from that. In a moment of anger I bit his ear as though I wanted to swallow it. We struggled, and the other one finally said, "Leave her alone! Let's go!" But my attacker told him to stay out of it. I think he was drunk. They started driving, and I hit the window with all the strength I had and I broke it. At that moment a police car came by and apprehended them. They really worked over that *bato*. The following day my arm was purple all over. After that I didn't ask for rides anymore.

. . . .

I worked independently, because if you worked for a bar, they would charge you for everything, even the toilet paper. Those of us who worked clandestinely [unregistered] could keep all the money we made. The only one we paid was the man in charge of the bar, who protected us from being taken in by officers of the Sanitation Department. He would give them a *mordida* [bribe] and they would let us hustle. It was a good deal for the bar owner because we would drink there. Before I worked out that deal, I was arrested by Sanitation frequently, almost every other day. At times I hardly had money to pay the fines. Once a new chief of sanitation wanted to increase the fines, but the Chamber of Commerce would not go for it. That day all the girls who worked at Curley's were ready to hide in the back just in case they came. But they would come in and find you, even in the bathroom.

For a time I worked at Virginia's, where we were checked by Sanitation every Thursday. They would arrive and give each girl a number and ask us to form a line. One by one we would be examined by the doctor. Part of the exam consisted of opening your legs and having the *pato* ["duck," or examination instrument] inserted to see if you were well or not. It's called a pato because it is shaped like a duck's beak. They insert it in you and then open it, and they are able to see with small mirrors. You have to know how they do it so you can assume the proper position so it won't hurt. Some girls didn't clean themselves, and the doctor would get a whiff of their odor. But he would put up with it. I think they are used to it. Sometimes the doctor would tell some of the girls to clean themselves more often, even with just water if soap was not available. After the exam we would get a card which proved we had passed. Sanitation would go around to the bars and call the girls by name and ask them for their cards. Those without cards would be fined 200 pesos. If you were not there when they came by, they would look for you again. You were obligated to let the bar or Sanitation know that you would not be there. You had to stay in your own bar, otherwise Sanitation would give you problems. Even if you just wanted to have a drink someplace else, you couldn't do that. I had a friend who finally got a special permit from Sanitation allowing her to go drinking by herself because she was tired of the harassment.

I went looking for work in the maquiladoras, but I was asked for a high school diploma and this and that. Why is that diploma so necessary? They put up those factories to provide work and to eliminate prostitution. But how are they going to eliminate it if the employers demand so much? Some of the girls who work in the maquiladoras make 500 pesos a week, others more. Five hundred pesos is not enough, but what one wants is permanent work. At the end of the week, you know they will pay you; your money is assured. Being a prostitute, sometimes you make it and sometimes you don't. When things go well, great. But when they don't, there's not much you can do about it. Prostitution is not easy. You run the risk of being beaten, of being robbed, or getting killed, or of having things done to you that you don't like. You have to do it because you need the money. I spoke with a lawyer who helped some camaradas get jobs in a factory, and he said he would help me. Maybe he will. At the Sanitation office they would tell us, "The president is going to put up some factories so you will stop being prostitutes." And we would say, "Well, build them. You've been saying that for a long time." Nothing happens.

"We had to work a whole week to earn what a worker in the United States could make in one day."
                                              —IRMA LETICIA LÓPEZ MANZANO

Hundreds of thousands of very young women have worked in foreign-owned maquila-
    doras on the Mexican border since the mid-1960s, prompting critics to accuse multi-
    nationals of engaging in widespread exploitation of the most vulnerable sector of
    the local labor force.[4] Unquestionably the companies have enjoyed great advantage
    over the workers, whose acute need for employment makes them ideally suited for
    assembly-line production. Fearful of losing their jobs, few are in a position to com-
    plain. But among the workers are women who have questioned the work environ-
    ment, production quotas, and low wages in the factories. Irma Leticia López Man-
    zano is a uniculturalist and former maquiladora employee who became concerned

about the policies and practices followed in plants where she worked during the late 1970s and early 1980s. She describes problems encountered with the work itself and with management, including harassment for discussing job-related issues with fellow employees. In addition, Ms. López Manzano describes sexual liaisons among female workers and male supervisors, suggesting that it was commonplace in the industry. Also of interest is her recollection of two assaults she suffered, one in Mexico and the other in the United States.

I started working in a maquiladora when I was seventeen. Working there became the thing to do. All my friends had jobs, and I wanted the same thing. At the time, going to school was not my goal. I had left school after the sixth grade and had spent my time helping out at home, sometimes caring for my younger brothers and sisters. I really didn't need to get a job because both of my parents worked, and they provided the essentials, but we lived very modestly. So I felt I could work and earn my own money. I liked having friends and going to dances.

The name of the maquiladora was Toko. It was owned by Japanese. I heard they were hiring, filled out an application, and showed them my birth certificate. They gave me a job immediately. About two hundred people worked there. We made electrical coils, but I never knew what for. We just made that one part and never saw the finished product. I was very happy to get that job. What I didn't realize at the time was that I would develop a big health problem. The soldering that went on irritated my eyes a great deal, and later I had to wear glasses.

After Toko, I worked at Coupon Redemption, where we sorted coupons from hundreds of American companies. Within a short time they promoted me to inspector. By then I had been attending night school and was more aware of my rights and the rights of others. I no longer viewed work just as something to do to earn money to buy things for myself or to help my parents. I had a different vision. We had to work so hard, and they would pay us so little. It was not enough to live on. We knew that the same kind of job in the United States paid a lot more. We had to work a whole week to earn what a worker in the United States could make in one day. I talked about that all the time with other workers at the plant. At the maquiladoras one finds many people who are very aware of what is going on and constantly seek to improve their situation. Not everyone is satisfied with the way things are.

Management became aware that I had those feelings, and they figured it was not in the best interest of the company to keep me. They began to harass me. They chewed me out for any little thing. They took away the privilege that had been given to me to leave work early to attend classes at the university. In some maquiladoras, employees were able to get that kind of permission as long as they were good workers. But when they found out that I was discussing wages and conditions at the plant with other employees and then when we asked for more money and more benefits, they took away the privilege. Also, if I was a few minutes late in the morning, they would not let me into the plant, and I would lose the whole day. At that time transportation to the maquiladoras was very difficult. I would have to leave my house at 5 A.M. to make it to work by 6 A.M.

I was a marked employee. My supervisor knew what was going on, and she would tell me that it would be best for me if I left. Eventually I did resign, but I put up with the harassment for a long time because my plan had been to remain at the coupon maquiladora until I got my degree in social work. There were times when I felt I couldn't take it anymore, but the thought of reaching my goal kept me going. I intended to get my degree no matter what they did to me, but I quit six months before finishing my studies.

One of the worst things I experienced during that period was an assault that occurred about three blocks from my house as I was walking toward the bus stop early one morning. Unfortunately, that day my father didn't walk with me. All of a sudden a car stopped right in front of me, and two men invited me to get in. They seemed to be on drugs. I got very frightened. I looked in all directions, but no one else was around. It was just beginning to get light. They got out of the car, grabbed me, and forced me to get in. I struggled with them and managed to jump out, but I injured myself. I remember hitting the ground, suffering cuts, bruises, swelling, and a loose tooth. But despite the fact that I was in such bad shape and so frightened, I didn't lose consciousness. The men sped off and crashed against a post; then they fled. Later, when we reported the incident, we found out it was a stolen car. The police didn't do anything to find the men. They asked my father for money to conduct the investigation, but we couldn't afford to pay them, so I never heard anything else about the case after that. I was left traumatized. When I would see a man, I would become fearful. Little by little I have been trying to get over it. That happened about ten years ago.

After I received my degree in 1984, I worked as an undocumented person in a factory in Compton, California. I had gone there to visit a brother and stayed three months. I was making $140 a week, which was about four times what I had made in a maquiladora. I was treated well and was impressed by the cleanliness and orderliness at the plant, but I didn't like the work. Since it was by the hour, we were not allowed to waste a single minute. Then I had an experience which really scared me. Two black guys grabbed me on the street. I didn't know if they wanted to rob me or what. I started screaming, and someone from one of the houses nearby came to my rescue. I then said to my brother, "You know, I am making lots of money here, but it's not my country and they don't speak my language. I shouldn't be here, so I'm leaving." I returned to Mexico and began my career as a social worker.

Those were very difficult years, even though not that many bad things happened to me, at least not in comparison to other workers, who have encountered all sorts of dangers, abuses, and bad times. I feel that the maquiladoras have actually promoted prostitution[5] because of the large numbers of women who work there and the favorable position that the men have. I remember there was usually one male supervisor for every twenty women, so that man could make the rounds with all of them. I think the majority of the men did that. I had friends who were supervisors. I saw it. I lived it.

At Ampex, another plant where I worked, I remember two married women who dated their supervisors on weekends. Then there was this woman who liked to have fun, but not in a healthy way. Her husband separated from her and went to the United States. She would leave her three children by themselves, and her mother-in-law took them away. Eventually she got divorced. I would visit her because she was one of my friends. Later she had twin girls, but one of them died. I saw those problems at close range because I liked to interact with the workers.

"I think that some girls consented out of necessity, while others, because of dignity or moral principle, did not."
—RICARDO NAVÁREZ

As suggested in the preceding interview, female maquiladora employees have typically worked on the assembly line, with men serving as supervisors or holding other administrative positions in which they exert control over them. Such authority has allowed the men to use their positions to pursue sexual relationships. Ricardo Navárez, a handsome and likable man who worked in the maquiladoras for twelve years, tells of his experiences with numerous women, offering further testimony of exploitation, promiscuity, and sexual harassment in the plants.[6] Much of the time, Navárez, a uniculturalist, worked as a production supervisor for several major American corporations. At one factory he was in charge of thirty-eight women operators.

The structure of work, the system at the maquiladoras made it easy for the men with authority to have relationships with the women. For example, supervisors had control over the tardiness and absenteeism of the employees under their charge. I had a girlfriend who worked on another shift under a friend of mine. I would ask him to let her go early and sign her card as though she had worked all day. He and others asked me for similar favors if friends of theirs worked on my shift. They would take the women out and bring them back later.

Other men involved in the "corruption of the flesh" were personnel directors and doctors who gave the women physical examinations. In one of the plants there was a personnel officer, an older man with grown children, who liked the young girls who came through his office. He would ask them a lot of stupid questions. I got into a fight with him when I recommended a girl for a job and he asked her if she had spots on her legs. Logically she answered no, but he told her he needed to be sure and for her to show him her legs. Of course, this girl refused. He also asked her if she had spots on her breasts and for her to show him. She refused again. Clearly he had other intentions. I think he was able to have a few relationships by doing that. The girls needed the work, and he was the person who said yes or no. I think that some girls consented out of necessity, while others, because of dignity or moral principles, did not. The doctor at the plant would get very friendly with the girls as he examined them. I think that he was especially talkative with the girls he liked. He would ask some of them out. Whoever accepted, fine, and whoever didn't, fine too.

The system of hiring lends itself even better than the system of supervising to do that kind of thing with the women. As a supervisor, one gets to know the workers very well; one sees them all the time; one has to work with them. You get so familiar with them that they almost become a part of you. On the other hand, those who do the hiring just see them once, or maybe a few additional times once they start working, so if they like a girl, they'll go ahead and make their move. They don't have to worry about constant contact. I saw that practice as a form of moral pressure. A physical as well as moral violation took place. Since the girls were so needful of a job, many of them were willing to do almost anything to get it.

At another factory where I worked, there was a scandal involving one of the supervisors. He practically raped one of the women after a company party or something like that. It seems she was unwilling to go with him, and he scared her; he threatened to fire her, or something like that. So under pressure she consented. She got pregnant and exposed him. They put him in jail. The company then got her to retract her accusation in exchange for 10,000 pesos. That was at the time when the exchange was 12.50 pesos for one dollar, so it was a good sum.

Over the years, I myself had the opportunity to carry on a number of relationships with women at the maquiladoras. In 1969 I was working as a line supervisor. I started dating operators who were not under my supervision. I would go to parties. The affairs I had were with single mothers and married women; I can't remember having affairs with young girls. One of the women was married to a policeman, and they had a daughter. One evening, during a company party, we were talking and she asked me if I would take her home. But on the way she said she didn't want to go home, that she wanted to be with me a while longer, that we should go wherever I wanted. I understood well what she wanted. So we went to a motel. She made me famous around the factory because later a bunch of other operators would joke around with me, asking me to take them home.

At another plant I had a couple of affairs. One of them was with a twenty-four-year-old single mother. She was a big, attractive woman who caught my attention right away. I invited her out and she accepted. From the beginning she knew what I wanted, and I knew she wanted it too. We understood each other well and continued going out for some time. Then she married a policeman who later went to jail for dealing in drugs. He must have treated her very badly because she really looked terrible after three or four years of marriage.

The other affair I had was with a nineteen-year-old married woman who had two children. She must have gotten married when she was thirteen or fourteen. I thought of her as a "child mother." She was a good operator, but sometimes she would do things that bothered me, and I had to bring them to her attention. I really didn't want to have relations with her, being that she was so young and had children, but I guess what happened had to happen. One problem was that she got very possessive. I couldn't talk with any of the other girls or bring them over to my desk to point things out to them because she would object. She would wait for me when I left work. I had to put up with jealousy scenes. That was one of the reasons I left that plant. The other was that I was offered a job at higher pay at another factory.

Throughout my years at the maquiladoras I went to many private parties, what we called *encerrones* [lock-outs]. My first experience with encerrones happened with a friend named Sylvia and a friend of hers named Lucy. I had already had an affair with Sylvia. On one occasion Sylvia, Lucy, and I went out drinking. We had a good time and decided to get together again the following day. We met at the place I had suggested. After a while Sylvia's friend said she didn't want to continue drinking, that she was tired, that she wanted to rest and sleep. She asked me to rent her a room at a nearby hotel so that the both of them could get some rest. We did that, but once at the hotel Lucy asked me to stay. Sylvia was opposed to that, but Lucy was very insistent. I had relations with both of them. After that Sylvia and I continued to see each other, as if nothing unusual had happened. I also went out with Lucy once in a while.

One day I committed an indiscretion: I mentioned my relationship with Sylvia and Lucy to a friend at work named Paco. He suggested that the four of us get together so we went out one day. Paco managed to convince Lucy to go to bed with him, and I had no trouble convincing Sylvia. About two weeks later a new girl at the maquiladora started hanging around with Sylvia and Lucy, and she became part of the group. We would get together regularly: three guys and three women, or two guys and three women. We did that for about a year. It became fashionable at that maquiladora to have those kinds of parties. I imagine that kind of thing went on in other maquiladoras as well. The women know each other; they meet each other on the bus and talk about their social life.

7

FUNCTIONARIES AND ACTIVISTS

This chapter brings together the reminiscences of individuals from two different camps: on one side are functionaries concerned with stopping or minimizing the surreptitious movement of people and products across the international boundary, and on the other are persons who seek to prevent abuses of human rights by zealous border enforcers or government institutions. Also included are memoirs of activists concerned with labor exploitation and ethnic discrimination.

From the point of view of the U.S. government and that of many Americans with a national rather than a transnational orientation, what is disturbing about cross-border migration is the massive number of people who enter the United States without proper documentation. Therefore, one of the major challenges for the authorities in the borderlands is to curtail illegal immigration. Another significant problem is drug trafficking. In the past several decades, many tons of marijuana, heroin, and cocaine have made their way into the U.S. border cities and far into the interior. Drugs have become an issue with very high visibility and a high priority for policymakers in Washington. In attempting to resolve these problems, the U.S. government has relied on various border law-enforcement bureaucracies. The agency charged with the task of stopping undocumented migration is the Border Patrol, an entity within the Immigration and Naturalization Service. Prior to 1924, when Congress officially established the Border Patrol, the prevention of immigration by undocumented people was carried out by a few dozen mounted immigration agents who received assistance from Texas Rangers and other local law enforcement officials. With the great increase in the undocumented traffic since World War II, the Border Patrol has grown substantially. Its offices and detention centers are now located in many communities on the border.

One of the most interesting developments in the organization of the Border Patrol in recent years is the rising number of Mexican American frontline officers. Many of them are children or grandchildren of immigrants, and in some

cases their parents and grandparents themselves entered the United States illegally. How ironic, then, that Mexican American agents now apprehend people
with whom they share an ethnic affinity and common history. At the policy-
making level, the individual who has personified that contradiction most dramatically is Leonel Castillo, a Mexican American politician from Houston who
served as the INS commissioner during the Carter administration. Despite (or
because of) his ethnicity, many Chicano activists found it exceedingly difficult
to maintain a positive relationship with him, since a major part of his responsibility as INS head was to oversee the Border Patrol. The hostility Castillo encountered in some Chicano communities puzzled him because he deliberately
downplayed the enforcement side of his job, emphasizing instead the improvement of services for immigrants within the INS bureaucracy. This policy not only
failed to placate his Chicano critics, it also alienated the Anglo community. Thus
Castillo was in a no-win situation. His own account of his experiences as INS
commissioner constitute the first selection in this chapter. Other interviews on
the issue of immigration include the perspectives of an "enlightened" Anglo
Border Patrol officer, Chicano activists who challenge the INS and its agents, and
a compassionate clergyman who provides asylum for undocumented refugees.

Another major border agency is the U.S. Customs Service, which is charged
with collecting tariffs and interdicting contraband. As far back as the 1850s,
horsemen with the Customs Mounted Patrol guarded the border, apprehending
horse thieves, cattle rustlers, and smugglers of all shades who hailed from both
Mexico and the United States. In time, horses gave way to automobiles and
airplanes, and the work of the Customs Service became much more complex.
Insights into the challenges posed by drug trafficking in recent years are con-
veyed by a U.S. Customs agent who has faced his share of dangers.[1]

Labor activism is another basic theme in the history of economic relations
along the border. In the past century, many unions have been formed, many
strikes have been called, and many leaders and spokespersons have led movements on behalf of frontier workers, but the task of improving conditions for the
workers has been a difficult one. Employers have had the upper hand because of
the abundance of labor, the easy availability of undocumented people who are
willing to work for low wages, and the regional political climate, which has
favored capital over labor. Consequently, conflict between management and labor has been constant. In the Arizona borderlands, the most serious confrontations have occurred in the copper mining districts, while in the California and
Texas border areas, strife in the agricultural fields has been widespread. In the
border cities, workers have organized strikes against factories, packinghouses,
smelters, refineries, and service establishments.[2]

Three interviews in this chapter focus on the experiences of leaders who have
struggled to improve the lot of industrial and agricultural workers, and a fourth

interview tells the story of an Anglo bishop who supported one of the most significant border strikes of recent times, the Farah strike in El Paso. These advocates of workers' rights carry on a long tradition of activism born of exploitation, poor working conditions, and hostility to unionism.

The final three interviews spotlight Chicanos who have been deeply involved in border community issues. Their activism began during the 1960s, when the Chicano Movement created awareness about the need for social change and the role that individuals could play in achieving it. At the time, activists loudly called attention to such problems as poverty, educational underachievement, the abuse of immigrants, and discrimination.[3]

"We used to joke that the only government official who got picketed more than me was Jimmy Carter."
— LEONEL CASTILLO

Houston native Leonel Castillo, a bicultural non-borderlander who served as the commissioner of the U.S. Immigration and Naturalization Service from 1977 to 1980, maintained a higher profile than many of his predecessors in that post. He confronted thorny issues directly, and he constantly visited trouble spots along the border. Castillo's term as the chief enforcer of U.S. immigration policy came at a time when Mexican undocumented immigration was commanding extraordinary attention throughout the United States. Given his Mexican American background, Anglo critics often accused him of being partial to the interests of immigrants, while Chicano activists at times denounced him as a traitor to La Raza (the Mexican people). Castillo's previous experience as a big-city politician helped him to weather the storm inherent in his job. His story affords a rare inside view of a functionary attempting to reform a hardened bureaucracy while confronting an emotionally charged public arena.

I wasn't interested at all in becoming INS Commissioner. As a matter of fact, I had been offered several jobs in Washington previously because I had been the state treasurer of the Democratic party in Texas and because (as comptroller of Houston) I was one of the highest elected Mexican Americans in the country at the time. The Carter administration had offered me positions involved in management, budget, and administrative types of responsibilities. I didn't want to leave Houston and go to Washington to do exactly what I did in Houston. Even though I would have a bigger budget, it would still be essentially the same problems, so I turned down those offers.

But one day in February or March of 1977, I got a call from Joe Aragón, the presidential assistant at the White House. He asked me if I was interested in being commissioner of the Immigration and Naturalization Service, and I told him that I did not believe in political suicide, that I didn't want any such gift, that it just made no sense. Joe said that he was very sorry to hear that because he had already recommended me. He added that I had a moral obligation to do all I could to help La Raza, and that if I didn't take it, somebody really bad was going to get it. After some discussion, I told him I'd discuss it with my wife but that it wasn't too likely I'd accept. After all, I had a good future in Texas. I was in line to be treasurer of the state. It looked very good; I had support from some very powerful groups. The treasurer at the time, Jesse James, was very clearly on his last legs, and it looked like I was the heir apparent. The governor was not against the idea, and neither was James. So, if I took the commissioner job, I would have to give that up.

I discussed the matter with several people and decided that, while it was not a very attractive job, it offered the opportunity to do something important, and it had a lot of moral imperative to it. Most people advised me, "Don't do it. It interrupts everything. It messes up everything. You're pretty safe in Houston as comptroller. You can go from there to a lot of other things. If you go to Washington, you will give up your great base for a thankless job, a job with no future in it. What are you going to get out of it?" The more idealistic persons, I call them more activist persons, like Joe Bernal [a Texas state representative from San Antonio], were the ones who urged me to take the job. Bernal said, "You've got to do it, because look at all the good we can do for La Raza. You have no choice." I listened to both sides and went to Washington. I don't regret it at all.

. . . .

During the swearing-in ceremony at the White House, the president said that I was getting one of the jobs that was as difficult as any in Washington, including his own, and that he was very glad I was getting it because of my background, and because he thought my sensitivity and knowledge of Mexican Americans would be very helpful in dealing with the other immigrants coming into the country. And that the administrative background as comptroller would be very helpful. He was very, very generous in his comments, I thought. He didn't have to be. He could've just said, "These are important posts which are being filled today, I'm delighted to have very qualified people." He went beyond that in my case.

. . . .

The official, formal reaction within government agencies to new leadership is always, "We'll work with the president's appointee," and "We're glad you're here," and "We're eager to help." But of course, the actual reaction at INS was . . . There was a view within INS that General Leonard Chapman [the outgoing commissioner] was right, that the focus should be on aggressive border policy and lots and lots more emphasis on enforcement. That was a very, very strong view within the agency, so I had to find my allies very quickly and issue orders relatively early on what I wanted done. The same afternoon that I was sworn in I issued orders to start working on the backlogs of the people who were legal immigrants but weren't getting service. I moved quickly on that. I'd even had the orders prepared in advance by an old-timer at INS who agreed with me. That gave a very clear direction to the agency that I wanted service as well as enforcement. It didn't sit well with a lot of people, because they wanted the first emphasis to be on enforcement.

Within a week I was embroiled in all the debates about enforcement and service, and that went on through the whole time I was commissioner, and it's still going on. Enforcement had always had the highest priority, and this made it clear that I wanted another priority as well. There was the usual bureaucratic infighting, where things just take forever to get done. In addition, some members of the staff, both at the national and local levels, started leaking stories to the press about things I was doing that they disagreed with. They immediately told the press that I was giving the country away to the Mexicans or that I was spending too much money on low priorities, and I should be spending money on enforcement, that they were being shortchanged—all sorts of things about me personally and about my priorities. It was all a way to get to me.

There were little jokes about how everybody would have to learn how to speak Spanish in the central office, or that personnel wouldn't get promoted if they didn't have Spanish surnames. Or, "Castillo is setting up the Mexican corner of the central office." Just all sorts of little things that would trickle back to me, snotty little things. Every now and then I'd get really nasty letters. I've gotten those all my life, ever since I've been in public office. These were Ku Klux Klan type of garbage, like, "Go back to Mexico or we'll kick you ass back." Or something less friendly than that. Some were anonymous; most were signed but had no address. Every now and then we'd find swastikas in some of the elevators. I got a lot of putrid mail. I've always gotten that. I always assume I'm going to get that if I'm combating racism or bigotry. I usually threw them away. They don't make for good reading.

I was sworn in on a Friday. By the next Tuesday I was in Los Angeles and San Diego, visiting offices and talking with people. The political climate was hot at the time. My news conference in San Diego was filled with reporters, all asking what I was going to do to stop the "invasion" of the undocumented. They were very upset, very excited, demanding action. On that tour I wanted to see things on my own. It was very enlightening. At the Los Angeles district office I found employees using ancient manual typewriters and adding machines that weren't produced anymore, really antique-type machines. Thousands of people were standing around waiting, trying to get in the office. I found no one able to answer the phone. It took two, three days to get a call answered. The mail couldn't be answered because they couldn't even get around to opening it. They had all these enormous administrative problems. There was no automation even though there were hundreds of thousands of files. A lot of employees didn't speak Spanish or other languages. The port-a-can toilets that were used for the people we were detaining and deporting were right in the federal building. It was *just one stinky, stinky place*. You couldn't imagine the smell and the stench that an indoor use of port-a-cans can have. I immediately ordered a lot of changes there.

While in office I traveled 50 or 60 percent of the time. I was constantly show-ing up in an office, sometimes announced, sometimes unannounced. It was really helpful. I was treated rudely or badly several times when I showed up unan-nounced. Once I tried to get an appointment at a district office, and they wouldn't see me. I wasn't dressed all that well, apparently, and they didn't know who I was, so they just told me to sit. I had to sit and be treated like everybody else. And that was good, because that way I was able to learn how everybody else was treated. I didn't want to know how the dignitaries were treated; I know how they're treated. I wanted to know how the average person was treated. I just sat there, until finally, one of my aides couldn't take it any longer and he had to tell them who I was. Later they expected it. One of my most delightful visits was one morning at the Bridge of the Americas in El Paso. I'd flown in from somewhere and I landed in El Paso at 3 A.M. There were a couple of Border Patrolmen there to meet me and drive me to the hotel because I had some meet-ings in the morning. On the way to the hotel, I told them, "Let's go to the bridge." They said, "Yeah, but they're not waiting for you." And I said, "I know that . . . and don't call ahead." I had a very delightful short visit with a couple of inspectors who were sitting there drinking coffee, waiting to inspect the traffic. I learned a lot about how to maintain the bridges, what they thought was important, and so on. I don't think they'll ever be visited by another com-missioner at 4 A.M.

I went to the San Diego border on several occasions. The first time I had a very weird, strange feeling because I wanted to see everything I could. I was put on a helicopter so I could see the people who were trying to cross. You're sup-posed to take the helicopter's spotlight and find Mexicans—shine the light on them. That way you tell the officers on land where to go catch them. It's like a herding. It's a *very* weird sensation when you get that spotlight and start looking for people under bushes. In effect, you're stalking human beings. You're part of this great big international drama. Later we landed and sat on one of the hilltops and looked through infrared scopes. It was really dark out there. These things are able to sense heat, so you can see people. By using that equipment you can tell how many persons are out there, and you can tell the Border Patrol where to go to apprehend the large groups. You pick up all these people and you put them in the Jeeps or vans and you take them to your central facility. Usually very shortly after that they're deported to Mexico. A short time later they're trying to cross again, so it's all an unbelievable exercise. The press had lots and lots of reporters down there who often compared the border to Vietnam. I think that's too much of an exaggeration. There isn't the bloodshed and violence of Vietnam, but there is the same kind of game involving people sneaking back and forth and going through the lines.

I once mentioned to a reporter from the L.A. *Times* that sometimes when you apprehend all these people you really manage to make yourself feel like a real shit even though you're enforcing the laws. In most cases you're deporting young men and women, and you know their sole reason for coming is work. They're not really a security threat; they're not a criminal element at all. So you have very bad feelings often when you do this. What most of the people on the line try to do is to say "It's my job," and just avoid feelings, which is probably the only way they can live with it. When the reporter wrote the story, he gave me a bad time, saying that policy was too lax. You can't sympathize with the person being apprehended or the one doing the apprehending until you're there.

I spoke with hundreds of undocumenteds. And in all the time I was with undocumenteds I never felt threatened. Whenever I was in a room that was full of undocumenteds, maybe forty or fifty of them and only one security officer and myself, I never felt like they were going to attack me. I just never worried or felt nervous, and I was, in some cases, in very demonstrative groups all over the country. I would walk in, and they would all want to know if I could help them, that the *coyote* misled them or took all their money, leaving them broke in San Diego or El Paso or New York City. What could they do to get their money back? Of course, they couldn't do anything. Others would ask for a cigarette, or if you could help them enter the country legally, or if you could please deport them quickly so they could go home. In some cases they complained about the food or the facility.

I remember one group of women in Chicago that was kind of interesting because it was so spunky. They had been apprehended at some factory. They were eating their lunch—tortillas and beans and what not. I was talking with the ladies about how they had been treated and things of that sort, and one of them said, "You're never going to catch me here again." I said, "Why is that? We're deporting you. You mean you're not coming back?" She said, "No, I just mean you're never going to catch me here again." All the other women had a ball explaining to me the obvious, that she was going to come back but would avoid being apprehended.

And then there was a group in Houston who included a young man, I think he was a Central American. He told me that he worked with a construction company and many of the workers were undocumented, that the *patrón* really liked the undocumenteds because when it came to working overtime or under hard conditions, the undocumenteds stayed until they were chased off the job. He was real proud of that. He said that the American workers would go home at the first *chispas,* drops of rain, but the undocumenteds would work until they were *told* to go home. He said that they were more honorable people than the Americans, because they worked harder and therefore they were better. He was very, very proud. I asked him why someone as articulate as he had not gone to a university. He said he wanted to, but there was no money; he was hoping to make enough money in the United States to study a profession. I don't know if he made it or not; we deported him.

Then there's the deportation of young children. I've interviewed some of them as well. Shortly before I left the agency, I made a trip to Mexico City on a regular flight. When the plane stopped in San Antonio, it was met by a Border Patrol officer, who brought on board some young men and women. They sat toward the back of the plane, and for all anyone knew they were just regular passengers. Obviously they didn't speak very much English. I went and spoke with three boys who were together. Their ages were seventeen, fourteen, and thirteen. We conversed for a good while about why they had come, what they had done, and so on. They had come from Colombia with the help of a *coyote.* They traveled from Medellin through Mexico and all the way to San Antonio, Texas. The seventeen-year-old, a bright young man, took responsibility for two younger brothers. At the time that he was apprehended, the seventeen-year-old was working full-time at a regular construction job and the kids were enrolled in school. He had enrolled the two younger ones in school and was supporting them; he was running the household. He was a very capable and impressive young man, the type you'd *really* like to have on your team, working for you. I'm sure that that young man, if he wants to, will be coming back to the United States, or will be an important figure in Colombia—if he isn't killed or lost somewhere.

. . . .

The people we apprehend are not dangerous, or the type to attempt escape. They don't have those instincts. There are only twelve cells in the whole United States for all undocumented aliens. At no time during the entire two and a half years that I was commissioner were all twelve cells filled. We kept the people in dormitory facilities. Those cells were used mostly to isolate people with contagious diseases or psychological problems, or to keep someone away from the other aliens. In a few cases, children or homosexuals were separated for their own protection. The apprehended undocumenteds outnumber the officers by tremendous percentages, and yet they are relatively mild-mannered. We had few instances of anyone being attacked or people overpowering the guard, or something of that sort.

. . . .

The Task Force on Immigration, consisting of Cabinet members and White House staff, had been working for some time to formulate a new immigration policy before I became head of INS in May of 1977. Predictably, the group had been met with skepticism among the old-timers, but there was great optimism on the part of the Carter people that they could resolve the immigration problem like they were going to resolve a lot of others. When I got there, much of the Carter plan had already been designed. I only sat in on a few meetings. Several concepts were easily established with little disagreement. One was the notion that we should legalize many of the people who had been here for some time with no papers. This unfortunately became known as amnesty. There was some hang-up about what to do with those people who didn't qualify for amnesty because they had been here too short a time and wouldn't benefit at all from the new policy. The resolution of this problem came about as a result of Attorney General Griffin Bell, who thought the best way to do it would be to create a new status called Temporary Resident Alien. The idea was to give people a form of temporary worker status without giving social service benefits. Bell's thinking was that they never asked for the benefits anyway, so the government would not be taking anything away from them. Some in the group argued that that would cause a great reaction among civil rights groups, but Bell's idea prevailed. The plan also called for a major beefing up of the enforcement, adding two thousand Border Patrol officers to the service. At that time that meant almost doubling the size of the Border Patrol, but as a result of budget cuts and budget balances and what not, only twenty-five or thirty Border Patrol officers were added in all the time I was commissioner. The plan drew attacks from both the left and the right. It didn't get much support from the Senate, and it never even got to a hearing in the House. Very few people even showed up. Members of the Senate themselves didn't show up for the perfunctory hearings.

I took part in some of the discussions of the task force. I was pushing hard at that time for streamlining the service and getting administrative support. I thought they were being too ambitious trying to get this huge plan in. It appeared to me the service could never run such a huge program. At one Cabinet-level meeting that I attended, the president was present. He convened the meeting and gave the group about forty minutes to discuss the key elements of the new plan. They went all around the table. After they had completed their discussion on what should be done, the president asked me what I thought about it. I said, "Well, Mr. President, I hate to disagree with my boss." Griffin Bell had just spoken on something, and he was my boss at the Department of Justice. The president answered, "Well, Leonel, I want you to know you have more than one boss." I said, "Yes sir. Well, my view is that what we really need at the Immigration Service more than all of these things, most of which are very critical issues, is typewriters. We need to have the capacity to process what we've got. There's no way we could handle another million people, an amnesty program, and all those other things. We aren't even able to answer our mail." He was very impressed with that and ordered some folks to help us with the administrative stuff, to get us some support, but very little happened. He was very interested in the fact that I was looking at administrative issues and that a lot of the other issues were just pie-in-the-sky.

The plan served the purpose of testing the waters. That is, it indicated just how tough things were going to be, and it gave us a clear view as to which ideas would sell and which ones wouldn't. It also gave us a good picture about who the allies were and who the opponents were. The plan was a compromise among many factions. The president tried to compromise with all the warring factions. He took midpoints on many of the issues. In hindsight, I feel like he would have been much better advised to have taken a position a little more to the left or a little more to the right and then presented it as the moral imperative, not as the "reasonable" plan. I think that would have attracted at least some strong allies. Taking a middle position on immigration issues angers everybody and pleases no one.

The problem was that the president and everybody else were selling the plan in a lukewarm fashion, in a reasonable fashion. That is a very bad way to present a proposal, because the way things work in Washington, you're either all for it or you're dead. You've got to push very hard as an advocate. If you're trying to present a reasonable plan, you know you're in trouble. And of course everybody had to find a focal point for kicking the plan. Obviously I was the focal point of demonstrators or protesters who would go to various places where I would be or to conferences on the issue. We used to joke that the only government official who got picketed more than me was Jimmy Carter.

Sometimes demonstrators would come inside where I was speaking, and sometimes they would stay outside. I knew those kinds of demonstrations were nothing new. There were so many that I just didn't bother with them lots of times. Every now and then I'd go out and talk to the demonstrators. In one case I even invited them up on the podium. The group was called the Council of Spanish Speaking Health Organizations. They were in Houston for their annual convention. They invited me to be a speaker the night of their final event. Some of them were demonstrating outside, but some came inside. Some walked out while I was speaking. A few called me names, and others started chanting. To avoid problems for the people in charge of the event—that is, so they wouldn't call the police or something—I invited the group that was against me to take fifteen minutes of my time, and I would even answer their questions. I did, and I turned into a pretty exciting after-dinner speaker.

Some of the other groups were pretty shabby in their approach—yelling, wanting to speak, trying to put up all sorts of signs, etc. Once I was in Laredo for a LULAC conference, and the protesters had up signs in which they accused me of being a murderer because a pregnant woman had died, and of course the baby had also died, as a result of problems she'd had at a border crossing point in Progreso, Texas. The irony of the whole thing was that the person who had inspected her had been from Customs and not INS. But still they sued me and raised a big stink. The Chicano group carried all kinds of signs calling me a baby killer, an assassin, and all sorts of things. One version has it that the woman was bringing over a maid who was undocumented. Her family's version was that the inspector was extra rough on her. They alleged the questioning was so rough that she got very nervous and that led to the problems. The inspector was trained as a paramedic and did try to provide first aid, and they did call for help. But Progreso is a little out of the way. By the time the ambulance came it was too late. That happened during the summer of 1978.

There were people who made a point of making wild statements and issuing news releases to the press. I thought some of the news releases were very irresponsible, but in some cases they said things that had to be said. I was often on the defensive, trying to explain policy. Some people, of course, were demanding more representation of blacks, Chicanos, and women.

I took all of that demonstrating with a grain of salt. I've been a demonstrator myself [during the civil rights days]. I tried to separate myself from the fact that they were demonstrating against a particular policy, a particular program, or a particular position, rather than against me personally. I guess the one situation that was most interesting occurred around November of 1977. I spoke in San Diego at the conference of the National Association of Social Workers. While I was speaking, a Chicano group was demonstrating. They were hitting the windows and making a lot of noise. Then they got into the hotel and chanted in the hallway. You could hear it right through the halls. Then one of them stormed in with a lot of petitions, demanded that I take them, and stormed out.

On my later trips to San Diego I almost always had bodyguards. I would even get out the back door of the plane. I would not go through the terminals. I'd get off the plane and then go into a waiting police car or a Border Patrol car. It wasn't because of my importance. It was because the police were worried about security. I had a number of threats. People would call up and say they were going to get me or call somebody else and say they were going to kill me. Some of my

staff would get nervous. In one instance in Arizona we had security people outside my hotel room all night, in the parking lot, and in other places.

I didn't go out drinking on trips. I had to be extra careful late at night. Some
of my assistants were also very careful. They would protect me, but not so much
from physical harm as from general intrusion. The commissioner of immigration
has an enormous amount of power, some perceived and some real. If I was in
New York City, I might get a call at 2 A.M. or 5 A.M. from people who wanted
my help, or someone hadn't seen his spouse in eight years. What could I do? I
would get notes under my hotel room door. I remember once I landed in the L.A.
airport and a woman asked me to prevent the deportation of her son, who was
being deported on drug charges. He had grown up in this country and had never
lived abroad. She wondered what I could do. I don't know how she ever found
out I was going to be landing in Los Angeles. It got to where I couldn't go to
certain places without people stopping me and asking for some benefit or some
help, or wanting to tell me their story, so my aides would sometimes check us
into a hotel under their name, and all the phone calls would go to their room, not
to mine. That way I would get a little sleep.

In some instances the press was merciless. I had a fellow call me once in San
Diego. It must have been 1 or 2 A.M., and I was asleep. The guy informs me
that I'm live on radio, that it's a talk show, and people will have some questions
for me. He heard I was in town, found out where I was staying, and hoped that
I didn't mind the intrusion. And there I was, sound asleep on radio. The press
was just eager to get the news.

. . . .

The Ku Klux Klan episode is a perfect illustration of how groups can use the
media and cause problems everywhere. The Mexican and American press gave
an enormous amount of space to the activities of the Klan. As best I could tell,
the Klan never had more than twelve people on the border at any one time. They
did have news conferences at different places. Apparently at times they would
get on a plane and have a news conference at one place, then go elsewhere and
have another one, and so on. The groups that protested against them always
completely outnumbered them, but the press outnumbered everybody.

When the Klan visited our facility in San Diego, the Chicano groups there
raised Cain. Yet you can't close the facility to anybody; it's a public place. The
Klan walked in, held a news conference, and said how they were going to help
us. Of course we said we didn't want their help and that they would be arrested
if they did anything, but they kept holding news conferences all up and down the
border. Different Chicano groups then said they were going to arm and go after
them. Rumors spread that the Mexican police were going to the border to deal

with the Klan. We spent hundreds of hours dealing with the press and looking for the Klan. As best we can tell, all the Klan ever did was to arrest one Mexican near San Clemente, California. They grabbed his Green Card, threw it away, and brought him into the Border Patrol office. The Border Patrol officers questioned him and found out he was in the United States legally. They went where he said the Klan had thrown his green card and found it. We prosecuted the Klansmen, and they were found guilty of false arrest.

That was the only case in which the Klan actually did something. Mostly they held news conferences. The Klan kept making statements, and the Mexican and American press kept buying them. The Klan was front page all over Mexico City for weeks. We told the press there wasn't much to it, that there were no arrests, but no one would believe us. It was just amazing. The Mexican newspapers included pictures of lynchings that had taken place in the 1920s and histories of the Klan and its role in segregation. They replayed all of this as if it had happened in the last week on the Mexican border when in fact it just wasn't so. The U.S. press obliged by reporting what the Mexican press said. For a while everybody in Mexico was convinced that the Klansmen were torturing and killing Mexicans all up and down the border and were a part of the Border Patrol. Some Chicano groups demanded that we arrest the Klan or that we issue strong statements saying we would not cooperate with them or have anything to do with them, and so on. There were some unbelievably emotional reactions to that issue. While one shouldn't play down the fact that the Klan has been horrible and can be horrible, in this instance the press stories were far more overreaching than the actual activities of the Klan. To our knowledge, they never showed up on patrol. We looked for them everywhere. We even had emergency plans all up and down the border just in case they did show up.

. . . .

In 1979, immigration inspectors at the Santa Fe bridge in El Paso stopped the buses coming from Juárez during a special program of raids. They found that a lot of people had no papers, so they started deporting them. They sent them all back through one bridge. That caused a traffic jam, and the traffic jam led to demonstrations. The first thing we knew, the three major international bridges were closed because of the demonstrations. We had a very serious question of what to do. The Mexican police were getting ready to use force to evict the protesters, while our police were reluctant to get near the bridge or to go beyond a certain point. The Border Patrol played it very quietly in that instance by simply collecting forces and staying out of sight behind the bridge. They weren't visible to the demonstrators; they were held more in ready than visibly present. The incident lasted almost a whole weekend. It might have been worse had not a very unfortunate thing happened. One woman somehow tried to drive through the crowd, panicked, and ran over a twelve-year-old girl, killing her. That defused the whole thing in a sad way. I don't know what would've happened had that woman not panicked. The violence could have been turned more outward than inward; there could have been a much more serious incident, in terms of more people getting hurt. The demonstrators suddenly began to ask, "What are we doing here?" and "Isn't this pretty horrible?" Many got worried that maybe they would get hurt or something. I don't know, it demoralized everybody. It was a very sad accident.

Had it been a death caused by an action of the Border Patrol or a U.S. police officer, then there could've been more demonstrations and much more action. There were, of course, protests that were immediately linked to the deportations that had nothing to do with the Immigration Service. There were people who showed up with signs asking for better treatment of taxi drivers, and there was a Marxist group that showed up right away with leaflets, blasting imperialism. My guess is that if the radical groups had any organizing ability, they could cause one *hell* of a mess along the border. Luckily for us they don't; up to now they've demonstrated very poor organizing ability. It's very easy to close a bridge; it's very easy to sabotage that whole process. It takes almost no brains and very little planning, and you don't have to injure people. We worry about terrorism all over the world, but one grenade dropped on a bridge at 3 A.M. on a delayed reaction would put it out of commission and would really, really hurt the economy of El Paso. And all you have to do is put one little explosive there; it doesn't even have to be at a place where anyone gets hurt. People don't realize how vulnerable we are to terrorism.

We developed emergency plans to deal with demonstrations, riots, and takeovers of bridges and Immigration Service facilities. We developed these as a result of some of the incidents that took place along the border. We started formalizing procedures throughout the whole country, because you have to decide on the relationship with the sheriff, or the relationship with Customs, and at what point to bring in the U.S. attorney. The plans were pretty much completed by the time I left office. We had some problems on the Canadian border. Some of the U.S. attorneys said they didn't have authority to do certain things. They have a slightly different problem on the northern border because people don't need documents to cross, whereas they do need them on the southern border. Also the traffic flows are different.

Our main concern at the El Paso demonstrations was that the Mexican police and army would use force more readily than we would had things gone on much longer. They were prepared to use force. Some of the Mexican officials told us that if they would have gotten the word, they would have cleared that crowd in a minute. They knew how and had the will to do it; they would've had no compunctions about moving everybody out very, very fast. They were getting in the mood to do that. Their method of dispersing crowds and dealing with demonstrations is a lot different than ours. We tend to let people go on and on, and they tend to take very direct action. Of course, almost all the demonstrations took place on the Mexican side. There were some tense moments when people threw the American flag in the river. That made the national television news and caused a very emotional response. But by and large the Mexicans contained the demonstrations, and we simply kept ourselves in readiness in case a large group of people did start to storm the bridge.

It may have been that we made a mistake in deporting the people through only one bridge, but it has to be remembered that the immigration officers on the spot were simply obeying the law of the United States on immigration, a law which they find to be as defective as the mayor of El Paso did. The mayor's immediate burst of anger at the Immigration Service was really not very productive, really not very helpful. It probably hurt efforts at coordination which were desperately needed then, more than serving any other purpose. I think the mayor made a mistake right at the start. It's true that we were the precipitating cause of the incident, but it's not true that what we did was illegal or even wrong. What the officers on the spot did was enforce the immigration law. The mayor put himself in an awkward position by asking us not to enforce the immigration law, which we were sworn to uphold. I think it would've been better had he not attacked us in public, but clearly the law is in need of revision; it just doesn't make sense. There should be a law allowing [non-immigrant] commuters to come to places like El Paso every morning to work. People shouldn't have to sneak over here every day and go home every night.

. . . .

I went to Southeast Asia in 1978 as part of my job. As commissioner I was in charge of refugee processing, and I had staff throughout Southeast Asia. I was invited to go see what was going on, to determine the need. I went with a person from the State Department and visited the camps in Thailand, Cambodia, and Malaysia. I wanted to visit the camps myself. It was a tremendous experience, but I don't recommend it to just anybody. At times everybody had machine guns. They even gave me one.

Some people drew an analogy between Cambodia and Vietnam and the U.S.–Mexico border, but I think that was overdrawn. Along our border there tragically is some life-and-death drama; there are some people dying on a far too frequent basis. Many people are trapped or pressed by misery and poverty, and there is a lack of economic opportunity. But the scale of the tragedy of Southeast Asia so totally overwhelms the tragedy along the U.S.–Mexico border that it's not even right to compare them. In Cambodia we're talking about a country where possibly one-fourth of the entire population was killed in a period of two years; we're talking about a country that had been at war for thirty years; we're talking about people being shot regularly as they try to cross the Mekong River, as they try to get into the camp at Aranea Patek. You can see the artillery or hear the artillery shells, and you can see the military, follow the military preparations, and so on. Along the U.S.–Mexican border, for all of our protestations, we really don't have anything like that. We do have electronic sensors, but I don't know anybody who's been mined along our border. We do have some armed troops, but I don't know anybody using a machine gun to go after undocumented aliens. There's just no comparison, none at all. And in even our facilities, for all of our complaining about their inadequacy, they are infinitely superior to what you see in Southeast Asia. For Cambodian refugees, survival is a major factor, whereas for Mexican immigrants, economic improvement is the major draw.

"How do you satisfy the law without causing people to be hurt?"
—RICHARD B. SMITH

Since the 1920s, U.S. Border Patrol officers have been the frontline forces charged with the task of apprehending undocumented immigrants. Cases abound concerning abuses committed by many of these agents against humble and defenseless *indocumentados,* but probably most Border Patrol officers perform their difficult duties professionally and some even with considerable sensitivity. The perspective provided by Richard B. Smith, a bicultural newcomer, falls into the latter category. A man in his late thirties, Smith had five years of experience in patrolling the border at the time of the interview.

I entered the Immigration Service in 1970. After six months of training at Fort Isabel, Texas, I went to Sierra Blanca [near El Paso], where I served for two and a half years. Our district covered a tremendous area, more or less from the Hudspeth County–El Paso County line to the Hudspeth County–Culberson County line, and from the Rio Grande north to within five miles of the New Mexico–Texas state line. It's an area that is much larger than many of the states within the United States. They had three men to cover that vast area, a senior Border Patrol agent and two journeymen. To say the least, it was an impossibility. Even with the later addition of five trainees, it was still an impossibility.

We had three basic operations. The line-watch men were stationed on the border to detect and stop illegals who entered the United States. The traffic check involved checking traffic along Interstate 10. In the farm and ranch check, a team was sent out to check local ranches and farms that were known to hire illegals. Our biggest problem was the small farming community of Dell City, Texas, which is one of the largest irrigated farming areas in Texas. The problem was that Dell City is approximately seventy-five miles from Sierra Blanca, and our men had the responsibility of checking that vast area with one vehicle and two officers. Once the agents filled their vehicle with illegals, they simply turned around and left the rest there at Dell City. They then called for a bus from El Paso to pick up the apprehended illegals after they had been processed at Sierra Blanca. The traffic checkpoint was manned only one shift a day, from four in the afternoon until twelve midnight. Anyone who found it necessary or profitable to become familiar with our operations simply had to sit up the road a ways and watch us when we opened and closed the checkpoint. If they wanted to smuggle aliens or drugs, all they did was come through when we didn't have it open, which was the majority of the time. So we were not performing that function adequately.

Another problem was that we only had four vehicles—a sedan, a Travelall, and two Jeeps. The sedan could not be used for anything but traffic check duty, the Travelall went to Dell City on farm and ranch check, and the two Jeeps were for rough duty—cross-country work. Along the Rio Grande in that area there are almost no roads. It is so rugged that you need mules to get around. It was not feasible to even try to operate close to the river, where we could make our presence known. We used to go fishing at several places down the river, and we could get within three miles of the river, but from there we had to use mules. By the time we became aware that illegals had crossed the border, they were already ten miles inside the United States.

. . . .

In El Paso there are two bridges intended solely for the crossing of trains to and from Juárez and El Paso. Illegals call one of them *el puente negro* [the black bridge], but some refer to it as *el puente más famoso* [the most famous bridge] because on given days more people will cross into the United States illegally across that railroad bridge than will cross legally across the Santa Fe Street bridge.[4] Of course, that's not literally true. It's just a joke. But the number of people who cross over the "black bridge" is considerable. I myself have observed great numbers of illegal aliens crossing on foot over that bridge. One particular morning at least 120 people came across *el puente negro* at one time and spread out among the buildings and the parking lots next to the river. They recognized my car, although it was unmarked. When my partner and I saw what was happening, we just drove into the crowd, honking the horn. Those closest to the bridge turned around and ran back across it. Others who were closer to the return lane of the Santa Fe Street bridge ran back to Juárez that way. We picked up four and put them in the back seat. Approximately thirty-five who had already made it to El Paso Street broke and ran toward El Paso. They simply scattered and were undetectable. We couldn't do anything about it; we already had our carload. That is caused by a lack of personnel on the part of the Border Patrol. It happens about the time that a shift change takes place. There's no one to relieve that shift that's on. While the outgoing shift goes to deliver their car to the on-coming shift, there's nobody on the bridge. That exchange takes about fifteen minutes, and the illegals know all about it.

I recall one group of four women that I caught at the same time in the same place three mornings running. The same four women! They came across to-gether. They obviously had jobs that started about the same time, but they didn't necessarily work in the same place. Each time, I wrote them up on a standard illegal-alien form and then let them return to Juárez voluntarily. The problem is that the Immigration Service has no facility in El Paso equipped to handle female aliens. We could place them in the county jail, but it would cost the government nine dollars a day per person. If they're caught early in the morning, we can take them to the office, serve them with an order to show cause why they should not be deported from the United States, and serve them with a warrant of arrest. Then we take them before the immigration judge, and he holds a hearing right then. They have every right that a U.S. citizen has, including the right of coun-sel. They are asked, "Do you understand the charges? How do you plead, guilty or not guilty?" In the majority of cases they plead guilty. You caught them in the United States illegally; they're not going to sit there and argue with you. They're then ordered deported from the United States. They're taken to the bridge and given a set of instructions as to what will happen to them if they reenter the United States without first obtaining permission from the attorney general of the United States. That means that these aliens cannot even come to that bridge and say, "I want to come into the United States" unless they first get that written permission. To say the least, it's a slight inconvenience.

. . . .

Our agency has been depicted by some as the service with a heart, meaning that we attempt to enforce the law but with understanding and compassion. We don't enforce the law like police officers. We're dealing with human beings who have families, who have possibly been here long enough to establish roots. If you find a family that has had sufficient time to establish itself to some degree and you find out they're illegal, the law says you must take them into custody. The father has a good job, the mother has cultivated friends in the neighborhood, and the children are in school. It's in the middle of the day and you go from school to school, picking up the children, and all the other children want to know, "What's wrong? What's going on?" It's very embarrassing for the children, especially the teenagers, and especially the females. It's literally horrible for them, and more so if the officer happens to be in uniform. Anyone who's lived in the Southwest knows what a Border Patrolman looks like. Immediately all of their friends know what the problem is—they're illegal aliens. As they leave the classroom they hear "pss, pss, pss," behind them, and it's degrading. I've done this sort of thing. How do you satisfy the law without causing people to be hurt, without causing embarrassment, and without giving others an opportunity to make disparaging remarks about you? How do I go and pull children out of school without appearing to some degree to be a Gestapo-type individual? It's extremely difficult, to say the least. I'm damned if I do; I'm damned if I don't. If I don't do my job, I should be fired. If I do my job, I'm going to make enemies.

When I took this job I didn't expect anyone to pat me on the back and tell me what a great fellow I was. There aren't too many other law enforcement officers who have to face this particular situation. There is a photograph that hangs on the wall in the office over my desk. It is a picture taken in the late evening hours by an immigration officer. It depicts an elderly Mexican gentleman who has a child on his shoulders, and his son and daughter-in-law are standing beside him. The elderly man is helping his wife out of the water. They're about to come up on the U.S. side of the Rio Grande River. It is a pitiful picture. If there is anyone who thinks that the Immigration Service doesn't genuinely feel the responsibility it has, they should look at the photograph.

. . . .

When this business about advising people of their rights came out, we ran into some funny situations. We had this statement written up on a standard form that stated [the rights of the accused] in Spanish, word for word, easily understood. The standard rule is that you allow the individual to read it for himself and then you take it and read it to him. Then you would ask him, "Do you understand your rights under the Constitution of the United States?" Some of them, especially the older men, would get the oddest look on their face, and many of them would answer this way: "Those are the rights that are inherent to all human beings, given by God. Why do you read them to me?" And this from uneducated, poor, ignorant people. When you get those kinds of answers from people like that, it says an awful lot for their understanding of the problem.

. . . .

Approximately eight or nine miles south of Sierra Blanca there is a pass through the Whitman Mountains that has probably been used by people coming from Mexico for centuries. The western slope, which is extremely steep, has a trail that was worn out of the rock by people walking through there. It's a major crossing point for illegals. Once I was in the area during the summer and decided to go into this canyon to see if any illegals were there, possibly resting and waiting for the cool hours of the afternoon and evening to continue on their way. I was by myself, on foot, because you can't even get a Jeep in there. I walked about half a mile to a place that has these old, gigantic cedar trees. Illegals lay under those trees during the hot hours of the day. This one particular tree had a real thick thicket of mesquite bushes all around it, so you couldn't see through to the base of the tree. The thicket was just a little higher than a man's head. All of a sudden I faintly heard men talking in Spanish. I could hear one laugh occasionally. Because of the stillness of the day, it was difficult to tell where the noise was coming from, because it was bouncing off all the walls in the canyon. Finally I decided that it was coming from that big tree, and I began walking in that direction. Sure enough, I came up on fresh tracks that led into that thicket. I got in there and, lo and behold, there were fifteen male illegal aliens there under the tree. They had been eating their lunch—sardines, crackers, corn tortillas, green chilies, and lots of limes. This is their diet when they're crossing the country on foot.

I walked right up the middle of them before any of them really knew I was there. Many of them were asleep. Eventually one of them saw me, and naturally he knew who I was. When he got quiet, the rest of them turned and looked. We awakened those who were asleep, got everybody's gear together, and I formed them in a single file. I was armed, but I didn't have to pull the pistol or anything. I have *never* had to pull my pistol in all my years of service. I placed myself at about the midway point in the line. At some spots the line began to scatter about because of sharp turns, to the extent that the head or the tail of the line would be out of sight from me. There was nothing I could do about that. If they wanted to run, what could I do about it? So I didn't worry. When I got to the Jeep, I still had fifteen aliens. There I was with only one Jeep, and I couldn't get anyone on the radio. I put the aliens in every available spot on the Jeep. I filled up the interior, put some on the tailgate, one on each fender, three on the roof right above the windshield, and three in the cab with me. Very slowly we started down the road. I'll never forget one old gentleman; he was sitting right over me on the roof. He began singing about Chicago. I could understand a little of the song, but some of it didn't make sense to me. I asked him if he knew Chicago, and he said, "Oh yes, I know Chicago real well. It's a good town, plenty of work, a good life, swimming in the lake." He just went on and on about the things you could do in Chicago. Finally he said, "Let's go to Chicago," meaning me and the Jeep and all the illegal aliens. I kidded with him and said, "But I don't have enough gasoline." He said, "Oh, we'll buy gasoline. I've got plenty of money." And this old man, who was illiterate, reached in his pocket and held down a roll of money about two inches thick. It wasn't Mexican currency; it was U.S. currency. He laughed. He was very jovial about this thing. And all the rest of them were laughing and kidding.

Their spirits impressed me because I realized they had come from the interior of Mexico. For the most part they had walked from their hometowns to the border, and I *knew* they had walked from the border to where I caught them because there are no roads in the area. They had put up with all that dirt and discomfort and cold nights. After all that, here comes an immigration officer and snatches them up to take them to El Paso and shove them right back across the river. All [their efforts] had been for naught, and yet they could kid and laugh and carry on. To me, it was a situation I could learn from. I did not feel apprehensive with them. These people were not criminals. They had not murdered, they had not stolen, they had not done any of these things. If you have committed such a crime, the urge to resist or to run is there. In this instance, the severity of their crime was minimal. They had violated the law, but they were not criminals as such.

"I participated in the confiscation of tons of drugs and arrests of hundreds of people."

—DAVID REGELA

One of the most dangerous jobs along the border is that of undercover agent in the "war" against drugs. David Regela, a biculturalist who worked for the U.S. Customs Service from 1972 to 1988, recalls some harrowing experiences at the Rio Grande during an era when the drug trade underwent change from a fairly informal to a highly organized system of smuggling, with a corresponding rise in the level of violence. Regela was continually frustrated at the seeming futility of trying to stop an unstoppable torrent of drug smuggling. He became resigned to the reality that the Customs Service, the Drug Enforcement Administration, and other agencies could hope to catch only a small percentage of the smugglers, distributors, and pushers.

When I arrived at the border I could not see how we could possibly succeed in stopping the drug trafficking. The Rio Grande was not what I expected. I thought it would be a big river and it would serve as a real barrier, but instead here was this narrow and shallow river that carried little or no water most of the year. I could see right away how easy it was for the smugglers to get across quickly. I had to accept that I would be involved in a losing proposition because the smugglers had the upper hand. The border was too long, and we had very few people working on the problem. I was prepared to spend my life watching jack-rabbits and never solving any cases. During my service I estimate that we were able to intercept only about 4 percent of everything that came across.

One thing that made the work very frustrating was that we spent half our time competing with other agencies such as the Drug Enforcement Administration and the Border Patrol. Cooperation was a joke. We were in heavy competition for federal monies and for public recognition. Customs wanted to be the lead agency in the drug war. We didn't want to share the glory or to wind up with less funding from the government than the other agencies. Our work was geared for getting immediate gratification, for making the "big bust" and getting substantial media coverage for our "heroic" deeds. The volume of drug traffic was so immense that I actually saw plenty of action. When I left Customs I had participated in the confiscation of tons of drugs and the arrest of hundreds of people.

My main job was to generate informants by convincing apprehended smugglers to give us information about future shipments and the people involved. In exchange for that information, they got reduced or dismissed sentences. I constantly tried to identify people who would lead us to the higher ranks of smugglers or buyers. Sometimes I played the role of drug purchaser to trap the traffickers. I also spent a considerable amount of time on the river, freezing my butt off waiting for something to happen. Typically we would receive information that a shipment was coming through, and we went to the designated crossing point, hoping for the best. A lot of the time nothing would happen, but there were times when all hell broke loose when we confronted smugglers.

Once we had a big shoot-out with smugglers who received protection from the Mexican police. We could see from our vantage point that the police were aiding and abetting the operation. When the smugglers crossed the river, we proceeded to arrest them, but they resisted and shooting erupted. We were shot at by both the smugglers and the police. When it was all over, two of the smugglers were dead. The rest ran back to Mexico, but we confiscated the dope. When things settled down, one of the Mexican officers came over and asked that we turn the dope over to him. He said he and the other Mexican policemen had been "chasing the smugglers." Having seen them helping the smugglers, we couldn't help but laugh at that guy. What balls he had to give us that crap! Sometime later one of those officers became an informant, and he and I reminisced about that battle. He admitted that the police had helped the smugglers, and we laughed at the officer who tried to recover the dope.

Another big shoot-out occurred in the Big Bend area, where lots of drug trafficking took place. On that occasion about thirty smugglers were protecting two pickup trucks full of dope. There were only five U.S. officers, but we had far superior weapons and also the element of surprise. The whole thing was kind of romantic because many of the smugglers were on horseback, and they wore the Pancho Villa type of bandoleers. It was a throwback to the days of the Wild West. Anyway, we were able to seize the truck following the shooting. We completely surprised them, and their pistols and rifles were no match for our fully automatic weapons. That night three smugglers were killed and another one died later of bullet wounds. Our informant was also killed.

In the seventies and early eighties, violence was actually the exception rather than the rule. Marijuana was the main drug being smuggled. It was rather bulky and fairly easy to spot. Later, cocaine and heroin came to dominate the drug trade. The stakes increased greatly, and the smuggling became more organized and the smugglers better armed. Drugs became big business, and the people in the trade got very serious. It was now a deadly game. I saw that evolution, and I consider myself lucky to have come out of it unscathed. But I saw plenty of violence and many people die right in front of me.

In the old days before things got so serious, many agents and smugglers used to look at the whole drug trade as a game. When we busted an operation the smugglers would joke around and say to us, "No big deal. You guys won this one. We'll win many others." And they did, because we were able to catch so few of them.

The amount of money involved in the trade was incredible. I can relate many stories of ordinary individuals who got rich from buying dope at the border, transporting it to some big city, and then distributing and selling it from there. For example, there were guys from Dallas who would come down to the border and buy $5,000 worth of drugs and wind up making $25,000. With that profit they would come back again and buy a larger quantity, getting a much higher return on their second investment. They kept making more trips, and their business kept getting bigger and bigger, and they made more and more money. Some of them became very rich. The practical ones made their fortunes and quit, but many greedy ones stayed in the business too long and wound up in jail.

One of the most interesting cases I worked on involved Anglo retirees who used RVs [recreational vehicles] to transport drugs. What happened was that some entrepreneurs from Dallas correctly figured out that retirees would make ideal transporters because they did not fit the usual profile of smugglers. Furthermore, during the winter it was normal for many of them to be on the road in the border area because it was the snowbird season. Agents at the different high-

way checkpoints would routinely let them pass without inspection. So the entrepreneurs acquired a fleet of RVs and then hired retirees to haul the dope away
from the border. That went on for years until we found out what was going on.
We penetrated the organization through informants and indicted seventeen
people for conspiracy to transport and sell drugs. Our investigation took about
two years.

Pablo Acosta, one of the biggest smugglers in Mexico, was one of my informants. He agreed to pass on information after we busted him. He represented
quite a catch because he had direct connections to the Colombia cartel. His
problem was that he became infatuated with his celebrity status. He was also
addicted to cocaine, and that impaired his judgment. He started giving interviews
to newsmen, bragging about his ties to the Mexican police, how he controlled
them. He embarrassed the police, and eventually they executed him in a big gun
battle. He found out too late that he was not bulletproof.[5]

I was always amused at the explanations and excuses that smugglers came up
with when they were caught in the act. One would think that they would be better
prepared to try to talk their way out of their predicament, but many came up with
preposterous stories that were totally unbelievable. For example, one night we
arrested these two young guys near the Rio Grande. They had driven their truck
by the river without the lights on, and we had seen and heard doors open and
shut. When we asked them what they were doing there in the middle of the night
and why they had driven around without their lights on, they said they were
looking for girls and that since there was a bright moon, there was no need to
use the headlights. We searched the truck, found drugs, and busted them.

On another occasion we caught this guy with several sacks full of dope in the
trunk of his car. His explanation was that he had driven off the road in the
direction of the river because he had to pee. He said that while heeding nature's
call several men popped out of the bushes and told him to open the trunk of his
car. Scared, he did as he was told, and they threw in the sacks. Then they told
him where to deliver the sacks, and he proceeded to follow their directions. He
had no idea what was in the sacks and didn't ask because that would have been
impolite. We laughed at his story and busted him for carrying 500 pounds of
marijuana.

We arrested another man who had seven spare tires in his truck that turned
out to be full of dope. When we stopped him and asked him why he had so many
spare tires, he said he got lots of flat tires driving around in rough terrain. He
said he needed to be well prepared. As I was inspecting his spares I asked him
what was inside, and he answered, "Air, of course." I said things were just too
suspicious and we would have to do a closer inspection. With a straight face he
said, "Well, go ahead and take the tires, and if you need me, give me a call."
Of course, we took him in and he wound up in jail.

"We attacked them with words, with rocks, with eggs, and with tree branches."

—SALVADOR MERCADO

In the late 1970s, the issue of undocumented migration commanded enormous attention in the border region and across the United States. The print and visual media constantly ran stories about the "silent invasion" by "aliens" intent on finding jobs and settling permanently on U.S. soil. The immigrants were often portrayed as big burdens for American taxpayers. Capitalizing on nativist sentiments in U.S. society, the Ku Klux Klan for a time joined the movement to put a stop to undocumented migration, holding well-publicized rallies and demonstrations in different parts of the border. One took place in San Diego in 1977, sparking an incident with local Chicano activists who defended the immigrants. Biculturalist Salvador Mercado, then a law student, played a leading role in the fracas.

In the last few years, I have become very aware of the migration problem. Part of my personal evolution was the result of a confrontation at the border. In October 1977, David Duke, the national leader of the Ku Klux Klan, announced on TV in San Diego that he was going to initiate a campaign to inform the public about what he considered to be the dangers of illegal migration for the United States. He wanted to blame to the undocumented for economic problems in the country. He wanted to divide the people. He visited several cities in California, spreading that message, but wherever he went he encountered resistance.

Duke and other Klansmen arrived in San Diego on October 17. I didn't find out about their visit until late that morning, but in a few hours we managed to organize about fifty people from different nationalities to hold a demonstration against the Klan. The Klansmen got to the border around 3 P.M. They were driving nice cars, and Duke and the local KKK leader, Don Metzger, wore suits, trying to pretend they were saints who wouldn't even kill a fly. The others, about ten of them, wore cowboy hats and T-shirts with white-power symbols on them.

We were waiting for them with picket signs outside the immigration offices. They parked their cars behind the bus station in San Ysidro, about 200 yards from where we were. As they approached, we attacked them with words, with rocks, with eggs, and with tree branches. Everything was flying. They ran into the immigration offices, and we followed them. The people in there became frightened; they didn't know what was going on.

The Klansmen then hid behind a counter. We wanted to go after them, but the immigration agents stopped us. When the Klansmen felt safer, they started spraying us with soda. I got sprayed on my shirt. That agitated the crowd quite a bit. The Klansmen then left via the back door, followed by immigration agents and reporters. We weren't allowed to go in that direction, so we went out the same way we came in and around the building. We wanted to stop the interview that the TV reporters wanted to do with the Klan. It was important to halt it because the objective of the Klansmen was to influence public opinion. Our objective was to publicly humiliate them, but we ran up against a wire fence and couldn't get to where the interview was taking place. The people were very angry.

Once again it rained rocks, eggs, and tree branches. Duke and his followers were taken to the garage where they park the *migra* cars, and they stayed there about twenty minutes. We resumed our picketing. Then they came out the main door, the one that the people of Tijuana use when they cross the border. We confronted them once again, accusing them of being cowards. They continued walking to where their cars were. That is where I broke the window of one of the cars and was arrested for it. But the driver, who was trying to run me down, was not arrested. The trajectory followed by the car from the moment it began to move was in my direction. I moved to the side, and the car followed me. Everyone clearly saw that he was trying to hit me, although he did step on the brakes.

I ran after breaking the window, but the policemen overpowered me. If there had not been cops in front of me, I would've escaped. I saw their huge nightsticks, and I thought, "They're going to beat me up if I resist." I was taken to jail, where I was subjected to police brutality. What happened was the following. On Monday morning a policeman arrived with a list of the inmates scheduled to appear in court. When he read my name, he looked directly into my eyes and said, "I know you! You're the guy at the border! You're a celebrity! You're very famous!" He started calling the other cops; he was giving me lots of publicity. I didn't respond. I just took my hands out of my pocket.

Later when I was walking through a hallway I felt someone grab my hand. It was a Chicano cop. He didn't say anything; he just guided me by the hand. I thought to myself, "Wow! I must have done something he didn't like!" I had seen him around there, but I didn't remember provoking him. He took me to the end of the hallway and put his arm on my neck and said, "Don't you ever take your hands out of your pocket again!" And then, wham! He choked me, and I fainted. I didn't resist because I had some experience in jail. Once I did thirty days for not having paid a traffic ticket, and I saw how they killed one of the inmates. They took him into the room where they put the drunks. There they beat him until he was dead. I was working on that floor at the time. I was in charge of taking the civilian clothes from the inmates and giving them jail clothing. That's why I didn't resist.

When I got up, everything was going around in circles. Then I heard a sarcastic voice behind me, "Well, you can't take it. You'd better eat more." I recovered my senses and joined the other inmates, but another Chicano cop came over and lifted my arm and said to his partner, "Do you remember this guy?" He was referring to the fact that when I was arrested I had lifted my arm in symbolic defiance. I didn't want to appear humiliated at that moment. I saw that a reporter was about to take a picture, and I thought of the impression that picture would create. To me, giving the impression of resistance has a lot of meaning. That's why I did it.

While I was in jail there was a demonstration outside on my behalf. I had a lot of support in the community. The case received a lot of publicity. As a result I was let go by Tuesday afternoon. The district attorney, who wanted to bring charges against me, actively looked for the Klansman driver so he would file a complaint. But at the time of the trial he was somewhere on the East Coast, and they couldn't find him. Nevertheless, the district attorney insisted on holding the trial. The charge was malicious mischief. Meanwhile, there were demonstrations against the district attorney. We took a *piñata* in the form of a Klansman with diabolical eyes to his office. Underneath it had a sign that said, "District Attorney in Disguise." That came out on TV, and the community got a big kick out of it. In my opinion it communicated well to the public whose side the district attorney was on.

When we finally went to court, my lawyer tried to get the case dismissed. He argued that the police acted with prejudice; that they arrested me but not the Klansman. I thought it was a good point, but the petition was dismissed. Then he filed a complaint against the police for having choked me and harassed me in jail. We asked for $5,000 in damages. There was an investigation of those incidents, but the complaint was dismissed. In the end I was tried by an all-Anglo jury. The district attorney eliminated all the potential Mexican American jurors and also a black juror. The result was that the Anglo jury found me guilty. In my opinion the instructions given the jury by the judge were out of line. He practically told them how to vote. It's another instance of discrimination in the courtroom. That is part of our history with Anglo juries.

"I feel more and more that the border should not exist."

—RUBEN GARCÍA

Human suffering on the border associated with poverty, undocumented migration, and refugees has long attracted the attention of charitable and religious organizations, leading to direct and highly visible involvement in these issues by some of their members. Thirty-eight-year-old Ruben García, a bicultural native of El Paso, has devoted years to serving the poor and the dispossessed through formal and informal social programs sponsored by the Catholic church. His most significant accomplishment is the establishment in 1976 of Annunciation House, a center in El Paso for undocumented people and political refugees. García relates how his involvement with the poor began and how certain circumstances, including the intervention of Mother Teresa, led to the creation of Annunciation House. He also narrates some significant events that occurred in the house during the first decade of its existence.

When I got out of college I went looking for work in Kansas City in the field of social services, but I had this nagging feeling that I could do more for people in my own hometown, that I was needed more at the border. I felt El Paso was more lacking in resources than Kansas City. When I returned home I called Father Thomas, the director of Our Lady's Youth Center, about the possibility of working with him for a while. He agreed, and I started running this employment office at the center.

I found myself wanting to get into something that had more direct involvement with people. I talked to the director of the Youth Department of the Diocese of El Paso, and he assigned me to doing weekend retreat work with young people. Within a couple of months, the person in charge of the retreats died from a heart attack, so there was an unexpected opening and I was offered the job. I accepted and worked with the youth for eight years. During that time I began to think that opportunities were lacking for youth to really give of their time, serving people in an in-depth way. I also began to ponder what God wanted me to do, what the gospel meant in my life. So the idea of opening up a house for poor people became an image in my mind, and with time it grew until it assumed the form of Annunciation House.

But the real push from imaging this house to actually establishing it came from Mother Teresa, who visited El Paso in 1976, the year of the U.S. Bicentennial. I even got the name for the house from her. What happened was that as the youth made plans for the 1976 Youth Convention for our diocese, we felt we could best celebrate the Bicentennial by speaking of the need to serve those who live in poverty, who are hungry, who live in oppression. We decided to extend an invitation to our convention to Mother Teresa, who personified better than anyone else complete devotion to serving the poor.

Getting her to come to El Paso was quite an accomplishment because we had to cut through a lot of bureaucracy set up by the U.S. Catholic Relief Services in New York, which handled the schedule for her visit to the United States. We were told that it would not be possible to schedule a stopover in El Paso. When I insisted, they suggested I write Mother Teresa a letter, but knowing bureaucracies I felt it would be intercepted and ignored, so I decided instead to call her directly. I called several cities in India until I finally tracked her down. I can't imagine what she must have thought, receiving a call from El Paso. She probably said yes to our invitation because she was shocked; it was something she never expected. When I told the people in New York what I had done, they were very upset, but they had to go along with it.

Mother Teresa took a fondness to El Paso. She spoke to about 5,000 kids at the civic center. Afterward I accompanied her to a couple of other places, and we talked about my idea of a house for the poor. She was very interested and really encouraged me to go forward. In one of her letters, she wrote that I would "be able to announce the good news and bring the children home." It was from her reference to "announce" that we came up with the name Annunciation House. We got an old abandoned building that belonged to the diocese, fixed it up, and moved in without a clear idea of what we would actually do there. At first there was nothing in the building, so we prayed that God might arrange to have beds and other furniture donated to us. That's what happened, and soon we had guests living with us. Little by little we had a house full of beds and full of people. We took in anyone who was homeless.

We began to discover other centers that could help many of these people, and we decided to concentrate on those who fell through the cracks, namely the undocumented. They couldn't go to emergency shelters, get food stamps or welfare, and they couldn't get into housing. So our focus became caring for those who had nobody else, people from Mexico, Guatemala, El Salvador, Nicaragua, and South America. Annunciation House became the single most active center offering hospitality to the undocumented. When full, we have accommodated about sixty-five people.

Over the years we have had many interesting guests. One was a poor fifteen-year-old boy from El Salvador who left his country when the guerrillas wanted him to join them and the army wanted to stop him from doing that. His father sent him to the mountains and wouldn't tell the army where he was, so the soldiers took the father away and almost killed him. The problem as I understood it wasn't that the military believed the boy was a guerrilla but rather that they wanted to deny the rebels every able-bodied young man. When the father was released, he went to his son and told him he wanted him to get out of the country. The father sold the family cow for about sixteen dollars, gave the boy the money, and pointed him in the direction of the United States. The boy walked, took buses, and hitchhiked all the way to Ciudad Juárez. Then he crossed the border and was quickly caught by the Border Patrol. One of the workers at the detention center called me, wanting to know if I would go to bat for him, and I did. With the help of a lawyer, I got him released under my guardianship and had him apply for asylum. Then I put him in school.

On another occasion, we took in a big group of refugees from Nicaragua. That happened in 1980, about six months after the triumph of the Sandinistas. A lot of people fled Nicaragua at that time. One day we got a call from immigration informing us that they had detained thirty-six Nicaraguenses and they needed help. Immigration had given them political asylum in less than twenty-four hours, and now they were loose on the street. They had no funds and no place to go. We agreed to take them, but there was no way we could accommodate all thirty-six of them. About twenty stayed at Annunciation House, and the rest stayed in private homes of friends of ours. Of the thirty-six, twelve were former officers in Somoza's army, and twenty-four were women and children. Included among the officers were generals and colonels, and there was even one spy who was disliked by the rest of the group. These people were now homeless and countryless. Some people were upset that we took them in because of what they represented, because of what Somoza had done to the people of Nicaragua, but we helped them because they were now the poor and the powerless.

One interesting sidelight to that story was this family that got separated when the Nicaraguenses initially crossed the border. Somehow the son and the daughter got ahead and crossed with the rest of the group, but the parents did not realize it and slowed down while looking for them. The father didn't want to cross without the kids, so the parents didn't make it and wound up detained in Juárez. Later, when U.S. immigration authorities apprehended the thirty-six who had crossed the border, they didn't release the two children because they were minors. We were asked to help find the parents and reunite the family. We eventually found the parents at one of the U.S. immigration offices. What happened is that the immigration official in charge at the main international bridge had tracked down where the parents were and had allowed them to cross the Rio Grande and then kept them in custody until we showed up to claim them. So we were able to reunite them with their children.

What struck me the most about these people was their inability to understand the realities in their country. The Somocista officers kept saying that the Communists, and primarily the Cubans, had taken over Nicaragua and that the only reason that had happened was because the United States had pulled the rug out from under the government. The women talked about being uprooted and losing their homes and their possessions. There was a tremendous amount of anger in the group. Eventually they made contact with other Nicaraguans in Florida, and money was channeled to them. They all went to Miami.

Another incident that stands out in the short history of Annunciation House is an immigration raid that occurred in 1984. One day around noon I returned from an errand to find the House surrounded by several Border Patrol vans. Agents were going through the entire building looking for everyone who was undocumented. They lined up the people against the wall, handcuffed them, and loaded them onto the vans. I asked the agent in charge, who was dressed in civilian clothes, if he had a search warrant. He answered he didn't need one because he had been given permission to enter the premises by one of the refugees. Indeed, that's what had happened, but the refugee, who didn't understand English, also didn't realize that the man was with immigration. The agent then told me that having all these undocumented people at the House was illegal and that I could be prosecuted, fined thousands of dollars, and sent to jail. He said, however, that he would recommend to his superiors that I not be prosecuted. About fifteen people were taken in that day. It was very sad to see them treated as if they were criminals. They were very scared; some were crying. It was one of those times when I wondered why my country had to treat people that way. We were lucky that some people were not at the house at the time of the raid and that others managed to evade the agents by hiding under beds, behind doors, and on the roof.

I've evolved to the point where I feel more and more that the border should not exist. Borders are arbitrary lines that people have set up for reasons that have to do with vested interests. It is to the advantage of the few who control the resources to have these lines. I look toward the day when we can live without borders. People should be allowed to move wherever they want to go.

"They wanted to deport me because I was accused of being an agitator."
—HUMBERTO SILEX

Union organizing among Mexican Americans in the border region has always been a difficult task, but there have been instances when workers have achieved significant victories. One example is the successful unionization in the 1940s of workers at the American Smelting and Refining Company (ASARCO) plant and Phelps Dodge refinery in El Paso. Under the banner of the International Union of Mine, Mill, and Smelter Workers, Mexican American unionists saw the fruits of a long struggle culminate in the recognition of their union and the achievement of better wages and working conditions. The central figure in the local unionization effort was Humberto Silex, a bicultural Nicaraguan American who settled in El Paso in 1930.[6] In the following account, recorded in 1978, seventy-five-year-old Silex describes the oppressive working conditions that sparked his activism and reflects on the triumphs and setbacks he and his comrades experienced.

I came to the United States during World War I, when there was a lot of work in this country. I planned to go to school, but I was very young and lacked experience. It was difficult to study, so I started working. In Nicaragua there was no opportunity to attend a university at that time. Only the rich could do that. I knew little English, only what I had learned at school. After working in San Francisco, California, for a year, I went into the army to learn English, but in eight months the war was over and I was discharged. I returned to San Francisco, then went to Dallas, then to Chicago, where I worked a few years. In Chicago I lived well because one could work eight hours a day and the wages were good.

But in 1930 I wanted to get married, and I went to El Paso, Texas, to look for a Latin woman. I had been told that in cities like San Antonio and El Paso it was like living in Mexico. When I arrived in El Paso, I found out that the people were working like slaves for $1.50 per day, but I got married and stayed there. In El Paso the best wage at that time was $1.90 for ten hours of work. Workers didn't know what overtime or vacation was. Only the superintendents and the big bosses could go on vacation. I worked the same as everyone else, making $1.00 or $1.50 per day under the same conditions. I saw that Hispanic Americans could not occupy high positions regardless of who they were. They could only be common laborers. It was pure discrimination.

The Mexicans in El Paso were second-class citizens. They could only live in one neighborhood. They couldn't even venture into the north side, where the Anglos lived. Within a few days after arriving in El Paso, I decided to go to the north side to find out what it was like. As I walked on the street I was stopped by the police, who asked me where I was going. I told them I was from out of town and wanted to get to know the city. They said, "You get back south of the tracks, where the Mexicans live." I wanted to work for the electric company and applied for a job as a fireman [full-fledged stoker]. I was told, "This is a job for a white man." I lowered my head and left. I started working as a laborer with the gas company.

. . . .

In the thirties I got a job with ASARCO as a fireman's helper. I applied for the position of fireman, but they gave me only that of helper. The fireman takes care of the fires, the ovens, and the temperatures. There were three levels for that kind of work: fireman, assistant, and helper. When an Anglo came in, it didn't matter if he was a hillbilly, he would enter as an assistant, not as a helper like me. The fireman earned a salary like an official. The assistant earned a dollar more than the helper, but between the helper and the common laborer the difference was only two or three cents. An Hispanic person could die there as a helper because they never promoted him to assistant. But an Anglo would come in as an assistant without knowing anything; the helper would have to train him and take care of him. In three, four months, if there was a vacancy the Anglo would rise to fireman. That was happening at the smelter as late as 1937.

A short time later the company gave an order that the three categories of fireman would no longer be used, that there would be only two—fireman and assistant. So they laid off the helpers, those of us who were at the bottom. One day they told me, "We no longer need helpers, just assistants." It happened that the assistant with whom I worked was new, but he was not laid off because he

was over me. I was the one who had to leave. The next day he died in an accident—not that I wished that to happen to him, but that's what occurred. They
called me right away to return to work. I was without work only for a day. I then
worked as an assistant but with a wage of a helper. Latins were not promoted. I
worked twelve hours a day, six days a week, and I earned a little over two dollars
a day. We had to buy our work clothes, shoes, etc. We also bought things in the
company commissary, so at the end of the week we owed six or seven dollars to
the company. The children of the workers at that time did not wear shoes, because there was not enough money to buy them. I would walk back and forth to
work to save the five-cent streetcar fare; I needed that money. It was a distance
of about five miles, more or less.

At the smelter the carpenters, mechanics, and masons were unionized. The
other workers—all Hispanic Americans—were totally forgotten. I read that the
CIO, the industrial organization, could organize all the workers into a single
union. I thought that's what was needed at the smelter. In 1938 I had the opportunity to talk to a labor organizer who wanted to organize the packers at the
Peyton Packing Company. I told him about the problem, and he said he knew
someone who could do something about organizing the workers at ASARCO. The
following year the International Union of Mine, Mill, and Smelter Workers sent
an organizer, James Robinson, to El Paso. When he arrived he contacted me so
I could inform him of the local situation. Since he didn't know Spanish and I
knew nothing about organizing, he told me we needed to find someone who knew
something about the labor movement. We went to the Mexican unions, and they
provided an individual who was later deported for organizing. We found another
Mexican organizer, but he too was deported. After stumbling like that, little by
little we started having meetings with a few workers.

We wanted to be treated as equals. We wanted ASARCO and Phelps Dodge,
which had mines, refineries, and factories all over the world, to pay us the same
wages they had in other places, for example in Nebraska or California. In San
Francisco the smelter workers made five dollars a day, but in El Paso they only
made two dollars. The work was the same in both places, and in El Paso working
conditions were perhaps worse. We wanted equal wages, equal treatment, shift
differential [different wages according to shift], and vacations. ASARCO ignored
us; they refused to recognize our grievances. We struggled a great deal to organize the first group. We tried different things—for example, underground work.
The people were scared. We had to go to the workers when it was dark so they
would not be afraid. We also sought the help of the Catholic church, given that
a great percentage of Mexicans were Catholic. We looked for sympathetic
priests, and we would say to them, "These workers are treated like slaves. If
they made decent wages, they would be able to contribute more to the church.

The church has an obligation to help them. Advise them to organize." We carried on the struggle in many different ways.

When we had meetings, the police would surround the block where we were. They would interrogate the people who passed by there, asking them what they were doing, what business they had, where they were going, and if they were Mexicans. They did that to scare them. To those known to be a part of the movement, the police would tell them to be very careful, that if they joined the union they would have difficulties. There were times when we had to paint over the windows and the doors and do everything in secret as if we were acting outside of the law. On various occasions the authorities entered the union hall and took all the papers they found there. They also arrested some of the workers, accusing them of being subversives. Even if nothing happened to them, the intent was to interrogate and to scare them. For a time there were labor spies paid for by the sheriff. We were able to prove that when we went to court, seeking recognition of our union. Once, during an investigation by the U.S. Labor Department, the sheriff accused one of the organizers of being a Communist. The labor official responded, "This is a labor issue; it is not a trial for Communists." And the stupid sheriff said, "I am so dumb that I see no difference between the CIO and the Communist Party."

. . . .

We won our first contract with the smelter in 1944, after five years of organizing. We also succeeded in organizing the copper refinery and the cement plant. The contract we signed with the smelter called for a minimum wage of $4.50 a day. It was a great victory, because before the minimum wage was $2.10 a day. The following year we asked for more money, but the company announced that it would never pay five dollars, that it would first close all its plants. The company justified its lower wages in El Paso by saying that Mexicans only ate beans, that the majority wore no shoes and didn't need shoes, and that they wore the cheapest clothes. Company officials made superficial and stupid arguments. But they didn't say that in public. They said that in the meetings we had with them. So we had to go on strike. We fought them and stood firm.

. . . .

In 1947 a group of union leaders and workers went to lunch in Ciudad Juárez. On the return to El Paso I was detained by the immigration inspectors. They put me in a provisional jail they had in the basement of the immigration building. At that time they were trying to deport me. I had applied for U.S. citizenship, but the federal court turned me down. Instead of granting me citizenship, they started proceedings to deport me. At the international bridge I was told that since I was a foreigner and my case was in progress I had no right to cross the border. They wanted to deport me because I was accused of being an agitator.

They based their allegation against me on a fight I had once with a foreman at the plant. The fight occurred because the foreman was responsible for my being fired from my job. He and other bosses were used to exercising strong control over the workers. Once he said to me, "The workers have too many privileges now. In the past we used to carry whips, but now we can't say anything to them. But when the war [World War II] is over, we're going to go back to the old days." When the first opportunity came along, he fired me. One day I met him at the entrance to the plant and grabbed him by the throat and hit him several times. He filed a complaint and they arrested me. I had to obtain a pardon from the governor of Texas to prevent deportation. But they refused to grant me U.S. citizenship, and I have remained a Nicaraguan citizen.

. . . .

After I left the union, I was blackballed. No one wanted to hire me. If a company hired me, the Chamber of Commerce would pass along information that I was a troublemaker, and in a few days I would be told that they were sorry but they had to let me go.

"I told them I wasn't afraid. Perhaps I **was** *afraid of engaging in violence, but I didn't tell them that."*
— ANTONIO ORENDAIN

Orendain, a bicultural settler migrant whose experiences as an undocumented worker during the 1950s are related in Chapter 6, joined the effort to organize farm workers in California when he met Cesar Chavez, the famous Chicano labor leader. In the 1960s the plight of the poor and ethnic minorities attracted the attention of the U.S. government and the American public. Leaders such as Chavez took advantage of the improved climate to promote the interests of farm workers, who occupied the lowest socioeconomic sector in U.S. society. Following the creation of a union in California in 1965 (which eventually became the United Farm Workers), Chavez sent Orendain to take charge organizing in Texas. Orendain arrived at the Texas–Mexico border during a period of great labor unrest.

In 1966 Cesar Chavez sent me to Texas to help out with a strike that had broken out in Rio Grande City. I got there on September 27, three weeks after a march that the farm workers had conducted to Austin, where they had hoped to see the governor, who as it turned out was not there to receive them. At first the purpose of the march had been to obtain collective bargaining rights for farm workers, but in the end it became known as a March for Justice, and the objective was to have the minimum wage raised to $1.25 an hour. With attention focused on the march, the strike in Rio Grande City was forgotten. We needed to figure out ways of calling attention to the strike once again.

I quickly found out that the local union members did not like to have a leader from California directing their struggle. They wanted a local leader. As a union administrator, I exercised my authority over the union finances, and they resented that. I knew that money always creates problems.

A few days after my arrival, this man named Librado de la Cruz said to me, "Antonio, I would like to speak with you. Let's go to the outskirts of the town." At that time I didn't know that in Texas, when someone told you he wanted to speak to you in the outskirts of town, it meant that he wanted to beat you up. I said, "Let's go." So we went and he said, "Look, Antonio. We want to give you a beating and send you back to California. You came here and took our money. You didn't march [to Austin]. You haven't done anything in Texas. Besides, you don't believe in violence, and here we are preparing ourselves to do something stronger than has been done in California. That's why we want to beat you up. But I told the others I would speak with you first."

I thanked him for giving me a chance, but I said, "Who told you I didn't believe in violence? It is one thing to do something stupid in the name of violence, and quite another to have organized violence. Are you organized? Perhaps you have a good plan and I will like it. Tell me the people who are ready and organized. I would like to see them. I would like that opportunity. Regarding money, I was sent here to be in charge. The only thing I can guarantee you is that I have not come to Texas to stay here forever. If you help me and we get a union contract, I will leave tomorrow and go someplace else, because there are many places in the United States where union contracts are needed." He said, "Well, let me speak to the others. Let's see if they would like to talk to you."

Later he arranged a meeting with about ten people, and I saw they had three rifles and about twenty-five sticks of dynamite that is used in construction. The dynamite was very dry, in very bad shape. I have used construction dynamite, and it has to be fresh in order to be useful and safe. When it gets dry it becomes very dangerous. Despite that, they carried it around in the trunk of a car, and it bounced back and forth. I had been driven around in that car without knowing the dynamite was back there. I said, "You dummies. Don't you know how to use this dynamite?" It turned out they didn't. Some guy had stolen it up north and had given it to them. I convinced them it was too dangerous to carry around, and we buried it in the sand by the river.

I asked them how they intended to use the rifles. They said, "Well, we'll shoot at the buses that are bringing in the strikebreakers."

"And what do we do after we shoot at them? Where do we hide?"

"Well, we'll go to Mexico."

"And how do we resupply ourselves? Who will give us more arms, more dynamite? If there is going to be organized violence, someone has to send us supplies."

"Well, that's what we have. The important thing is to do something."

"Yeah, but that isn't organized violence. That's a dumb thing to do."

I won their trust and got to know them. Five days after my arrival we were united. I told them I wasn't afraid. Perhaps I *was* afraid of engaging in violence, but I didn't tell them that. I kept saying, "Let's develop a plan." We began to look for ways of trying to convince or force the strikebreakers not to go to work. On October 14 we had our first demonstration, and one of our people, a gringo named Bill Chandler, was arrested. They put him in jail for inciting to riot. Imagine that! He was accused of that and he couldn't even communicate with the people. He didn't know Spanish, and the people did not understand English.

On October 24 we shut down the international bridge between Roma, Texas, and Miguel Alemán, Mexico. I selected about fifteen people, and we placed ourselves right at the international line and began stopping traffic. We were there thirteen hours, and we stopped all the workers headed for the fields that had been struck. That day only seven workers made it to the fields, and three of those swam across the river. The American police tried to arrest us, but I pointed out to them that they had no authority to do so because we were about three feet inside Mexican territory. So the county attorney said, "Okay, we won't arrest you. Now let us through so we can speak with the Mexican police." But we didn't let them pass, and they became very angry. They went back to Roma and called the Mexican police, who came over to where we were. So we stepped back to American territory, and the Mexican police couldn't arrest us either. We continued moving back and forth across the international line until the Texas Rangers got together with the Mexican police and we found ourselves in between both of them. We placed one foot in the United States and one foot in Mexico, but the Mexican police pushed us toward the Rangers and they began arresting us. We resisted by laying down and singing "Solidarity Forever." All sixteen of us were arrested that day.

Shortly after we got out of jail, we shut the bridge again, this time by locking these gates at the bridge that were no longer used. This time three of us did the job during the night. My two compañeros went ahead of me by foot and cut the locks that kept the gates tied to the sides, and when they lit a cigarette, that was my signal to proceed across the bridge and bring them new locks and chains to shut the gates. I drove onto the bridge, dropped off the locks and chains, and kept going rapidly to the Mexican side. When the compañeros locked the gates, they walked to the Mexican side, where we met about two blocks from the customshouse. We then headed toward Camargo, where we planned to recross into the United States. But the bridge there didn't open until 8 A.M., so we had some time to kill. My compañeros were curious about what was happening at the bridge at Miguel Alemán, so we went back to find out. When we got there the police were waiting for us. They identified us as the last people to cross the bridge and accused us of locking the gates. In short, they threw us in jail and kept us there until two in the afternoon. Then they let us go because they said the Texas Rangers would arrest us as soon as we crossed into Roma. To avoid arrest we swam across the river. We made it to Roma without any problem and were feeling good because Cesar Chavez was scheduled to arrive that day. When he got there I informed him of everything that had happened, and he said, "I sent you to Texas to organize workers, not inmates. You're in jail all the time."

On November 3 we stopped a train loaded with green chiles on its way out of town. We convinced the engineers to respect the picket line. That was about 6 P.M. By 10 P.M. we heard that the Texas Rangers were on the way. They arrived an hour or two later with machine guns and accompanied by engineers from the railroad company. They started to move the train, but then they discovered that a nearby bridge that crossed an arroyo was burning. They could go no farther. They immediately tried to blame us, and they deputized all the farmers in Rio Grande City. The county attorney went on television, saying he knew who had burned the bridge but that he planned to make no arrests until after the elections on November 7. On November 8 the Rangers came over to arrest us. When they got to me, I asked to see the warrant, but they said they didn't need one in my case. I asked them why not, and they didn't say anything. Then they asked me if I had any weapon on me, and I said no. Then I remembered reading a newspaper article back in California that said there is nothing to fear from a Mexican with a gun, but watch out for a Mexican with a rock or a knife. So I looked at them and said, "Yes, I do have a knife." All five of them jumped backwards as though they had springs on their feet. They took out their guns and said, "Give it to us!" I was trembling from fear, but I laughed at them. I took out a small knife that had a nail clipper and gave it to them. I realized that they too were afraid despite their reputation of being so brave.

They took me to jail, and soon I was joined by the other fifteen compañeros. When they served us breakfast, I refused to eat. One of the compañeros asked me when I intended to eat, and I told him not until they informed us why we were being held there. Then I said, "You know, back in California I used to catch jackrabbits, and I would put them in a cage. I would take them the best grass I could find. And the jackrabbits would not eat the food I took them; they would rather starve to death than live in captivity. Animals know very well what freedom is. They haven't told us why we are here. When I hear why, and if I am guilty, then I'll eat. Until then, I won't." Pretty soon all of us were on a hunger strike, and we didn't eat for fifteen days, when they let us go.

After six months, Cesar Chavez pulled me out of Rio Grande City because it was too dangerous there. I went back to California to help direct the strike there. The movement stalled in Texas once again. In 1968 the Texas Rangers were taken to court, charged with brutality and violations of civil rights against the farm workers. They were found guilty of joining with the growers and against us. The state of Texas appealed, and in 1973 the U.S. Supreme Court upheld the finding that the Texas Rangers had not acted properly.

Orendain eventually founded a new union, the Texas Farm Workers Union, which by the 1970s was competing with Chavez's United Farm Workers in the organizing effort in Texas. Orendain split with Chavez because, according to Orendain, the California-based union would not commit sufficient resources to sustain the movement in Texas.

"It may take us ten or twenty years, but it can be done. The people are tired of being exploited."

— ÁNGELA BÁRCENA

In recent decades, trade unions have made many efforts to organize border workers in garment factories but have had only limited success. The account that follows focuses on a struggle waged in a plant in Deming, New Mexico, in the late 1970s. The lead organizer was Angela Bárcena, a twenty-six-year-old Mexican immigrant whose awareness of border conditions and sensitivity to the plight of workers were aroused early on by suffering in her family and her own work experience. Bárcena can best be described as an upwardly mobile bicultural immigrant.

My parents met each other in Chihuahua during the 1930s, when the United States started deporting Mexicans to Mexico because of the Depression. My mother has told me about the thousands and thousands of Mexicans they deported on trains and buses, many of them people who had been born in the United States, who had lived all their lives here. All my mother's family was sent to Mexico even though they were all U.S. citizens. Her father was Mexican, but he had lived in California since the 1890s. They sent them to the state of Chihuahua, where the Mexican government gave them some land. But they could not make a living in the countryside, so they moved to the city. My mother relates the story of the family's repatriation with a great deal of resentment because it was a big change for her—from going to school in California to all of a sudden living in the Chihuahua mountains, where conditions were terrible. She felt her family had been thrown out as something which was no longer needed or wanted in the United States. She was about ten years old at the time.

Years later, after she married my father and I was born, we moved to the border area on the Mexican side. We lived in an interesting neighborhood. There was a mixture of poor people, middle-class people, and rich people. I was one of the poor ones. I began forming impressions of class differences. When I was about seven, I noticed that I didn't have such things as a bicycle or a Sunday dress, but other girls I played with did have those things. The class differences were clear; children have the capacity to see that. When you are suffering, when you are living through that, you notice it because it is part of your daily existence.

When we moved to the United States, part of the family had the problem of needing papers. Half of my brothers, the younger ones, were born in the United States, and the rest, including myself, were born in Mexico. Soon I had problems with *la migra*. I used to ride the bus, and on one occasion I was waiting for it along with some other people. The officers stopped at the bus stop and started asking me questions in English, and I didn't understand them because at that time I didn't speak English. I thought to myself, "Who are these people?" They asked me in Spanish, "Where do you live?" and I answered, "Well, I live right there, next to the bus stop." They wanted to know where my mother was, and I told them she was working. They said they needed to talk to someone; they wanted to know where my papers were. I didn't have any papers; I had nothing. But they did not apprehend me; they left me alone. I guess they just stopped to find out who I was. That was a bitter experience because I didn't know what was going on. I reacted emotionally. I was very angry, furious.

Something else that bothered me was the attitude I noticed on the part of Mexican Americans toward people from Mexico. They would say things like, "Hey, you Mexican. What are you doing here? This is not your country." I felt sad about that. I asked myself why such differences existed.

When I was seventeen I got a job in a restaurant helping to make salads. The other Mexican workers washed the dishes and did the sweeping. The majority did not have documents. I had a lot in common with them. By then I had papers, but I was also from Mexico. Once *la migra* raided the restaurant and left the kitchen without anyone to cook or clean the dishes. The manager and supervisors had to do all the work, and that pleased me a lot. Later they switched me to waiting on tables. I worked there for only five months, but that was long enough to find out that things worked the same in the United States as they did in Mexico.

In 1968 I spent some time with relatives in Mexico City. It was during the big student demonstrations. I was influenced by that. I became aware of many things. It was very exciting for a young person like me. I was also influenced by my older brother. He was always talking about exploitation, using that kind of terminology. I didn't know what those words meant, but they sounded good to me. I also read his books. That's how I began to form my ideas. Later I was influenced by my first husband, who was involved in the Chicano student movement. I didn't know anything about Chicanos, but I learned by going to various functions like theatrical presentations and demonstrations. I noticed that the working class was not participating in those activities and that their conditions remained the same. Exploitation continued. I felt there was no movement if the workers did not participate. There could be no change.

I worked in a garment factory for a year and a half. Conditions were ideal in those factories to raise one's consciousness. I became a quality inspector on the assembly line. I wanted to join the union at the plant, but they told me I couldn't because I was considered supervisory personnel. I thought I had the right to join, but they didn't let me. I couldn't even talk to the operators; it was prohibited in the Quality Control Department. I could really feel the class differences in that factory: owners, managers, supervisors, operators, and laborers. It was sort of understood that part of my work consisted of checking the work of the operators with a whip in hand. I was not about to do such a thing, first because of my convictions and second because those women had much more experience at what they were doing than I did. Who was I to tell them what they were doing wrong? Many of them had been sewing for twenty years, and I had never even been near a sewing machine.

At first they resented me, but I eventually became friends with most of them. I didn't bother them. I felt I had no right to bother the workers. The other thing that had a bearing on my relationship with the workers was that I stood up for them in their dealings with a German woman who was also an inspector. She could barely speak English, but she had a reputation of being tough with the workers. She was very demanding of them. She returned a lot of their work. The Quality Control Department loved her. It is true that the quality of the clothes improved a lot with that woman around, but she was one of the most racist people I've known. She treated Mexicans with disparagement. She was offensive. We didn't get along. I had many arguments with her, and we were called to the office a few times. At that time I was very nationalistic. I wasn't going to permit her to talk that way about my people. It was a racial conflict.

When I became a labor organizer with the International Ladies Garment Workers' Union, I was sent for training. The trainees were told that organizing was the same with all workers, that all workers are the same, that one can organize any worker regardless of race. I was not in agreement with that. I had experience with my people and felt that an Anglo or black could not organize in El Paso. To be effective, one must speak the same language as the workers, be at the same level socially, and have a good relationship with them. I have heard organizers contradict themselves. First they say it is very easy to organize Mexicans, then the next minute they say the border will never get organized because the people have no experience. That is like saying that Mexicans are so used to being exploited that they will accept that as a fact of life, that they are content, and that's it. That attitude is discriminatory and racist. Mexicans have to fight strongly against it within the union so it will end. We may not organize border Mexicans in one or two years. It may take us ten or twenty years, but it can be done. The people are tired of being exploited.

One mistake made by unions is the way they try to educate Mexican workers. For example, after my training I returned to the border to begin an organizing campaign. I was joined by an experienced organizer. She had been organizing for nine years, and she was supposed to continue training me [in the field]. We started visiting factories and passing out leaflets and cards, about 900 of them. Only one person returned her card to us. That is no way to organize workers. The first contradiction is that the leaflets were completely in English. Only about 5 percent of the workers could read or communicate in English. I told myself, "I will not pass out any leaflets that are not in Spanish." On one occasion I disobeyed an order to pass out leaflets that were not in my own language. That is an insult to our people. You can't just pass out leaflets and then wait for people to sign their cards and send them to you. You don't begin organizing with a piece of paper. Anyone can stand outside a factory and pass out papers. As an organizing technique that does not work. The only way to organize is to agitate and talk with people personally. You have to go to their homes and talk with them. In the beginning you socialize with them, and that way you will get them to like you; they will respect you, and you will gain their friendship. Then you begin agitating. You have to use leaflets that excite the people, not passive ones. Bland leaflets may work in places like Illinois, where unions have a long history and where people are used to that technique. Along the border things are different.

In November 1978 a letter written to union headquarters by Clement Scott, a retired teamster from Deming, New Mexico, was forwarded to me. In that letter Mr. Scott described working conditions in a local textile factory. I went to Deming to find out what was going on. I quickly found out it was a town controlled by Anglos. It really was no different from other similar towns, but in Deming the control was more obvious because the town was small. The factory described by Mr. Scott employed lots of people from the town. I went to talk to him and then to a worker he had mentioned in his letter. She told me she no longer worked at the factory because she couldn't stand it and left. But even though she didn't work there anymore she still knew everyone. She could tell me everything I wanted to know about the factory. She gave me lots of names, including those of the supervisors. At first I didn't even go by the factory; I didn't want anyone to know I was with the union. I stayed at a motel, most of the time by myself. It was very boring because there was little to do. I spent most of my time getting to know the town and where the workers lived.

As I visited workers in their homes, they complained about the working conditions, the wages, and the racism toward Mexicans. The work quotas were high; the workers could never reach them. Many women were working as many as fifty-five hours a week. There was lots of work. The company had sold much more than it was producing. The women would get home so tired that they could do nothing. Sunday was the only day they could spend with their families. All that work, and the pay wasn't that good. And neither were the conditions. At the end of the day, each worker had to clean up her own little space. The company supplied the operators with small brooms which they kept by the sewing machines. That bothered the workers a great deal. The company's policy was that whoever didn't like it could leave.

The workers were not treated very well. For example, once an operator got a phone call that her son was very sick, but because she was working at the time, she was not given the message. Phone messages were delivered only at lunchtime or at the end of the day, when the operators were not working. Another case involved a seven-months pregnant woman who asked to be switched to another station where she could do the work while standing, because her own machine was cramping her and she was not feeling well. They told her that, because of her condition, she should leave her job, But she needed to keep working. She took a note from her doctor saying that she could no longer work in a sitting position; her womb was being damaged. Nothing was done, and she became very ill. Eventually they had to take her from the factory in an ambulance. Her baby was born dead, asphyxiated. The machine had pressed her organs in such a way that the baby was asphyxiated. On top of that the company didn't want to pay her maternity leave benefits. Racism was very, very strong. The workers told me that the plant manager would frequently make statements like, "Stupid Mexicans." Mexicans never became supervisors. The bosses were all Anglos, and most of them were brought in from Arizona or other places.

I kept visiting the women in their homes for about three months and kept reporting back to the union. I averaged three visits a day; things were going too slowly. I asked the union to send another organizer to help me out, and they did. Sandra Solis from San Antonio joined me. We divided the work. We began our organizing campaign in April 1979. Up to that time we had done everything in secret to avoid having the company find out about us. But the company found out right after we went to talk to the priest at the church where most of the workers went to Mass. We asked him if we could use the church to have the first meeting of the union, and he said yes. Somehow the company found out about the meeting. I concluded the priest had called them; that was the only way they could've found out. At that time the priest was remodeling the church, and the company had made a contribution. So he was very interested in pleasing them.

In any case, we thought we would have only a few people at the meeting, but 130 showed up. They were very interested in the union. They were tired of the conditions under which they worked and no longer believed what the company told them. We organized a committee of forty-seven workers. Then we made a leaflet in which we denounced the company. We also sent a telegram to the company and the National Labor Relations Board informing them which workers were involved in the organizing; we said we hoped their constitutional rights would be respected. The following morning we began distributing the leaflets along with cards that the workers could return to the union. Instead of having a lot of words, the leaflet had drawings. One had a picture of a ferocious-looking supervisor chewing out an operator.

The company started a campaign against the union, which is illegal. They did all kinds of stupid things, however, which benefitted us. They would talk to the workers and make all kinds of promises. We would have someone tape record those sessions, and the same day we would prepare our response. One day I had a confrontation with one of the supervisors in front of the factory. He was accusing the workers of breaking the law by engaging in union activities on company property. It was the workers' right to do that, but they were confused and looked to me for leadership. They still were affected by the respect they had for their employer. I took on the supervisor so the people would have more confidence in me. We started arguing, and he threw a "finger" at me. I said to the workers, "You are all witness to that." The following day we had a leaflet that said, "Here is the respect this man has for you."

On May 25 we had the election, with 158 workers favoring the union and 97 opposing it. That was fabulous. It was the first time in twenty years that the International Ladies Garment Workers' Union had won an election in the area by that margin. Shortly thereafter the company started laying off and cutting the hours of workers. All of a sudden, operators who had been working fifty hours a week were cut down to fifteen or twenty. The company then informed the union that they would have to close down the factory for economic reasons. They closed it in June. The people understood that it was a tactic to avoid paying union wages and to move the operation to Mexico; that way they would avoid problems. The company could do that. How could we prove that they were closing down because of the union? Within a short time the union pulled me out of Deming.

"When workers are unfairly treated, anger and despair set in, and this is when trouble and potential for violence start."

—BISHOP SIDNEY M. METZGER

Since the 1960s, increasing numbers of clergymen in the Catholic church have become involved in social issues in the United States. With poverty, discrimination, segregation, and exploitation of workers widespread in the border area, intervention from local religious leaders has become commonplace. Bishop Sidney M. Metzger, who retired in El Paso in the 1970s, followed his conscience in matters of social justice. A biculturalist, he is best known for his strong support of the strike against the Farah Manufacturing Company, a clothing firm that at the time of the strike (the early 1970s) employed large numbers of Mexican Americans. In the following memoir he explains his commitment to workers' rights and reveals some of the dynamics surrounding his controversial stance on that famous labor conflict.

I became interested in labor issues when I was a young priest in Rome. Pope Pius XI prescribed that students should be given a course in social justice based largely on the encyclical letters of Pope Leo XIII. We learned about the condition of the working man and so on. I had that background when I returned to the United States from Rome.

My very first strike that I was involved in in El Paso was back in 1943 or 1944, just shortly after I became bishop. It involved the Mead Bakery. A Mr. Hardesty, an AFL-CIO organizer from Oklahoma City, came to me and said that since all the workers were Mexican Catholic people, I should probably help them out. I said that I didn't quite know what I could do but that I would be glad to talk to the person in charge at the bakery. Mr. Hardesty gave me the name of the man in charge, and I called him up and offered to talk with him, to give him some advice. He came to see me one evening and we talked. I pointed out that when workers are unfairly treated, when wages are not enough to live on, and so forth, anger and despair set in, and this is when trouble and potential for violence start. I believe that eventually the workers and management came to an agreement about having some kind of wage scale with gradual increases so as not to put too much strain on the business.

Over the years I came to know some of the labor leaders in El Paso. George Webber, local head of the AFL-CIO, was a very close friend. We had many discussions on labor issues. One of the first encounters I had with labor was with the International Union of Mine, Mill, and Smelter Workers. Some of the members of that union belonged to St. Patrick's Church. They came to tell me about the union, that it was Communistic. I told them they should join another union, a good union, and I actually fought the Mine, Mill, and Smelter Workers, fought them openly. As it turned out, the Mine, Mill, and Smelter Workers simply deteriorated. They had so many legal expenses they couldn't exist. The man who was causing a lot of the trouble at that time was Clinton Jenks. He was a card-carrying Communist. There is no question about that. Later he was tried in federal court in El Paso, and he was convicted. Finally the case went to the Supreme Court, and the case was overturned because some evidence was not introduced, and that supposedly was a violation of his constitutional rights. But he was absolutely an out-and-out professional Communist. The story goes that he went to Silver City, New Mexico, and other places after the acquittal, and the workers told him never to return or they would shoot him.

Later I was involved in the strike at the Hilton Hotel. The bellboys and the maids and so on were picketing the place. Long before the strike, a dinner had been booked there by people who had a drive underway to build Jesuit High School. I was asked by Father Donnely what he should do, and I said, "Well, don't have the dinner there. If you have it, keep me out. I never cross a picket line." He understood that. That got into the newspapers and, oh boy! The evening paper said, "Bishop Refuses to Cross Picket Line," or something like that. I had my foot in it again.

[In 1972] I became involved in the biggest labor dispute of my career, one that became an issue of national importance. This happened when some of the workers at Farah Manufacturing Company went out on strike and asked me for my support. About this time a bishop from the East wrote to me asking for an in-depth report on the situation at Farah. I spent two weeks gathering information and documenting all of the charges against Farah. I sent the bishop a three-page letter concluding that conditions at Farah were not in accordance with what we would call the principles of good social justice. This letter was printed verbatim in the *National Catholic Reporter*.

A lot of people felt that I shouldn't involve myself in labor affairs, that perhaps church funds were being spent on non-church matters. Catholics who disapproved of my involvement reacted by organizing boycotts, refusing to contribute financially to church programs. Very few people were willing to come and talk over the issues with me. My position was that I was happy to calmly discuss everything with anybody. I had to be very sure of my ground. I never butted into anybody's business, only when I was approached.

Later when I attended a bishop's meeting in Washington, D.C., I discovered that Willie Farah [president of the Farah Manufacturing Company] had flown in a contingent of lobbyists and other supporters, including some Protestant ministers, to lobby against the strike with the bishops. One of the other bishops asked me to seek permission from the cardinal in charge of the bishops' meeting to speak to the assembled bishops and explain my views on the Farah situation. I gave a twenty-minute talk to all the hierarchy of the United States that were there. I got an ovation such that I had never gotten anywhere in my whole life. Now, I'm saying this to give you an idea of what the church hierarchy were thinking, even though many were quite conservative. Some didn't like the idea of church involvement with unions, but I guess they thought I had guts if nothing else. In time, a committee from the bishops' meeting who were experts on issues of social justice came to El Paso, went to the Farah plant, talked over the issues with both sides, and reported back to the bishops, confirming the stand that I had taken.

On another occasion the former secretary of labor, Arthur Goldberg, came to town to address a civic function. He was the featured speaker, and I had been asked to give the invocation. Before launching into his prepared remarks, Mr. Goldberg commented to the audience that he was glad to have met me, and then this is what he said. He said, "You know there're all kinds of issues that are before the public these days. There is the question of a living wage, for instance, how the workers should be paid. There's racial discrimination and all such things as that. There's housing, and all the things we're supposed to do. Now, some people consider those political. They may be political issues in a sense, but there is an element of justice involved in all of them. Whenever justice is involved, religion has its function. And therefore if your rabbi or your minister or your priest speaks out on these issues, even though you may not personally agree with him, do not persecute him or anything of that kind. That is his duty." They couldn't get it more clearly than that.

On another occasion Sargent Shriver was campaigning for the Democratic presidential nomination, and when he came to El Paso he asked to see me. He told me that he agreed with the things I had written about the strike. He said that back east I was a hero and that I was one of his. I told him that some of the local people were rather bitter about me, that some had written critical letters to the pope and had otherwise criticized me. He advised me to pay no attention to that because I had done the proper thing.

Well, that Farah strike went on for a long time, and the unions organized a boycott of Farah products all over the country. Finally, economic pressures forced Farah to accept the unionization of its workers, along with collective bargaining, better wages, benefits, and working conditions. After the settlement, Farah went through several years of severe economic distress, which union foes blamed on the effects of the boycott. I believe that the boycott did hurt Farah, but after the strike they were on their way back, financially, for awhile. I myself sent a letter to all the bishops in the U.S., advising them that Farah's labor problems were settled and requesting that they do what they could to encourage trade with Farah. I think that the financial decline suffered by Farah for a few years after the strike was largely due to bad business practices on the part of Farah management. Willie Farah made no secret of his unhappiness with the union settlement. I think his customers may have felt that with Willie unhappy there might be another breakout of some kind. That type of thinking could very easily hurt business.

"More and more, I've seen the border as an obstacle to peace and good will."

— ROBERTO MARTÍNEZ

San Diego–Tijuana has been the site of many border confrontations and incidents since undocumented migration and drug trafficking emerged as major issues in the 1960s. U.S. federal agencies as well as local law enforcement entities have aggressively sought to curb illegal activity, all too frequently treading on the rights of people identified as suspects. Ethnic friction involving Chicanos, African Americans, and Anglos has added to tensions in this area. Among border activists concerned with these issues, none is better known than Roberto Martínez, who heads the American Friends Service Committee's U.S./Mexico Border Program in San Diego. Martínez is a bicultural fifth-generation Californian whose involvement in community affairs was motivated by some unpleasant personal experiences as a teenager and young adult. His activities are widely known, as he has appeared on many media programs and has been quoted extensively in major newspapers.

In the 1950s I experienced what a lot of Chicanos experienced: the police stopping me, throwing me up against the wall, pointing guns at my head, and taking me to jail. The only reason they stopped me was because of the way I looked, although I didn't dress outlandishly or anything. I worked after school in restaurants and in hotels, and the owners would call the Border Patrol so I would be deported and they wouldn't have to pay me. I went through this week after week through my high school years.

In the 1960s I moved my family out of a barrio that had many problems. There were a lot of blacks there, and there was a lot of bitterness among them. It was the time of the Watts riots. A lot of drugs were coming in, so I wanted to get my family out. We moved to East County. I was very naive, and I didn't know that East County was a redneck area. It wasn't a couple of days after we moved into this house that vandals broke in. They pounded my living room and marked it up with racial slurs like "Wetbacks Get Out" and all kinds of obscenities. When the first blacks moved in up the street about a month later, they burned crosses on their lawn and spray painted swastikas on their doors. At night they would break their windows. When more Mexican American families moved in, we formed a support group around the church.

Most of the problems were centered in the high school. Unbeknownst to us, the Ku Klux Klan was sending the Klan Youth Corps into the schools to recruit members, so they were stirring things up. Consequently, fights started between white and Chicano kids. My kids didn't have a problem because they are very fair. My first wife was Chicana, but she is really fair, so my kids have almost blond hair and blue eyes and very light skin. But the darker kids had real problems.

One day I got a call from a Mexican lady who wanted to bring over some people from the community and some students to discuss an incident that had taken place at the school. The boys had lumps all over their heads, and one of the girls had blood coming out of her mouth. One of them said that after school some white kids started yelling racial slurs—"Go back to Mexico" and stuff like that. Then they started beating up the kids, so the vice-principal called the sheriff, and he arrested all the Chicanos but not the white kids. They took the Mexicans away, claiming it was for their own protection, but once they got them into the car they started beating them up. They took the older ones away, and the younger ones came to my house. They were looking to me because they considered me a community leader.

I couldn't hide my anger. I called the school and requested a meeting the following morning, but the principal said no, that the problem had been taken care of. Then I called the sheriff's department and asked for a meeting, but the lieutenant in charge said there was no problem and therefore no need to meet. I threatened to hold a news conference right at the police station, and they agreed to a meeting. I called their bluff and it worked. They told me that the sheriff's deputy involved was disciplined. We didn't have any more problems for a while.

But there were worse problems going on in other parts of San Diego County. Friends asked me to attend meetings, and very soon I was really involved in real bad racial problems and in police brutality cases. Whole families were rounded up and beat up by sheriff's deputies. Riot squads would barge in on birthday parties, baptisms, weddings, everything. They were just going around clubbing and swinging and trashing. They love to trash houses just because these people are poor. They pretend they're looking for drugs or something, and they destroy everything. So I formed what we called the East County Community Sheriff's Task Force, and in the 1970s and early 1980s we filed big lawsuits on behalf of Mexican families.

In the late 1970s I got involved in problems in North County, an agricultural area where Mexicans were being attacked. Some workers were shot by white groups, and police harassed and assaulted immigrants in restaurants, in bars, and on the street. By the early 1980s I was working for the Chicano Federation, a coalition of Chicano attorneys, community leaders, and what have you. We were better organized—we marched and we filed lawsuits. Then in late 1983 I began to work for the American Friends Service Committee, focusing my efforts on the migrant workers but also handling complaints and lawsuits against the police. So here we are, in 1991, fighting the same battles that we had in this county in the 1960s.

In the early 1980s I received death threats when I was organizing in North County. I was younger and I didn't take them seriously, but I would go around in different cars. In 1990 I received more death threats from the White Aryan

Resistance, a group of skinheads. They came after me when I was organizing counterdemonstrations against the Light Up the Border campaign, calling it racist.[7] We formed a coalition comprised of people from Tijuana and San Diego and confronted the anti-immigration demonstrators at the border. We held mirrors and aluminum foil in front of their cars and reflected the lights they were shining back on them. While we were doing that, a whole bunch of police on motorcycles went up and down between the two groups to prevent physical contact. But there was only pushing and shoving and people throwing stuff and yelling at us. I criticized the Border Patrol for letting them do this. So the White Aryan Resistance targeted me, warning me that if I didn't stop criticizing the Border Patrol, they would kill me. But the threats were traced, and the guys who did it were arrested, and in March 1991 they were sentenced.

I have also been involved in incidents in Calexico–Mexicali, where people have been killed or wounded. In 1990 a fourteen-year-old boy who was climbing the border fence was shot in the back by a Border Patrol agent. He was running back to Mexicali, and when they shot him he fell into Mexico. A bullet exploded inside of him and damaged his lungs, liver, kidneys, and colon. He's almost paralyzed. How he can still be alive I don't know. The Calexico police said there was no reason to shoot him, that it was unjustified. The Border Patrol agent said the boy had a rock in his hand.

The weekend of the shooting, the women at the orphanage where the boy lived organized a big protest. Something like 4,000 people were mobilized, and a rally was held against the INS. They invited me to talk. The demonstrators actually shut down the border for nine and a half hours. The Mexicali city council helped to organize people. The Mexicali police set up roadblocks so shoppers couldn't cross into Calexico. The economy in Calexico and in the Imperial Valley shut down. No farm workers could cross; nobody worked on the farms for two days. Statements flew back and forth between Mexico and the U.S. State Department. The National Guard in Calexico were dressed in riot gear; they expected the worst.

INS, the Border Patrol, and the Customs Service have consistently denied that they're responsible for the violence at the border. They say the main problem is crime involving Mexicans against Mexicans, which of course is not true. They continue to say our allegations are unsubstantiated, but the Office of the Inspector General in Washington, D.C., has conducted an audit of all the shootings along the border, and the report clearly states that 45 percent weren't justifiable. For the first time Americas Watch, in its report on Mexico, has included human rights violations on the U.S. side of the border. Amnesty International is now documenting human rights violations on the border. So all this has served to put INS, the Border Patrol, and Customs on notice. This supports what we've been saying in our own annual reports and in hearings. This vindicates us and our work. We have the data to support what we say, plus the fact that we've won so many lawsuits.

That has really ticked them off, and the Border Patrol is sending a lot of undercover people to monitor my house. They constantly pull up across the street in unmarked cars, trying to be inconspicuous; they take pictures and stuff like that. They have these new cars, these ugly green Chevrolet Caprices, and they act like little kids with their toys. Last week a Border Patrol vehicle parked in my driveway, and they were taking notes, so I went out and took pictures of them. I did a piece for "48 Hours" at the border, and the Border Patrol followed us around with binoculars. That evening, when I came home, they [the Border Patrol agents] stopped in front of my house; they were all honking and waving.

More and more, I've seen the border as an obstacle to peace and goodwill. The worst part is that the border is militarized from San Diego to Brownsville, with the presence of National Guard, marines, and the army. We're not at the point where we can see each other as real neighbors, as two countries that are interdependent. The border itself is a contradiction in the broadest sense of the word. It was an open border for generations, and now suddenly they have decided to create all these laws to control it. In Europe they're looking for ways to open up borders and to eliminate them; here they're constantly reinforcing the border, experimenting with fences, with stadium lights [to illuminate the Tijuana–San Diego border], and with military sensors. That sends the wrong message to Mexico.

"We still do not have an open society. A lot remains to be done."

—CÉSAR CABALLERO

The Chicano movement of the 1960s made a deep impact on the Mexican American population along the border. As elsewhere, much of the activism began among university students, who challenged campus practices that brought few benefits to Chicanos. Community institutions, organizations, and officials also came under the critical scrutiny of Chicano activists anxious to rectify many wrongs long perpetrated against La Raza (the people). César Caballero, a forty-two-year-old bicultural librarian from El Paso, was caught up in the frenzy of that era, first as a student and later as a community leader. His activism against "the system" has centered on educational, political, and immigration issues. Although disappointed with the slow pace of progress, Caballero acknowledges that significant changes have taken place in the last two decades and that border Chicanos have more power and influence than before.

My first leadership position in the United States was as the leader of a gang called *los* "tigers." I was about ten years old at the time, and my family had just arrived from Mexico. We settled in a low-income area in South El Paso and lived in a small, crowded apartment. There I learned the struggles and challenges faced by people from the barrio. We were the new immigrants and were ostracized and harassed by the old immigrants, who had their own gangs. We were called names and not included in games. So, to better defend ourselves, we followed their example—we formed our own gang.

My adjustment to the United States was not easy in that tough environment, but the fact that I knew who I was helped me to survive. My identity as a Mexican was strong because I had lived in Mexico until 1958, and once we crossed the border my parents made sure that I kept my Spanish language skills. You might say that they created a customized bilingual program for me because at home we always spoke Spanish, and even when we lived in Ciudad Juárez I went to a Catholic school in El Paso and was able to learn English at an early age.

My involvement in community affairs started as a teenager when I participated in projects that would help poor people, such as canned-food drives. Later, as a freshman in college I was involved in an incident that made me realize that Chicanos had few rights, that encouraged me to become a student activist. What happened was that one evening a friend and I went to a dance, and a policeman would not let us in. My suspicion was that he was deliberately trying to keep Chicanos out, and I made some comment about the fact that this was supposed to be a free country. He accused me of trying to incite a riot and of possessing pot, then beat me up and took me to jail. I got a lawyer, and eventually the charges were dropped. That taught me a good lesson about fighting for my rights.

At the University of Texas at El Paso [UTEP] I became a charter member of MECHA.[8] The students felt a need to organize on campus and in the community. I began to learn about issues and to meet local leaders. We advocated greater recruitment of students from our community and a better campus environment. We pushed hard for a Chicano Studies program and for more Chicano faculty and administrators. In 1972 when university officials canceled an important meeting with us, we organized a demonstration involving several thousand students. We then took over the administration building for several hours. The police came after us, but many of the demonstrators managed to get away, including me. We surrounded a bus that was supposed to haul off lots of students to jail; we immobilized it by letting the air out of the tires. We had a big laugh because it had to be towed away from the campus. But the police did arrest about thirty members of MECHA.

After I completed my graduate training and took a job as a librarian at UTEP, I became involved in Reforma, an organization made up of librarians concerned with developing library services for Chicanos. We tackled that issue, plus we fought hard to get more representation on the local library board. We succeeded beyond our wildest expectations in a very short time. We got Chicanos elected to the board and got the services our people needed. I became chairperson of Reforma, so I was in the middle of the struggle. I got myself elected to the library board as well. The Reforma experience was crucial for many of us because it served as a springboard for other political activity in the community. It was excellent training for those Chicano librarians with an activist orientation. Several people who served as chairpersons of that organization have since become important political figures. One of them is currently the head of the local Democratic party. As chairperson of Reforma I became a representative to El Concilio de El Paso, a broad coalition of twenty-five Chicano organizations. The purpose of El Concilio was to bring together the activist Chicano leadership for the purpose of addressing community issues with one unified, strong voice. El Concilio also offered a forum and great networking opportunities.

From 1982 to 1984 I served as chairperson of El Concilio. At that time we tackled a number of problems that were very important in the city. One was political redistricting. Through our activism we were able to get the power structure to draw district lines that were more favorable for Chicanos. As a result, more of our people became involved in the political process. A related issue was getting the boards of the El Paso Independent School District, the El Paso Community College, and the Ysleta Independent School District to shift from at-large elections to single-member districts. The city council had made the change to single-member districts in the late seventies, and we felt these boards should follow that example. It wasn't easy, though. It took a lawsuit to get the El Paso Independent School District to make the change. The board was dominated by Anglos who disliked the idea, since they would lose a lot of their power. With the help of Texas Legal Aid attorneys, we won the lawsuit. The El Paso Community College Board settled the issue before going to court, and the Ysleta Independent School District took it upon itself to change the election system without legal action. El Concilio also went to court when the El Paso Independent School District tried to back away from implementation of desegregation orders arising out of the Alvarado case of 1975, which determined that the district was guilty of fostering an educational system that discriminated against Chicanos. We tried to keep the desegregation plan on track, but we were only partially successful. The district was able to free itself from some of its obligations.

Another issue that we tackled was abuses perpetrated by the U.S. Immigration and Naturalization Service. The Border Patrol went around conducting raids wherever they thought they would find the undocumented. They acted like a paramilitary force and even had dogs to intimidate people. They would barge into public places like bars or restaurants, secure the doors, and demand that everyone prove their citizenship. Conflict arose when some of the people refused to do that.

During one of the raids, a Vietnam veteran who knew his rights responded with questions of his own. He asked one of the agents, "Who are *you* to ask *me* for my citizenship? Are *you* a citizen?" As a result he was roughed up and arrested. What really hit the fan, however, was an interrogation conducted with a dishwasher in a restaurant. He was a frail and timid young man. He responded to their questions in Spanish, explaining that he was a U.S. citizen and that his father owned the restaurant. But the agents did not believe him and arrested him, failing to even leave word in the restaurant where they were taking him. Of course, he had told them the truth, so he had a good case against the INS.

When we found out what was going on, we protested and held a news conference. We accused the Border Patrol of "unconstitutional and Gestapo-like behavior." We met with the local INS director, but he ignored us, so we filed a class-action lawsuit, and we won. The judge ruled that the Border Patrol was wrong in the way they conducted the raids and in their interrogations, that such tactics constituted violations of the civil rights of individuals. The INS was forced to pay several thousand dollars in damages to each plaintiff. To my knowledge, it was the first time that the INS had to pay people for abusing them.

Apart from my activism in El Concilio, I have also held a number of positions on city and county boards. There I have been able to see how the system works, how Chicanos are left out of the process most of the time. In some circles there is still a lot of resistance to change. The majority of city leadership positions are still in the hands of rich Anglo males. Banks and other financial institutions have very few Chicanos on their boards. There are some wealthy Mexicans from Chihuahua, but those people cannot be counted as U.S. Hispanics, as the banks try to do.

In the cultural arena we have been clobbered because Anglos have been able to establish mechanisms and procedures to maintain their dominance. For example, the board of the El Paso Museum of Art is totally controlled by twelve elite Anglo families, so museum exhibitions and activities reflect Anglo culture. Those people have been spending public funds to promote the culture of the minority of the population in the city. Sure, they have had some Chicano-oriented exhibitions, but it has amounted to tokenism.

I have to admit, however, that in the last twenty years things have changed a great deal in El Paso. Many Anglos have modified their attitudes and their behavior, although I am not ready to say they accept us totally. But it is a big change from the sixties, when their main concern was how to keep us out of the system. Now we are partially in. Before, we were trying to kick the door down because it was closed. Now the door is basically open, but in truth only a chosen few can go in. Wherever we are present in positions of influence and power it is because we have forced our way in there. We still do not have an open society. A lot remains to be done.

"I've always felt that there's a lot of help that needs to be given to the people."
—SANTIAGO MALDONADO

For many young Mexican American activists, poverty and myriad other problems in their communities became powerful incentives for involvement in social causes. When he was growing up, Santiago Maldonado felt angry and resentful at the inferior status of Chicano children and the preferential treatment accorded Anglo students. Raised by his grandparents in the El Paso area, Maldonado, a biculturalist, developed a strong sense of identification with the plight of the poor and became well known locally as an advocate for Chicano civil rights. At the time of the interview, he was a university student and a VISTA volunteer. Maldonado's experiences as a farm worker are related in Chapter 6.

When I was in the second grade, my grandparents moved from El Paso to Dell City, Texas, a nearby town that was 50 percent Anglo and 50 percent Mexican American. I recall that my teacher, Mrs. Billingsly, used to scold all the Mexican Americans. She used to yell at us more than the Anglo girls and boys. I could see that we were segregated. We were placed behind them; they were always at the front. Instead of being seated in alphabetical order, we were seated by race.

I can recall when Easter came around, we were taken to a cotton field to hunt Easter eggs. All the Anglo pupils were in the front, and we were in the back. We couldn't hear what the teacher was saying; she was giving clues as to where they could find the Easter eggs. When we went out into the field, we just didn't know where we could find them. As it turned out, all the Anglo pupils found the Easter eggs and we didn't.

The Anglo kids at school were rich, well-dressed. I always went to school in a T-shirt. The reason I liked the T-shirt is because the temperature was so hot, and I just didn't like the idea of a long-sleeved shirt or anything that would keep me hot. The Anglos would always come in dressed nicely, with ties sometimes, and expensive clothes. This made me feel real poor. The other Chicano kids were in the same situation. We always used to hassle the gabacho kids because of the way they dressed and talked.

The Anglo kids had the very strong cowboy influence. I guess their parents taught them that it was bad to associate with the Mexicans, and I guess they applied that in school also. I recall I used to fight a lot with a guy named Lody, who was the head of a bunch of Anglo kids. I didn't like him because he thought he was the king. He would push everybody around. That kind of got to me. I just didn't like the way he talked behind everybody's back. He would always be talking bad about the Chicano kids, but when he was in front of a Chicano kid he would be very quiet. Then, as soon as he was with his friends, he would be making all kinds of noises. So the day came when I found out that he was talking bad about me. He thought he could beat me up. I fought him twice. The first time I lost; the second time I won.

When I attended Bowie Intermediate School in El Paso, they had a "no Spanish speaking" rule. If you were caught speaking Spanish, they had several forms of punishment, such as being detained after school for an hour for several days, being inflicted with physical punishment—being hit with a ruler on the hand, being swatted, or being forced to do pushups, like I was, in front of the class. It wasn't only me; everybody got the same treatment. Sometimes it got really bad; you had to bring your parents to talk to the assistant principal and explain why you were acting that way.

I recall that there was an uproar at the school in 1967. The students banded together behind some activists who were pushing for the elimination of such rules. The activists belonged to the Mexican American Youth Association (MAYA). At that time I wasn't a member; I was only on the sidelines. Those students started an awareness, and it spread. It got to the point where the parents got involved, the social workers from the area got involved. Protests were initiated. They got the assistant principals at that time, who were Anglos, to testify before the Commission on Civil Rights as to why the trouble was happening. After that some changes took place. The assistant principals were transferred to other schools, and the Anglo principal was promoted. They were replaced by Mexican Americans, who were more sensitive to the problems. Then the "no Spanish speaking" rule was eliminated. Now students could speak Spanish in the hall, in the classroom, or on campus, whereas in the past they could not.

I got involved directly with MAYA when I was in high school, during the Chicano Movement. At that time a lot of people were becoming politicized. A lot of people were getting active in social affairs, in school affairs, in civic affairs. Chicano publications were starting to come out. I used to read them all the time. I even sold them in high school. I recall once that certain teachers complained about it to the principal, and I was called to his office to explain why I was selling the magazines. I told him why, and he said I couldn't do it. He said that any publications not published inside the school were forbidden to be sold, with the exception of the school newspaper. So I sold them outside the school grounds.

After that I became very community service oriented. I became a VISTA volunteer, and that gave me the opportunity to work in the barrio and help in any way possible. The experience that I recall the most is my role as an organizer of

a "tent city" demonstration in South El Paso. Due to the neglect and the ignorance of politicians, we set that up to get the attention of the general public that
there was a housing crisis and that it did merit attention. With several other
activists, I organized the campaign to get exposure through the media. We sat
down with many people in meetings; we set up conferences; we set up work-
shops. We talked with people not only from the community but also from the
state and federal levels. We finally got the attention we deserved. The mayor
went to Washington, and he was guaranteed that $1.7 million would be sent to
our city for construction of future public housing. Later we went before the El
Paso city council to get funds for painting murals. We got several thousand dollars to pay for the cost of the paints, brushes, and so forth. We felt that the
concept of murals was really embedded in the culture of Mexican Americans and
that they had a lot of talent that should be exposed to the community at large.

The majority of my friends have not made it like I have. I'm still poor, but
they're poorer than I am. I am a university student, and I have a job as a VISTA
volunteer, whereas the majority of them are unemployed. They just hang around
street corners and run around in gangs. A lot of them are pushing drugs. A lot
of them are always drinking and fighting. Each street corner is against the other.
They're just victims of unemployment. They're victims of the drug culture. A lot
of them have dropped out of school or are "push-outs." I like to use that term.
The ones who are involved with the gangs are kids in their teenage years. Their
concept of machismo, of being *el más chingón* [the toughest], is very prevalent.
Every street corner has its group, its gang. There is always friction over a girl,
or maybe over somebody who is pushing bad stuff like drugs, marijuana. For
any little reason a fight will break out. It is common; it is natural.

When I was growing up in that environment, I was afraid. I would always be
witnessing people being hit with beer bottles, people being stabbed, people always being locked up in jail. It was a bad time. I recall when the Chicano gangs
would go fight with Mexican gangs at the border. I also recall that many tourists
would be assaulted. I never participated in that. I participated in a different way.
My feelings and motivations have been instigated by the Chicano Movement, by
MAYA, by my parents, my neighbors, my friends. I've always felt that there's a
lot of help that needs to be given to the people. A lot of services and improvements are needed. I also have liked to do something with my life, do something
constructive with it.

8

MIXERS

Mexicans and Anglos first established meaningful contact with one another in the borderlands during the 1820s with the arrival of thousands of U.S. citizens in Texas, then a province of Mexico. Initially, cordial interactions prevailed, but as the Anglo immigrant population overwhelmed the Mexicans, the latter became a marginalized minority in their own land. Race relations deteriorated following Texas independence and the U.S.–Mexico War as a result of protracted confrontation. Racism, segregation, and economic colonialism became the established pattern in Texas for the rest of the nineteenth century and for most of the twentieth. In New Mexico, Arizona, and California the experience of Mexicans and Mexican Americans was similar, but none of these states matched the deplorable record compiled in Texas.[1]

Ethnic conflict in Texas was most acute along the border, where incidents precipitated by the troubled relationship between Mexico and the United States constantly stirred nationalistic passions, driving the dominant Anglos to subordinate people of Mexican descent ever further. The population of the Lower Rio Grande Valley suffered the most, enduring heightened persecution at various times between 1836, when the Texas rebellion began, and 1920, when the violent phase of the Mexican Revolution, which frequently spilled over the border, came to an end.

As the twentieth century progressed, the instability of the borderlands subsided and friction declined appreciably. Economic growth offered new opportunities for many members of minority groups to achieve middle-class status. With higher social standing and expanded access to the political and legal systems of the United States, they also increased their effectiveness in fighting discrimination. Simultaneously, Anglos became more tolerant and less abusive of minorities, and the U.S. government became more responsive to minority needs. The passage of significant civil rights legislation in the 1960s and 1970s represents a landmark development for minority rights. Thus, by the late twentieth century,

substantial improvements had been realized in the nation's racial climate, leading to more extensive and more intimate interethnic relations along the border.
Nevertheless, the legacy of past conflicts remained, and the differences between
the Anglo and Mexican ways of life supported a clear cultural dividing line.

Before the social breakthroughs of the 1960s and 1970s, the limited contact
between Anglos and Hispanics occurred mostly in the workplace, and many
cases of such interaction reflected the patrón-peon system then widespread in
the borderlands. When Mexican Americans climbed up the economic ladder in
significant numbers, cross-cultural relationships began to assume a different
character. More Hispanics moved into Anglo neighborhoods, attended Anglo
schools, participated in the Anglo-controlled political system, and took part in
mainstream cultural activities. In short, Mexican Americans achieved greater
integration into the dominant society, and in turn Anglos learned more about the
Hispanic world.

The intensity of the effort by Mexican Americans to master Anglo culture has
varied from community to community along the border. Generally speaking,
pressures to assimilate have been most pronounced in Anglo-dominated areas
such as San Diego and El Paso, and most relaxed in Hispanic-controlled places
such as Laredo and Brownsville. In the latter cities, Anglos have tended to be
more tolerant and benevolent and have often even been willing to become acculturated to the Mexican way of life. Many Mexican Americans have experienced
stress and emotional discomfort in their interaction with Anglos, and mastering
the English language has often been traumatic. Aside from the vast cultural gap
that separates the two groups, class differences have also acted as powerful di-
viders. Yet, however difficult and complicated the process has been, Mexican
Americans in large numbers have made the adjustment. In the process they have
had to give up portions of their native culture, but that has been common in the
experience of all ethnic groups that have pursued integration into the U.S. mainstream culture.

Of the three groups discussed in this book, it is Mexican Americans who,
because of their status as an ethnic group in the United States, have experienced
the most acculturation and assimilation, and consequently most of the people
whose stories appear in this chapter are Mexican Americans. The need among
Anglos to absorb cultural traits from their neighbors has been rather limited, and
relatively few of them have left the comfortable confines of their society to experience the world of Hispanics on either side of the border. Nevertheless, as
was illustrated in Chapter 5, a portion of the Anglo population has been driven
by economic or social circumstances to interact closely with the Hispanic community. Among Mexican nationals, substantial interaction with Anglos and with
Mexican Americans has been confined to biculturalists and binationalists, and as

indicated in Chapter 3, these two sectors have remained numerically small. For most transnational Mexicans, contact with the United States has been driven by employment considerations or consumerism, yielding at most superficial cross-border acculturation.

The people featured in this chapter are "mixers," or individuals who have ventured into other cultural worlds to such a degree that their lives have been changed significantly. Their stories reveal the joys as well as the frustrations that accompany the crossing of cultural and social boundaries. Among the memoirists are four Mexican Americans who recall many struggles along the road to integration into U.S. society, and two Mexican Americans who emphasize favorable circumstances in their hometowns that facilitated their entry into the mainstream culture. An Anglo man offers a positive view of transculturation, and his narrative is followed by an Anglo woman's story that focuses on the discomfort she has felt in living as a "minority" person in a predominantly Mexican American community. The special challenges encountered by persons assumed to be Mexican Americans are explained by a woman who is culturally Anglo but whose physical appearance is distinctly Hispanic, and the unique circumstances of ministering to Mexican American parishioners are discussed by an Anglo priest. Two interviews focus on inter-ethnic marriage, with a Mexican American woman recalling the problems she had with her African American ex-husband and an Anglo woman discussing the many adjustments she had to make after she married a Mexican national. The final memoir is that of a Mexican American male homosexual whose nocturnal world transcends the boundary.

"One good thing about us Mexicans is that we adjust to everything."
—FRANCISCO HIDALGO

Family and job-related circumstances thrust many Mexican children into a constantly changing life pattern, challenging them to overcome the myriad problems they encounter in new and strange cultural and social environments. Francisco Hidalgo, a biculturalist and now a successful professional, recalls experiences from his sometimes unpredictable childhood that brought him face to face with U.S. society. The trauma of living away from home over extended periods was compounded by innumerable cultural shocks in schools and other milieus that were different from his own environment. Hidalgo drew on survival skills developed in Ciudad Juárez to overcome one difficulty after another created by his status as a "foreigner" and an "outsider." Above all, his story illustrates the spirit of versatility and adaptability characteristic of many transnational borderlanders. Hidalgo's experiences as a border taxi driver appear in Chapter 6.

I was born in California. I was "made in the USA" by wetbacks, because my *jefe* [father] had gone there to work as a "track man" for the Southern Pacific Railroad Company. My mother joined him with my two older brothers. One had been born in Camargo, Chihuahua, and the other in Ciudad Juárez. At that time my father had papers that belonged to one Francisco Cabrera, so our assumed name was Cabrera. My name became Frank Cabrera at the hospital where I was born. The nurse saw that my mother had written "Francisco" on the forms, so she said, "His name is Frank," and that's the name they put on the birth certificate. When we returned to Juárez, my mother wanted to change the name back to Francisco, but she was told that it cost a lot of money. The *coyotes* [hustlers] in Juárez wanted a lot of *feria* [money] just to write letters to Sacramento. They wanted to take advantage of my mother. Later, when we returned to California, we got that taken care of without paying a cent. We went to see the priest, and he quickly made available to us my birth certificate and this and that. Of course, my papers had the name Frank Cabrera so we had to get an affidavit changing the name to Francisco Cabrera. (My real name was Francisco Hidalgo.)

When we were in California, my *jefita* [mother] was very influenced by my grandmother, who wrote to her from Camargo, telling her to go back to Juárez to get our papers. She persuaded my mother, and we returned to Juárez. We lost all the furniture we left in Selma; my aunt sold all of it in a rummage sale very cheaply when she herself went to El Paso. My jefe never got his papers because they put up all kinds of obstacles—that he needed to ask for a pardon in Washington for having lived illegally in the United States and for having used a different name, and blah, blah. My father accumulated a big stack of immigration documents, and they never let him get his papers.

But my father soon returned to California anyway, and my mother joined him. I was left in Camargo with my grandmother, where I remained until I was five. My father would come and go just like an American citizen. He had learned quite a bit of English and everything. You might say that at that time the *migra* was not very strict. Then my father decided to settle in Juárez, and the family joined him. I started kindergarten in Juárez after having gone to a private preschool in Camargo, where supposedly we had feria because my father worked in the United States and because my grandmother was not bad off. In Juárez my father got a job in a gasoline station and I went to school. That year I was chosen "king" because I was the "prettiest" kid in kindergarten. Actually I sold more votes than anyone else for a fund-raiser for the school. That's why I won.

We lived in a house in an isolated, fenced-in area used to store old tires. We were about a mile from the closest neighborhood. While we lived there, we were cleaned out, robbed, three times. They even took some birds that my mother had in a cage. We were paid to live in that corral because it was like a warehouse. They stored tanks there before putting them in gas stations, and we were paid to watch them. The tanks belonged to my father's boss. When we were robbed the third time, we moved to another house that also belonged to the boss. We lived there for seven years.

In 1966 an uncle came from Michigan driving a new station wagon. My father persuaded him to lend us the station wagon to take our family to California with a tourist permit. My sister and I, of course, didn't need papers, since we had been born in the United States. Our godparents lived in Selma. My godfather was managing a farm at that time, so he gave us work picking grapes, peaches, and plums. We made good feria.

In Selma, my father was told by friends and relatives that since he had U.S.-born kids, he could easily fix his papers. Then he was advised that it would be even better if my sister and I stayed in California, and in time we wrote to the consulate asking that they "give" us our father so he could support us. My parents decided to stay at that farm during the summer and return to Juárez after the picking season, so they returned to Mexico, leaving us with my godparents. I liked it there because I saw lots of grapes, orange trees, and lemon trees. I would see peaches, pears, plums. Everything was *a toda madre* [fantastic], things I had not seen in Mexico. I was a child; I became fascinated with all that. I thought to myself, "Here I've got it made." But after our parents left, things got tough. We did a lot of crying, but not the crying that spoiled kids do. I thought of myself as someone who had been toughened by all that experience in Juárez. I had sold all kinds of things on the street: newspapers, burritos, gum. I also shined shoes. I had done all those things that poor kids do. The kids with money don't have to do anything; they just say "Papa" and "Mama" [give me this, give me that].

I went to the sixth grade in a school I first saw during the summer, when there were no kids there. My first reaction was, "¡Híjole, que pinche escuelota tan 'a toda madre'!" [Wow, what a bitchin' big school!]. Things were swell until school started, when the kids arrived. I then spent the six most miserable months of my life up to that point. I had suffered from hunger and many other things, but I had never suffered psychologically. I felt unwanted. Most of the kids at the school were Japanese and gabachos. There were only a few Mexican Americans, but they didn't know Spanish. I was told, "Go back to where you came from, wetback, dirty Mexican." Even the Mexican American kids said that to me. Since I didn't know English, the only thing I could do was to hit them. If someone would look at my school record, he would find that I spent about 90 percent of the time at school in the principal's office. As soon as I stepped off the school bus, the bus driver would turn in his report about me, because I had already hit three gabachillos. Every day I would arrive at home all beaten up. In Juárez one was taught in the streets to be a fighter, to throw rocks and whatnot. When I got to California, nobody was going to push me around and treat me badly. I didn't

understand what they were saying to me, but someone would more or less translate for me.

After I was called a wetback and all that, I was taken to the office and punished. I was given swats with big boards, but by then I was ready for that. In
Juárez they used to hit us with rulers on the hands, so I didn't care. There was
one thing that got me down, though. A gabacho would come with two or three
friends and want to beat me up, but since I was a pretty good fighter, I fought
like a beast. I would soon bloody someone's nose, and they would take me to
the office. There I would lose because no one knew Spanish. The gabachito
would just explain, "He attacked me," and all that stuff. And I would just keep
quiet. The only thing I could do was to laugh along with the principal. I think he
thought I was some kind of idiot. I only knew how to say "Hi," "Bye," and
"Somebody came." There at the farm where we lived, whenever a car was heard
the dogs started barking and I heard people say, "Somebody came." Those were
the first English words I learned.

When they gave me my report card, they didn't put in grades or anything. It
just said, "He's showing progressive attitudes." They couldn't evaluate me since
I understood nothing. It was a disaster for me. I cried just the way machos cry.
Things must have been really bad! We couldn't take it anymore after four
months. My godmother heard about a family that was driving to Juárez, so she
arranged for my sister and me to go along with them. I think my aunt paid twenty
dollars for us. My poor little sister also had a rough time. She was in the second
grade, and she had the same experience. Frequently she too had to fight the
gabachillos.

When we got to Juárez, I couldn't go to school because they would not accept
students in the middle of the year. I told them, "But I was going to school in
California!" They answered "Well, there you could enter school anytime, but
not here. There is no more room." I was going to lose that year, when an aunt
who lived in Mesilla, New Mexico [forty miles from Juárez–El Paso], said I
could go live with her and go to school there. So I went to Mesilla and visited
my family in Juárez every week. Things were all right, but I had to work, as
always. I picked pecans and cotton in the afternoon, and onions during the summer. I also thinned cotton plants once, but I really blew it. Since I was big and
skinny, they must have thought I was older than my age, because they gave me
a long hoe, just like the ones they gave the adults, those with experience. The
kids got a short hoe so that they could bend and be close to the ground and not
hit the wrong plants. I figured I would just watch what others did, and I would
do the same thing. I stuck close to this old man who just kept smoking and
talking and hitting those plants, wham, wham. I thought, "I'll just do what he
does." And I started, bam, bam, bam. When we got to the end of the row (the
rows were about a mile long), the foreman came over and said, "Oh, sonny. You

have a beautiful swing. You walk real good. I can tell you know how to do the work. But your aim is pretty bad. Look, you haven't left me a single plant." He was an old man, and he had taken a liking to me right away because I talked to him really nicely. I was quite a talker, and I would ask him about his love affairs when he was young. I think I left only about fifteen plants in the whole row. I would swing and hit, but man, I couldn't leave a single plant standing. I only worked that day, because the next morning I couldn't get up.

Whole families would work out in the fields. Kids would be placed under trucks or cars so they could sleep. There were young children who could really work. For example, my aunt had two girls in the second grade who would pick everything. In the wintertime the family picked pecans for three cents a pound. The kids could do that work. It's just a matter of gathering the fruit from the ground after it's been shaken off the tree. A five-year-old kid can pick up six pounds in a few minutes, just playing there. "Just throw those nuts in the little can, my son." A kid could pick thirty pounds or more working every day after school and make ninety cents or a dollar a week. Everybody had to work; there were no lazy people around there. My aunt earned eighty cents an hour peeling, cleaning, and packing geese on her regular job. After she got off, she would take us to pick pecans every afternoon, and we would pick about 500 pounds a week. We could pick from the time we got out of school until dark. At times we couldn't make out which were nuts and which were rocks.

At school I was placed in the fifth grade, which was a grade below where I had been in California. They demoted me because I didn't know English. I felt like a dummy because I already knew everything they were teaching; it was just that I didn't understand what was being said. I would look at the pictures in books, whether it was history, natural sciences, or geography, and I would tell the kid sitting next to me what it was about. I knew more or less. In Mexico they teach you a lot. He would say, "That's right, that's what the book says." But I couldn't tell the teacher or answer questions on tests. Spelling and that kind of stuff; that was easy—easy. I just had to learn words. I began to catch on. There was a Mexican teacher, I think she had come from Mexico, and she liked me a lot. She began to teach me a lot of things, and I learned a bundle. Soon she said they could put me in the sixth grade. I was in the sixth grade for a month and passed the tests, so they put me in the seventh grade.

I finished the seventh grade and was into the eighth when my father came by to borrow money from my aunt because he and a friend from Juárez were on their way to Chicago as *mojados* [wetbacks]. He asked me if I wanted to go along, and of course I tagged on pretty quickly. That was the first time I went to Chicago. We had a limited amount of money, but there we went. On that trip I became very aware of racial discrimination because both my father and his friend were very scared of going through Texas. According to mojados, Texas immi-

gration agents are the worst in the United States, so we avoided Texas and traveled instead through New Mexico, Colorado, and Kansas. We stopped in a little
town in Kansas to buy some used tires because the ones we had were worn out.
We found a gas station where we could buy them, so we left the station wagon
there and went to a restaurant next door. We ordered something to eat, and the
waitress said, "But that costs $1.25," as though she thought we didn't have any
money. We waited a long time to get served. I think she figured that if she waited
long enough, we would take off. But we were killing time at the restaurant,
because outside it was colder than hell. It was around November, at the end of
the football season. (I remember that because I played football in Las Cruces. I
was assigned to be a defensive player, since I really didn't know much about the
game.) So she took about an hour to serve us. I would look at the clock and ten
minutes would go by, then another ten, and another ten. In reality we didn't want
to eat; we just wanted to be in a warm place while they fixed our station wagon.
At last the waitress returned and asked, "What do you want?" So we ordered
something, I forget what. Again she told us what it cost. I think people around
there had never seen Mexicans. They looked pure redneck to me.

We finally got to Chicago. My dad and his friend had run out of money, but I
had $2.70 in my pocket. I hadn't spent anything on the trip because they paid
everything for me. We were almost on empty and we put in two dollars' worth
of gas. Then we had some coffee because it was really cold. We called our aunt
and got instructions on how to get to her house, but we were going crazy trying
to find it. We didn't know our way around, and Chicago is such a big city. Finally
we used up our last dime to call her again. She told us to stay where we were,
that she would come get us when her husband, my uncle, got out of work. We
had to wait a long time because he didn't get out of work until two or three in
the morning. There we were, shivering in the car. I thought the whole world was
like Juárez, that it didn't get that cold. I had heard that it got quite cold in the
north, that it snowed, but I thought that was an exaggeration. The only clothes I
took with me was what I was wearing, just summer clothes that I was used to
wearing at home. We just huddled together to keep warm.

My aunt and uncle actually lived in Hammond, Indiana, just east of Chicago.
That's where we lived for three weeks. I attended school there during that time,
but my father could not find work. It was wintertime, and they were not hiring.
Production was very slow, and all that jazz. But my dad had a brother living in
Saginaw, Michigan, and he asked him for some money so we could go there.
My uncle had it made there. He worked at the Gray Iron Chevrolet Foundry,
where they made car motors. In just two or three days my dad was able to get a
job there, just through sheer luck. So I started school there. That was the first
time blacks tried to beat me up; I guess I was too white for them, and I looked
like a gabacho. We lived on the north side, where all the blacks lived, and that

was the year of the riots and the year they killed Martin Luther King. They had riots in Detroit, and they burned some houses in Saginaw. Once someone tried to run me over with a car. They called me honky and I didn't know what to say because I didn't know what that meant. I asked at home and they told me it meant gabacho. "¡La Madre! [Damn!]." No wonder they were trying to kill me!

I got a job after school. One good thing about us Mexicans is that we adjust to everything. If they need farm workers, Chicanos are there. If they need factory workers, Chicanos are there. It was the same with me. There was no work in the fields, but there was quite a bit of work shoveling snow. I earned a lot of feria—at least it was a lot for me because I could keep it all, since everything was paid for me at home. I would make twenty-five or thirty dollars in just about four hours. I would take a wide shovel and a broom and go to the west side, where the gabachos, the rich, lived. I rang doorbells and asked if they wanted their walkways and sidewalks cleared for two or three dollars, depending on the amount of work. Most houses also had steps and porches, so I cleared those too. So five or ten minutes of swinging my shovel back and forth would earn me two or three dollars, and I was off to the next house. Of course, I could only earn that kind of money when it snowed heavily. During light snows I couldn't charge that much, but I still worked. After a while I had many regular customers, including a store and a doctor's office. I would notice snow in the morning, and in the afternoon I quickly went and cleared all those places. Each one would give me ten or fifteen dollars a week. I liked it there.

When school was over that year, my dad got an idea to go to Traverse City, Michigan, to pick cherries. My uncle had told him that in the summer of 1966 he had taken his whole family to pick cherries, and they had made a lot of feria, enough for a down payment for a new station wagon and for a trip to Mexico to visit us. My dad became excited because my uncle had six girls and only one boy. He was told that the girls, who hardly worked, filled up fifty or sixty boxes every day, and each one earned ten dollars. My dad figured that if those girls did that, then his boys could do much, much more, since we had lots of experience picking grapes and onions. So he sent money to my mom and my older brothers to come to Saginaw, as "tourists." When they got to Saginaw my dad got an old car and we were off to pick cherries. We were able to make lots of money because together we could earn eighty to one hundred dollars a day, and we liked it because we lived on a farm and there were lakes around there. It wasn't like in Texas, where there was nothing to do after work. When we were through we would head for one of the lakes and go take a bath. We didn't have a place to bathe where we lived.

At the end of the summer, my brothers returned to Juárez to continue high school, and I returned to Las Cruces to enter the ninth grade. That year some *comadres* [close friends] told my aunt in Las Cruces that she could get a better place to live in Arizona with a certain farmer, so she decided to move, and I went with her. But once a rattlesnake almost bit me, and I decided to return to El Paso, where I lived with another aunt so I could go to school there. I eventually graduated from high school and then enrolled at UTEP.

"I really found myself in a box, being kind of neither/nor."
—LEONARD PACHECO

Mexican Americans brought up in a predominantly Anglo environment face personal
situations fraught with ambivalence because of their cultural distance from their Hispanic heritage. Dark-skinned individuals in particular often find little acceptance in
Anglo society and at the same time feel disengaged and even alienated from other
Mexican Americans with a strong Hispanic identity. Leonard Pacheco, a biculturalist
whose parents immigrated from Mexico to the United States in the 1910s, illustrates
this pattern. He grew up in a U.S. border city in the 1930s and 1940s, and he remembers many instances in which he was not sure of his place in society. His ambivalence drove him to be very cautious in dealing with Anglos lest he be subjected
to discrimination. But to his surprise and delight, his ethnicity and physical appearance actually became assets in a different social environment away from the border.

When my father was discharged from the army, he got married and settled in an Anglo neighborhood. Previously he had lived in different Mexican parts of town, and I think the only reason he moved was that he felt his children would have a better life and get a better education. He never lost any of his Mexican feeling or anything like that; he just felt that was the best thing for us, and so he did it. So we grew up with nothing around us but Anglo families and Anglo kids.

My parents would speak to us equally in Spanish and in English, and they probably spoke more correct English than a lot of the people around us even though they were supposedly uneducated. I know that my mother wrote better than 90 percent of the people around us. Whether purposely or not, we would generally answer them in English. I don't know if we consciously thought, "If I do this, I will not be as much of a Mexican," but we seldom spoke Spanish to our parents, even though they spoke Spanish to us at least half of the time. Since we started speaking English from the beginning, we didn't have anything to un-learn like some people who come from Mexico and have learned a full vocabu-lary of Spanish and no English, and then they have to do the switch. We never had to do that; we were just learning up one track.

At that time, instead of feeling uncomfortable that I was a Mexican in an Anglo neighborhood, I felt more uncomfortable going to visit relatives in a Mexican neighborhood. All my friends were Anglo. There weren't any Mexicans living in my neighborhood, although after a while there was one who lived about three blocks away.

About the time I got into grade school, I started feeling a little different because there was always someone to remind you that you were different. These were generally the kids that one might classify as the bullies, who would say or start something. When I got to junior high and high school, I really started noticing it more because then you get the social separation—who you can go out with and who you can't. Then I really found myself in a box, being kind of neither/nor. Socially I felt uncomfortable going to the Mexican houses, but I also started having this feeling with the Anglos. I would have my friends all the time, but then when they would have parties I would not be invited. I was never invited to a high school party of any variety, but I didn't go around dragging my head in the sand. There were certain times when I really thought about it and felt bad, but maybe I was a good rationalizer and maybe after a few years I sort of got used to it. "That's the way it is, that's what's going to happen." Cheerleaders, the National Honor Society, school clubs, those were Anglo things. I don't think I belonged to anything in high school, none of those things. You just didn't.

My parents taught us to take care of ourselves and to work. I got a paper route when I was thirteen and kept it till I went to college, and my sisters did pretty much the same thing. One of them started supporting herself, I guess, since she was about twelve, working at Kress's [department store] and places like that where . . . Well, there were certain places you could get a job and certain places where you couldn't. She applied at the telephone company, and Mexicans didn't get jobs there; she applied at Standard Oil, and Mexicans didn't get jobs there either. Those companies and others didn't want any accents, even though my sister never had anything that you could classify as a Spanish accent.

At the gas company I had a good friend who was a big wheel; I used to deliver his paper. Well, he got me a job and I thanked him for it. But even there, where I had a friend, the jobs that I got were as a yard man in their pumping stations or out in the pipeline. You didn't get an office job or a clean job. Mexicans do now, but they didn't then. When I think of things like that, my sister is the one I look at, because she was in front of us, and I didn't try what she had done if she ran into trouble. She was kind of blazing the way a little and made things a lot easier. My choices were based to some extent on the reception she had gotten at different places.

At the time we didn't call that kind of treatment discrimination. You'd get sort of mad, but you didn't think about it quite as much as you do now. We sort of thought, "Well, that's the way it is. In the springtime, leaves come out, and at that place you don't get a job." One was as natural as the other. It's funny, because it really didn't leave you with the feeling, "I'm being cheated." You knew that you were, but you felt that it was sort of inevitable, and what was the point of upsetting your breakfast over it. This happened in the middle and late 1940s.

Along the same line, yet a little differently, I remember when I went off to school in Kentucky in September 1949. When the bus stopped in Odessa so the passengers could eat, I made sure that I ordered breakfast in good clear English so they knew I spoke English. I don't know that they could have thrown me out, but it's a perception I had because of the things that had happened previously, which made me conscious that I might run into trouble. So I paid my insurance money by making these outward sounds or motions or whatever to clean myself up, if you want to call it that. I was never mistreated in that way, really, but I knew those things happened. One or two years before, a softball team that included a Mexican player had gone to Odessa, and he had to stay in a different place than the rest of the team and eat in particular places. These things were in my mind. I watched where I went and how I acted. Maybe that sounds chicken, but that's what people did without feeling bad about it.

In Kentucky I encountered a different situation. There prejudice was directed against people darker than myself and of a different background. There I found myself seen as an oddity, in the image of Spaniards seen by Americans in the movies, the Spanish lovers and so on. For a while I wasn't sure how to take it. One day I was sitting in class and this sweet young thing came over and plopped in my lap. I thought, "My God!" Not that it was an unusual sort of behavior for an eighteen-year-old girl and an eighteen-year-old boy, but it wasn't the sort of thing that would've happened to me on the border. On another occasion I was walking in this park and some girls started a kind of forward flirting which I hadn't experienced. I knew what was coming off, but it was just unusual for me. It was very interesting that these girls, who would not even be seen talking to a black, would then be attracted by pigmentation to a different person. I felt like a new brand of snake.

"And what the devil are you doing in the U.S. Army?"

—JUAN RODRÍGUEZ

Historically, military service has been one of the most significant avenues for acculturating members of minority groups to American culture. People of Mexican heritage have served in large numbers in all branches of the military throughout the twentieth century, compiling a meritorious record and at the same time coming into closer contact with Anglos from different parts of the United States. As in civilian life, the military has not been immune to racial and ethnic discrimination, and it is very common for veterans of Hispanic descent to relate such experiences when they recall

their days in the service. The selection that follows is of interest because of the elo-
quence with which a former soldier tells us why he joined the U.S. Army and what
he felt during his tour of duty in Vietnam. It is especially significant that Juan Rodríguez, a Mexican national, volunteered for military service in the United States as a
way of becoming a U.S. resident. Few people are aware that U.S. immigration policy
permitted Rodríguez and many others like him to enter the "land of opportunity" in
this manner. Born in Guanajuato, Rodríguez migrated to the border with his family
in the 1950s. While living in Mexico, young Juan managed with sacrifice to attend a
low-tuition, Protestant high school in the heart of a poor Mexican American barrio
on the U.S. side. In 1960 he made his decision to leave Mexico permanently, using
the military as his ticket to pursue the American dream. At the time of the interview,
he was a salesman, but he later became an educational administrator. Rodríguez can
be classified as an upwardly mobile bicultural immigrant.

I came to the United States hoping to have a better life. Unfortunately, Mexico
was not doing very well economically. Being so close to the United States, one
is naturally interested in something better, and one crosses the border. When I
finished my studies I had to make a decision what I was going to do. The U.S.
Army offered me the opportunity to come to the United States. The other alter-
native, staying in Mexico, was not very attractive. Had I stayed in Mexico, my
plan was to go to a big city like Guadalajara or Mexico City, where I could earn
a good living. I wanted to find work with some government agency or perhaps
in a hotel, where I could use my knowledge of English with tourists. That was
the best I could hope for, since I didn't have a career.

But I couldn't put my idea into action because I had no money to cover my
initial expenses in a big city. My family's economic situation was pretty pathetic.
There were seven kids in my family. We were not well connected. There was no
one who could offer help. That's the reason I had to do what I could with what I
had. In Mexico, if your economic situation is no good, you will stay that way. It
doesn't matter if you have lots of determination. Contacts are what counts. When
you are poor, all your friends are also poor, so you remain poor. That's why I
started thinking of coming to the United States.

The idea of joining the U.S. Army originated with some Mexican friends who
had done just that. They had joined the military earlier that year [1960]. I was
aware they had completed basic training. I started thinking I should do the same
thing. A friend and I went to talk with the army recruiters. They told us to think
it over and if that was what we wanted, that we should return the following day.
The next day we went back and spent about two hours in the office. They then
took us to the American consulate on the Mexican side, and things moved very
quickly there. The military recruiters had direct and immediate access to the
consul, so we didn't have to put up with stuff like, "Wait a while," "Bring your
card," "Come back on Wednesday." In less than half an hour, all the documents

were signed. To this day, I don't know exactly what I signed, but I signed many papers.

They told us to say goodbye to our families in Mexico and to report to the office on the U.S. side the following day. They gave us some document to cross the border. That's what we did, and the next day we reported in. They gave us a voucher so we could stay in a second- or third-class hotel that night. They also gave us vouchers for meals. I was excited because I thought I was coming to a better life in the United States, but in reality I didn't know if that would indeed be the case. The following day we were processed, and we left for Fort Ord, California. We arrived there at 2 A.M. To my surprise, at 5 A.M. we heard this loud voice, "Get up! Get up! Up! Up! Up!" And you had to get up quickly; otherwise they would throw you off the bed. Thus began my experience with the U.S. Army.

We spent two months in basic training. It was tough for me because I wasn't used to that, but at least we had a place to sleep. We made it all right through basic training, and they let us go home for two weeks. Man, I was happy! Of course our hair was very short, and I was embarrassed by that. In Mexico if you run around with little hair on your head, it means you have spent time in jail.

They told us we could not cross into Mexico with our uniforms on, so we put on civilian clothes. But one night my friend and I decided to wear our uniforms to this place where they had dancing. I guess we did that because of vanity. We wanted to be seen in our uniforms, especially by the girls. But some [Mexican] guys didn't like the idea of having us around wearing those uniforms, so they started insulting us, calling us "little chocolate soldiers" and things like that. I thought we would have problems there, so we decided to leave. I have never liked aggression. I didn't like the idea of getting into a fight, so we left.

After our two weeks of leave I was sent to supply school, and my friend was sent to electronics school. Then I was sent to Korea, and he was sent to Germany. I was full of envy. I also wanted to go to Germany, not to Korea. We spent twenty-two days on a boat crossing the ocean, and I didn't like it one bit. I had to wash pots and pans and peel potatoes. I didn't like it, but what could I do? I spent thirteen months in Korea, and I didn't enjoy it. Korea was too backward. There were no places to visit, no places to have a good time, no places to go dancing. From Korea they sent me to Fort Hood, Texas, and I didn't like that place either. It was an isolated post; there was nothing around there. But it is near San Antonio and Austin, and one could go there on weekends.

One of my mistakes in the military which I greatly regretted was changing my MOS [Military Occupational Specialty] from supply specialist to infantry-man. I could have stayed in the supply field. I didn't have to run around like a crazy man scaling mountains or running across fields with a rifle or a machine gun on my back. But I fell for what the gringos told me. They said, "Don't be dumb. You won't be able to accomplish much in the supply field. There are no promotions there. Get into the infantry." So I did that, and later I was sorry because I couldn't change again to something else. I tried to get out of the infantry many times. I thought with my abilities and my knowledge of English and Spanish I could be useful to the Army someplace else. But no, they kept me in the infantry for the eight and a half years I was in the military.

During my time in the service I was a good soldier. I did my work and stayed out of trouble. I was surprised at the attitude of many Anglos, who didn't seem to care. Many of them avoided responsibility. I would think to myself, "How can it be that I as a foreigner am more conscientious about being a good soldier than the Anglos?" Of course, many Anglos were there involuntarily. They had been drafted for two years. As far as discrimination is concerned, I did experience it in the military. Anglo soldiers from the South would take notice of my color and marked accent, and I was made to feel at a disadvantage. They would ask me, "And what are *you*?" And I would answer, "I am a Mexican." And they would say, "And what the devil are you doing in the U.S. Army?" "Well," I would tell them, "I just wanted to join the U.S. military."

In Vietnam there was a period when I was the leader of a squad, and all [the squad members] were Puerto Ricans or Mexican Americans. It seemed to me it was that way because someone in Washington had decided that's the way things should be. I couldn't help thinking it was some form of racism. It also appeared to me that Mexican Americans, Puerto Ricans, and blacks were concentrated in the toughest fields—in the infantry, artillery, and tank units. By contrast, there seemed to be few minorities in such fields as quartermaster and communications. I remember I was passed up for a promotion in Vietnam. I was the next one in line to get it, but they gave it to an Anglo. I complained to the captain, saying, "Look, this promotion belongs to me. I have been a sergeant for such and such period of time, and I have spent plenty of time in Vietnam. I think I am the one who merits the promotion, but they have given it to someone who does not deserve it." In about a month, when more promotions arrived, they promoted me. I am almost sure that if I had said nothing they would have ignored me.

One of the things that bothered me the most was that they did not let me become an officer. My ambition was to become a lieutenant colonel. I made my calculations and thought to myself, "Well, even if things go badly, if I serve twenty years I should at least be able to make lieutenant colonel. By working, studying, and just trying hard I think I can do it." I got excited about becoming an officer and started getting together the necessary paperwork to apply to OCS [Officer Candidate School]. I got everything ready with the exception of one form, something that had to be approved in Washington, D.C. I can't remember what the devil it was. I was waiting for that form to come back so I could take everything to my company commander for his signature. In my mind I was already at OCS. I even bought new uniforms and new boots. At the time I was stationed at Fort Bliss, Texas.

All of a sudden I was informed by the personnel office to get my things ready, that I would be shipped to Vietnam in a few days. This was in December 1965, and the Vietnam War was getting hot. I said, "Wait a minute. I've got this application to OCS pending." But they told me that since the company commander had not yet signed the papers, my application wasn't valid. I was left with all my papers, my new uniforms, and my new boots. I got to Vietnam on December 24, 1965. What a Christmas Eve! As I arrived we came under attack! There were shells falling all around us! There was thunder and shaking everywhere! That was the first thing I experienced in Vietnam.

Later I was informed that the form from Washington had arrived, and I continued to press my case to go to OCS. But I was told that I would have to wait until I returned to the States. When I did get back I was asked if I still wanted to go. I said, "No, I don't want to go anymore." And I was told not to be foolish, that now I had a year of combat behind me and that would be a big plus for me. But by then I had decided to leave the service. I knew if I went to OCS they would send me back to Vietnam, and I didn't want to go back there. That was a very bad experience for me. What stands out the most in my mind about Vietnam is the physical and mental suffering that I went through. I had a sense of desperation because I wanted the thirteen months I was there to go by rapidly, but it turned out just the opposite—time went by very slowly. I remember things . . . such as the time we were attacked by mistake by our own helicopters. Several friends fell dead and wounded all around me. I don't know why I was saved. I remember unpleasant scenes such as being engaged in conversation with others and all of a sudden they would be hit and fall dead. One moment they were alive, and the next one they were dead. And then I couldn't talk to them anymore.

I remember having to sleep in foxholes half-filled with water and walking through the jungle at night in total darkness and with rain falling. I remember getting malaria and being in the hospital for over a month. It was good that I got malaria because if I hadn't, perhaps I would have died in combat. While I was in the hospital, 75 percent of my company was wiped out. I came to the conclusion that the big fish in Washington, D.C., ran the war without caring how many lives were being lost, without caring if I or a hundred thousand others like me slept in foxholes filled with water, or if I survived or died. While we were going through all those experiences in Vietnam, the big fish in Washington were having big parties and big feasts. All those things bring unpleasant memories.

I would also get upset at the fact that many gringos got out of the responsibility of going to defend their country by using religious beliefs as their excuse. To me that was not a valid reason. I was disgusted at the lack of patriotism on the part of many gringos. But on the other hand, they may have refused to go to Vietnam because they knew things I didn't. As a foreigner I felt a certain loyalty, a certain gratitude to this country. I don't regret coming here, but now I would refuse to go to Vietnam, because now I know it was just politics. It was a matter of manipulation. The lives that were being lost didn't matter.

"I was treated that way because I was half German and half Mexican."
—CARLOS STRUMM

Individuals of mixed ethnicity face many difficult problems because of the differences that separate them from other people. Rejection and discrimination are felt particularly strongly by those whose physical appearance makes them stand out. The dilemma of people who are between cultures has been brilliantly explained by Everett V. Stonequist in his classic work *The Marginal Man.* Carlos Strumm, a forty-year-old man of German-Mexican descent, recalls painful experiences, particularly during his childhood, that are rooted in his dual identity. What has been especially heartrending for Carlos, an upwardly mobile bicultural immigrant, is the rejection he has encountered in both Mexican and Anglo societies. The fact that his German father was racially prejudiced and neglected family responsibilities only added to Carlos's predicaments.

I remember well that wherever I went to school in Mexico, the teachers hated me. I use the word *hate* because some teachers called me "Damn German" or "Damn American." When I was in the second grade, there were seats for everyone except me. I was thrown out of several classrooms. They would send me outside for the whole day in the hot sun. They would say "Carlos now knows his place." I was treated that way just because I was half German and half Mexican. I don't remember being so bad to deserve that kind of treatment. There was hatred toward Germans. Kids would stop me on the streets, raise their hands, and say, "Heil Hitler." I was ashamed to be seen with my father because they drove it into my head that I was inferior because I was the son of a German. At the same time, however, everyone respected my father.

In 1951 my father, my sister, and I moved to the United States [to a U.S. border city]. We lived in a slum area that was totally Mexican American. We had nothing. Back in those days everyone wore short hair except me. Every six months my father would take me to Mexico and I would get a haircut for fifteen cents. At that time he would get very drunk. There were times when he would beat me, even with a chain. He would say, "You stinking, goddamn, dirty Mexican." I think my father treated me badly because of his excessive consumption of alcohol, and also because of lack of education. Despite the fact that he knew a great deal about mathematics and mechanics, that he spoke about six languages, and that he traveled all over the world, he was sadly lacking in social culture. He could not accept religious or racial differences in people. He hated Protestants, Catholics, Jews, blacks—everyone. To him I was just a Mexican. He liked my brother William, who looked like a gringo, better.

In elementary school I encountered hatred. The Mexican American kids called me names. The teachers were all Anglo American, and they pushed a lot of anti-Mexican propaganda on us. I remember being asked, "What is your name?" I looked at the teacher and answered, "What is *your* name?" Since I didn't know what that meant, I just repeated. I thought I was being asked to repeat it. On one occasion an Anglo music teacher came to the school to give us lessons. She had a little pitch pipe. One day I took it and played it. She grabbed it from my mouth and said something like, "You pig. How dare you?" Then she threw it in the trash, I guess because she couldn't stand the thought that I had touched it. That was the kind of Anglo teachers we had in school.

I was also treated badly in high school. All the teachers there were also Anglo. They used to beat me because I spoke Spanish. They wanted to make a gringo out of me by force. My mother wanted me to become an electrical engineer. When I was in the ninth grade I went to see a counselor about that, and he told me, "That's not for you. You can be a good carpenter or a good mechanic." I said, "I study what I want. I want mathematics." Later I transferred to a technical school, but I had to drop out because my father left us and I had to work. I worked in a hotel as a busboy but made little money. When I turned seventeen I decided to join the Air Force. They paid $87 a month and provided food and clothing. At the same time I could get rid of my military obligation.

It was in the Air Force where I learned to speak English and where I got to know the way of the Anglo-Saxons. I found out that many of the Anglos came from the countryside and had limited education. I met sergeants who had served for twenty or thirty years and couldn't write. I found out about how Anglos feel toward other groups. I learned that Anglos would always put down Mexicans, blacks, Chinese—everyone who was different. I used to hang around with Anglos, but I always remembered that I was Mexican. I didn't want to lose my culture or my language. Despite my name, Strumm, I didn't want to mix with them in such a way that the real me would disappear. By contrast, I saw some Mexicans who made it a point to change. There was one whose name was Jáquez, but he would say his name was Haykes. He was one of those Mexicans who admire Anglos so much that they lose their principles and their customs.

Being in the air force really opened my mind. Suddenly I encountered people who were totally different from me. I came to find out the worst about Anglos, but I also learned that not everyone was the same. There were many who had their good points, especially those who came from the North. They were astute, better educated, and had an ample view of things. Those from the South were more closed-minded. As I learned English and Anglo customs, I found out the Northerners had different values from the Southerners. I saw enough differences to be able to function in both groups and survive. I was stationed in Louisiana for a time, and there I learned more about racial hatred. Once I boarded a bus to get back to the base. As I headed to the rear of the bus, the driver turned around and said, "Hey boy, come over here. Don't sit back there, sit up front. Negroes sit in the rear." I was stunned. I learned that the civilian employees at the base hated blacks. Some would say, "Don't call the negroes blacks, call them niggers." That remark reminded me of a comment my father made the first time I saw a black man. It was at the border, when we had crossed the international bridge. He said, "They are niggers, not blacks." While I was in the air force I worked out a system to be better accepted. I managed to be different, to take things in stride, and to get along with others.

When I got out of the air force after four years, I was going to stay in New York, but I got a letter informing me that my mother was very sick, that she had had a heart attack. I returned home and stayed there. I started to work in a gas station and had plans to go to school. At that time I was officially twenty-one years old, but in reality I was only twenty. My father, who must have been drunk at the time, had registered me as one year older years before. With the GED certificate I had earned while in the service, I was able to go to college. It was very hard for me because, although I could speak English, I could not write it. I got bad grades and was kicked out. I then worked as a waiter from four to eleven at night, leaving me time to return to school. But I had to take a full load because they no longer let me take less than twelve hours. At that time [1961] there were very few Mexicans at the university. There were Mexicans from Mexico and Mexican Americans, *pochos,* or Chicanos. The Mexicans from Mexico would keep to themselves; they did not associate with the pochos or the Anglos. Mexicans and Mexican Americans did not belong to fraternities. They usually sat in the back of the classroom.

Once a professor in a business course read an announcement about a job opening with an insurance company. He told us that those who were interested should see him in his office. Since I needed work I decided to apply. The professor took everyone's name except mine. He told me in a very nice way, "Look, Carlos, I don't think it's to your advantage to apply for this job." What I understood he was saying was, "You're a Mexican. You can't compete with the Anglos."

I graduated from college in 1973 with a degree in economics, and I went to work with the welfare department. I think my major contribution there was to find ways of helping people who needed the services of the agency. That was difficult to do because of the bureaucracy. I noticed that the department had been completely invaded by Mexican Americans. Unfortunately, too many Mexican Americans seek public jobs like that and don't aspire for anything higher. They find their "bone" and stay there. Because they make careers out of jobs like that, they become bureaucrats. Their main objective is job retention and building a pension rather than providing services for the people. I suppose we have Anglo Americans who do the same thing.

I remember one employee who used to spend a lot of time decorating doors with Christmas ornaments in an attempt to win a bottle of liquor. They had a contest in the office for the best decorations. He finally won, but he should have spent that time helping people. I saw that as a lack of professionalism, of interest, of dedication. I was against a lot of these practices and policies of the agency. I started writing letters making recommendations for changes. That got me into trouble. I spoke to the supervisor, a very powerful Mexican American woman married to an Anglo. A higher-ranking boss, a Mexican American man, was also present. Above them there were nothing but Anglos. I guessed he was there only to back her up, because he said nothing. She told me that if I didn't like it, I could leave. Eventually that's what I did.

"It's a long way from the banks of the Rio Grande to the banks of the Potomac."
—ELIGIO "KIKA" DE LA GARZA

Integration into Anglo society has been difficult for many Mexican Americans because of economic and social marginalization. In some parts of the border, however, certain favorable circumstances have allowed some members of the group to experience relatively rapid assimilation as well as social mobility. Eligio "Kika" de la Garza, a congressman from South Texas since 1964, was one of those select borderlanders who rose from poverty to prominence in politics. De la Garza, a biculturalist, credits the healthy social and ethnic environment that prevailed in his hometown of Mission, Texas, for his success, but he is quick to recognize that in other parts of Texas conditions were far different and that Mexican Americans faced innumerable obstacles that impeded advancement.

As a youngster I had different jobs. I sold newspapers and had my own shoe-shine stand. I caddied at the golf course. I worked at a grocery store and a department store. My main ambition was to join the navy. I don't know why, but I wanted to be a sailor, which I did as soon as I became seventeen. There was an old attorney in Mission named D. F. Strickland; they called him Judge Strickland. I used to shine his shoes in his office. This is when you got a nickel for a shoe shine, but he always gave a quarter, so I was in the money there. He was a sort of a big man and smoked a cigar. He appeared to be a rough individual, but he wasn't. He was very kind. I'd sit on the floor and shine his shoes. I noticed that he never looked down to see if I was doing a good job with his shoes. He always looked above me or across the room but always spoke to me as an equal. We spoke about grown-up things, and somehow I always felt at ease. I thought, "This man isn't looking down at me and I'm shining his shoes. I don't know what he is, but whatever he is, I think that's what I'd like to be." When I found out he was lawyer, I wanted to go into the law profession.

The small town where I grew up was a good place. It simply was. There a kid could shine shoes and get to be a congressman. Among my contemporaries are very prominent doctors and teachers. The prevailing atmosphere was family life, closely knit families with respect for law and order. This is the sort of background that makes success possible. There wasn't that much opportunity, but there was no obstruction to the opportunity. I don't recall noticing differences in wealth in our town. There were families that were wealthy, but the kids in school didn't show great wealth. Everyone was alike. People didn't go around showing that they did or didn't have money. I think that wasn't as noticeable as in a large city. I was never able to notice and say, "This is a rich neighborhood and this is a middle neighborhood and this is a poor neighborhood."

Our town was basically divided by the highway running east and west. The Anglos lived on the north side, and the Mexican Americans on the south side. There was only one junior high school and one high school, so at a very early age, you didn't have that daily, continuous separation. When I was growing up I would say that the population breakdown was 50 percent Anglo and 50 percent Mexican American. Now [1975] it is probably at least 75 percent Mexican American. I attended a parochial grammar school in our parish. We had two parishes then, one on the north side and one on the south. Ours was 99 percent Mexican American, and our teachers were mostly Irish nuns.

There are some experiences that stand out in my mind from my high school years. In my freshman year, I remember I was elected vice-president of my class. I was beat out for president by a very good looking, nice Anglo girl. In this case, beauty beat me. I participated in football, basketball, and track. I did fairly well even though I was quite small and didn't weigh much. I guess the feeling of success just develops. It's an inward feeling that you can't explain, but somewhere down the line perhaps my being smaller than the rest of the group made me try harder. I had to keep up and compete with them.

One of the interesting things about my hometown is that I don't recall any instances of discrimination against me. I understand that before my time there had been overt cases of discrimination in the schools. I'm told that there was the Lion's Park with a sign that said, "Whites Only," or something like that. During my school years there may have been some subtle discrimination against me but no acts of direct discrimination that I can remember. There may have also been some subtle discrimination against grown-ups pertaining to availability of jobs or to education. My generation was probably the first in our area that had students going to college. Before that time, very rarely would anyone from Mission, whether Anglo or Mexican American, go to college, with the exception of the wealthy people.

Mission was founded by a few families, and basically those few families knew each other as friends and acquaintances, whether they were named Conway or Garza. The children of the community, myself included, *were* the children of the community. The place was so small that there wasn't really the opportunity for someone to discriminate. I believe this is one of the reasons why we didn't have that kind of problem. By contrast, this particular city in West Texas (I won't name the city) that was *all* Anglo American was very different. The first Mexican Americans who went there were cotton pickers. Having outsiders who were poor lent itself very readily to segregation. Hence the Anglos initiated the separate school, the separate neighborhood, etc. In Mission, where you lived was basically by choice. There was no outward sign of "The north side is better than the south side" because at that time, we had as many poor on either side. The few Anglo business families—Conway, Bentsen (the family of Secretary of the Treasury Lloyd Bentsen), for example—were not wealthier than the Longoria, Martínez, or Guerra families. There was equilibrium with the wealth, and it made it easier for all people to live together.

In certain areas of West Texas, the Anglo was not really educated at a much higher level than the Mexican American who came to pick the cotton. This is one of the sad things about discrimination: it's ignorance, and I think many people will agree. In order for the Anglos to show their superiority, they had no other recourse but to discriminate. We are still seeing some of the products of that type of discrimination that existed in West Texas and even in the Lower Rio Grande Valley.

I have been very fortunate. I know the Lord has been good to me. Probably my greatest success is to have been elected a member of the Congress of the United States. It's a long way from the banks of the Rio Grande to the banks of the Potomac, from shining shoes on the streets of Mission to the Congress. It's a long way. Life has been good to me. I have no complaints.

My view on assimilation has been the following: all individuals have a basic inherent heritage they want to keep. Basically it's family pride. This is probably more so in the Spanish-speaking or Spanish/Mexican culture, as contrasted to some other ethnic backgrounds. It has always been important that one knows from whence he came. We take pride in saying "We are Mexican Americans." Our people discovered the whole Western Hemisphere. It was the Spaniards who sent Columbus. The founding of important institutions in the Western Hemisphere is a part of our ethnic background. Before the white man came, we had (and I say "we" collectively, as a descendant of someone who was born in Mexico) the pyramids; we had organized society; we had zoological gardens; we had medicine; we even conducted surgery. Our contribution is twofold. One is having discovered the whole hemisphere. The other is the advanced civilization that *our* Indian ancestors in the south had.

Our heritage must be preserved but not to the extent that we segregate ourselves. Pride in our ethnic background can only be shown when we are with those who are not of our ethnic group. It won't do us any good to pound our chests and say, "You're Mexican American and I'm Mexican American, look how great we are." We achieve nothing by doing that. The inherent pride that everyone has should be fostered and developed so that we can then assimilate with other groups and be able to *show* that we have made contributions. In the assimilation process, whether involving intermarriage or moving to areas that have very few Mexican Americans, one should be able to say, "I am proud of whence I came, but I am not letting that separate me from my involvement in American institutions as we know them today."

My feelings toward Mexico have always been very close because I live right on the border. Our family, because of history, was split down the middle, and we have relatives on both sides of the Rio Grande. Hence, one feels kindlier towards a country where one's relatives live. Also, since our area was once part of Mexico, we basically have a feeling of closeness and association with Mexico. I think Mexico has come a long way in spite of all the obstacles it has had. Certainly no major country in the world has had the setbacks and upheavals that Mexico has had.

"We are fairly isolated and have 'geographic immunity.'"

—MERCURIO MARTÍNEZ

Because of a long historical presence and contemporary demographic superiority vis-à-vis Anglos, Mexican Americans in several towns on the U.S. side of the border have been able to wield significant political and economic power and to feel relatively secure in their social milieu. Laredo, Texas, is one such community. As the dominant group, Mexican American Laredoans see the structure of their society as having produced patterns that differ greatly from centers where Hispanics are marginalized minorities. Businessman Mercurio Martínez, a biculturalist in his forties, elaborates on this theme, emphasizing the interaction between Mexican Americans and Anglos and between Mexican Americans and Mexicans. As a native Laredoan, Martínez has had extensive direct experience with transnational interaction and cross-cultural relationships.

In Laredo you don't see ethnic discrimination between the Anglos and the Hispanics. Anglos, who constitute about 15 percent of the population, have been raised with a strong Mexican influence. Hispanics, who make up the other 85 percent, have not carried a chip on their shoulders, as you find in other areas of the United States. The Hispanics in the interior have a complex; that chip on the shoulder is very dominant. The positive identity of the Hispanics in Laredo is explained by a combination of things. We are a majority of the population. We are fairly isolated and have geographic immunity. Laredo is located about 150 miles from the major cities in the region: We are about 150 miles from San Antonio, 150 miles from Corpus Christi, 150 miles from McAllen, 150 miles from Monterrey, Mexico, and about 180 miles from Del Rio. Anglos born and raised in Laredo end up speaking Spanish just as fluently as the Hispanics. For example, one former district attorney, an Anglo, even used Mexican *dichos,* sayings, in the courtroom. There is, of course, economic discrimination in Laredo. People who are economically well off are part of the elite and belong to a certain social circle. But the elite includes both Anglos and Hispanics. The division between the Anglos and the Hispanics just isn't there. Many have integrated and intermarried.

I have never been exposed to discrimination. I guess that is due to a number of factors. One of them is that I have never looked for it. When you have a tendency to be sensitive to discrimination, you immediately sense it. When you're not looking for it, you don't notice it even if it's there. That has been my attitude. I never grew up with the consciousness of being Mexican or of being different from the mainstream. This was never a part of our growing-up experience at all. I consider I grew up in a clean atmosphere in Laredo. I was educated in a Catholic school. Many of the students were from Nuevo Laredo, Mexico. For twelve years I had constant exposure to my Mexican classmates. We could not ignore the fact that they were from another country, yet we didn't have any animosity toward them—at least I didn't, because I considered them my classmates. I must admit we felt insulted when the Mexican students called us *pochos,* because we were not completely fluent in either English or Spanish. Hispanics have a tendency to switch back and forth between the two languages. But we were also critical of *them* because they spoke English with a strong accent.

I improved my Spanish when I played semiprofessional basketball in Nuevo Laredo. Four of us from Laredo played in Mexico. We learned how to say things correctly in Spanish. For example, we used to say *driboliar* for "to dribble the ball." The correct term is *botar la bola.* We learned to say *fintar* for "to fake," instead of *feikiar,* and *el arbitro* for "the referee," instead of *el ref.* It took a while to realize it, but we learned that *la cancha* meant the basketball court. I'm glad I went through the experience because I saw how deficient I was in Spanish.

In my experience working for the International Bank and the Laredo National

Bank, I had frequent contacts with customers not only from Nuevo Laredo, Mexico, but from all parts of the interior of Mexico. I discovered Mexicans are extremely sharp. I had dealings with people from holding companies such as Grupo Alfa, Grupo Televisa, and Grupo Chihuahua. They are very shrewd, very knowledgeable, very astute businessmen. In order to understand the behavior of Mexican businessmen, you have to understand the culture. When you extend credit, for instance, you have to understand that *el mexicano jinetea el dinero y jinetea la persona a quien le debe*; The Mexican rides the money and the person to whom he owes it. That means that if you extend credit for thirty days to someone, he will "ride" you for sixty days. He will tell you, "Yes, I'll pay you in thirty days," but he will probably ride you for an additional period of time. When you get paid will depend on how persistent you are, but eventually you'll get paid. You have to understand that's part of their culture, and that's part of doing business.

That kind of thing is also done in the United States, but the Mexicans are more astute about it. *Si, hombre, te voy a pagar*; yes, man, I'm going to pay you. *Cuando*; when? That's something else. The Mexicans use your money for their own personal gain and for their own business. They will ride you as long as they can get away with it. I have learned that they don't usually play by the rules, like we have a tendency to do in the United States. The ethics are there, but they are colored. While playing semipro basketball in Mexico, I learned that the rules were there, but we didn't actually play by them. In the first game we learned that we had to be just as aggressive as the opposition—and in some instances just as dirty—in order to survive. That was the way we had to play, and we eventually ended up winning the conference. I can cite another situation where the rules are not applied. When you read a financial statement of a Mexican businessman or business, you can only accept a part of it. You cannot accept the whole thing as being gospel or actual fact. I once took a course with a visiting business professor from the Universidad Nacional Autónoma de México, and he told the class that if we had a financial statement from a Mexican businessman, we should discount 50 percent of it and challenge the other 50.

Sometimes you get burned. I remember an interesting experience at the bank when I was in charge of the loan department. I met this extremely attractive young lady from Nuevo Laredo who had had two previous loans from us to finance two used cars. She had obtained the loans with the help of a cosigner who had good credit. In both instances the loans had been financed over a period of twenty-four months, and she paid them off in less than ten months. The third time she came to the bank she approached the junior loan officer asking for a loan to trade up to a brand new automobile. This time she did not have a cosigner. The junior officer approached me and showed me her record of payment, which was excellent. We discussed the matter, and based on the record, we decided to go through with the third loan over a three-year period. Within a short time she appeared in the past-due list. The junior loan officer came to me and showed me her name, and we decided to wait an additional thirty days to see if she would take care of the payment. Thirty days went by and she was still delinquent. We decided to pay her a visit and actually had in mind repossessing her car. We went to a residential area of Nuevo Laredo, knocked on her door, and this matronly lady answered. As soon as we walked into the house we knew exactly where we were—in a house of ill repute, so to speak. Soon the young lady appeared, wearing maternity clothes. She was pregnant. She couldn't make her payments because she wasn't working. She knew exactly why we were there. She said, "You came to repossess the car," and gave us the keys. We brought the car back to Laredo. When we sold it she still had quite a bit of equity left, so the bank sent her a money order for the difference.

In another case, I financed a Ford Mustang for this very influential man from Nuevo Laredo who had an account at the bank. After a period of time, he showed up on the delinquency list. I tried to contact him but was unsuccessful, so I went through a bank in Nuevo Laredo. Finally I got to him and was able to repossess the car. As I drove the car across the bridge, the U.S. customs officer sent me to secondary inspection. Two narcotics agents approached me with a dog and asked me what I was doing with that car. I told them I had repossessed it. Fortunately, one of them knew me quite well. He said, "Well, I'll have you know that this car was given in payment for a large marijuana haul in Saltillo, Mexico. We had an all-points bulletin on this vehicle. I'm sorry, but we're going to have to confiscate it." Of course, I wasn't about to challenge that. They checked the car thoroughly but found no illegal merchandise. I ended up losing the car. Fortunately, nothing happened to me.

Having been burned a few times, I got very apprehensive and challenged people who came to the bank for one thing or another. Take the case of people who would want to cash personal checks or money orders. Once this individual asked me to approve a postal money order that had been sent to him. In a polite way I asked him for personal identification, but he had none. He explained that he had gotten mugged in Mexico and had lost everything, including identification papers. He had gotten hold of his family somewhere in the interior of the United States, and they had sent him the money order so he could get back home. I told him there was no way I could approve that money order. He became a little abrasive and said, "How do you expect me to show identification when everything was stolen from me?" I responded, "How do you expect me to be sure you're so-and-so, when in fact you might be somebody else?" After a few choice words, he took off, but as he reached the door he turned around and quickly came back. He said, "You told me that as long as I showed you something that proved to you who I was, you would cash the money order for me." I said, "Yes, that's right," He then took off his false teeth, which had his name engraved in them. That was proof enough for me to give the okay for that check to be cashed.

"I lived in a world where we spoke English and Spanish interchangeably."

— AMBER MILTON YEARY

Bicultural Anglos are found in all U.S. border communities, and especially among families who have businesses that cater to Mexican Americans and Mexican nationals. Forty-year-old Amber Milton Yeary is a third-generation resident of Laredo, Texas, who has acculturated to the Mexican way of life to a significant degree and is therefore a biculturalist. His grandparents arrived in Texas in the early 1900s. Yeary, who owns an auto repair and parts shop, shares his experiences living in a bicultural environment. His astute observations on the social milieu of Laredo provide valuable insights into the nature of biculturalism, including problems confronted by people who must function in different worlds.

Laredo has a very large racial mix—a rather sizable Arab community, a rather sizable Jewish community, a predominantly Latin American community, and a large number of Anglos such as myself who fall into a pot which seems not to have any distinctions. I feel like it's a great place to raise children because of the mixed atmosphere and tolerance that people learn here for each other's peculiarities. Growing up in the west part of Laredo, I was the only *gringito* [little Anglo] in school until the fourth grade. We were fortunate to have Mexican maids in our home, and consequently we spoke Spanish before we spoke English, so there was no inhibition at school. The first time I came in contact with other Anglo children was when I went to another school, the United Day School, sponsored by the Baptist church. Through high school I lived in a world where we spoke English and Spanish interchangeably as a matter of course during the day. We were taught to think in two languages. Sometimes English vocabulary would not be descriptive of a particular situation, and it was not a problem switching back and forth in the two languages.

When I went off to college at Texas Tech I was thrown into a West Texas society that was predominantly Anglo and very intolerant of people of other racial backgrounds. One of the things that stands out in my mind is a quote in the school paper from the athletic director. This was in 1957 or 1958. He was asked if he would recruit black athletes. In those days they called them Negroes. His retort was, "I would rather have one Mexican than ten Negroes." It was a slam against both racial groups and very difficult for me to handle. I had gone to Tech with a good friend from Laredo, and we would find ourselves speaking

Spanish to each other because it was more comfortable for us. But when we did that in the company of others, we ostracized ourselves from them. They would usually make some racial slur like, "Hey, you two Mexicans, cut that out." In time it ceased to be a racial thing with them; it was more a statement made in jest. They began to appreciate the fact that we were bilingual, but it took some time. Even our peers in the fraternity we joined thought we were different. They knew our cultural background was different, but I don't think there was any less respect for us as individuals. It was just kind of hard for them to handle. Cultural differences are not easy things for people to accept. I would say it took the full four years of college to be able to live in that kind of environment.

My daughter went through the same thing when she went off to college. She has brought home a number of friends who have a difficult time understanding the environment here. Many of my daughter's friends have Latin surnames. Her college friends notice things that we don't even think about. To us, things are very natural here. Anglos and Mexican Americans share the same problems, the same lack of public services, the same business problems. Our problems become theirs, and theirs become ours; there is no distinction. The distinctions are made by people outside of the Laredo environment who do not understand our ability to transcend racial categories. Many people who have been transplanted here because of employment reasons have chosen not to integrate themselves into the local society. They have not appreciated the uniqueness of the bicultural situation because their preference has been to deal primarily with their own immediate group.

Of course, many of the local Mexican Americans have been very much aware of discrimination in Anglo society. People I went to school with felt subtle discrimination, like not being accepted into things. Mexican American students who went to college in East Texas or at the University of Texas at Austin during the 1950s had a difficult time. A lot of them preferred to go to St. Mary's University in San Antonio because they found real camaraderie with other Mexican Americans from South Texas. They found the atmosphere at St. Mary's to be very comfortable for them.

Most people I know who are contemporaries of mine who have intermarried have had a few problems, especially outside Laredo. The same is true for children of mixed marriages. For example, there is the case of a young woman who was from a mixed marriage who went to a university in North Texas and got a degree in education. She taught school up there for two years but decided to come back to Laredo. She was very blond, but she had a Spanish surname. She could not make it up there; she was not accepted by that society. When she returned, she married a young man, a Mexican American. Because of their differences, the marriage lasted for only a little over a year. She had some problems adjusting to her situation. I think the lack of stability would probably be directly traced to the fact that she came from a mixed family. I am not saying that is the normal situation, because I know other people from mixed marriages, and their lives go right on. In Laredo it generally makes no difference whether they come from a racially mixed marriage or not.

One interesting situation about mixed marriages is the names people give their children. We have a little joke in Laredo that when our athletic teams go play in San Antonio, the Laredo roster will have names like Ricardo Johnson and José Clark, but the roster of the San Antonio team will have names like Roland García and Jerry García. The Spanish first name and English last name reflect the intermarriage that has taken place between Anglo men from the local air base and Mexican American women. We notice those differences when we see that people who have moved from Laredo to San Antonio have adapted to the Anglo society by changing the first names of their children, say from Gerardo to Jerry. In Laredo, Spanish first names are generally retained. You do find that distinction between the two areas. It is also interesting that as some of the Anglo military men have been transferred out from Laredo, the wives have not wanted to go with them. This is their home; they have felt they cannot assimilate into the other [Anglo] society. Often marriages have broken up and mama has stayed home with her Anglo-surnamed kids, but their first names are very definitely Mexican American.

One of the things that enables you to operate comfortably in either society is the ability to communicate and understand the colloquialisms that are peculiar to Mexican Americans. If I walk into your home and you speak Spanish, and you know that I understand everything you say, and that I understand how you feel because I've been a part of that, then you're not uncomfortable with me. I think the success of my business is very much related to that. We have been in the auto repair and parts business in Laredo for fifty-two years. Had my family not been able to become a part of the [Mexican American] society, we would not have been as successful. We would not have lasted so long had people not felt comfortable with the Yeary family. We probably have twenty-seven competitors in Laredo, all Mexican Americans. We are the only Anglos in the business.

Being an Anglo and speaking Spanish sometimes brings on interesting situations. One day I was in a department store, and some men said to the clerk in Spanish, "Leave the gringo alone and take care of us because we need to do such-and-such." The clerk was someone I knew, someone I had grown up with, and he knew that I understood what was going on. He was doing his best to try to keep them from saying any more. Finally I couldn't resist the temptation to answer them, and I explained that my needs were just as great as theirs and that my time was as limited as theirs. They were all embarrassed. One of them was amused enough to inquire who I was and what I did. He turned out to be a really good customer and a good friend.

There are many amusing stories and jokes that we tell among ourselves. Among those of us who have grown up in Laredo, ethnic jokes are not considered racial slurs. We tell stories on each other with no problem whatsoever. If it's a funny story, we recognize it as a funny story. The sense of humor of the Mexican Americans is probably what has carried them over some rather difficult situations. If we were not able to laugh at ourselves as well as we do in our bicultural situation, many of the things that have gone on would have been intolerable.

"Perhaps we are singled out because we are 'them,' or güeros [blondies]."
                                                              —DIANE DAVENPORT

Contrary to the standard pattern, in which Hispanics feel marginalized by mainstream society, in several relatively small, Hispanic-dominated communities, Anglos—especially newcomers—are the ones who often feel discriminated against. Many of them have a hard time dealing with the reality of minority status in an environment that seems strange and difficult to understand and penetrate. Diane Davenport is a forty-one-year-old Anglo originally from Dallas who has lived for fifteen years in a Texas border town where Mexican Americans constitute 85 percent of the population. She is a high school teacher and artist who speaks some Spanish and who has traveled in Mexico and Central America. Her husband, who is also an educator, likewise has spent considerable time south of the border. Although sympathetic to Hispanics, Mrs. Davenport has encountered varying problems in her predominantly Mexican American community. She understands that the simple fact of being a "minority" person explains some of the difficulties, but she also feels strongly that her fair skin and striking blonde hair have exacerbated her dilemma, for she has stood out dramatically among the dark-skinned, dark-haired Hispanics. In some ways Mrs. Davenport is a uniculturalist and in others a biculturalist.

We came to the border because my husband got a job here. We had been here once before, and we had gone to the beach and crossed into Mexico. It was a quick visit, so I didn't have a good sense of how thing really were in this town. My initial impressions were not negative, and before moving here I thought that perhaps it would be fun to live on the border, that we would have a chance to enjoy Mexican culture, that we would go to different fiestas. I didn't want to leave the big city, but I had expectations that things would go okay, that there would be interests we could pursue. I guess I had a romantic notion of the local lifestyle. As soon as we arrived I suffered culture shock. I had a hard time shopping for groceries. Everything was arranged differently, and I couldn't find anything. Also, I couldn't get waited on, and that really bothered me. Once when

I went to one of those big Mexican stores I was waiting to check out and this woman pushed my basket out of the line. She said something in Spanish, but I didn't understand her. I said to her, "What are you doing?" She fussed at me, but I had no idea what she was saying. The other women just laughed. I complained to the manager, but he just said, "Never mind, just get back in line."

I've had experiences at the 7-Eleven store waiting to pay, and I've been ignored by the clerks. It doesn't matter if I'm first in line. If there are other people around, I will usually be the last one to be waited on. I remember taking my daughter to buy her first bra. This is a traumatic experience for a young girl. What made it worse is that we were totally ignored by the clerks at this store that specializes in lingerie. We could not get waited on, so she could not be fitted. Perhaps some of the clerks are afraid they don't speak enough English, or perhaps they don't want to fool with us because we don't spend enough money in their stores. Maybe they are used to waiting on affluent people from Mexico who come here and buy in large sums. One Anglo buying in small quantity perhaps is not worth their time. In the nice dress stores, Mexican women often spend several thousand dollars all at once, whereas one of us will look for the sale rack.

Anglos have a hard time around people who are always speaking Spanish. If you are with a group of Hispanics, they have a tendency to speak Spanish at all times. I have been at dinner parties where people around me are having a conversation, and I am not a participant because I don't understand what is being said, and they know that. This is equivalent to whispering in someone's ear in front of someone else. At school, in the office when I ask the secretary something she will immediately turn around and say something in Spanish to the other secretary. You don't know whether they're continuing a conversation and you're being ignored or they're saying something about you. It's a very awkward and frustrating situation. I don't really know why Anglos are ignored. Perhaps we are singled out because we are 'them,' or güeros."

Unlike Hispanics, Anglos who are newcomers to this area find it difficult to fit in or to be accepted. It is very hard to break into local groups. The best bet for Anglo newcomers is to have other Anglos show them around because they know how difficult things are here. You very seldom see an Hispanic showing an Anglo around. If an Anglo couple were to move here and ask me where to send their children to school, I would choose either a certain public school that handles more Anglos or a certain private school with a high Anglo enrollment. The local public schools are really geared toward bilingual education, so if your child winds up in that kind of a classroom with all Spanish speakers, chances are the teacher will also speak Spanish most of the time. These are problems I confronted with my own kids until I finally found the right schools for them.

My daughter in particular had trouble fitting into the schools. She is very beautiful but also high strung and dominating. She found herself ostracized.

Even some of the teachers didn't like her. I tried several schools and finally found a private one where she did well. Ironically, most of the students in that school were Mexican nationals and U.S. Hispanics. She got along particularly well with the Mexicans, most of whom came from middle- and upper-class families. I guess they accepted her because she was from Dallas and they figured she could add something to their group. But I've dealt with parents of Mexican students and have found that they don't give equal respect to women teachers. I've been in situations where the men have made it clear that they do not believe that women should be working, that if you're working, your husband is not really providing for you, that your place is in the home.

Sexual harassment of Anglo women is fairly common at the border. Many times when I have pulled into my driveway Mexican men have said things to me. I used to work in the front yard and I would have to contend with men who passed by the house. Once a car pulled up and I ignored the man in it; he came back and kept making comments in Spanish, calling me güera. I'm not sure what he said, but I picked up a clod of mud because I didn't know what else to do, and he left.

I like to jog, but of course I don't do it by myself. I always run with other women. Once five of us were running in the country club area, and a car with three men who had been drinking pulled up and said something to us in Spanish. We didn't answer. It's better not to confront them in a situation like that. We were all Anglo women in our thirties and forties, and most of us were blondes. One of the guys reached out the door and tried to pull down the pants of one of the women. She got very angry and kicked the door. Then they drove off. Another time an Hispanic male followed us while we were running. He got real close and tried to run us off the road. He kept appearing every day and continued to do this, so we reported him to the country club officials. When he came back again I said something to him because I was furious. Then he really wanted to run us off the road. He even put his car in reverse as he came toward us. I don't know why he did that. We just took off running.

I have also had problems at the border. One evening my daughter asked me to drive two of her friends back to their homes in Mexico. It was late and she didn't want to drive them by herself. They had been to a football or basketball game. As we pulled into the Mexican checkpoint, a border guard approached us. He saw these two blonde women in the front seat and the two young men in the back seat, and who knows what he thought. My daughter and I had shorts on, and he leaned over into the car to look at our legs, especially at my daughter. He was almost halfway in the door. He started saying things in Spanish. Then one of the young men leaned forward and said something to him. The border official backed up immediately and almost clicked his heals and saluted. He was extremely embarrassed. The young man was the son of the mayor of the town, and he must have told the guard his father would hear about this. On the way back, we were also hassled by U.S. border guards. They teased us about why two blonde women in shorts had gone to Mexico.

Despite all these incidents, I don't live in fear here. I can go anywhere by myself. I don't feel threatened or in danger. I feel harassed at times, but not in danger. I have come to feel very comfortable in large groups of Hispanics. They're actually very friendly, soft-spoken, and mild-mannered. Since we arrived here, things have improved to some degree. The beach is great, and we really like the easy access to Mexico. We are not very far from the interior of Mexico, and we like to go there. We have established some roots. Nevertheless, if I had the opportunity to go elsewhere, I would have no qualms about leaving tomorrow.

"There are definite limits to the extent to which I can fit in."
— HILDA BECKER

To ease communication and interpersonal interaction, culturally different people on the border have developed appropriate accommodation strategies, but generally speaking Anglos act like "Anglos," and Mexican Americans like "Mexican Americans." The assumption that anyone of Hispanic descent in a predominantly Mexican American area necessarily speaks Spanish and practices Mexican culture is widespread among both groups. This notion poses difficulties for non-Hispanics who look Hispanic but do not speak Spanish and are in fact unfamiliar with Mexican culture. Hilda Becker, a twenty-seven-year-old newcomer and professional librarian, unmistakably has the physical features of an Hispanic woman, but in reality she is culturally Anglo, and as a newcomer to the region she is unfamiliar with the border milieu. Her case reveals the problems that arise when others assume she is a native Hispanic. What makes her experience particularly poignant is that biologically she may in fact be a Mexican American, but that remains a mystery for her because she was given up for adoption by unknown parents whom she suspects were Hispanic. Her adoptive Anglo parents brought her up in a culturally different world. Now she wonders if her new environment at the border is like that of her real parents.

My adoptive parents are of French Canadian and German descent, so I grew up in an Anglo environment, and I have always thought of myself as an Anglo. I have been told that is my ethnic heritage, but because of my appearance I have considered the possibility that I am really Mexican American or Native American, or both. I wonder if, because of the negative racial climate of the early 1960s, my adoptive parents wanted to spare me possible feelings of inferiority or discrimination at the hands of others, so they figured the best thing for me would be to assume I was of the same ethnicity as they. For many years I have wanted to know what I really am. When I was eighteen I was gung ho to find out, but I was persuaded not to pursue it at that point because too many things were going on in my life. I was in the process of maturing, and I was beginning college and thinking a lot about my future. It was not a good time to complicate my life. I am disappointed I still do not know, but I am thinking the time may be right now to find out.

Throughout my life I have tended to go in and out of the Mexican American culture. My father was real open to mixing with other groups. Growing up, I associated with Chicanos, and for several years we attended church in a poor Mexican American neighborhood in Pueblo, Colorado, called Dog Patch. Later, at Colorado College I majored in Southwestern Studies, and I felt I needed to be involved with other cultures. I became a member of MECHA and of the Indian Student Association. I took part in many student activities, including social and educational events. Once I organized a film series, and on another occasion I took a leading role in protesting the presence of Senator Alan Simpson as commencement speaker in 1986. As the leading advocate of discriminatory restrictions against Mexican immigration, we felt he was not an appropriate speaker. So I organized a teach-in on immigration, as well as a rally and armband protest.

It was easy for me to be involved in those things at Colorado College. I was readily accepted by the minority students, most of whom tended to be Anglicized. So I fit in quite well. Later, when I went to UT Austin for graduate work, it was harder to be a participant in Mexican American activities. The Chicano students there were different. Many were from South Texas, and they were much more Mexicanized. I was left with the feeling that I did not fit in.

Since coming to the border I have become involved with a group that speaks out for the rights of immigrants. I feel a little uncomfortable because I do not know much about the issues, but I am learning. I am helping them set up a data base. Now I want to immerse myself in Mexican American culture. I enjoy having Chicano and Mexican friends. Lately I have been dating a Mexican anthropology graduate student who has helped me understand cultural differences. He has also taught me things about the Mexican side of the border. I plan to improve my Spanish by taking classes. I know a little, but there are many things that throw me off. For example, recently I was embarrassed when a lady in a parking lot asked me in Spanish if I had change. Not understanding what she was saying, I did not realize she was talking to me. But she was, and she felt offended I ignored her. She assumed I was a Mexican.

Often I feel like I am straddling a fence—that I am Anglo and Mexican American at the same time. There is no question in my mind about my Anglo heritage, and I have seen myself at the point of being a part of Mexican culture. But then something will happen, and I realize I am different. I am not Mexican

American. I know there is a wall there. There are too many things that make it clear I am not part of the group. There are definite limits to the extent to which I can fit into Mexican American society. My experiences at the border have sharpened the focus in my mind of how Anglo I am. People pull me into their cultural spheres, but my background pulls me out. Fortunately my training in anthropology helps me understand my situation, and that is useful in dealing with these challenges.

"The parishioners . . . really didn't care whether I was Hispanic or not and that I couldn't speak Spanish that well."
— FATHER BRUCE ORSBORN

Our Lady of Guadalupe Church in Chula Vista, California, is far from a typical Catholic congregation in the United States. It is located in a tough neighborhood less than ten miles from the border, and its members are almost all working-class Mexicans and Mexican Americans. Further, it is headed by Father Bruce Orsborn, a flamboyant, bicultural thirty-six-year-old Anglo priest whose "hip" appearance (complete with abundant curly blond hair), unconventional ministerial style, and love of surfing have attracted attention throughout the San Diego area. To the youth he is known as Father Rad. The community was introduced to Father Rad when some Chicanos protested his appointment to the parish, charging that an Anglo priest was inappropriate for an Hispanic congregation. But his unusual way of doing things and his ability to relate well to the local ambiance have apparently overcome whatever opposition he encountered initially. His background included growing up in San Diego, having previous contact with Mexican Americans, and studying Spanish in high school, and these experiences helped to ease the adjustment to his new position.

I was assigned to Our Lady of Guadalupe Church in the summer of 1990. The pastor who had been here for years retired. He was an older Mexican priest in ill health. He wanted someone younger and with more energy to replace him because he couldn't keep up with what was going on. Somehow the assignment fell to me. I'm not sure of the politics involved in my selection.

When I arrived I heard there had been some opposition to my coming here. One of the parishioners told me he had been asked to sign a petition protesting the assignment of an Anglo as the new pastor. There was a lot of stuff about this in *La Prensa,* a local Hispanic newspaper run by a single family. It has its own editorial policy. Seemingly it stands up for Hispanic causes. My understanding was that *La Prensa* said that an Anglo shouldn't be a pastor of an Hispanic parish. It implied that it was a racist move to keep Hispanics down. It was nothing personal against me; they just didn't want an Anglo to be the pastor. The issue picked up when a big article appeared in the *Los Angeles Times*. To me it was racism in reverse.

But matters had been pretty much cleared up by the time I arrived, so I didn't even notice it. The previous pastor calmed them down. He made the transition very easy for me. He welcomed me by introducing me to everyone. The parishioners themselves accepted me with open arms. They really didn't care whether I was Hispanic or not and that I couldn't speak Spanish that well. What they cared about was whether I would be there for them. Very soon the barriers seemed to disappear. It's been good ever since.

Getting a little crazy and joking with the parishioners has helped. I've no shame. I always stand up and say, "The answers to the two most frequently asked questions are: yes, I'm 36 and yes, my hair is naturally curly." I don't preach at the pulpit. I walk down into the crowd. I'll ask questions. I'll talk to the kids. I'll barge right in. I get involved with the parishioners, having a beer with everyone. Someone will say, "Look, Father drank a beer." It sounds scandalous, but everyone goes, "All right!" I'm still into surfing, although it's getting to be less and less, but whether I surf or not I look like I belong to that culture. The youth seem to like it; they think it's cool. I guess it's really surprising to find a priest who surfs. The older Mexican priest would not even have considered it.

Our Lady of Guadalupe Church is practically 100 percent Mexican. It doesn't have boundaries. Theoretically, anyone of Mexican descent in the whole area can come here. Many of the parishioners go back and forth across the border because their families are split by the border. Most of them were born in Mexico and immigrated at a young age. We also get lots of people from Tijuana. They come to shop and do mass on the way. When new people come here, they're surprised by me. They ask, "Where is the priest?" and I say, "I am," and they don't believe it.

It's a pretty violent neighborhood. There's lots of drugs and lots of gang activity. If you want crime, just go three houses down the street and it's there. You get used to it. When I first came, teenagers would not come into the church. They would just stand around outside, so I would leave the altar and say to them, "Get in! We're here to do church. Either you participate or just go. None of this kind of 'hanging out' stuff." They looked shocked. They stood there, and I stood there and waited, and they eventually came in. My view was that they actually wanted to go inside. I think the peer pressure was keeping them out. I went out and yelled at them, "Freedom from peer pressure!"

As far as undocumented people are concerned, it's not much of an issue within the parish. It's a blur. I don't worry about it. I have no idea who's documented and who's not. Years ago, some Jesuit wrote an article about the border, and his basic theory was that it just be opened up. He felt that would probably ease the tensions. I tend to go along with that thinking. I guess I have a radical streak in me. I've heard stories about my grandfather housing immigrants. It's in the blood, I guess. I'll run into Anglos and they'll complain that a lot of people don't even speak English. They get angry with that. I remind them that the state constitution was originally written in Spanish, so we're the invaders, not the Mexicans.

The parishioners don't make distinctions either. They don't go around asking people where they're from or checking documents. If anything, parishioners see the border as an inconvenience; they'd just as soon it didn't exist. When people from the other side come here with problems, they put them up for the night and take care of them. Then they send them on their way. The only trouble I have is with *coyotes* who sometimes drop off people in front of the church. I've seen forty people standing out there, and I think to myself, "Is there some meeting going on that I don't know about?" The coyotes are very cruel to the immigrants. They are supposed to take them to Los Angeles, but then they demand more money, which the immigrants don't have, so they get stranded. I inform them they can walk two blocks and catch the trolley, which will take them back to Tijuana for a quarter.

At Our Lady of Guadalupe Church pretty much everything is in Spanish. All the masses on Sunday are in Spanish except the last one, which is in English. I knew some Spanish when I came here, but I've made my share of mistakes, and sometimes it gets humorous. I said to the parishioners, "When I make a mistake, first laugh, then correct me gently." But sometimes they all scream at once, and I can't hear a thing. I usually just give up and say it in English or whatever and end up laughing. At times the parishioners rattle off in Spanish, thinking that I don't understand, and then when I respond they look shocked. The women sometimes talk about my hair, and I'll pick up a little bit about what they're saying and just say, "Thank you." They get very embarrassed. When I speak to the kids in Spanish and they answer in English, I say to them, "What are you doing? I'm the gringo here, not you."

The parishioners are always trying to make me into a Mexican, and I go along with it. For example, they've been trying to get me to eat menudo [soup with red chile broth, tripe, and hominy]. I've eaten it, but they don't know that. They're always trying to push it on me, saying that I will have to eat menudo for lent, to do penance. So I'll say, "Okay, I'll eat menudo for lent."

When I first heard I was coming to this parish, my first response was, "Isn't there somebody else you can send?" I was reluctant to come here because I didn't know Spanish that well. I always have the fear in the back of my mind that someone is going to come with some really big problem and I'm not going to understand, and there won't be anyone around to translate. The best thing that

could happen here is for a young Hispanic priest to replace me, someone ener-
getic who could take over the parish. But there just aren't many young Hispanic
priests. That's the problem.

"He wanted to humiliate me because I was a Mexican."

—PATRICIA JONES

The presence of large military installations in the U.S. borderlands has brought American servicemen in contact with Mexican women. Many interracial marriages have
resulted, often creating difficult situations because of the formidable adjustments
required. Patricia Jones, a bicultural disadvantaged immigrant who met her future
husband while living in a Mexican border city, endured particularly trying circumstances. Apart from the language and cultural differences that had to be transcended,
both of the partners and the children experienced trauma owing to the significantly
dissimilar moral codes the two partners preferred. The marriage dissolved after a
separation of eight years. At the time of the interview, Jones was working as a janitor
in a U.S. border city.

I got married at age sixteen to an American soldier of the black race. I met him
through a friend. He was visiting her one day when I came home from work,
and she introduced me to him. Sometimes one falls in love without knowing
what will happen later. We didn't go together very long; we got married within
two weeks. He wanted me to go away with him, and I told him that if he really
loved me, to marry me. He said okay. He didn't know how to speak Spanish,
and I didn't know how to speak English. We had a hard time talking to each
other. Before we got married I had to bring an interpreter to tell him that I didn't
have much education, that I didn't know many things. I told him I didn't think I
would be a good wife for him. He said he didn't care, that he would educate me
his own way.

   I don't wish anyone the kind of marriage I had with him. I lived with him for
eleven years and had three daughters by him. He was the one who proposed that
I go to the United States with him, but when all the paperwork was ready, he
tried to keep me in Mexico. Someone had told him that I had married him only
to enter the United States. We had an argument, but he sponsored me anyway.
About five years later he went to the Immigration Service and told them that he
wanted me sent back to Mexico, that he no longer wanted me as a wife, that I
didn't deserve to live in the United States. The immigration officer told him, "No
sir, you cut your own throat. She hasn't done anything against the law. We can't
do anything against her."

   Three months into the marriage, he started hitting me. He even hit me when

I was pregnant. He wanted to humiliate me because I was a Mexican. Instead of feeling proud that I had married him, he was ashamed of me. He would talk about me in front of his friends. I suffered through beatings, humiliations, and putting up with women who would come looking for him. When we lived in California, I once came home from work for lunch and found him in bed with another woman, right in our own bedroom. At that moment I felt like burning down the house, but I just left immediately. I couldn't stand it.

For a time I worked in a restaurant as a busgirl and dishwasher. One night as I walked home around 11 P.M., three men kidnapped me. One looked like a Mexican, one Cuban, and the other Anglo. They were on drugs. One of them held a knife and said, "You'd better not do anything if you don't want to die." I was very scared. They pushed me into an old car and took me to an old hotel. It was a horrible place. They did with me what they wanted until they got tired. They beat me all over. I had to do whatever they said in order to survive. They held me until noon of the following day, then let me go. They threatened me that if I reported them they would cut my throat. God willed that they didn't liquidate me.

When I got home my husband hardly noticed me. I said, "You don't even ask what happened to me." He answered that he thought I was with my girlfriends. I said, "Sure, as if I habitually stayed out all night. I never fail to come home at night." My daughter noticed my face and mouth and asked me what was the matter. It was then that he noticed how I looked, and I explained what had happened. He said, "I think you accepted their invitation to get into the car." He didn't believe my story, so I said, "Let's go to the police. I want to report this." We took the police to that place, and they found traces of marijuana and needles the men had used to inject drugs. I saw them do those things, but at the time I didn't know what they were doing. I had not been exposed to those things. That was quite an experience for me.

I continued having problems with my husband. Once he was going to strangle me. We fought a lot because he had no respect for his daughters. He would walk around the house naked after taking a shower, with all his things hanging. Our oldest daughter was about four years old, and she was beginning to notice. He said that his daughters needed to know about life so that they would not be afraid. I said they would learn about those things in time, and besides, they had me to teach them about men and women. The day he almost strangled me he insisted on taking a shower with our oldest girl. I said no, and we started fighting. He slapped me, and I cussed him out. That's when he grabbed my throat and was strangling me. I said, "Dear God, if I have done something wrong, please forgive me and help me with this man." At that moment everything went dark and we heard a loud noise, like thunder, and he let me go. Then my husband said, "God is speaking to us." I think I was spared because I believed what I had read in the Bible, that when one has a problem, if one asks God for help, He will respond.

Later the law was after my husband. He had a car accident, and he refused to pay damages to the other party. He also got involved in taking nude photographs and doing bad things. He would get himself photographed making love to other women. He would play with sex. He would sell those pictures. He wanted to make a business of that. He was afraid that if the law caught him, they would find out he was taking those kinds of pictures. I told him it would be better to leave California, and he agreed. We moved back to the border. Then he left me for good. He left without paying the rent or other bills. I was receiving unemployment benefits because of the work I had done in California, and that's how I managed. I had to support my daughters.

Shortly after this, Ms. Jones got a permanent job as a janitor in a university. One daughter joined the U.S. Army, another married an architect, and the third became a truck driver.

"I think I adjusted easier to his culture than he did to mine."
—MARGARET PETERSON SÁNCHEZ

The ultimate "mixers" on the border are individuals who marry into another nationality without prior knowledge or experience with the culture of their spouse. Many surprises and conflicts arise as the couple discovers the profundity of the differences that separate them. In the case of Margaret Peterson Sánchez, a native of East Texas who became a biculturalist, the adjustment was particularly difficult because initially she spoke no Spanish and her Mexican husband, Miguel, spoke little English. More disturbing, however, was Miguel's upbringing, which conditioned him to think and behave in an extremely conservative manner in matters pertaining to male-female relations. His expectations shocked Margaret, but gradually they both learned to cope with each other's ways. She changed her perspective on many things, and Miguel became more flexible and in some ways more liberal. Their tendency to adjust and modify their views has kept their marriage together for eighteen years.

I was teaching in an elementary school in a U.S. border city. I was the only unmarried teacher and the youngest one, and all the teachers were always getting me blind dates. One of the women in our church was a medical librarian at a hospital, and Miguel would go there to read journals. He couldn't speak English at the time, but he could read fluently, because he grew up on the Mexican border and learned English in school, but he had no practice speaking it. The librarian there was very impressed with him. She told me she wanted me to meet him, so it was set up that we would go to a party in Mexico. I was supposed to meet Miguel there. It was a birthday party in a home. All the women visited in one room, and all the men in the other. We didn't get to talk to any of the men at all. I didn't know that they [Mexicans] did these things at parties. At the time it was difficult for me because so many of those women didn't speak English. I was kind of stuck there, being able to talk to only one or two. It got boring some-times, just staying with women and talking about what they were interested in. I saw Miguel, and he knew who I was. Finally, after about an hour, my friend, who was real aggressive, said, "Come over here. I want you to meet Dr. Sán-chez." She just took me by the hand and went to the other side of the room and introduced me. I don't know how we talked because he knew very little English, and I didn't know any Spanish. But, we talked for about two hours, ignoring everyone else. I had to ask him to repeat a lot of things many times.

Two weeks went by, and he called me. We went dancing and then started dating gradually. We spoke in English but had problems communicating. He would misunderstand a lot of the words. One time I explained to him that I enjoyed adventure, that I liked that type of a life. I had saved my money from teaching school and traveled in the summer. I lived a summer in Turkey and had been to Europe. When I said *adventure* to him, that meant having an affair or something. I had a hard time explaining that word.

I didn't have any trouble with his friends because they seemed to like me real well. Most of my friends were pretty liberal, and they liked him very much, but I did have a little difficulty with both sides of our family. My parents were not too happy for me to be marrying someone from another country and going to live in Mexico. We dated for about eight months before we got married. He went down to Mexico to visit his parents and took a picture of me. His father imme-diately said, "Well, that's good. Then you'll learn English." That was the only thing he was worried about. He didn't say anything about how I looked. He was very pro-American. He admired the U.S. very much. He was a master mechanic and had been sent to San Antonio for training, and he could read English, al-though he didn't speak too much. The first thing that the mother asked was, "Is she Catholic?" She was a very strict Catholic. The father said, "That's not im-portant!" So evidently that wasn't a problem.

My parents wrote me a letter wanting me to come home to visit that summer and think about it. I figured that at twenty-three I was old enough to make my own decisions. They had never met Miguel. I wasn't sure if my stepfather was coming to the wedding. He was very unhappy. My mother came out first before we married, and when she met Miguel and all his friends she was very favorably impressed. Of course, he was highly educated, and I guess that overweighed the fact that he was Mexican. So she called my father to come out a little early before the wedding. He did, and she kind of paved the way. Of course, now they just love him.

At the time they didn't have too many mixed marriages where the man was Mexican and the woman was Anglo. It was more common for an Anglo man to be marrying a Mexican girl. My principal at school, a little old maid, was very worried. She would come by my schoolroom and wanted to be sure I knew what I was doing before I married. I had a lot of good advice. I guess people thought it wasn't going to last very long, but we've been married eighteen years. We married in the Methodist church. All of my family and friends came, and all his friends came. No one from Miguel's family came; they don't travel much. Then we had a civil ceremony in Mexico, because we were going to live there. Three months later we married in the Catholic church, mostly for his mother, so she would think we were really married. Miguel was not a strict Catholic, so it didn't make any difference to him.

We went to Europe for two months on our honeymoon. They were having an international congress of pediatricians in Lisbon, Portugal. We went to about eight different countries with a group of doctors from Mexico. Of course, our guides would be Spanish-speaking, and I couldn't understand them, so I would hunt around and try to find an English-speaking group and kind of stand on the outskirts and listen. That's the way I tried to find out some information. After two months I could say some things in Spanish.

I thought I knew the Mexican culture, but I wasn't prepared for the extreme jealousy that is displayed in Mexican men. One morning in Madrid, our bus driver, Pepe, was eating breakfast with a huge, fat woman. She must have weighed about 300 pounds! I said to Miguel, "I think that must be Pepe's mother, because he said he was from Madrid." Well, my husband clammed up, and he wouldn't talk to me the rest of the day. I didn't know what I had said or what I had done. I was crying and worried and trying to please. Finally, at the end of the day he said, "Well, here we are, on our honeymoon, and you are interested in another man." I wasn't prepared for that type of extreme jealousy. We had several instances like that, so finally I just wouldn't look at any men or talk to them. I didn't want to upset him. That was a very smothering experience.

When we came back from our honeymoon, we moved to Mexico, and we lived in a tiny room that my husband rented in a kind of boardinghouse. We lived there about a month till we found an apartment. They had about five people living there, and there was only one toilet for the whole top floor. I was still teaching and would go back and forth across the border. I taught about three years in the United States when we were living in Mexico.

When we did find an apartment and started buying furniture on the U.S. side, we needed to get permission to move it to Mexico. We bought this new stove, and my husband "arranged" to move it in a hospital ambulance that belonged to the Seguro Social [Mexican Health Agency]. I don't know how he got permission. He knew a couple of people who worked on the Mexican side of the bridge. They were his patients. I'll never forget one of them, Sr. Domínguez. He had three jobs—one at the bridge, another upholstering cars, and he would clean rugs. He also had a wife and two mistresses. We used to tease him that he had a job for each woman he had. One time he brought his wife and son to Miguel's office, and Miguel asked, "Señora, how is your little baby?" She said, "No, this is the youngest one I have." Sr. Domínguez was behind her making faces to hush. Miguel would get all the children mixed up, which ones belonged to his wife and which ones to his mistress. Finally Miguel decided he better not say anything anytime Sr. Domínguez brought children to the office. Sr. Domínguez would "fix it up" so we could pass these things across the bridge. They never looked in my trunk. They thought I was a tourist. I took over two TVs and all my wedding presents. I used to take everything across. They would ask me, "¿A donde va? [Where are you going?]" And I would answer, "Al salón de belleza [To the beauty parlor]."

As I mentioned before, I wasn't prepared for the severe jealousy of my husband. I don't know if it was because he grew up in a very conventional little Mexican town. Maybe it was a combination of the Mexican culture and his particular family. His mother told me that his father was extremely jealous. She married when she was fourteen and the father thirty-five. She was still playing with dolls. I guess it was like a father-daughter relationship, which many marriages in Mexico were at that time. The wife had to get permission from the husband to do everything. Miguel's mother had very rosy cheeks then, and when she went to church her husband would accuse her of putting rouge on her cheeks to attract men. After a lot of this, she finally just didn't leave the house. In ten years she never left her front door. She would go in the patio, but there no one could see her because it had a wall around it. The husband or the maid would go buy the groceries. He would not even let her go two blocks to visit her own mother. The mother and her sisters had to visit her. She said she didn't get a divorce because she was afraid her husband wouldn't educate her children. I think he was extremely neurotic over the whole matter. I'm sure that's why he married someone so young, because an older woman with an education would not have tolerated that. So Miguel grew up with that type of example.

I liked the color red, and Miguel said I couldn't wear red dresses. He never mentioned this until after we got married. He believed that other people thought that I was trying to attract men. So I gave my red clothes away. I couldn't wear pants; I always had to wear dresses. One time I went out in jeans to get the mail from the postman, and my husband got upset. I grew up very independent, yet I was trying to adapt myself to the Mexican culture. It wasn't until ten years later that I was able to wear pants. But even then when we'd walk down the sidewalk together and some men were also walking by, I had to look down to the sidewalk so that he wouldn't think that I was looking at other men. Once I went to visit my husband at his office, and he had a friend there. I conversed with him and asked him, "Where were you born? Where did you grow up?" When he left the office, Miguel told me that I was never supposed to ask those questions because they would think that I was sexually interested in them.

I recall one instance before we were married. I went to a medical banquet with him. We sat beside an elderly couple the whole night. My husband never introduced himself since you're not supposed to say anything to a stranger until you have been introduced. I felt very uncomfortable because my stepfather is a Methodist minister and I learned to introduce myself and be friendly in a strange situation. That's the way I grew up. Miguel told me, "People in Mexico don't introduce themselves." It was very hard for me to learn because I was an outgoing and aggressive person.

Another time we were riding in the car and I noticed Miguel wouldn't say a word. I asked him, "Miguel, what's wrong with you? You're not talking. You're not saying anything." He said, "I saw you looking out the window at that man when we went around the corner." I asked, "Where? I don't remember doing it or even know what man you're talking about." He told me where it happened and what I did. I had no idea what he was talking about. He was a little paranoid. I eventually learned to cope with it.

When we would go to parties on the U.S. side I would be myself and it was all right. I was like two different people. When I was on the Mexican side I was one type of person, but when I'd come to the United States I was another type because I had more freedom. I belonged to the American Association of University Women. Once they were going to have a fashion show and wanted me to model the costume that I had brought back from Turkey, which consisted of a long dress and a veil. I mentioned this to Miguel, and he wouldn't let me wear that because he felt that I would be exhibiting myself. I was not able to do it, so I let somebody else wear my costume and be in the fashion show.

We were married over a year when our son, Mike, was born. His name was Miguel, and so when he was older we called him Mike. I noticed the difference in the cultures concerning how to treat children. When Mike was born I couldn't take him anywhere. My husband wouldn't let me go out of the house with him, the reason being that he might get sick or do "something." It was almost like being in jail. We were just really confined. In the United States, after children are a few months old you take them in the car and go shopping with them, but evidently not in Mexico. I guess they had maids to leave them with. The custom is not to take them everywhere like it is done in the United States. Every time Mike would get sick I would be responsible because I wasn't careful and this and that. I don't know if Miguel felt this way because he was Mexican or because he was a pediatrician and he was exposed to all those germs and diseases, thus making him more apprehensive. Finally he made me so nervous that I said, "Look, Miguel, I'm going to take Mike to a doctor in the United States and you have got to quit treating him . . ." He just made me so nervous.

When my son was older I went back to teaching. I would go back and forth across the border. At least that alleviated some of the stresses I was having with my life at home. I think I would have had real marital problems if I hadn't had my own career. It would have been harder for me to adjust. I was lucky that my husband let me work. He said, "If you want to work, work. If you don't, stay home." He was conservative in some ways and yet liberal in other ways because his sister is a doctor and he was used to aggressive women.

As long as I had a certain amount of freedom in my teaching and going and coming over to the United States to teach, I was able to put up with some of the other things that I didn't think were as important—for example, not wearing the red dresses and being submissive to my husband. I think having my own career and interests helped me to adjust better to living in Mexico because I didn't have to concentrate my whole energies just to my home and family. We lived four years in Mexico. My husband had always wanted to study in the United States. After he learned English he wanted to go to the United States to do his residency, so that's what he did. We lived a year in Austin, Texas, and a year in Temple, Pennsylvania. Then we went to Philadelphia and lived there two and a half years.

It was so hard for Miguel, especially in Austin because he thought Austin was a real prejudiced town against Mexicans. Of course, he didn't know much English and he was struggling. It was hard for him to know the customs and so forth. Now it was different because we were on the United States side and he was the one who had to adjust. I think I adjusted easier to his culture than he did to mine. It was easier for him in Philadelphia, perhaps because it was a bigger city and there were more nationalities. In Philadelphia, gradually he became more Americanized. With time he was exposed to the culture. One thing that was interesting to me that Miguel told me was that people in Mexico thought that American women were very lazy and that the maids did everything. He even thought that same thing until he moved to the U.S. He believed a stereotype, and he had to change. I guess he thought I was the only American who worked hard. It became a little easier in our marriage after he became Americanized.

We moved back to the border in 1972. By that time I wore pantsuits and red clothes, and Miguel had confidence in me. He was not as jealous as he used to be. We bought a home from my sister and brother-in-law. I continued teaching school, and he opened an office on the U.S. side of the border. We still went over to Mexico to visit friends, and I enjoyed shopping over there. We lived in the area where I had had my first teaching job. The neighborhood had changed a lot in ten years. It used to be 20 percent Mexican American, and now it seemed to be predominantly Mexican American. Our son, Mike, who was thoroughly Americanized after his six years away from the border, began to have problems in the Mexican American school. He didn't know much Spanish even though he looked Mexican and had a Spanish name, and the other boys teased him.

Mike went through a stage where he'd come back from school and he would act like he had some kind of germs on him. He would take his jacket off and would not wear it again. The next morning he would put on a different jacket to go to school. After running through a bunch of jackets, he wouldn't have any unused ones left to wear. I also noticed that his hands had become red and chapped, and soon discovered that he washed them constantly. It was a psychological thing, so we took him to a psychologist and he gave him a battery of tests. The psychologist's findings were that Mike was not seriously ill, but his father and I continued to be so disturbed by his behavior that we finally sent him to East Texas, to live with my mother. The original plan was that he would stay with them to finish out the fifth grade, but he did so well and was so happy there that he never did return to the border to live with his father and myself.

Mother told me later that people would ask him what his last name was and he'd say, "Well, it's none of your business." His full name was Mike Peterson Sánchez, but in signing his name he preferred to leave off the Sánchez. My maiden name was Peterson. Mother told me that she thought he was having an identity crisis because he was half Mexican and half Anglo. He had blondish hair and dark, dark black eyes. He is a very good looking boy. In retrospect I feel that the strain of being thrown into the Mexican culture after six years away from the border was too much for Mike. His only contact with Mexicans during that time were vacations spent on the Mexican side with his upper-class cousins. Coming back to the old school and a different class of Mexican Americans, plus perhaps the fact that both his father and I were working and he was in the care of a maid, perhaps the combination was just too much for him. Probably we left him alone too much. One of the reasons I was content to let him live permanently with my parents was because I recalled that a professor in one of my psychology classes had said, "Sometimes when there is an immediate crisis, removing the person from the situation physically helps."

Perhaps it was just as well that Mike was happily situated with his grandparents because my husband and I began to have marital problems again. I think one of our problems was coming back to the border after I had the freedom and everything in Philadelphia. My husband resumed his jealous, possessive attitudes, and several unpleasant incidents occurred. But now I was a changed person, and I was not willing to put up with that mode of behavior from him. After several visits with a marriage counselor, things got better between us, but I think that this was the first time I really asserted my authority.

I think all of us have come a long way in accepting each other in the different races. When Miguel and I married, you didn't hardly see any mixed couples. I think that our marriage has lasted because we were both from middle-class families and both well educated. This helped a lot. And I think that this city is one of the best places for a mixed marriage to succeed, because you can get the best of both cultures. My impression is that the Mexican Americans here are less prejudiced against Anglos than they are in other cities because of the proximity to Mexico. The city has a larger proportion of middle-class Mexicans, whereas in places like Houston most of the Mexican Americans are poorer and the newly arrived Mexican immigrants are mostly all poor job-seekers.

I have felt privileged in my opportunity to live in another culture. I feel that my life has really been enriched in being able to be part of a Mexican family, to visit for extended periods with his family, and to have lived in Mexico for several years. By marrying Miguel I was not just a visitor to the Mexican culture; I actually became part of it. I learned the language and really broadened my experience. And the same is true of my husband. He has become part of the American culture through his marriage to me. A long time ago he thought that he might want to settle in Houston or San Antonio, but once we came back here we never even went to visit the other cities. We just felt that we belonged here. Neither of us has ever experienced any prejudice here or in Mexico. It's a comfortable place to live. The two cultures add so much to each other.

"Here people are more open-minded."

— "MUÑECA" (DOLL)

As a subculture that functions in the shadows of society, the homosexual community on the border is of substantial interest because of the different levels of tolerance that are found in the two nations. Homosexuality is expressed much more openly and is more accepted in the United States than in Mexico. Consequently gay and lesbian borderlanders have adapted themselves to the local system, carrying on some activities on one side and others on the other. As is true of the general population, gays have also developed attitudes about variations in sexual behavior between people from the two nations and among different ethnic groups. In this interview, "Muñeca" (a self-given nickname), a bicultural twenty-eight-year-old Mexican American gay man who works in a cafeteria in a major U.S. border city, relates personal experiences that reveal yet another dimension of cross-national and cross-cultural interaction and at the same time provide glimpses into the environment in which homosexuals function. The memory of painful and traumatic moments has not diminished "Muñeca's" ability to laugh at himself, easing somewhat in his own mind the uncertainties and risks inherent in his unique way of life.

I first felt I was gay when I was about eleven years old. At that age one begins to notice such things. I didn't feel bad, but I did feel out of place. I was a loner [as far as boys were concerned], but I hanged around with girls. I had many girlfriends. I was fascinated by makeup and women's fashions. The first time I dressed like a woman I was fifteen. I never thought I would always be like this. I felt there would come a point when I would be attracted to girls [in a sexual way]. Sometimes boys from the neighborhood would get together and show their penises, but I just watched. I was embarrassed and would not show mine. I was very timid. I felt strange. The other boys started calling me names like *joto, maricón, cócono,* and *puto* [disparaging terms equivalent to "queer" and "faggot"]. That's why I was always alone.

I thought I was the only one who felt this way. I didn't see anyone else who seemed to be like me—that is, until I went to high school. There I saw other boys who seemed similar to me, but at first I didn't think they felt the same way I did. I had met one of them in junior high school, and I was glad to see him in the high school. I thought to myself, "I won't be the only one they yell at." Another one was very open about his homosexuality, and one day I approached him. [Apparently he was Anglo.] We talked, and he told me he would take me to these places downtown [gay bars] where I would see many others like myself. I noticed that his family was very accepting of his homosexuality. His parents and brothers didn't care. His mother was very nice to all his friends. She bought him makeup, whatever he wanted. His father would let him leave the house dressed like a woman. The only thing he would say was, "Don't come home late." My [Mexican American] friends and I wondered how it would be if we talked openly with our parents. I said I would not do that. I knew they would not accept me. We all agreed it would be impossible to do that with the parents we had. I think Anglo parents are more accepting of homosexuality than Mexican parents. I have known gays, lesbians, and transvestites who lived with their parents. I have visited the homes of Anglo gays and have noticed the difference. I could never take friends dressed like women to my house. If I did, my father would kick us all out.

When I was seventeen my father threw me out of the house. He couldn't stand the way I was. He felt ashamed. He got angry when relatives and friends made comments about me. I moved in with a friend, a truck driver. He was my lover. When he went to New York, he had drug problems, and they killed him. He was a pusher. Later I lived with two other transvestites, and we would go out "prostituting" and made money. We did that simply to pay our bills. For a time I worked in a gay bar, and I made some good money. Any bartender can make money by hustling drunken customers. I would shortchange them. A customer would give me a twenty-dollar bill, and I would keep some of the change, say five dollars. I thought to myself, "What the heck, when he leaves the bar he's going to get robbed anyway. I might as well do it."

The guys who rob them outside are mostly bootblacks and others who come over from Mexico. They're hungry and badly dressed. Many of them get into prostitution. They start by allowing themselves to be picked up by older homosexuals who can give them money and buy them clothes. But a relationship like that won't last because the older homosexual will usually drop the Mexican when he spots a younger guy. Then the one who's been dropped, who's now used to having homosexual relations, will wait for someone else to pick him up. When no one picks him up, he might become an "impersonator," performing in gay nightclubs. If it works out, he will continue doing that; if not, he'll go back to the streets, hoping to get picked up even if only to make five dollars for a one-night stand. It's very ugly. That's why I decided to get a regular job. Even if I make very little, at least I'll have something. The other way it's very risky. One might get nothing, except perhaps a disease.

Transvestites from Mexico hustle on this side because it is easier for them. Here people are more open-minded. On their side they are not accepted. In the United States I can walk on the street dressed like a woman and they will not throw me in jail, although I will be arrested if I walk around the square trying to make money. In Mexico they will pick you up simply for walking around. That's why I don't walk around over there. But I have gone to Mexico many times in a car, usually to bars and discotheques. I have known quite a few Mexicans who come to gay bars on the U.S. side, including doctors, lawyers, and bureaucrats, men who have money and important positions. They like the ambiance, and they are very nice, but if they see me on the street, they will avoid me. I understand their situation. They have told me, "Look, Muñeca, we like you. We know you don't care what people say, but we have to protect our jobs. We have to maintain our respectability." And that's fine with me. When I spot them in public I'm not going to yell out, "Hey *joto, maricón!*" Not at all. They are very nice to me.

The worst experience I've had as a transvestite was when I was beaten by a Mexican who had asked me to go with him for a ride. He was very handsome. He took me to a lookout point above the city. When we finished doing what we went there to do, he took out a knife and stabbed me on the arm and on the side. I was really scared. Nothing like that had ever happened to me. Then he took me out of the car and started hitting me. He left my face really battered. I told him to leave me alone, that if he was not satisfied with what we had done or if he felt I had tricked him into thinking I was a woman, that I was sorry. I told him I thought he knew I was a man. He was one of those people who appear to be nice, but after they've had their pleasure they react in a strange way. He must have known I was a transvestite, otherwise why would he have gone to that gay bar?

Six or seven months later he came back to the bar, and I took revenge. He didn't recognize me at first, but I recognized him immediately. I could not forget his face. I had thought that sooner or later I would have a chance to get even. I had told my friends at the bar what he had done to me. There were about twenty "impersonators" there at that moment, so we agreed that when I gave the signal we would jump him. And that's what we did. We stabbed him with our sharp and pointed combs and with these little knives that many of us used to cut our hair. Some of my friends also pounded him with their high heels. We drove him away, and he never returned.

My best relationship was also with a man from Mexico who I met in a gay bar. I never thought I would meet a man like him. He was a very good person. I had a great time with him. We shared and enjoyed everything, but then his family found out about us and he couldn't continue with me. His family had money. His father sent him to a "school for men." I didn't think that would help him any; I thought he would remain the same.

The first time I had relations with an Anglo was when I was eighteen. I really was not attracted to Anglos because they are different from Mexicans in the way they make love. They are good at it, but I prefer Mexicans or Puerto Ricans. I like men who are more masculine. To me Anglos are very simplistic, very cautious. Mexicans are more willing to do whatever comes along. And they will do it well. One feels more love with Mexicans. Anglos require a lot of help to get excited. It's not worth the effort because by the time they're ready to do it, I no longer feel like it. But Mexicans, if they feel like doing it, they will go for it right away. One even gets tired because as soon as they are finished they want more. The same is true for Puerto Ricans and blacks.

I had a relationship with a Mexican customs official for about a year and a half. I met him one evening when three of us went to dance at a nightclub in Mexico. Of course, we were dressed as women. This man kept looking at me, and I looked at him from the side. He finally asked me to dance. He bought me drinks and took me to dinner. All that time he thought I was a woman, and then he asked me to bed. At that point I felt the best thing to do would be to tell him the truth. I didn't want to have problems and wind up in jail. I apologized for having misled him, but I said I thought he knew the score. I asked him if he still wanted to find a room, and he said no. I said okay. I thanked him for the good time he had given me and told him I had felt very comfortable with him. He said he also had felt comfortable with me. Then he commented that in a crowd one knows nothing about other people, that under those circumstances he could just as well have wound up with the devil. I said I didn't know about that, but I assured him I wasn't the devil. I thanked him again and started to get out of the car. I said, "I suppose you don't want to kiss me goodbye." He said no. He asked me how I would get home, and I said I would walk. He gave money for a taxi, and that's how I got home.

Later this man went around the gay bars, finding out what was going on. He was also looking for me, but he didn't find me for some time. One day one of the bartenders told me he had been asking about me. Finally he found me and told me he wanted to take advantage of the opportunity to find out what relations with a homosexual would be like. He said I had given him a different kind of affection, something he had not experienced with a woman. So we talked several times for about a week but without having relations. He wanted to know all about the gay scene. He was very observant and asked a lot of questions. I thought he was preparing himself for the moment when we would go to bed. We really developed a strong mutual trust.

One day he invited me to a party in Mexico, wanting me to play the role of his girlfriend. I was reluctant because I feared I would be recognized, but he assured me no one there would know that I was not a woman. So I went and everything turned out great. I had the time of my life. I danced with several of his friends, who kept making comments about how pretty and sexy I was. I didn't think they could be so dumb as to not realize I was a drag queen, an impersonator. When I went to the women's room, the women in there also didn't catch on. Several of them even complimented me about my dress, my makeup, and my hairdo. One asked me to let her use my lipstick. No one knew what was happening. I was laughing inside at how I was fooling everyone. My friend would glance at me and he would also laugh. I couldn't believe it. It was great fun. After the party he said he was ready [for sex] and took me to a very elegant hotel. We spent two days there. He asked me to keep pretending I was a woman, and he would try doing things with me that he did with a woman. We did that, but I also taught him new things, and he liked them. We have continued seeing each other, but only about once a year. He calls me from time to time. His family situation does not permit him to see me more frequently. Every time we see each other he gives me money and very nice gifts.

As far as embarrassing experiences are concerned, I've had a few. One day I was dancing in a nightclub in Mexico and my breasts fell off, landing on the floor. I wanted to pick them up, but everyone was stepping on them. When the dance was over, several people noticed me, and my friends and I were thrown out. After that they would not let us go into that nightclub. That happened to me because at that time I had very little experience with wearing the proper clothes so the breasts could be secure and not fall out. Once in a bar I forgot I was dressed as a woman and went into the men's room. I must have been a little drunk. I was standing there urinating when five men came in and just stared at me. They couldn't decide whether to stay or leave. So I took off. But those guys told the bartender, and he told the manager, who came to our table to find out what was going on. As he talked to me my friends scolded me for messing up, hitting me with their purses. I apologized and everything was okay. Later as we drove home in the car we laughed and laughed at what had happened. To this day they kid me about it, and also about the time my breasts fell off.

CONCLUSION

Physical isolation, frontier conditions, transnational frictions, ethnic rivalries, and a sense of separation from heartland areas have all contributed decisively to the special identity of people in the U.S.–Mexico borderlands. But it is the ambiance of internationality and intense cross-border interaction that stand out as the major shapers of the unique personality and flavor of the region. Notwithstanding local variations in landscape, climate, demography, economic activity, and urbanization, the borderlands in their entirety constitute a single transnational system that functions essentially the same from Brownsville–Matamoros to Tijuana–San Diego, joining two societies and producing distinct life experiences and population groups defined by their ties to the "other side." The Mexicans, Mexican Americans, and Anglo Americans examined here are products of that singular milieu.

This study has focused on the way of life of borderlanders, pointing out its vitality and rich diversity. The information provided by people themselves has illustrated the capacity of borderlanders from differing nationalities, ethnic backgrounds, and cultural perspectives to coexist, adapt, and flourish. Rich detail contained in the life experiences of interviewees has furnished revealing insights into the character of borderlands society, touching on many situations and challenges encountered in daily living. The emphasis of the discussion that follows is on central questions that have been raised throughout the book pertaining to the behavioral characteristics of borderlanders, a matter of considerable interest. We begin by underlining the need to view the borderlands in context.

The Borderlands in Perspective

The acute interdependence found in the borderlands mirrors recent global trends toward greater integration across continents and countries, yet no international boundary in the world divides two nations so economically unequal and so culturally different. Asymmetry in living standards and attendant opportunities account for most of the extraordinary growth experienced by the area throughout the twentieth century as it evolved from an isolated and underdeveloped region to become one of the most dynamic zones in North America. In the process, borderlanders overcame the extreme polarization that prevailed decades ago, when chronic political instability in Mexico and pronounced racism in the United States produced many confrontations. Modernization eventually set in all along the boundary, the economy took off, border cities expanded rapidly, and transnational interaction became highly institutionalized. In 1990 about 9 million people lived adjacent to the boundary, deriving myriad benefits from proximity to another nation. To be sure, border-related controversies have continued to cause stress, but in daily life the prevailing tendency has been toward a harmonizing of differences and, among many borderlanders, even cultural coalescence.

A transnational community clearly exists on the border, yet this concept has sometimes been stretched too far. Some have expressed the view that the borderlands constitute a "Third Country," neither Mexican nor American but a combination of the two.[1] Obviously the region is not a country but rather two contiguous geographic entities that are highly interdependent yet that remain inextricably bound to their respective nations. In the first half of the nineteenth century, a strong sense of independence and even separatism existed in different parts of the far northern Mexican frontier, but following the establishment of the modern boundary in 1848 and 1854, that sentiment faded. In the U.S. borderlands, neither secessionism nor even a political drift toward Mexico has surfaced in any serious way.[2] Borderlanders north of the dividing line, both Anglos and Mexican Americans, are steadfast and loyal members of U.S. society, and Mexican *fronterizos* remain proud and faithful citizens of Mexico. All signs point to continued political separation of the two borderlands far into the future.

The Third Country analogy is also incorrect when viewed from the perspective of institutional organization and the use of space. The structure of society in the U.S. borderlands reflects the federalism inherent in the United States, while on the Mexican side it manifests centralization. Public and private institutions on each side are highly dissimilar, and the physical appearance of the two sides is strikingly different. Each mirrors the architecture, landscape, and spatial patterns of its respective nation, although some hybridization is present.[3]

It is in the realm of transnational interaction that the Third Country concept assumes validity. As this study has shown, powerful economic, social, and cultural forces bind the borderlands. In a functional sense, two systems have blended to produce an order that is quite distinct from the structures of the two parent societies and a population whose lifestyles differ considerably from those of the heartland zones. Economic activities that epitomize the Third Country orientation of the region include tourism, assembly industrialization, job commuting, binational consumerism, and smuggling. Transnational social and cultural activities that promote hybridization include bilingualism, biculturalism, intermarriage, and cross-border school attendance.

The Border Perspective and Issues of Identity

Basic to the experience of borderlanders is a variability that is deeply rooted in the phenomenon of duality. The border is predictable and unpredictable; it divides and unifies; it repels and attracts; it obstructs and facilitates. In a bipolar environment, it is not surprising that border society manifests such contrary tendencies as conflict and accommodation, poverty and wealth, social rigidity and fluidity, racial animosity and tolerance, and cultural separation and fusion. Mexico pulls from one direction and the United States from the other, and while the border exerts a force to separate the two national systems, it also generates a power to bring them together. In contrast to people in the heartland, who live at great distances from the border and who are therefore largely immune from direct influence from abroad, borderlanders structure much of their lives around their interaction with foreigners. Yet the effect of the border varies substantially among different sectors of society. People with a national orientation are able to minimize influences from the other side by maintaining a domestic economic base and by avoiding direct involvement with foreigners or foreign-related activities. Such an approach is common on the U.S. side, where large numbers of Anglos, and even some elements in the Mexican American community, have shielded themselves from substantial contact with Mexico.

Transnational borderlanders, however, thrive on cross-border interaction, building bridges that sustain the symbiosis starkly evident in the twin-city complexes along the boundary. People with strong ethnic, cultural, or economic links with the other side are the ones most profoundly affected by such ties because they promote intimate association between two national societies. That orientation is the essence of people categorized as core borderlanders, those transnationals who most exemplify the way of life implicit in the borderlands milieu and who are most involved in overcoming barriers posed by political and human divisions. Core borderlanders abound in the Mexican American population, and they are also found, albeit in smaller numbers, among Mexicans and Anglos. What unifies these otherwise distinct subgroups is a common international mind-set and a binational form of behavior resulting from an intense involvement in transnational, transethnic, and transcultural processes. It is core borderlanders who adhere most to the notion that the boundary should be perceived not as a barrier but as a bridge to greater human contact, not as a divider but as a unifier of different styles of life, not as a symbol of rejection but as one of acceptance.[4]

Core borderlanders have successfully adjusted to the instability generated by a boundary born of territorial and cultural conflict and sustained in more recent times by great economic disparity between the two nations. They have molded their thinking and their human relationships to conform to a binational social environment that needs visionary and open-minded individuals to guide and direct it. Core borderlanders have found ways of making the border permeable and different cultural worlds accessible. They have developed attitudes, values, and behavioral strategies that allow them to move swiftly between two nations and from one cultural group to another; they are able to speak Spanish one moment and English the next. These Mexicans, Anglos, and Mexican Americans have formed a triangular partnership to promote cross-border cooperation and good-neighborliness, and to facilitate trade, migration, economic growth, and sociocultural interaction. At times they have sought to change national statutes deemed detrimental to border interests; on other occasions they have worked together to circumvent official obstacles to cross-border interaction. They have also established informal mechanisms to accomplish what is not ordinarily possible under nationalistic laws dictated by Washington and Mexico City.[5]

In day-to-day relations, core borderlanders have collaborated to keep the channels of international communication open and to keep border-related conflict within manageable levels. Individuals with extensive knowledge and experience in the workings of the border economy have played extremely significant roles in promoting binational growth and development. Others with a high degree of cultural versatility have provided leadership in the networks that bind the area's major groups to one another. Constant movement among different cultural milieus has allowed core borderlanders to develop expertise about the ways of others and sensitivity to their concerns. Aware of the feelings, interests, and perspectives of people from both sides of the border, many core borderlanders have been prompted to look beyond their own national interest, examine problems in broad perspective, and take into consideration the implications of parochially motivated policies and actions. In pursuing transnational interaction and multiculturalism, they have overcome persistent rivalries between the two nations and the sting of racial and cultural biases. Because they live in an environment of uncertainty and unpredictability, they have developed a high tolerance for ambiguity and mechanisms for coping with it. Core borderlanders have discarded fears, inhibitions, and prejudices that afflict people with a national rather than a transnational orientation. Receptivity, flexibility, and adaptability are strategies they commonly employ in conducting cross-boundary and transcultural interaction.

A lack of data makes it impossible to determine the proportion of the population that subscribes to the core borderlander perspective, but undoubtedly it is not very large. For most people in the region, the challenge of functioning effectively in two nations and multiple cultures is overwhelming and fraught with predicaments and dilemmas. Despite a tendency toward consolidation, borderlands society—especially on the U.S. side—continues to echo strong national sentiments that militate against cultural fusion. Both Mexicans and Anglos are subject to great pressure from the heartlands to maintain a unicultural style of life and to minimize external influences. Thus to a significant degree becoming transnational and transcultural entails annoying or even alienating one's countrymen.

People with a national orientation often equate bilingualism, biculturalism, and the consumption of foreign products with a dilution of national identity. This is an erroneous interpretation. Clearly, mutual borrowing and blending have resulted from the mixture of the two cultures, but borderlanders have absorbed external traits and values selectively. Each country has left its imprint on the other, but the essence of Mexican and American cultures and the foundations that sustain the two societies have not been compromised. If anything, the prevailing tendency among borderlanders has been to retain and even strengthen their identification with and loyalty to their parent societies. In the case of Mexican borderlanders, one perceptive observer aptly described the dynamics of that phenomenon almost half a century ago:

> Mexican [*fronterizos*], while rubbing shoulders with Americans, feel in their soul and their heart affection for their country; their nationalism is fortified; they feel more Mexican; they filter patriotic sentiments and purify them; they are transformed from strident patriots into tempered patriots, acquiring greater conscience and clarity about the meaning of the concept of fatherland. . . . *Fronterizos,* in order to be in tune with the civilization and culture of their neighbors, to triumph over them in the end, must dress themselves with a different plumage: they need to speak English to conduct business more effectively, they need better apparel, they need to be more erudite. . . . It is a contest in which *fronterizos* must adapt so they can strengthen their position against opponents [affluent Americans] who have the advantage.[6]

Ethnic and Cultural Conflict

As intimated above and delineated in the body of this work, people of Mexican extraction and people of Anglo heritage have engaged in a protracted competitive struggle, with the latter enjoying the dominant position by virtue of a higher political, economic, and social status. Nationalists and uniculturalists, who predominate in the Anglo community, have often expressed alarm at the permeability of the border and the interplay between Mexican and Anglo cultures. In particular, they continue to be irritated by continuing Mexican immigration, by social conditions among Hispanics, and by the use of the language from the other country on the U.S. side of the border. For many Anglos, not understanding conversations and transactions in a foreign tongue precipitates frustration, resentment, and an inescapable feeling of being on the outside in their own turf.

Throughout the U.S. borderlands, this reaction has given rise to English Only movements that are widely supported by nationalist Anglos and even some assimilationist Hispanics.

The recent expansion of the Hispanic population accounts in part for Anglo cultural antipathy and even flight from the borderlands. The combined Anglo population in the sixteen counties on the Texas border decreased from 293,795 in 1980 to 285,928 in 1990, a 2.7 percent decline. By contrast, Hispanics numbered 1,210,139 in 1990, a 36.8 percent gain from the 884,710 counted in 1980. El Paso County, with the largest population on the border, recorded the greatest Anglo decline (see Table 2.3).

The dramatic demographic shift has been accompanied by an increase in Hispanic political power and a corresponding sense of disenchantment among many Anglos who had previously maintained tight control of local offices and institutions. Anglos with a national orientation are uncomfortable having Hispanics in leadership positions, at worst viewing them as intellectually unfit and at best as foreigners or outsiders who do not belong in such offices. Other developments related to the quality of life have also disturbed Anglos. For many, the borderlands have become less attractive because of growing congestion, chronic border incidents, an increase in crime, a rise in poverty, a decline in wages, greater competition for blue-collar and professional jobs, and the "Hispanicization" of public schools and universities.

As Hispanics consolidate their newfound strength, confrontations with Anglos may increase. Current interethnic tensions in El Paso and San Diego are easily identified in recurring controversies and in letters written to local newspapers that are full of virulent ethnic attacks. Yet even in the worst cases conflict remains well within manageable levels, and accommodation prevails. Long ago, Anglo and Hispanic borderlanders learned the art of compromise, and they continue to practice it. In places like Brownsville and Laredo, for instance, where Mexican Americans have long been the dominant population, the recent record displays substantial mutual adjustment rather than heightened antagonism. In all likelihood, newly empowered Mexican Americans and the numerically smaller but still economically and politically strong Anglo community will build bridges of understanding and cooperation.

Because of demographic superiority, Hispanics are now under less pressure in many communities to justify and defend their way of life, but as they seek to become full participants in the larger U.S. mainstream they will continue to face difficult problems because of their linguistic and cultural deviation from the national norm. At a personal level, the consequence of minority status in a world based on Anglo-Saxon culture and institutions has been psychological marginality for large numbers of Mexican Americans. In his classic study *The Marginal Man,* Everett V. Stonequist defines a marginal person as "one who is poised in psychological uncertainty between two (or more) social worlds reflecting in his soul the discords and harmonies, repulsions and attractions of these worlds, one of which is often 'dominant' over the other.'' [7]

Inner tension and ambivalence are constantly felt by Mexican Americans who are torn between adherence to their traditional culture and conformity with the ways of Anglo society. At times, the Anglo world appears attractive and desirable; at others, it seems cold and hostile. The Mexican American milieu itself produces contradictory reactions: one moment it assumes the character of a secure haven and the next it feels limiting and confining, seemingly slowing the process of integration into the larger society. Instinctively, Mexico is perceived as the "old country" that will unconditionally embrace its children who live abroad, but Mexican Americans soon learn that they do not fit well in the Mexican milieu. In short, Mexican Americans are made to feel that they do not fully belong in either U.S. or Mexican society, and they cannot avoid grappling with issues and questions associated with the phenomenon of marginality.

For many Mexican Americans, this anomalous condition breeds acute self-consciousness and sensitivity about their heritage, ancestry, family, and community. In an attempt to escape this uncomfortable position, some gravitate away from their culture and toward the dominant society, but their physical features, Spanish surname, and general background inhibit full acceptance among Anglos, especially among those who hold Mexicans in low esteem. The most determined Mexican American assimilationists often conceal their past, Anglicize their names, and jump into the melting pot, hoping to melt with dispatch. Those who experience rejection from Anglos after a concerted effort to integrate feel the pain of marginality most acutely.

The predicament of being caught between two nations and two cultures has been captured by numerous Mexican American writers from the border region. Three who depict the problem in especially perceptive and sensitive terms are Américo Paredes, Gloria Anzaldúa, and Pat Mora. Paredes, a noted scholar of borderlands folklore, wrote a timeless poem in 1935 that illustrates the rejection felt by *tejanos* (Mexican American Texans) in both Anglo and Mexican societies. To underscore the problem of nonbelonging, Paredes included in the language of the poem the broken English pronunciation heard among many tejanos. A portion of the poem follows.

> For the Mexico-Texan he no gotta lan',
> He stomped on the neck on both sides of the Rio Gran',
> The dam gringo lingo he no cannot spik,
> It twisters the tong and it make you fill sick.
> A cit'zen of Texas they say that he ees,
> But then, why they call him the Mexican Grease? . . .

If he crosses the reever, eet ees just as bad,
On high poleeshed Spanish he break up his had,
American customs those people no like,
They hate that Miguel they should call him El Mike,
And Mexican-born, why they jeer and they hoot,
"Go back to the gringo! Go lick at hees boot!" [8]

More recently, Pat Mora explored the same theme in her poem "Legal Alien," which reads in part:

American but hyphenated,
viewed by Anglos as perhaps exotic,
perhaps inferior, definitely different,
viewed by Mexicans as alien. . . .

an American to Mexicans
a Mexican to Americans
a handy token
sliding back and forth
between the fringes of both worlds . . . [9]

Gloria Anzaldúa, also a contemporary writer, reflects on the difficulty of maintaining a strong Mexican identity in an Anglo-dominated environment: "Nosotros [We] los Chicanos straddle the borderlands. On one side of us, we are constantly exposed to the Spanish of the Mexicans, on the other side we hear the Anglos' incessant clamoring so that we forget our language. . . . Deep in our hearts we believe that being Mexican has nothing to do with which country one lives in. Being Mexican is a state of soul—not one of mind, not one of citizenship. Neither eagle nor serpent, but both. And like the ocean, neither animal respects borders." Anzaldúa notes that Mexican American women in particular face countless confusing situations that often leave them "floundering in uncertain seas." They cope "by developing a tolerance for ambiguity," by learning "to juggle cultures," by operating "in a pluralistic mode." [10] Anzaldúa's final poem in *Borderlands: La Frontera* concludes with some powerful images regarding the stripping away of one's cultural heritage and ethnic identity to which Mexican Americans are often subjected:

To live in the Borderlands means
the mill with the razor white teeth wants to shred off
your olive-red skin, crush out the kernel, your heart
pound you pinch you roll you out
smelling like white bread but dead;
To survive in the Borderlands

you must live *sin fronteras* [without borders]
be a crossroads.[11]

In the case of Mexican immigrants, a cushioning process along the border eases integration into American society and reduces marginality. Upon arrival in the United States, most immigrants are able to intermingle with people of their own background, shielding themselves from the shock of a sudden direct encounter with Anglo society. In effect, immigrants first assimilate Mexican American culture and then Anglo culture, making the transitional stage easier. The children of the immigrants, however, confront a contrasting situation because their environment is different from that experienced by their parents, and their orientation is toward the United States, not Mexico. This situation creates conditions that produce greater cultural conflict and feelings of marginality in the second generation. In discussing this phenomenon, Stonequist explains the divergence that can occur between immigrant parents and their native offspring. His observations are applicable to Mexicans:

> The tension in the mind of [a member of] the second generation is more pervasive and profound than appears on the surface. He is bound to his parents by the usual family sentiments. But his loyalty to them clashes with his loyalty to his friends and to the American culture which they symbolize. The ways of his friends stand for his future, the ways of his parents for his past. . . . The foreign origin of his parents, their lack of education, their ignorance of American standards all tend to give him an attitude of superiority. This reverses the usual relationship of the generations. In rejecting his parents' advice or authority he has the moral support of the American community. He may even come to despise his parents as "foreigners" and to repudiate the family name. . . .
>
> When . . . [members of the] second generation are the objects of race prejudice and discrimination, their position is particularly difficult. Their tendencies toward assimilation arouse the anxiety and opposition of their parents; their lack of assimilation incurs the antipathy of the native-born. *They are between two fires.* [Emphasis added][12]

Questions of identity and assimilation, then, are central concerns for Mexican Americans and Mexican immigrants along the border. Choices about old and new cultural expressions are often difficult and painful, and unquestionably some individuals become estranged, demoralized, and disorganized. But it must be emphasized that most Hispanics in the U.S. borderlands have successfully adjusted to the stresses of cultural transformation. They have overcome the problems created by marginality, arriving at a rational balance in their lives between continuity and change. The resilience of Mexicans and Mexican Americans is amply illustrated in the interviews and oral histories presented in this book. Out of necessity Hispanics have built bridges between themselves and the dominant society, diminishing isolation and deprivation. Viewed within the larger story of the assimilation of a multitude of ethnic groups into U.S. society, the struggles experienced by Mexican Americans are certainly not unique. Europeans, Africans, Asians, and others have traveled a similar path.

On the Mexican side, marginality is expressed differently than on the U.S. side because the Anglo–Mexican American dichotomy does not exist. The relatively homogeneous Mexican mestizo population precludes internal ethnic or cultural frictions. Nevertheless, it is clear that the Mexican border population as a whole finds itself in a marginal situation vis-à-vis U.S. society. Living next to the richest and most powerful country on earth and enduring myriad foreign economic and cultural influences have bred a love-hate relationship with Americans. A history of conquest and economic subservience has instilled resentment and feelings of inferiority. Mexicans find much to admire in U.S. institutions and culture but also much to disdain. They greatly value easy accessibility to American products but are disturbed by the growing U.S. presence in their economy. Many Mexican parents want their children to become educated in the United States and to master the English language and American culture, but they insist on maintaining the native culture intact and undiluted. In other words, border Mexicans want to preserve a strong national identity but at the same time desire to partake fully of the enticing fruits available north of the boundary. Their inability to regulate effectively the overwhelming cultural impact from north of the boundary is a source of continuing concern. Nevertheless, the prevailing response among Mexicans has been acceptance and resignation to a reality that is very difficult to change. Not surprisingly, in their dealings with gringos as well as with nationalistic countrymen, Mexicans often express sentiments that reflect marginality, sometimes silently and sometimes overtly. But that is not unusual in a border environment.

The Creative Spirit of Borderlanders

While marginal status entails considerable inner tension and discomfort, the ability of marginalized people to adjust to their complex and often difficult surroundings can make them more creative human beings. Ultimately, says Stonequist, it is the marginal individual who, because of his or her circumstances, must rise above self-interest and ethnic parochialism to build a better world for all. "The fate which condemns [the marginal person] to live, at the same time, in two worlds is the same which compels him to assume, in relation to the worlds in which he lives, the role of a cosmopolitan and a stranger. Inevitably he becomes, relatively to his cultural milieu, the individual with the wider horizon, the keener intelligence, the more detached and rational viewpoint. The marginal man is always relatively the more civilized human being." [13]

In various ways the incertitude and restlessness spawned by marginality have served as sources of energy and inventiveness for many individuals determined to overcome the questionable status bestowed upon them. The experience of being on the outside looking in has given such persons an uncommon vantage point from which to analyze and conceptualize solutions to human problems. A restive state of mind is conducive to cultivating sensitivity and awareness of how society works. Marginal people develop strategies to overcome imposed limitations and hurdles, experiment with different forms of behavior, and try new approaches to dealing with people from other groups. Gradually they internalize a mode of resourcefulness and use it when challenging or ambiguous situations arise. Marginal people are conditioned to view problems from different angles, to identify alternatives, to capitalize on advantages, and to search for opportunities not readily apparent to others. In particular, those with an imaginative mind have found fertile ground in the border environment for interpreting the human condition through music, art, and prose; the lens through which they view the world has been shaped and colored by the struggles they and others have waged in their quest to find acceptance beyond their own communities.[14]

One of the most interesting forms of creativity on the border involves smuggling, an illegal activity that borderlanders easily rationalize. To be sure, there is dishonor in smuggling strictly forbidden and harmful substances such as drugs, but not in smuggling ordinary consumer goods. Engaging in smuggling petty contraband is widely viewed as culturally acceptable behavior and a necessity for carrying on daily life. Few borderlanders miss the opportunity to take part in this surreptitious game at some point in their lives. Significant numbers make a life-long habit of it. Many make their living from it. The casual attitude toward small-scale smuggling springs from the acceptance of the borderlands as an interdependent binational system and from the belief that officials in distant places are wrong to impose unreasonable restrictions on transborder trade. This permissive view extends into other economic and social spheres as well, leading border society in general to tolerate myriad indiscretions and violations of sundry laws. Not surprisingly, the borderlands have attracted adventurers, hustlers, and lawless elements who prefer to conduct their business outside the norms of government and societal institutions.

For those with entrepreneurial instincts and skills, the potential gains from conducting illegal transborder operations can be extraordinary. Local people have found innumerable ways to profit from contraband trafficking, and bureaucrats at all levels have participated in the bonanza as well. Together they have devised mutually acceptable mechanisms to facilitate the flow of prohibited commodities across the boundary. This understanding between the authorities and the citizenry is a central component of the psychology of border communities.

Smuggling to satisfy personal needs emerged as a standard topic of discussion in many of my interviews with borderlanders. What I found most remarkable in those conversations, as well as in direct observation of life on the frontier, is the ingenuity that border people have shown in getting what they want regardless of legal obstructions. Present-day borderlanders who introduce foreign products at unauthorized points along the boundary, who fail to give truthful declarations at official ports, or who pay bribes to inspectors are carrying on a local tradition that began in the nineteenth century. Over time, the only changes in the contraband game have been in the volume of merchandise making its way from one country to the other and in the strategies invented to circumvent the law.

A recent example of the creative defiance of regulations is the manner in which Mexicans during the 1992 Christmas season evaded the fifty-dollar-per-person import limit set by their government. One popular strategy was to increase the number of persons in U.S.-bound shopping parties by taking along all available family members, employees, and friends and thus multiplying the import amounts. U.S. resident aliens, who were permitted to retain the old $300 limit, were eagerly sought out as partners by Mexicans. One devious tactic called for obtaining receipts from U.S. merchants showing smaller amounts than the actual prices paid for purchases. Many merchants gladly obliged. Another trick entailed people putting old clothes in suitcases after they had made their purchases and then wearing the newly acquired items when crossing the border. A variation of the same strategy called for braving the cold weather by going shopping without a coat, then returning wearing a new one and not declaring it.[15]

For decades, many Mexicans have craftily avoided paying tuition for children who attend U.S. public schools by having them live with relatives or friends on the U.S. side or by giving false U.S. addresses at the time of registration. Undocumented people have devised ways of evading the U.S. Border Patrol, holding jobs, and utilizing such services as the health care provided in U.S. clinics and hospitals. Though they are technically in violation of the law, many U.S.-born Mexicans have retained dual citizenship in order to have access to benefits and privileges in both nations. On the U.S. side, employers are noted for their ingenuity in avoiding prosecution for hiring illegal aliens. As well, Mexican Americans and Anglos of middle- and upper-class standing have been adroit at bypassing Mexican legal restrictions on obtaining hard-to-get commodities, owning property, and conducting businesses.

Those at the bottom of the social order, who constitute the largest sector of the border population, feel the greatest need to be resourceful and enterprising. For them it is often a matter of survival. Making a living on the street, crossing the border illegally, or searching for a job in another country requires boldness, ingenuity, and courage. Dealing with strangers from another culture requires them to act out roles that are nonthreatening. Making it in a foreign and hostile environment demands substantial inner strength.

The borderlands, then, are conducive to a great deal of creative thinking and innovation at all levels of society. Much of what goes on in the economy, in human relations, and in cultural interchange leads to new ideas, new ways of doing things, and new social trends. These patterns of behavior are the product of powerful historical forces that have long been reshaping the two societies and bringing them ever closer together. The pace of creativity is rising as the free-trade movement further restructures the region. More borderlanders—especially industrialists, merchants, and professionals—are adopting multinational per-spectives. What is transpiring now yields insights into what is in store in the future on a grander scale. As the United States and Mexico forge a closer rela-tionship, transborder contact will become more and more intense. Borderlanders will feel the effect of the increased interaction most acutely, but fewer and fewer people who reside in the interior of both countries will be left untouched as the force of transnationalism radiates beyond the frontier.

REFERENCE MATERIAL

NOTES

Introduction

1. My previous research focused on the social, economic, and political history of the borderlands since the mid nineteenth century. Relevant titles appear in the bibliography.

2. The institute's 1987 *Guide to the Oral History Collection* lists 760 interviews in the collection on a wide range of subjects with highly diverse interviewees.

3. On the general functioning of borders viewed from various disciplinary perspectives, see Asiwaju, *Borderlands Research;* Asiwaju, *Artificial Boundaries;* Boggs and Bowman, *International Boundaries;* Ladis K. D. Kristof, "The Nature of Frontiers and Boundaries"; Martínez, *Across Boundaries;* Prescott, *Boundaries and Frontiers* and *The Geography of Frontiers and Boundaries;* Strassoldo, *Confini e Regioni;* Strassoldo et al., *Cooperation and Conflict in Border Areas;* and Sven Tägil et al., *Studying Boundary Conflicts.*

4. For example, see Asiwaju, *Western Yorubaland Under European Rule, 1889–1945;* Burghardt, *Borderland;* Fraser, *The Steel Bonnets;* Martínez, *Border Boom Town;* Price, *Tijuana;* and Sahlins, *Boundaries.*

5. See Asiwaju, *Borderlands Research* and *Artificial Boundaries.*

6. The following are excellent guides to the literature on the U.S.–Mexico borderlands: Cumberland, *The United States–Mexican Border;* Stoddard et al., *Borderlands Sourcebook;* and Valk, *Borderline.*

PART I   THE BORDER PHENOMENON

Chapter 1. Borderlands and Borderlanders

1. A. I. Asiwaju, a historian and member of the Nigerian Boundary Commission, has forcefully pointed out the need to recognize the universality of border phenomena. Asiwaju's eloquent arguments flow from his studies of African border communities and comparisons with the U.S.–Mexico border. Asiwaju, *Borderlands Research* and *Artificial Boundaries.*

2. My conceptualization has benefitted from ideas on borderlands interaction posited

by Raimondo Strassoldo and C. S. Momoh. Strassoldo has briefly sketched three models—nation building, coexistence, and integration—while Momoh has outlined the functioning of what he calls Zero Borderlands, Minimum Borderlands, and Maximal Borderlands. See Strassoldo, "Border Studies: The State of the Art in Europe," and Momoh, "A Critique of Borderland Theories," in Asiwaju and Adeniyi, *Borderlands in Africa*, 383–95, and 51–61 respectively.

3. The intensity of transnational cooperation in integrated borderlands is revealed in the large numbers of workers who commute across the international boundary to their jobs. Anderson, *Frontier Regions in Western Europe;* Coombes, "The Impact of International Boundaries on Labour Markets in Europe"; Tuppen, "A Geographical Appraisal of Transfrontier Commuting in Western Europe."

4. Ronald Eyre et al., *Frontiers*.

5. Every year, many millions of Mexican Americans cross from the United States into Mexico for personal and business reasons. An even larger number of Mexican nationals cross into the United States for similar purposes, as well as to work.

6. Asiwaju, *Artificial Boundaries*, 19–24; Asiwaju, *Partitioned Africans*.

7. Strassoldo, *Confini e Regioni;* Strassoldo et al., *Cooperation and Conflict in Border Areas;* Anderson, *Frontier Regions in Western Europe*.

8. Hansen, "Border Regional Development and Cooperation," 37.

9. This is the population that resides in the U.S. border counties and the Mexican border municipalities. See Tables 2.1 and 2.3.

10. The articles listed below emphasize the close interdependence of the border communities. The "overlap" quote is attributed to Ellwyn R. Stoddard of the University of Texas at El Paso and is found in the *Newsweek* article, while the "Siamese twins" comment is credited to former El Paso city planner Nestor Valencia and is in the *New York Times* article below. "Towns Together, Douglas–Agua Prieta, *Arizona Highways*, September 1975, 32–37; "The Border: A World Apart," *Newsweek*, April 11, 1983, 36; "An International Tale of Two Cities" [Nogales–Nogales], *Los Angeles Times*, February 9, 1986, sec. 6, p. 22; "Two Laredos," *Washington Post*, June 29, 1986; "Separated by Border, Two Cities Are United by Need" [El Paso–Ciudad Juárez], *New York Times*, December 17, 1988, sec. I, p. 8; "Columbus Discovers Mexican Town, Border Cities Form Bond" [Columbus–Palomas], *Arizona Daily Star*, February 18, 1990, sec. C, p. 2; "Where the Border Starts to Blur" [El Paso–Ciudad Juárez], *El Paso Times*, May 20, 1990, sec. E, p. 1.

11. Asiwaju, *Borderlands Research*, 15.

12. For a useful overview of theories on border conflict, see Sven Tägil et al., *Studying Boundary Conflicts*.

13. Fraser, *The Steel Bonnets*, 4. Writing on the same theme, John Graham notes the impossible position in which the "native of the Borderland" was placed: "His family, his home, and all his belongings were ever within the zone of military operations, where there was little respite from the clash of arms, and where his good sword was the only guarantee for his life and his property." Graham, *Condition of the Border at the Union*, 1. The term *Borderers* is widely used to refer to the people of the Scottish-English

border. While *Borderers* seems perfectly appropriate in referring to people of any border area, my own preference is for *borderlanders*.

14. Juan Seguin is a prominent example of a *tejano* who left his home in South Texas and lived in Mexico, choosing to return many years after the signing of the Treaty of Guadalupe Hidalgo, which established the Rio Grande as the Texas–Mexico border. Unlike tejanos who simply left Texas for the safety of Mexican territory and stayed out of the war, Seguin actively fought with the Mexican forces against the Texas rebels. Seguin, *Personal Memoirs* (typescript in the Barker Library, University of Texas at Austin).

15. Concise overviews of U.S. attempts after 1854 to acquire more Mexican territory and filibustering expeditions during the late nineteenth century are found in Martínez, *Troublesome Border*, 21–24, 38–46.

16. Sahlins, *Boundaries*, 161–63, 231–32, 271–72; Martínez, *Troublesome Border*, 131–32.

17. Reed, *The Border Ballads*, 41. Transboundary raiding involving Indians, bandits, filibusters, and revolutionaries is an important historical theme on the U.S.–Mexico border. See Martínez, *Troublesome Border*, chaps. 2, 3. Today, feuds between clans competing for control of drug trafficking along the U.S.–Mexico border periodically erupt into open warfare, as occurred in Ojinaga, Mexico, in 1982. Poppa, *Druglord*, chap. 7.

18. Fraser, *The Steel Bonnets*, 376.

19. Lang, *A Land of Romance*, 291–95, 391–92; Fraser, *The Steel Bonnets*, 376.

20. Along the U.S.–Mexico border, contemporary tensions often prompt Mexicans to recall U.S. invasions of their country in the nineteenth and early twentieth centuries.

21. For discussions of approaches to border problem solving at the local level, see Sloan and West, "Community Integration and Policies Among Elites in Two Border Cities"; Sloan and West, "The Role of Informal Policy Making in U.S.–Mexico Border Cities"; West, "Informal Policy-Making Along the Arizona-Mexico International Border"; and Martínez, *Across Boundaries*.

22. Minghi, "From Conflict to Harmony in Border Landscapes," 29.

23. Lang, *A Land of Romance*, 177.

24. Ibid, 179. Group loyalties notwithstanding, in that lawless environment both Scots and English also conducted raids against their own countrymen. Fraser, *The Steel Bonnets*, 7–8.

25. Sahlins, *Boundaries*, 220.

26. Paredes, *"With His Pistol in His Hand,"* 243.

27. Ibid., 244.

28. Ibid., 144–50.

29. Ibid.

30. The literature on Chicano history includes substantial information on events along the U.S.–Mexico border, although the pivotal role of the border as a precipitator of conflict is seldom discussed. General overviews include Meier and Rivera, *The Chicanos;* Acuña, *Occupied America,* and McWilliams, *North from Mexico*.

31. Fraser, *The Steel Bonnets*, 65.

32. Sahlins, *Boundaries*, 215–17.

33. Murgía, *Chicano Intermarriage*.

34. Burghardt, *Borderland*, 211–13, 275, 278.

35. Strassoldo et al., *Cooperation and Conflict in Border Areas*, 152.

36. Sahlins, *Boundaries*, 221.

37. Emecheta, *Destination Biafra*, 194.

38. Sahlins, *Boundaries*, 222–27, 268–69, 292; quotation is from p. 292.

39. "A World Apart," *Newsweek*, April 11, 1983, 36.

40. Johnson, "Border in French and French-African Literature," 152.

41. Gordimer, *A Sport of Nature*, 58–59.

42. Allen, *Southwest*, 82.

43. Greene, *Another Mexico*, 13.

44. Ellison, "On the Mexican Border," *Potter's American Monthly*, September 1880, 176.

45. Keller, "The Image of the Chicano in Mexican, United States, and Chicano Cinema," 30.

46. Apart from *The Pilgrim*, other films that focus or touch on the border include *Bordertown* (1935), *Border Incident* (1949), *The Tijuana Story* (1957), *Across the Bridge* (1957), *Touch of Evil* (1958), *The Border* (1982), *Losing It* (1983), *Born in East L.A.* (1987), and *La Bamba* (1987).

47. Discussions and references to the portrayal of the border in U.S. literature, films, and television may be found in the following works: Martínez, "Advertising and Racism: The Case of the Mexican American," 48–58; Robinson, *Mexico and the Hispanic Southwest in American Literature;* Pettit, *Images of the Mexican American in Fiction and Film;* and Maciel, *El Norte*.

48. Examples of Mexican films with border themes include *Frontera norte* (1953); *Espaldas mojadas* (1953); *El pocho* (1970s) *El Chicano justiciero* (1970s); and *Los mojados* (1977). Discussions of these and other Mexican films that feature the border appear in David R. Maciel, "Visions of the Other Mexico: Chicanos and Undocumented Workers in Mexican Cinema, 1954–1982," in Keller, *Chicano Cinema*, 71–88, and Maciel, *El Norte*, 7–53.

49. Lang, *A Land of Romance*, 132.

50. Klymasz, "Folklore of the Canadian-American Border," 231.

51. Kristof, "The Nature of Frontiers and Boundaries," 272.

52. Smuggling is a standard theme in studies of border areas that examine transboundary interaction. See, for example, Asiwaju, *Western Yorubaland Under European Rule, 1889–1945;* Martínez, *Border Boom Town;* Sahlins, *Boundaries;* Fraser, *The Steel Bonnets*.

53. Rampant smuggling, and the money it generates, can sometimes overwhelm a border community and create a lawless environment. This occurred, for example, in Ojinaga, Mexico, in the 1980s during a period of significant drug trafficking into the United States. Drug lords practically took over the town, controlling the authorities and having complete freedom to carry on their nefarious trade. Frequent shootouts between rival smuggling factions created a reign of terror for the local population. Poppa, *Druglord*, passim.

54. Lattimore, "The Frontier in History," 374.

55. Sahlins, *Boundaries,* 108, 115.

56. Kristof, "The Nature of Frontiers and Boundaries," 271–77. Encouraged by the receptivity of Sinkiang to outside influence, Britain, Japan, and the Soviet Union promoted secessions among the Sinkiangese. From the 1930s to the 1950s, the Soviet Union capitalized on the strong ethnic ties between its own frontier population and the people of Sinkiang, exerting considerable economic and political influence beyond its own border. This situation led to prolonged conflict with the Chinese government, which accused the Soviets of fomenting subversive activities inside China. Until recent times, border relations between China and the former Soviet Union remained tense. Jukes, "Political and Military Problems of the Sino-Soviet Border," 11–32.

57. Martínez, *Troublesome Border,* 40, 109–11.

Chapter 2. The U.S.–Mexico Borderlands

1. This evolutionary scheme expands on the periodization sketched in my earlier book, *Troublesome Border,* 6–7.

2. For a detailed historical overview of the delimitation of the U.S.–Mexico boundary, see *Troublesome Border,* chap. 1.

3. The literature on these topics is extensive. See *Troublesome Border,* chaps. 1–3, and my article "La frontera en la conciencia nacional, 1848–1920."

4. An interesting narrative of the initial entry of Anglo Americans into the Southwest is found in Lavender, *The Southwest,* 69–98. See also Meinig, *Southwest.*

5. After the United States secured the Southwest in 1848, many Anglo American entrepreneurs acquired farms, ranches, and mines whose products ended up in eastern U.S. markets. Mexicans provided much of the labor for these enterprises. For an interesting study of one of the key industries in the region, see Paul, *Mining Frontiers of the Far West, 1848–1880.*

6. Zoraida Vásquez and Meyer, *The United States and Mexico,* 72–92.

7. Hall and Coerver, *Revolution on the Border*; Martínez, *Fragments of the Mexican Revolution.*

8. For an overview of U.S.–Mexican relations during the Revolution, see Zoraida Vásquez and Meyer, *The United States and Mexico,* 103–25.

9. Relations between El Paso and Ciudad Juárez during the period are examined in my book *Border Boom Town,* 38–56.

10. Luan-Miller, "U.S. Direct Investment in Mexico, 1876–1978," 46–51.

11. The powerful economic presence of foreigners in Sonora and Chihuahua during the Porfiriato is detailed in Ruíz, *The People of Sonora and Yankee Capitalists,* and Wasserman, *Capitalists, Caciques, and Revolution.*

12. Cardoso, *Mexican Emigration to the United States.*

13. The growth of commercial agriculture throughout the western United States in the early twentieth century is discussed in Nash, *The American West,* 22–26.

14. Nash, *The American West,* 67; Reisler, *By the Sweat of Their Brow,* 78–87.

15. The following works contain useful information on the migration debate between

the two nations since the early twentieth century: Galarza, *Merchants of Labor*; Hoffman, *Unwanted Mexican Americans in the Great Depression*; North, "The Migration Issue in U.S.–Mexican Relations"; Reisler, *By the Sweat of Their Brow*; and Samora, *Los Mojados*.

16. Piñera Ramírez, comp., *Panorama histórico de Baja California,* 430–59; Langston, "The Impact of Prohibition," 326–37; Martínez, *Border Boom Town,* 57–77.

17. See the following works by Gerald D. Nash: *The American West,* chap. 4; *The American West Transformed*; and *World War II and the West*.

18. On the Sunbelt phenomenon, see Abbott, *The New Urban America,* and Rice and Bernard, *Sunbelt Cities*.

19. The labor functions of the Mexican border cities in relation to the U.S. borderlands are discussed in my article "Chicanos and the Border Cities."

20. The Border Industrialization Program, more popularly known as the *maquiladora* program, has attracted significant attention from scholars. A valuable guide to the literature is Sable, *Las Maquiladoras*.

21. Herzog, *Where North Meets South,* 139–40.

22. The figures cited in this paragraph are based on official census reports, which tend to underestimate the population in the area, especially on the Mexican side. For example, it is commonly assumed by researchers that Tijuana and Ciudad Juárez each have a population of more than a million.

23. As English-speaking Americans, blacks have the same kinds of experiences as Anglos in their general interaction with Mexican Americans and Mexican nationals, and have much the same response to the borderlands milieu. At the level of personal relations, there are differences in kind and degree, but the concern here is with broad transnational and intergroup patterns.

24. Useful overviews on the Kickapoos, Yaquis, and Tohono O'odham are given in Gibson, *The Kickapoos*; Latorre and Latorre, *The Mexican Kickapoo Indians*; Spicer, *Pascua*; Spicer, *The Yaquis*; and Fontana, "History of the Papago."

25. For interesting discussions of border culture viewed from different perspectives, see the selections in Part I of Ross, *Views Across the Border,* 25–96. Useful schematic depictions of border culture and biculturalism are found in Weaver, "The Social Effects of the Ecology and Development of the United States–Mexico Border," 246–49.

PART II   BORDER TYPES

Introduction

1. Some Hispanics even lump African Americans into the Anglo category because they understand the term *Anglo* to refer essentially to people whose language is English and whose culture is derived predominantly from the Anglo-Saxon Protestant tradition. This is not to say that such Hispanics fail to appreciate the profound racial and social differences between African Americans and white Americans. The gist of their thinking is that African Americans on the border, who are generally few in number and largely

lower and middle class (as opposed to overwhelmingly poor and marginalized), tend to have lifestyles that resemble those of Anglos more than those of any other native group. Hispanics perceive Native Americans to be quite distinct from other populations except those Indians in urban areas who are highly Hispanicized and closely associated with Mexican American communities.

2. In the world-systems and dependency literature, *core* means the locus of power or control, and *periphery* refers to areas that are subordinate to that core. At the international level, the industrialized nations have historically been at the core, and the underdeveloped countries have occupied the periphery. At the national level, the heartland, representing the center of economic and political power, is the core, and the outlying provinces, including border areas, constitute the periphery. Viewed in this context, the U.S. borderlands might be thought of as the periphery (the distant and subordinate subregion) of the core (the world-dominant United States) and the Mexican borderlands as the periphery of the periphery or semiperiphery (Mexico, a Third World developing country). Useful introductions to the vast and complex world-systems and dependency literature include Shannon, *An Introduction to the World-System Perspective*, and Kay, *Latin American Theories of Development and Underdevelopment*.

3. On the question of marginalization, nationally oriented people generally feel a sense of exclusion by local borderlanders in those areas where the borderlands culture is felt more than the national culture (for example, in Brownsville and Laredo), but this is not the case in areas where the national culture is strong and dominant (as in San Diego and El Paso). For example, most Anglos from San Diego, who constitute the local majority, are largely indifferent to being a part of the transnational system because they perceive no need to extend their lives beyond their own world. In Brownsville, however, where Anglos are a small minority, isolation from transnational and transcultural interaction marginalizes them. On the Mexican side, the marginalization of borderlanders with a national perspective is manifested primarily in provincial discrimination against people from central Mexico (especially Mexico City) and the extent to which such individuals feel unable to function in the binational milieu. Ethnic or culture-based marginalization is not an issue on the Mexican side, as it is on the U.S. side.

4. See García, *Desert Immigrants;* Madsen, *Mexican-Americans of South Texas;* Martínez, *The Chicanos of El Paso;* Montejano, *Anglos and Mexicans in the Making of Texas;* Paredes, *"With His Pistol in His Hand";* Rubel, *Across the Tracks;* and Taylor, *Mexican Labor in the United States.*

5. Studies conducted in the 1960s revealed that in selected border counties in Texas, New Mexico, and Arizona an average of 10 percent of all Hispanics married Anglos, while in interior areas of Texas, New Mexico, and California the average was 23 percent. Intermarriage was the lowest in those areas where Anglo prejudice was strong and where the Hispanic middle class was small, which was precisely the situation along the border, especially in the Lower Rio Grande Valley of Texas. Undoubtedly the percentages of intermarriage are higher now, but a significant gap remains between the border zone and the interior. See Martínez, *The Chicanos of El Paso,* 27; Moore and Pachón, *Hispanics in the United States,* 108–9; and Murgía, *Chicano Intermarriage,* 48–49.

Chapter 3. Mexicans

1. For a discussion of the unique history of Mexican *fronterizos,* see Martínez, *Troublesome Border,* chap. 4.

2. *Coyotes* is a true account written by a journalist and writer.

3. Margulis and Tuirán, *Desarrollo y población en la frontera norte,* 154; Castellanos, *Ciudad Juárez,* 130; Herzog, *Where North Meets South,* 106.

4. The presumed low incidence of Mexican nationalists at the border is explained by the region's prolonged, close-range exposure to U.S. culture and external economic dependence. This reality has significantly moderated the attitudes of many borderlanders in the direction of greater tolerance and in many cases even acceptance of U.S. economic influences and the gringo way of life. Firsthand experience with U.S. society has convinced fronterizos that the United States is a complex country and that contrary to some commonly held assumptions, there are many positive things to be said about the system fashioned by the gringos. For ordinary fronterizos, the most appealing thing about the United States is the tremendous economic opportunity it offers workers, which serves as a powerful neutralizer of anti-American attitudes.

5. Hopkins, "The Economic Impact of Mexican Visitors to Arizona," 1–3.

Chapter 4. Mexican Americans

1. The history of Mexican Americans along the border is discussed in Martínez, *Troublesome Border,* chap. 5.

2. For simplicity's sake, I have lumped all Mexican immigrants into the Mexican American population. No doubt it takes most of them years to *become* Mexican Americans, but their physical presence in the United States makes them a *part* of the Mexican American milieu, and it is that milieu that is under examination here.

Chapter 5. Anglo Americans

1. Given the long history of Anglo-Mexican conflict and accommodation in the borderlands, the old-timer–newcomer dichotomy deserves serious research, as do questions that relate to attitudes and behavior among the various Anglo populations along the border at different points in history. But other personal factors like place of origin and socioeconomic class and societal influences like international conflicts and economic fluctuations have undoubtedly played important roles in the variety of responses to the border situation that is found in the Anglo community.

2. According to the 1980 census, 13 percent of the white population in the Brownsville–Harlingen–San Benito SMSA, 10.4 percent in the El Paso SMSA, and 23.4 percent in the San Diego SMSA had resided in a different SMSA in 1975. U.S. Bureau of the Census, *Census of Population, 1980.*

3. Augie Bareño, director of the Department of Transboundary Affairs for the County of San Diego, believes that a majority of San Diego's Anglo population subscribes to the nationalist perspective. Interview, January 6, 1993.

Introduction

1. The wide acceptance of oral history led to the organization of the Oral History Association, which over the past two decades has held annual conferences that have focused on a wide variety of topics and methodological issues. The association sponsors the *Oral History Review,* which regularly publishes bibliographies of recent works. Among useful guides to oral history are Havlice, *Oral History; Oral History Index;* and Gallagher, *Oral History Collection in the Southwest Region.*

2. The earliest border-related oral history work is Manuel Gamio's *The Mexican Immigrant.* In this classic book, Gamio provided an outstanding collection of fifty-seven autobiographical statements on the immigrant experience of the 1910s and 1920s. Paul S. Taylor also interviewed many immigrants in the late 1920s and early 1930s as part of a comprehensive research project on Mexican workers in the United States. The result was a series of detailed studies of selected regions in which Taylor sprinkled extensive quotes from Mexicans and Anglos, many of them borderlanders, to supplement statistical and documentary data. Taylor's works have been reprinted in *Mexican Labor in the United States.* My own book *Fragments of the Mexican Revolution* includes many interviews with Mexican and Anglo refugees who left Mexico during the upheavals of the 1910s.

3. Most of the original interviews are deposited in the Institute of Oral History at the University of Texas at El Paso. Copies are also available in the Department of Special Collections and Archives in the university's main library.

4. Thompson, *The Edwardians,* 6.

Chapter 6. Migrants and Workers

1. Useful overviews of the trends in migration since World War II are provided in Corwin, *Immigrants and Immigrants;* Cross and Sandos, *Across the Border;* and Samora, *Los Mojados.* The personal side of the migration experience is included in Conover, *Coyotes;* Halsell, *The Illegals;* and Nelson, *Pablo Cruz and the American Dream.*

2. American Friends Service Committee, *Sealing Our Borders.*

3. A longer version of this statement appeared in Beezley and Ewell, *The Human Tradition in Latin America,* 195–206.

4. For contrasting viewpoints on the debate regarding the exploitation of workers, see Fernández-Kelly, *For We Are Sold, I and My People,* and Stoddard, *Maquila.*

5. Ms. López Manzano uses the word *prostitution* to convey the idea that circumstances at the maquiladoras were very conducive to promoting promiscuity and also to suggest that many women used sex to gain favor with male supervisors and/or to retain their jobs.

6. Empirical evidence is insufficient to conclude that promiscuity is rampant in the maquiladoras or that it derives from pressures on women that may be commonplace in the industry. Obviously this is a topic deserving of more attention from researchers.

Chapter 7. Functionaries and Activists

1. Three recent exposés of the drug smuggling imbroglio are Mills, *The Underground Empire;* Shannon, *Desperados;* and Poppa, *Druglord.*

2. Works on border labor history include Clark, *Mexican Labor in the United States;* Coyle et al., *Women at Farah;* Victor Nelson Cisneros, "La clase trabajadora en Tejas, 1900–1940"; Park, *The History of Mexican Labor in Arizona;* Taylor, *Mexican Labor in the United States;* Weber, "The Organization of Mexicano Agricultural Workers"; and Zamora, "Chicano Socialist Labor Activity in Texas."

3. On the Chicano Movement, see Muñoz, *Youth, Identity, Power.*

4. The Santa Fe Street bridge is one of the two heavily used downtown bridges connecting El Paso and Juárez. *El puente negro* ceased to be a major crossing point for undocumented persons in 1977 when steel doors were placed at the bridge's midpoint to stop foot traffic.

5. Pablo Acosta's story is told in Poppa, *Druglord.*

6. The story of the Mine Mill unionization movement in El Paso, including the landmark 1946 strike, is told in García, *Mexican Americans.*

7. For a discussion of the Light Up the Border movement, see the interview with Muriel Watson, in Chapter 5.

8. Movimiento Estudiantil Chicano de Aztlán, or the Chicano Student Movement of Aztlán. Aztlán refers to the mythical ancestral homeland of the Aztecs, thought by Chicanos and others to be the U.S. borderlands.

Chapter 8. Mixers

1. Overviews of the history of Mexican-Anglo relations are provided in Acuña, *Occupied America;* Meier and Rivera, *The Chicanos;* Weber, *Foreigners in Their Native Land;* and Montejano, *Anglos and Mexicans in the Making of Texas.*

Conclusion

1. Garreau, *The Nine Nations of North America;* "One River, One Country" ("CBS Reports," 1983).

2. Two twentieth-century movements involving Chicanos that had secessionist overtones were the Plan de San Diego insurrection in South Texas in 1915 and 1916 and the Chicano Movement of the 1960s, with its rhetoric of recreating "Aztlán" (the mythical homeland of the Aztecs) as a modern-day "nation." In both instances, however, few people took the idea of seceding from the United States seriously. See Sandos, *Rebellion in the Borderlands,* and Muñoz, *Youth, Identity, Power.*

3. See Arreola and Curtis, *The Mexican Border Cities,* for an insightful analysis of the cultural geography of the urban centers south of the boundary.

4. To my knowledge, empirical research on the values and behavior of core borderlanders does not exist, and my conclusions are necessarily suggestive rather than conclusive. I base these interpretations on years of study, observation, and participation in

border phenomena, as well as dozens of interviews with a wide variety of border people. In two speculative papers, Kathleen Fairbanks-Rubin has argued that borderlanders possess unique personal qualities and an ability to overcome obstacles to transnational and transcultural cooperation. Her hypotheses have yet to be tested in the field, but I concur with her analysis. See Fairbanks-Rubin, "Bilateral Fronterizos," and " 'Border People' in Organizations."

5. Sloan and West, "The Role of Informal Policy-Making in U.S.–Mexico Border Cities."

6. Graue, "La delincuencia en las fronteras," 700–701, my translation.

7. Stonequist, *The Marginal Man,* 8. Marginal personalities are found throughout the world wherever different groups and societies are in close association with one another. As crossroads of human contact, borderlands then may be said to be prime areas for the development of culturally versatile individuals. This has been particularly true in the late twentieth century, when increased world economic integration has catapulted border zones into the center stage of cultural interaction.

8. Paredes, *Between Two Worlds,* 27.

9. Mora, *Chants,* 52.

10. Anzaldúa, *Borderlands: La Frontera,* 62, 79.

11. Ibid, 195.

12. Stonequist, *The Marginal Man,* 99, 101.

13. Ibid., xvii–xviii.

14. In the field of music, for generations the border experience has inspired many stirring and fascinating *corridos* (ballads) that focus on such subjects as ethnic conflict, migration, smuggling, and drug trafficking. Highly creative artists and fiction writers have used the same themes in their work. Recently along the Tijuana–San Diego border the volatile politics of undocumented migration has given rise to a dynamic art movement that has received international attention. See "Art Crosses the Line," *Calendar,* October 20, 1991, pp. 6–7, 82–83 (supplement to the *Los Angeles Times*).

15. *Arizona Daily Star,* December 21, 1992.

BIBLIOGRAPHY

Primary Sources

Interviews

The interviews below, many of which are listed under pseudonyms, were conducted by the author and various research assistants. Interviews intended to illustrate border "types," as summarized in Part II, are based on notes taken by the author. Interviews that depict the "border experience," namely the oral histories included in Part III, were tape-recorded, and with a few exceptions the tapes and transcripts are deposited at the Institute of Oral History (IOH) at the University of Texas at El Paso (UTEP). They are identified in the list that follows. Translations from Spanish to English are by the author.

Anderson, Gladys. January 12, 1991.

Bárcena, Angela. August 2, 1979. Translation. IOH.

Becker, Hilda. March 11, 1991.

Brewer, Hank. April 13, 1991.

Caballero, Cesar. April 5, 1991.

Carrasco, Roberto. January 8, 1990. Translation.

Castillo, Leonel. June 21–24, August 24, 1980. IOH.

Cruz Davidson, Diana Patricia. January 20, 1990.

Davenport, Diane. January 13, 1991.

De la Garza, Eligio "Kika." October 22, 1975. IOH.

Diamos, Michael Peter. May 18, 1990.

Domínguez family. June 18, 1988. Translation.

Fisher, Daniel. March 11, 1991.

Fuente, Soledad. January 27, February 1, 1976. Assisted by Arturo Hernández. Translation. IOH.

Gabaldón, José. December 13, 1979. Translation. IOH.

García, Ruben. March 23, 1986. IOH.

García Montenegro, Mónica. May 19, 1990. Translation.

Gonzáles, Lillian. January 10, 1990. Translation.

González, Sebastian. March 4, 1985.

Hidalgo, Francisco. March 15, 1975. Translation. IOH.

Hinojosa, John. May 15, 1992.

Jones, Patricia. July 29, 1979. Assisted by Virgilio Sánchez. Translation. IOH.

Lizárraga, José Diego. May 8, 1990. Translation.

López Manzano, Irma Leticia. August 4, 1992. Translation.

McKnight, Frank. January 5, 1990.

Maldonado, Joe. October 19, 1990.

Maldonado, Santiago. August 28, 1975. IOH.

Martínez, Mercurio. March 13, 1984. IOH.

Martínez, Roberto. November 10, 1991.

Matthews, Elena. January 10, 1990. Translation.

Mercado, Salvador. April 13, 1978. Translation. IOH.

Metzger, Bishop Sidney M. August 8, 1978. Assisted by Anne Reidmiller. IOH.

Montes, Cristina. May 19, 1990. Translation.

"Muñeca." March 11, 1981. Translation. IOH.

Navarez, Ricardo. October 23, 1980. Translation. IOH.

Nuñez, Alfredo. October 20, 1990. Translation.

Ochoa, Samuel. January 12, 1991. Translation.

Orendain, Antonio. April 18, 1977; March 31, September 24, 1978. Translation. IOH.

Orsborn, Father Bruce. November 8, 1991.

Osante Zubia, Ana María. January 8, 1990. Translation.

Pacheco, Leonard. September 15, 1976. IOH.

Padilla, Manuel. December 21, 1974. Translation. IOH.

Peterson Sánchez, Margaret. November 12, 1980. IOH.

Regela, David. August 14, 1991.

Resendez, Margarita Ayala de, and Antonio Resendez. May 18, 1990. Translation.

Richeson, Ann. March 11, 1991.

Rocha, Greg. August 14, 1991.

Rodríguez, Juan. December 2, 1980. Translation. IOH.

Sanders, Archie, and Arlene Sanders. January 12, 1991.

Sandoval Caples, Gloria. January 20, 1990. Translation.

Silex, Humberto. April 28, 1978. Translation. IOH.

Simmons, Ray. May 16, 1990.

Smith, Richard B. December 18, 1975. IOH.

Strumm, Carlos. May 11, 1978. Assisted by Virgilio Sánchez. Translation. IOH.

Tolbert, Jack. March 13, 1991.

Vargas, Juanita. November 10, 1991. Translation.

Villanueva, Teresa. May 29, 1979. Translation. IOH.

Watson, Muriel. October 18, 1990.

Yeary, Amber Milton. March 14, 1984. IOH.

Newspapers and Magazines

El Paso Herald Post. Summer 1983. Special report on the border.

The Texas Humanist. March–April 1984. Special issue "The Borderlands: Grappling
with a Dual Heritage."

Other Primary Sources

Mexico. *Censo general de población y vivienda, 1980*. Mexico City: Dirección General
de Estadística.

———. *Censo general de población y vivienda, 1990: Resultados preliminares*.
Mexico City: Dirección General de Estadística.

Seguín, Juan. *Personal Memoirs of John N. Seguín*. San Antonio: Ledger Book and Job
Office, 1852. Typescript in the Barker Library, University of Texas at Austin.

U.S. Bureau of the Census. *Census of Population*, 1980, 1990. Washington, D.C.:
USGPO, 1980, 1982, 1983, 1990.

———. *Statistical Abstract of the United States, 1991*. Washington, D.C.: USGPO,
1991.

U.S. Immigration and Naturalization Service. *Statistical Yearbook, 1989*. Washington,
D.C.: USGPO, 1990.

Secondary Sources

Unpublished Materials

Bustamante, Jorge. "Identidad nacional en la frontera norte de Mexico: Hallazgos preliminares." Tijuana: Colegio de la Frontera Norte, 1983.

Coombes, Mike. "The Impact of International Boundaries on Labour Markets in
Europe." Paper presented at the conference International Boundaries: Fresh Perspectives, International Boundaries Research Unit, University of Durham, Eng., July
18–21, 1991.

Fairbanks-Rubin, Kathleen. "Bilateral Fronterizos: Keys to Transborder Cooperation?"
Paper presented at the Segundo Congreso Sobre Fronteras en Iberoamerica, San José,
Costa Rica, November 14–17, 1990.

———. "'Border People' in Organizations: Tapping Current Staff to Bridge Cultures."
Paper presented at a meeting of the Association for Borderlands Scholars, Reno,
Nev., April 25–26, 1991.

Langston, Edward L. "The Impact of Prohibition on the Mexican–United States Border:
The El Paso–Ciudad Juárez Case." Ph.D. diss., Texas Tech University, 1974.

Luan-Miller, Patricia Dolores. "U.S. Direct Investment in Mexico, 1876–1978: An Historical, Theoretical, and Empirical Analysis." Ph.D. Dissertation, University of Texas at Austin, 1980.

Vila, Pablo. "Everyday Life, Culture and Identity on the Border: The Case of Ciudad Juárez–El Paso," Paper presented at the Colegio de la Frontera Norte, Tijuana, October 24, 1992.

Documentaries and Docudramas

Chulas Fronteras. Produced by Chris Strachwitz. El Cerrito, Calif.: Brazos Films, 1976.

The Global Assembly Line. By Lorraine Gray, produced with María Patricia Fernández Kelly and Anne Bohlen.

The Lemon Grove Incident. Written and produced by Paul Espinosa. Directed by Frank Christopher. San Diego: KPBS, 1985.

Neighbors: The United States and Mexico. Produced and directed by Jesús Salvador Treviño and José Luis Ruíz. Los Angeles, 1985.

The New Tijuana. Produced by Paul Espinosa. Directed by Frank Christopher. San Diego: KPBS, 1990.

The Nine Nations of North America: Mexamerica. Written and narrated by Joel Garreau. New York: PBS, 1988.

One River: One Country. New York: "CBS Reports," 1983.

The Trail North. Produced by Paul Espinosa. Directed by Thomas Kario. San Diego: KPBS, 1983.

Books, Articles, and Reports

Abbott, Carl. *The New Urban America: Growth and Politics in Sunbelt Cities*. Chapel Hill: University of North Carolina Press, 1981.

Acuña, Rodolfo. *Occupied America: A History of Chicanos*. 3d ed. New York: Harper and Row, 1988.

Alegría, Tito. "Ciudad y transmigración en la frontera de México con los Estados Unidos." *Frontera Norte* 2:4 (July–December 1990): 7–38.

Allen, John Houghton. *Southwest*. Philadelphia: J. B. Lippincott, 1952.

Alvarez, Robert R., Jr. *Familia: Migration and Adaptation in Baja and Alta California, 1800–1975*. Berkeley: University of California Press, 1987.

American Friends Service Committee. *Sealing Our Borders: The Human Toll*. Third Report of the Immigration Law Enforcement Monitoring Project. Philadelphia: American Friends Service Committee, 1992.

Anderson, Malcolm, ed. *Frontier Regions in Western Europe*. London: Frank Cass and Co., 1983.

Anzaldúa, Gloria. *Borderlands: La Frontera*. San Francisco: Spinsters/Aunt Lute, 1987.

Arreola, Daniel D., and James R. Curtis. *The Mexican Border Cities: Landscape Anatomy and Place Personality*. Tucson: University of Arizona Press, 1993.

Asiwaju, A. I. *Artificial Boundaries*. Inaugural Lecture. Lagos, Nigeria: University of Lagos Press, 1984.

————. *Borderlands Research: A Comparative Perspective*. Border Perspectives, no. 6. El Paso: Center for Inter-American and Border Studies, 1983.

————. *Western Yorubaland Under European Rule, 1889–1945: A Comparative Analysis of French and British Colonialism*. New York: Humanities Press, 1977.

Asiwaju, A. I., ed. *Partitioned Africans: Ethnic Relations Across Africa's International Boundaries, 1884–1984*. London: C. Hurst and Company, 1984.

Asiwaju, A. I., and P. O. Adeniyi, eds. *Borderlands in Africa: A Multidisciplinary and Comparative Focus on Nigeria and West Africa*. Lagos: University of Lagos Press, 1989.

Bannon, John Francis. *The Spanish Borderlands Frontier, 1513–1821*. New York: Holt, Rinehart and Winston, 1963.

Beezley, William A., and Judith Ewell, eds. *The Human Tradition in Latin America: The Twentieth Century*. Wilmington, Del.: Scholarly Resources, 1987.

Bock, James. "The Border." (Baltimore) *Sun*, August 2–7, 1987. Six-part series.

Boggs, S. Whittermore, and Isaiah Bowman. *International Boundaries: A Study of Boundary Functions and Problems*. New York: Columbia University Press, 1940.

Burghardt, Andrew F. *Borderland: A Historical and Geographical Study of Burgenland, Austria*. Madison: University of Wisconsin Press, 1962.

Buss, Fran Leeper, ed. *Forged Under the Sun/Forgada bajo el sol: The Life of María Elena Lucas*. Ann Arbor: University of Michigan Press, 1993.

Cahill, Rick. *Border Towns of the Southwest: Shopping, Dining, Fun & Adventure from Tijuana to Juárez*. Boulder: Pruett Publishing Company, 1987.

Cárdenas, Gilbert, and Charles Ellard. *The Economics of the U.S.–Mexico Border: Growth, Problems and Prospects*. Edinburg, Tex.: Division of Inter-American Affairs and School of Business Administration, Pan American University, 1982.

Cardoso, Lawrence A. *Mexican Emigration to the United States, 1877–1931*. Tucson: University of Arizona Press, 1980.

Castellanos, Alicia G. *Ciudad Juárez: La vida fronteriza*. Mexico City: Editorial Nuestro Tiempo, 1981.

Clark, Victor S. *Mexican Labor in the United States*. Washington, D.C.: Department of Commerce and Labor, 1908.

Connor, Walker, ed. *Mexican Americans in Comparative Perspective*. Washington, D.C.: Urban Institute, 1985.

Conover, Ted. *Coyotes: A Journey Through the Secret World of America's Illegal Aliens*. New York: Vintage Books, 1987.

Corona Rentería, Alfonso, and Juan Sánchez Gleason. *Integración del norte de México y la economía nacional: Perspectivas y oportunidades*. Mexico City: Secretaría de Programación y Presupuesto, 1989.

Corwin, Arthur F., ed. *Immigrants and Immigrants: Perspectives on Mexican Labor Migration to the United States*. Westport, Conn.: Greenwood Press, 1978.

Coyle, Laurie, Gail Hershatter, and Emily Honig. *Women at Farah: An Unfinished Story*. El Paso: Reforma, 1979.

Cross, Harry E., and James E. Sandos. *Across the Border: Rural Development in Mex-

ico and Recent Migration to the United States. Berkeley: Institute of Government Studies, University of California, Berkeley, 1981.

Cumberland, Charles C., ed. *The United States–Mexican Border: A Selective Guide to the Literature of the Region*. Supplement to *Rural Sociology* 25 (June 1960).

D'Antonio, William, and William H. Form. *Influentials in Two Border Cities: A Study in Community Decision-Making*. Notre Dame: University of Notre Dame Press, 1965.

Demarci, B., and A. M. Boileau. *Boundaries and Minorities in Western Europe*. Milan: Granco Angeli, 1982.

Demaris, Ovid. *Poso del mundo*. New York: Pocket Books, 1971.

Ellison, R. F. "On the Mexican Border." *Potter's American Monthly* 15 (September 1880): 171–76.

Emecheta, Buchi. *Destination Biafra*. London: Allison and Busby, 1982.

Estudios fronterizos. Mexico City: Asociación Nacional de Universidades e Institutos de Enseñanza Superior, 1981.

Eyre, Ronald, et al. *Frontiers*. London: BBC Books, 1990.

Fernández, Raúl A. *The Mexican-American Border Region: Issues and Trends*. Notre Dame: University of Notre Dame Press, 1989.

———. *The United States–Mexico Border: A Politico-Economic Profile*. Notre Dame: University of Notre Dame Press, 1977.

Fernández-Kelly, María Patricia. *For We Are Sold, I and My People: Women and Industry in Mexico's Frontier*. Albany: State University of New York Press, 1983.

Flores Caballero, Romeo R. *Evolución de la frontera norte*. Monterrey: Centro de Investigaciones Económicas, 1982.

Fontana, Bernard L. "History of the Papago." In *Handbook of North American Indians*, edited by Alfonso Ortiz, 10:137–48. Washington, D.C.: Smithsonian Institution, 1983.

Fowler, Gene, and Bill Crawford. *Border Radio: Quacks, Yodelers, Pitchmen, Psychics, and Other Amazing Broadcasters of the American Airwaves*. Austin: Texas Monthly Press, 1987.

Fraser, George MacDonald. *The Steel Bonnets: The Story of the Anglo-Scottish Border Reivers*. London: Collins Harvill, 1989.

Galarza, Ernesto. *Merchants of Labor*. Santa Barbara: McNally and Loftin, 1964.

Gallagher, Cathryn A., comp. *Oral History Collections in the Southwest Region: A Directory and Subject Guide*. Los Angeles: Southwest Oral History Association, 1986.

Gamio, Manuel. *The Mexican Immigrant: His Life Story*. Chicago: University of Chicago Press, 1931.

García, Mario T. *Desert Immigrants: The Mexicans of El Paso, 1880–1920*. New Haven: Yale University Press, 1981.

———. "La Frontera: The Border as Symbol and Reality in Mexican American Thought." *Mexican Studies/Estudios Mexicanos* 1 (Summer 1985): 196–205.

———. *Mexican Americans: Leadership, Ideology, and Identity, 1930–1960*. New Haven: Yale University Press, 1989.

Garreau, Joel. *The Nine Nations of North America*. Boston: Houghton Mifflin Co., 1981.

Gibbins, Roger. *Canada as a Borderlands Society*. Orono, Me.: Borderlands, 1989.

Gibson, Arrel M. *The Kickapoos: Lords of the Middle Border*. Norman: University of Oklahoma Press, 1963.

Gibson, Lay James, and Alfonso Corona Rentería, eds. *The U.S. and Mexico: Borderland Development and the National Economies*. Boulder: Westview Press, 1985.

González Salazar, Roque. *La Frontera del Norte: Integración y Desarrollo*. Mexico City: El Colegio de México, 1981.

Gordimer, Nadine. *A Sport of Nature*. London: Jonathan Cape, 1987.

Graham, John. *Condition of the Border at the Union*. New York: E. P. Dutton and Co., 1917.

Graue, Desiderio. "La delincuencia en las fronteras." *Criminalia* 22 (1956): 694–709.

Greene, Graham. *Another Mexico*. New York: Viking Press, 1939.

Gross, Feliks. *Ethnics in a Borderland*. Westport, Conn.: Greenwood Press, 1978.

Hall, Linda B., and Don M. Coerver. *Revolution on the Border: The United States and Mexico, 1910–1920*. Albuquerque: University of New Mexico Press, 1988.

Halsell, Grace. *The Illegals*. New York: Stein and Day, 1978.

Hansen, Niles. *The Border Economy: Regional Development in the Southwest*. Austin: University of Texas Press, 1981.

———. "Border Regional Development and Cooperation: Western Europe and the U.S.–Mexico Borderlands in Comparative Perspective." In Martínez, *Across Boundaries*, 31–44.

Havlice, Patricia P. *Oral History: A Reference Guide and Annotated Bibliography*. Jefferson, N.C.: McFarland, 1985.

Herzog, Lawrence A. "Border Commuter Workers and Transfrontier Metropolitan Structure Along the United States–Mexico Border." *Journal of Borderlands Studies* 5 (Fall 1990): 1–20.

———. *Where North Meets South: Cities, Space, and Politics on the U.S.–Mexico Border*. Austin: Center for Mexican American Studies, University of Texas at Austin, 1990.

Herzog, Lawrence A., ed. *Changing Boundaries in the Americas: New Perspectives on the U.S.–Mexican, Central American, and South American Borders*. La Jolla: Center for U.S.–Mexican Studies, 1992.

Hoffman, Abraham. *Unwanted Mexican Americans in the Great Depression*. Tucson: University of Arizona Press, 1974.

Hopkins, Randall G. "The Economic Impact of Mexican Visitors to Arizona." *Arizona's Economy* (Tucson: University of Arizona) (November 1992): 1–5.

Horgan, Paul. *Great River: The Rio Grande in North American History*. 2 vols. New York: Rinehart, 1954.

Johnson, M. A. "Border in French and French-African Literature." In Asiwaju and Adeneyi, *Borderlands in Africa*, 151–60.

Jukes, G. "Political and Military Problems of the Sino-Soviet Border." *New Zealand Slavonic Journal* 10 (1972): 11–32.

Kay, Cristobal. *Latin American Theories of Development and Underdevelopment*. New York: Routledge, 1989.

Keller, Gary D. "The Image of the Chicano in Mexican, United States, and Chicano Cinema." In Keller, *Chicano Cinema*, 13–58.

Keller, Gary D., ed. *Chicano Cinema: Research, Reviews, and Resources*. Binghamton, N.Y.: Bilingual Review/Press, 1985.

Klymasz, Robert B. "Folklore of the Canadian-American Border." In *Handbook of American Folklore*, edited by Richard M. Dorson, 227–32. Bloomington: Indiana University Press, 1983.

Kristof, Ladis K. D. "The Nature of Frontiers and Boundaries." *Annals of the Association of American Geographers* 49 (September 1959): 269–82.

Lang, Jean. *A Land of Romance: The Border; History and Legend*. London: T. C. and E. C. Jack, 1930.

Langewiesche, William. "The Border." *The Atlantic* 269:5 (May 1992): 53–92; 269:6 (June 1992): 91–108.

Latorre, Dolores L., and Felipe A. Latorre. *The Mexican Kickapoo Indians*. Austin: University of Texas Press, 1976.

Lattimore, Owen D. "The Frontier in History." In *Theory in Anthropology: A Sourcebook*, edited by Robert A. Manners and David Kaplaw, 374–86. Chicago: Aldine, 1968.

Lavender, David. *The Southwest*. Albuquerque: University of New Mexico Press, 1984.

León-Portilla, Miguel. "The Norteño Variety of Mexican Culture: An Ethnohistorical Approach." In *Plural Society in the Southwest*, edited by Edward H. Spicer and Raymond H. Thompson, 77–114. New York: Weatherhead Foundation, 1972.

Lorey, David E. *United States–Mexico Border Statistics Since 1900*. Los Angeles: UCLA Latin American Center, 1990.

McGreevy, Patrick Vincent. *The Wall of Mirrors: Nationalism and Perceptions of the Border at Niagara Falls*. Borderlands Monogaph Series, no. 5. Orono, Me.: Borderlands, 1991.

Maciel, David R. *El Norte: The U.S.–Mexican Border in Contemporary Cinema*. San Diego: Institute for Regional Studies of the Californias, San Diego State University, 1990.

———. "Visions of the Other Mexico: Chicanos and Undocumented Workers in Mexican Cinema, 1954–1982," in Keller, *Chicano Cinema*, 71–88.

McKinney, Lauren S. *Borderlands Reflections: The United States and Canada*. Orono, Me.: Borderlands, 1989.

McWilliams, Carey. *North from Mexico: The Spanish-Speaking People of the United States*. Updated by Matt S. Meier. New York: Praeger, 1990.

Madsen, William. *Mexican-Americans of South Texas*. San Francisco: Holt, Rinehart and Winston, 1964.

Margulis, Mario, and Rodolfo Tuirán. *Desarrallo y población en la frontera norte: El caso de Reynosa*. Mexico City: El Colegio de México, 1986.

Maril, Robert Lee. *Living on the Edge of America: At Home on the Texas-Mexico Border*. College Station: Texas A & M University Press, 1992.

———. *Poorest of Americans: The Mexican Americans of the Lower Rio Grande Valley of Texas*. Notre Dame: University of Notre Dame Press, 1989.

Martínez, Oscar J. *Border Boom Town: Ciudad Juárez Since 1848*. Austin: University of Texas Press, 1978.

———. "Chicanos and the Border Cities: An Interpretive Essay." *Pacific Historical Review* 46 (Feburary 1977): 85–106.

———. *The Chicanos of El Paso: An Assessment of Progress*. Southwestern Studies Monograph No. 59. El Paso: Texas Western Press, 1980.

———. "La frontera en la conciencia nacional, 1848–1920: Comentarios historiográficos sobre temas selectos." In *Estudios fronterizos*, 21–48.

———. "México-estadounidenses de la frontera: Una tipología." *Revista Mexicana de Sociología* 53 (July–September 1991): 291–303.

———. "Soledad Fuente." In Beezley and Ewell, *The Human Tradition in Latin America*, 195–206.

———. "Transnational Fronterizos: Cross-Border Linkages in Mexican Border Society." *Journal of Borderlands Studies* 5:1 (Spring 1990): 79–94.

———. *Troublesome Border*. Tucson: University of Arizona Press, 1988.

Martínez, Oscar J., ed. *Across Boundaries: Transborder Interaction in Comparative Perspective*. El Paso: Texas Western Press, 1986.

———. *Fragments of the Mexican Revolution: Personal Accounts from the Border*. Albuquerque: University of New Mexico Press, 1983.

Martínez, Tomas M. "Advertising and Racism: The Case of the Mexican American." In *Voices*, edited by Octavio L. Romano, 48–58. Berkeley: Quinto Sol, 1971.

Meier, Matt S., and Feliciano Rivera. *The Chicanos: A History of Mexican Americans*. New York: Hill and Wang, 1972.

Meinig, D. W. *Southwest: Three Peoples in Geographical Change, 1600–1970*. New York: Oxford University Press, 1971.

Messmacher, Miguel. *La interdependencia de la frontera norte de México*. Mexico City: Centro de Investigaciones y Estudios Superiores en Antropología Social, 1983.

Metz, Leon C. *Border: The U.S.–Mexico Line*. El Paso: Mangan Books, 1989.

Miller, Tom. "On the Border: Life Begins on the Other Side." *GEO* 1 (November 1979): 6–36.

———. *On the Border: Portraits of America's Southwestern Frontier*. New York: Harper and Row, 1981.

Mills, James. *The Underground Empire: Where Crime and Governments Embrace*. New York: Doubleday and Co., 1986.

Minghi, Julian V. "From Conflict to Harmony in Border Landscapes." In *The Geography of Border Landscapes*, edited by Dennis Rumbley and Julian V. Minghi, 15–30. New York: Routledge, 1991.

Miranda, Mario, and James W. Wilkie, eds. *Reglas del juego y juego sin reglas en la vida fronteriza*. Mexico City: ANUIES/PROFMEX, 1985.

Momoh, C. S. "A Critique of Borderland Theories." In Asiwaju and Adeniyi, *Borderlands in Africa*, 51–61.

Montejano, David. *Anglos and Mexicans in the Making of Texas, 1836–1986*. Austin: University of Texas Press, 1987.

Moore, Joan, and Harry Pachón. *Hispanics in the United States*. Englewood Cliffs, N.J.: Prentice-Hall, 1989.

Mora, Pat. *Chants*. Houston: Arte Público Press, 1984.

Moyano Pahissa, Angela. *México y Estados Unidos: Orígenes de una relación, 1819–1861*. Mexico City: Secretaría de Educación Pública, 1985.

Muñoz, Carlos, Jr. *Youth, Identity, Power: The Chicano Movement*. New York: Verso, 1989.

Murgía, Edward. *Chicano Intermarriage: A Theoretical and Empirical Study*. San Antonio: Trinity University Press, 1982.

Nash, Gerald D. *The American West in the Twentieth Century: A Short History of an Urban Oasis*. Englewood Cliffs, N.J.: Prentice-Hall, 1973.

———. *The American West Transformed: The Impact of the Second World War*. Bloomington: Indiana University Press, 1985.

———. *World War II and the West: Reshaping the Economy*. Lincoln: University of Nebraska Press, 1990.

Nathan, Debbie. *Women and Other Aliens: Essays from the U.S.–Mexico Border*. El Paso: Cinco Puntos Press, 1991.

Nelson, Eugene. *Pablo Cruz and the American Dream*. Peregrine Smith and Eugene Nelson, 1975.

Nelson Cisneros, Victor. "La clase trabajadora en Tejas, 1900–1940." *Aztlán* 6 (1975): 239–65.

North, David S. "The Migration Issue in U.S.–Mexican Relations." In *United States Relations with Mexico: Context and Content,* edited by Richard D. Erb and Stanley R. Ross, 121–34. Washington, D.C.: American Enterprise Institute for Public Policy Research, 1981.

Oral History Index: An International Directory of Oral History Interviews. Westport, Conn.: Meckler, 1990.

Paredes, Américo. *Between Two Worlds*. Houston: Arte Público Press, 1991.

———. *George Washington Gómez*. Houston: Arte Público Press, 1990.

———. *"With His Pistol in His Hand": A Border Ballad and Its Hero*. Austin: University of Texas Press, 1958.

Park, Joseph F. *The History of Mexican Labor in Arizona During the Territorial Period*. Tucson: University of Arizona Press, 1961.

Paul, Rodman W. *Mining Frontiers of the Far West, 1848–1880*. Albuquerque: University of New Mexico Press, 1974.

Pettit, Arthur G. *Images of the Mexican American in Fiction and Film*. College Station: Texas A & M Press, 1980.

Piñera Ramírez, David, comp. *Panorama histórico de Baja California*. Tijuana: Centro de Investigaciones Históricas UNAM-UABC, 1983.

Poggie, John J., Jr. *Between Two Cultures: The Life of an American-Mexican*. Tucson: University of Arizona Press, 1973.

Poppa, Terrence E. *Druglord: The Life and Death of a Mexican Kingpin*. New York: Pharos Books, 1990.

Prescott, John R. V. *Boundaries and Frontiers*. Totowa, N.J.: Rowman and Littlefield, 1978.

———. *The Geography of Frontiers and Boundaries*. Chicago: Aldine, 1965.

Price, John A. *Tijuana: Urbanization in a Border Culture*. Notre Dame: University of Notre Dame Press, 1973.

Randall, Stephen J., Herman Konrad, and Sheldon Silverman, eds. *North America Without Borders? Integrating Canada, the United States, and Mexico*. Calgary: University of Calgary Press, 1992.

Reed, James. *The Border Ballads*. London: University of London, The Athlone Press, 1973.

Reisler, Mark. *By the Sweat of Their Brow: Mexican Immigrant Labor in the United States, 1900–1940*. Westport, Conn.: Greenwood Press, 1976.

Rice, Bradley R., and Richard H. Bernard, eds. *Sunbelt Cities: Politics and Growth Since World War II*. Austin: University of Texas Press, 1983.

Rives, George L. *The United States and Mexico, 1821–1848*. 2 vols. New York: Charles Scribner's Sons, 1913.

Robinson, Cecil. *Mexico and the Hispanic Southwest in American Literature*. Tucson: University of Arizona Press, 1977.

Ross, Stanley R., ed. *Views Across the Border: The United States and Mexico*. Albuquerque: University of New Mexico Press, 1978.

Rubel, Arthur J. *Across the Tracks: Mexican Americans in a Texas City*. Austin: University of Texas Press, 1966.

Ruíz, Ramón Eduardo. *The People of Sonora and Yankee Capitalists*. Tucson: University of Arizona Press, 1988.

Ruíz, Vicki L., and Susan Tiano, eds. *Women on the U.S.–Mexico Border: Responses to Change*. Boston: Allen & Unwin, 1987.

Sable, Martin H. *Las Maquiladoras: Assembly and Manufacturing Plants on the United States–Mexico Border: An International Guide*. New York: Haworth Press, 1989.

Sahlins, Peter. *Boundaries: The Making of France and Spain in the Pyrenees*. Berkeley: University of California Press, 1989.

Samora, Julian. *Los Mojados: The Wetback Story*. Notre Dame: University of Notre Dame Press, 1971.

Sandos, James A. *Rebellion in the Borderlands: Anarchism and the Plan of San Diego, 1904–1923*. Norman: University of Oklahoma Press, 1992.

Sepúlveda, César. *La frontera norte de México: Historia, conflictos, 1762–1975*. Mexico City: Editorial Porrúa, 1976.

Shannon, Elaine. *Desperados: Latin Drug Lords, U.S. Lawmen, and the War Americans Can't Win*. New York: Penguin Books, 1988.

Shannon, Thomas Richard. *An Introduction to the World-System Perspective*. Boulder, Colo.: Westview Press, 1989.

Sklair, Leslie. *Assembling for Development: The Maquila Industry in Mexico and the United States*. Boston: Unwin Hyman, 1989.

Sloan, John W., and Jonathan P. West. "Community Integration and Policies Among Elites in Two Border Cities." *Journal of Inter-American Studies and World Affairs* 18 (November 1976): 451–74.

———. "The Role of Informal Policy Making in U.S.–Mexico Border Cities." *Social Science Quarterly* 58 (September 1977): 270–82.

Smith, Clint E. *The Disappearing Border: Mexico–United States Relations to the 1990s*. Stanford, Calif.: Stanford Alumni Association, 1992.

Spicer, Edward H. *Pascua: A Yaqui Village*. Chicago: University of Chicago Press, 1940.

———. *The Yaquis: A Cultural History*. Tucson: University of Arizona Press, 1980.

Stenberg, Richard R. "The Boundaries of the Louisiana Purchase." *Hispanic American Historical Review* 14 (February 1934): 32–64.

Stoddard, Ellwyn R. *Maquila: Assembly Plants in Northern Mexico*. El Paso: Texas Western Press, 1987.

Stoddard, Ellwyn R., Richard L. Nostrand, and Jonathan P. West, eds. *Borderlands Sourcebook: A Guide to the Literature on Northern Mexico and the American Southwest*. Norman: University of Oklahoma Press, 1982.

Stonequist, Everett V. *The Marginal Man: A Study in Personality and Culture Conflict*. New York: Charles Scribner's Sons, 1937.

Strassoldo, Raimondo. "Border Studies: The State of the Art in Europe." In Asiwaju and Adeniyi, *Borderlands in Africa*, 383–95.

Strassoldo, Raimondo, ed. *Confini e Regioni: Il Potenziale di Sviluppo e di Pace Delle Periferie (Boundaries and Regions: Explorations in the Growth and Peace Potential of the Peripheries)*. Trieste: Edizioni LINT, 1973.

Strassoldo, Raimondo, G. Delli Zotti, and Franco Angeli, eds. *Cooperation and Conflict in Border Areas*. Milan: Franco Angeli Editore, 1982.

Tägil, Sven, et al. *Studying Boundary Conflicts: A Theoretical Framework*. Oslo: Scandinavian University Books, 1977.

Tamayo, Jesús, and José Luis Fernández, eds. *Zonas Fronterizas*. Mexico City: Centro de Investigación y Docencia Económicas, 1983.

Taylor, Paul S. *Mexican Labor in the United States*. 2 vols. New York: Arno Press and the *New York Times,* 1970. Reprint of studies originally published between 1928 and 1934.

Thompson, Paul. *The Edwardians: The Remaking of British Society*. Bloomington: Indiana University Press, 1975.

Timmons, W. H. *El Paso: A Borderlands History*. El Paso: Texas Western Press, 1990.

Tuppen, J. N. "A Geographical Appraisal of Transfrontier Commuting in Western Europe: The Example of Alsace." *International Migration Review* 12 (Fall 1978): 386–405.

Urrea, Luis Alberto. *Across the Wire: Life and Hard Times on the Mexican Border*. New York: Anchor Books, 1993.

Valk, Barbara G., ed. *Borderline: A Bibliography of the United States–Mexico Border-lands*. UCLA Latin American Center Publications. Los Angeles: The Center, 1988.

Vanderwood, Paul J., and Frank N. Samporano. *Border Fury: A Picture Postcard Record of Mexico's Revolution and U.S. War Preparedness*. Albuquerque: University of New Mexico Press, 1988.

Voss, Stuart F. *On the Periphery of Nineteenth-Century Mexico: Sonora and Sinaloa, 1810–1877*. Tucson: University of Arizona Press, 1982.

Wambaugh, Joseph. *Lines and Shadows*. New York: Bantam Books, 1984.

Wasserman, Mark. *Capitalists, Caciques, and Revolution: The Native Elite and Foreign Enterprise in Chihuahua, Mexico, 1854–1911*. Chapel Hill: University of North Carolina Press, 1984.

Weaver, Thomas. "The Social Effects of the Ecology and Development of the United States–Mexico Border." In *Ecology and Development of the Border Region*, edited by Stanley R. Ross, 233–70. Mexico City: Asociación Nacional de Universidades e Institutos de Enseñanza Superior, 1985.

Weber, David J., *The Mexican Frontier, 1821–1846: The American Southwest Under Mexico*. Albuquerque: University of New Mexico Press, 1982.

———. *The Spanish Frontier in North America*. New Haven, Conn.: Yale University Press, 1992.

Weber, David J., ed. *Foreigners in Their Native Land: Historical Roots of Mexican Americans*. Albuquerque: University of New Mexico Press, 1973.

Weber, Debra Anne. "The Organization of Mexicano Agricultural Workers: The Imperial Valley and Los Angeles, 1928–1934, An Oral History Approach." *Aztlán* 3 (Fall 1972): 307–47.

Weiner, Myron. "Transborder Peoples." In *Mexican Americans in Comparative Perspective*, edited by Walker Connor, 130–58. Washington, D.C.: Urban Institute, 1985.

Weisman, Alan. *La Frontera: The United States Border with Mexico*. Photographs by Jay Dusard. Tucson: University of Arizona Press, 1991.

West, Jonathan P. "Informal Policy-Making Along the Arizona-Mexico International Border." *International Review of Public Administration* 1 (1979): 435–58.

Wieczynski, Joseph L. *The Russian Frontier: The Impact of Borderlands upon the Course of Early Russian History*. Charlottesville: University Press of Virginia, 1976.

Windling, Terri, ed. *Life on the Border*. New York: Tor Books, 1991.

"A World Apart," *Newsweek*, April 11, 1983.

Zamora, Emilio, Jr. "Chicano Socialist Labor Activity in Texas, 1900–1920." *Aztlán* 6 (1975): 221–36.

Zoroida Vásquez, Josefina, and Lorenzo Meyer. *The United States and Mexico*. Chicago: University of Chicago Press, 1985.

INDEX

ABOUT THE AUTHOR

OSCAR J. MARTÍNEZ   has spent most of his life in the U.S.–Mexico borderlands, taking part in and observing transboundary and cross-cultural interaction at close range. His family migrated from the interior of Mexico to Ciudad Juárez in the 1940s, moved to El Paso in the 1950s, and eventually settled permanently in Los Angeles. Before becoming Professor of History at the University of Arizona in 1988, he taught and directed research programs at the University of Texas at El Paso for more than a decade. He has written or edited five other books and numerous articles and chapters of books on the history of the borderlands, including *Troublesome Border* (University of Arizona Press, 1988). Professor Martínez is also a former president of the Association of Borderlands Scholars.